A Critical
History of French
Children's Literature

Children's Literature and Culture

Jack Zipes, Series Editor

A Critical History of French Children's Literature

VOLUME TWO: 1830–PRESENT

Penny Brown

Routledge
Taylor & Francis Group
New York   London

Routledge
Taylor & Francis Group
270 Madison Avenue
New York, NY 10016

Routledge
Taylor & Francis Group
2 Park Square
Milton Park, Abingdon
Oxon OX14 4RN

Printed in the United States of America on acid-free paper
10 9 8 7 6 5 4 3 2 1

International Standard Book Number-13: 978-0-415-97327-4 (Hardcover)

Library of Congress Cataloging-in-Publication Data

Brown, Penny, 1944-
    A critical history of French children's literature / by Penny Brown.
        p. cm. -- (Children's literature and culture)
    Includes bibliographical references and index.
    ISBN 978-0-415-97326-7 (hardback : v. 1 : alk. paper) -- ISBN
    978-0-415-97327-4 (hardback : v. 2 : alk. paper)
    1. Children's literature, French--History and criticism. 2. Children--Books and reading--France. I. Title.

PQ845.B76 2007
840.9'9282--dc22   2006101149

Visit the Taylor & Francis Web site at
http://www.taylorandfrancis.com

and the Routledge Web site at
http://www.routledge.com

CONTENTS

ACKNOWLEDGMENTS

This project has been supported by two periods of research leave generously funded by the Arts and Humanities Research Council of Great Britain (2002 for volume 1; 2006 for volume 2) and by two corresponding semesters of research leave awarded by the School of Languages, Linguistics and Cultures at the University of Manchester.

SERIES EDITOR'S FOREWORD

Dedicated to furthering original research in children's literature and culture, the Children's Literature and Culture series includes monographs on individual authors and illustrators, historical examinations of different periods, literary analyses of genres, and comparative studies on literature and the mass media. The series is international in scope and is intended to encourage innovative research in children's literature with a focus on interdisciplinary methodology.

Children's literature and culture are understood, in the broadest sense of the term *children*, to encompass the period of childhood up through adolescence. Owing to the fact that the notion of childhood has changed so much since the origination of children's literature, this Routledge series is particularly concerned with transformations in children's culture and how they have affected the representation and socialization of children. While the emphasis of the series is on children's literature, all types of studies that deal with children's radio, film, television, and art are included in an endeavor to grasp the aesthetics and values of children's culture. Not only have there been momentous changes in children's culture in the last fifty years, but there have been radical shifts in the scholarship that deals with these changes. In this regard, the goal of the Children's Literature and Culture series is to enhance research in this field and, at the same time, point to new directions that bring together the best scholarly work throughout the world.

Jack Zipes

INTRODUCTION

Blyton, Dahl, Horowitz, Pullman, Rowling, Tolkien: these writers feature prominently on the children's fiction sections in bookshops in France in 2007. Characters from American comics and animated cartoon films populate French children's comics. Yet this apparent invasion of translations and adaptations may obscure, in the eyes of an Anglophone observer, the wealth of excellent material being produced by French writers today, and the complex history of children's literature in France. The aim of this volume is to examine the development of French children's books in the nineteenth and twentieth centuries, and at the beginning of the twenty-first, in order to establish the richness and variety of a field little known and little studied in Anglophone countries although the latter have been at the forefront of the study of children's literature.

The choice of 1830 as a starting point for this volume is not an abitrary one. Historically, the date marks the revolution that brought Louis-Philippe to the throne in France and the beginnings of the July Monarchy (1830–1848), which saw a period of relative social and political stability and prosperity. The normative model of the development of North Western European children's literature articulated by Emer O'Sullivan and discussed in the introduction to volume 1 of this study continued to be true of France in the nineteenth century.[1] In this model, children's literature is seen to evolve under the impact of a conjunction of specific factors: the rise of the middle classes and the emergence of a new bourgeois reading public, the development of new technologies and new strategies in publishing and marketing, with publishers specialising in books for the young, and changes in perception of the family group and the role of parents as educators. The second quarter of the nineteenth century in France saw economic and technological developments in the book trade and a diversification in literary genres that were to have a considerable impact on the production of children's

1

books. New initiatives in publishing—notably, the enterprises of such publishing houses as Hachette, Hetzel, and Mame—affected significantly the contents, materiality, marketing, and dissemination of children's books. Increasing literacy and a demand for both educational and leisure reading amongst a flourishing bourgeoisie created a wider market than ever before for both high-quality and affordable books, and young readers were recognised by publishers as a huge potential market with its own special needs and interests. The implications of these factors for the development of French children's literature will be addressed in the course of this study.

After the Restoration of the monarchy in France in 1815, there was a renewed and increased emphasis on the family and on the collaboration of mothers and fathers in the upbringing of their offspring. Throughout the nineteenth century, society invested heavily in its children in emotional, economic, educational, and existential terms, because they represented the future in an age that privileged family, property and status.[2] Contemporary art favoured images of calm, domestic interiors, in which children and parents shared living space and activities. Books on child rearing, like P. Janet's *La Famille* (1855), proliferated and were required reading for devoted parents, and by the latter half of the century, childhood was a favourite theme in fiction for adult readers and in autobiographical memoirs.[3] Childhood was perceived as a time to be cherished and nourished but also carefully monitored and controlled. This concept derived in part from the views of Jean-Jacques Rousseau in *Emile, ou de l'éducation* (1762) which were taken up in the first half of the century by the Romantic writers who eulogised not just the innocence of childhood, but saw that period of life as a time of spontaneity, imagination, and wonder that was forever lost in adulthood. This view, exemplified in the poems of Marceline Desbordes-Valmore and Victor Hugo, for example, presents to the eye of the observer distanced in time a familiar paradox when the literary construct is compared to reality. For socially and economically privileged children, their welfare, education, entertainment, and general upbringing were important concerns for the family and educators, while at the same time working-class children were undergoing terrible privations and drudgery as cogs in the wheels of the Industrial Revolution. Although to a lesser extent than in Britain because of the relatively late introduction of industrialisation in France, children as young as six worked long hours in factories, mills, and mines and, given the importance of agriculture, on farms and in the fields. Protection and control of child labour, let alone cosseting, were slow in coming.[4] It is significant that just as these children had little or no opportunity for access to stimulating reading material, so their plight was rarely featured realistically in literature for child readers.

The nineteenth century in France also saw the continuation of passionate debates about the scope, content, and mode of education and the gradual assumption of responsibility by the state for schooling and hence for literacy and children's introduction to books. Successive education laws broadened the potential readership for children's books, yet, for much of the century, children's books continued to be read by, and for the most part were targeted at, the offspring of bourgeois families and were informed by bourgeois ideals. The evolution of children's books in France had, since the seventeenth century, always been firmly associated with education and the process of socialisation, and, as will become evident in the course of this study, the production of these books remained closely linked with a pedagogical agenda of one sort or another until after World War II. A didactic element is, in effect, one of the characteristics commonly adduced to distinguish 'children's literature' from 'literature' at large.

The problems of arriving at a precise definition of *children's literature* (or indeed, of *children* or of *literature*) are even more acute in the period under consideration in this volume than in earlier periods. The frontiers of what might be considered 'children's literature' were, and continue to be, shifting and permeable.[5] By 1830, nevertheless, the concept of a juvenile readership as a discrete entity was well established, even though in reality the dividing line between child and young adult still varied considerably depending on class, economic status, education, and gender. Publishers and authors were becoming aware of the need to cater for young readers of different ages and reading ability, although the concept of adolescence as a period of physical and psychological upheaval that might be explored specifically for young readers in a literature of their own was not, of course, to be fully recognised or exploited for many decades to come. The nineteenth century also saw the continuation of a gender-specific trend in the marketing of children's books that had begun with the growth in the late eighteenth century of a literature directed specifically at young female readers. Many of the novels of domestic realism and the adventure stories that dominated the market in the second half of the nineteenth century addressed and were marketed at female or male readers, respectively, although they were certainly not read exclusively by one audience. After 1830, children's books began to mirror more closely developments in literature addressed to adults. The impact on children's literature of Romanticism, of the realist novel's portrayal of contemporary social concerns, and of the discourses of patriotism, empire, and colonial expansion is addressed in successive chapters in this study. At the same time, the second half of the nineteenth century saw an increase in genres—like adventure or travel narratives and those popularising science—that were informed by a broader didactic agenda and were overtly targeted at, or were appropriated by, a dual audience of adults and young readers. Of course, there has never been a simple correlation between material written specifically for children and what children have actually read, and perhaps the most obvious example of this in the nineteenth century is the *roman-feuilleton* of popular literature. These romantic, sensational, and often lurid novels serialised in newspapers were readily available to competent readers of all ages. This study, however, limits its focus to works where there is a demonstrable desire to target young readers. (The implications of such 'crossover' literature has become an intriguing issue in recent times when books written ostensibly for children have been appropriated by adult readers, and comics are enjoyed by both.)

Before 1830, children's books revealed a clear aim on the part of authors to construct an ideal child reader through their narratives. Wolfgang Iser's concept of the 'implied reader', a reader constructed by the text who 'embodies all those predispositions necessary for a literary work to exercise its effect' is particularly interesting in respect of children's books.[6] Both school books and leisure reading assumed, in their content and mode of address, a reader who shared or would respond in the desired manner to the social and cultural values inscribed in the text. A more or less explicit didactic agenda manifesting itself most obviously in initiation narratives that encouraged conformism to the values of the dominant culture of the time was still of central importance in the later nineteenth and early twentieth centuries but underwent significant transformations in response to urgent social, political, or religious imperatives. Children's books have always evolved to reflect the changing times, and therefore offer considerable insights into the culture of which they are a product. The first half of this study traces the religious and social agenda underpinning prize books and the novel of domestic realism, the educational agenda best exemplified by Hetzel's *Magasin d'éducation et de récréation*, and the patriotic, lay agenda that dominated after the disaster of France's defeat in the Franco-Prussian War in 1870 and throughout more or less the whole of the first half of the twentieth century.

Views on childhood and the status of the child changed dramatically in the twentieth century in the wake of studies on child psychology and paediatrics and the work of educationalists and sociologists. Attention in pedagogical theories, like those of Jean Piaget in *Psychologie et pédagogie* (1969), was focussed increasingly on understanding children and helping them develop their own individuality and capabilities rather than on imposing a set of uniform ready-made adult values. In 1959, the General Assembly of the United Nations gave its blessing to a Declaration of the Rights of Children. The Convention on the Rights of the Child, thirty years later, reiterated the aims of the declaration in a binding treaty for member nations, celebrating childhood and codifying in international law the rights due all children in order to protect their physical, mental, and spiritual development. The 1960s saw the development in all social and cultural areas of a cult of youth that has increased to this day, and acquired particular social and political significance in France after the events of May 1968. The extent to which such factors influenced writing for the young will become apparent in the course of this study. Most important for the development of children's literature, children have become major consumers with increased spending power, capable of exercising autonomy and choice, and hence the objects of intensive commercial advertising of toys, clothes, magazines, music, computer games, and the latest technological devices. They are also now more demanding and selective in their choice of reading matter (if they read at all, for there are so many rival distractions for their education and leisure time). The long-standing top-down approach of adult authors mediating wisdom to impressionable readers is no longer seen as the only desirable or appropriate narrative model. Children's books have other, diverse, agendas to satisfy, and those agendas are increasingly determined by market forces. The identification of an implied reader and the role of such a construct thus becomes increasingly complex in juvenile literature in the second half of the twentieth century.

The experience of the two world wars strongly influenced the direction, content, and tone of children's books in France. The most profound changes in children's literature have come about since World War II, although the acceptance of social and cultural norms continued to be encouraged in children's books in the 1950s, even when fictional children were beginning to enjoy greater emancipation from the constraints of the adult world in narratives in which they acted independently and autonomously in exciting adventures. With the new flowering of children's literature in the second half of the twentieth century, there has been a radical shift from this unquestioned and unquestioning position towards, in many works, an interrogation and even subversion of these norms and a refusal of adult authority, one of the most significant changes in its history. The disruption of long-established codes of an author/reader relationship in which the former assumes a responsibility to enlighten and guide has resulted in a much more thoroughly child-centred literature. Although the authors of children's books are still for the most part adults, the teacherly narrative voice has been displaced by a more informal tone and even, in some cases, by a voice complicitous in a gleeful anarchy. There has been a move away from a single (adult) narrative viewpoint with which the reader is expected to identify. Instead, a child or adolescent protagonist is frequently employed as the chief focaliser in an attempt to communicate a youthful view of the world to young readers in a language with which they can identify. Readers may be positioned in a viewpoint that closely resembles their own or, conversely, one that challenges their own personal feelings or inherited cultural assumptions (a strategy used, for example, in narratives concerning ethnicity and culture shock) or they may be exposed to a multiplicity of conflicting viewpoints.

Since approximately the 1970s, emphasis in fictional plots has been placed increasingly on individual psychology and the problems of accommodating the needs and desires of the self to existing family and social structures, particularly in texts in which the targeted readers are adolescents. Subjects that had been seen in the first half of the twentieth century as problematic in children's books (death, politics, religion, or money), or that, like sex, had always been a taboo topic, are now regarded as acceptable and are treated openly in fiction for different ages. Such a virtual abolition of taboos inevitably creates new problems for authors, publishers, and purchasers of children's books. It is, of course, debatable as to whether such frankness about all aspects of human experience reflects the real interests of young readers or whether it relates to adult concerns or even the financial motives of publishers. It also inevitably raises questions about the desirability of exposing children to such matters at a young age, an issue that has continued to preoccupy parents, teachers, and commentators on children's literature alike.

The most significant literary innovation to impact on children's books in the period under consideration in this volume was the increased role accorded in books and papers to the image. The importance of images as creators of mood and meaning is, arguably, a more crucial one in children's books than in books for adults. For the preliterate young, whether being read to or browsing alone through a text, the image may be the primary generator of meaning, and educationalists (from John Locke onward), writers, and publishers have long recognised the power of illustrations to capture the interest of and hence influence a child reader. The post-1830 period saw an exceptional increase in the sophistication of illustrative techniques and in the number and quality of illustrations in books. The rise of the illustrated journal, the *histoire en images*, and, in particular, in the twentieth century, the *bande dessinée* or comic book led to a new type of reading experience that has revolutionised ways of reading for the young (and for many adults as well). The implications of this phenomenon, its evolution from the late nineteenth century in France, and the development of a francophone genre that has achieved worldwide popularity are important aspects of the history of French children's books. An associated element is, of course, the role of humour in children's books (in both text and image) that has undergone a transformation in the last hundred years from gentle, polite satire or farce to caricature, the scatalogical or violent, and the use of the comic to defuse anxieties and fears.

Children's books in Europe have constantly interacted with the products of other countries. The importing of children's books and comics from Britain and America in particular has had a fundamental influence on the direction of French publications throughout the two centuries covered in this volume and are continuing to do so. Moreover, the interlinking in recent years of fictional works for children with other media—notably, the bande dessinée, cartoon films, and television—has produced a new genre of crossover literature in which the characters and situations depicted in one medium have been transplanted and adapted to another. Together with an unprecedented marketing of character-related commodities (toys, clothes, bed linens, videos, DVDs, computer games, and even food) this phenomenon imparts to books a role as part of a whole fictional universe a child can enter and enjoy in a variety of ways—of which reading is only one. It also, in the case of the acculturation of material from abroad, tends to create a degree of homogeneity and universality in children's books.

Children's literature has always been 'radically intertextual' and the recycling of traditional models of narratives has not ceased to be an attractive strategy for writers despite the widening of the social, moral, and literary parameters within which children's books now operate.[7] The function of a 'retold story' has traditionally been 'to initiate children into aspects of a social heritage, transmitting many of a culture's central values and a body of shared allusions and experiences'.[8] Thus, apart from the many adaptations and abridged versions of existing texts, the appropriation of images and plots from traditional narratives like myths or folktales to promote concepts and ideologies is a powerful tool for imprinting values and desires on impressionable minds. The plot structures and narrative devices of fairy tales, in particular, have continued to be exploited in children's books in the period under consideration here in a variety of sometimes surprising contexts, as the discussion of novels of domestic realism and adventure stories will demonstrate. Intertextual strategies, whether explicit quotation or reference to an earlier children's book or the borrowing of a structure or familiar scenario, are frequently used simply to generate enjoyment, increased by the pleasure of recognition, or to prompt reflection and encourage a critical stance.[9] Moreover, in the last fifty years or so, traditional narrative models have also been deployed in an innovative manner to interrogate and challenge both social and cultural assumptions and the literary conventions they invoke. Of course, it cannot be taken for granted that young readers possess the experience of both life and literature needed to recognise and respond to intertextual references, and the inferences may be skewed by adaptations, through different media, of the pre-text.[10] However, such allusions may generate a response on a later reading of the text or enhance the reading of other texts later in life.

Although children's literature began to be seen as meriting serious study in France only comparatively recently, a substantial body of work that focuses on specific periods, genres, or authors is now accumulating.[11] The majority of critical commentaries have focussed on the literature of the nineteenth and twentieth centuries. Studies of aspects of French children's books by Anglophone critics are, however, few in number, and even studies of Jules Verne, for example, tend not to explore the implications of the specificity of a young readership. It is self-evident that a wide-ranging study of two centuries cannot pretend to be all-encompassing, and therefore this volume will entail some degree of selectivity amongst the wealth of primary material. This is particularly true of the last fifty years, when there has been an explosion of children's books of all kinds and for all ages; this period merits a study of its own. My approach, as in the first volume of this work, has been to present a contextually grounded overview of the development of French children's literature, illustrating the argument with discussion of texts that are either representative, of widely agreed significance, or of particular interest in terms of their content or narrative approach. The discussion is not, however, limited merely by received notions of the classics of children's literature. In some cases, the selection has also been occasioned by personal preference, and in others governed by availability, since extant copies of some early children's books are difficult to trace. The discussion has been restricted to books produced in metropolitan France, as the study of other francophone literature is beyond a work of this length and requires a further large-scale project.

It must always be borne in mind that a problematic aspect of discussing children's books from the position of an adult critic is the danger of facile assumptions about the 'success' and popularity of a book with its targeted audience. It is impossible to make sound judgements about reader response in respect of children's literature from previous centuries because of the lack of a body of first-hand evidence. While children's books may reveal what authors and publishers have deemed to be attractive to young readers, and it is sometimes possible to surmise how young readers in the past might have reacted, this is to a large extent an unknown factor. Success of a given text in financial terms or by its inclusion in the canon does not necessarily tell us that it was enjoyed by the children who read it, since most books, until comparatively recently, were still recommended and bought for children by adults. Sales figures today, although often revealing, are still in some cases unreliable as a guide to the popularity of a book with young readers as they may derive from advertising campaigns directed at parents or the appropriation of a work as a set text on a school syllabus. These issues will certainly resurface in the course of this study.

The history of French children's books since 1830 has been one of tradition and innovation. The aim of this study is to present a picture of the evolution of French children's books to the present day and an exploration of the reworking of old narrative models and the invention of new ones that will contribute to a reassessment of France's contribution to children's literature and serve as a resource for further investigation.

1

OLD FRIENDS, AND CHILDREN'S BOOKS ON THE MOVE

The decades of the 1830s to 1850s were a significant period in the history of French children's literature. Like the varied range of publications in the transitional period of the first three decades of the nineteenth century, many of the children's books published at this time tended to combine features of pre-revolutionary texts with newer approaches.[1] But there were also significant developments that heralded the beginnings of a new era, commonly seen as the 'golden age' of children's books. Writers and pedagogues had already begun to be aware of the need to write differently for the young and, indeed, for the young of different ages, addressing them directly and catering for their abilities and their perceived interests and needs. The balance between the two imperatives of instruction and amusement, which had dominated children's books since the seventeenth century, and the ways in which they found expression, were now to shift and change, although a didactic aim still remained essential in most authors' minds. Developments in children's literature began to mirror those in literature for adults, with the involvement of Romantic writers and, above all, the rise of the realist novel, which was eventually to displace the old-fashioned moral tales in the style of Arnaud Berquin and Mme de Genlis.

There were several factors that influenced the direction that the production of children's books was to take in France in the years after 1830. After the upheavals of the French Revolution, the Napoleonic Wars, the years of Empire, and the unsettling political events of the first decades of the new century, which saw three monarchs in just over fifteen years, France during the July Monarchy of Louis-Philippe (1830–48) was enjoying a period of relative stability and expanding economy. Paris was widely regarded as the cultural centre of Europe. With increasing prosperity, the period marked the beginnings of the consumer revolution, and profitable enterprises like printing were encouraged. The book trade generally had entered upon a significant period of expansion.[2] The developments in education aimed at an increase in literacy had a significant impact on the potential market for children's books, and the increased demand for reading matter suitable for the young resulted in exciting new specialist publishing initiatives. This chapter considers the implications of these factors and introduces the new directions in reading that stimulated the exceptional growth of children's literature in the second half of the century.

CHILDREN READING

Despite the many plans and projects for the reform of the education system put forward during the years of the Revolution and its aftermath, the scope and provision of education remained largely the same in the early years of the century as at the end of the ancien régime. A comparatively low number of children regularly attended schools, even elementary schools, in some areas. The serious situation as regards the lack of schools in some parts of the country; the poor quality of much of the teaching; and the totally unsuitable, and even insanitary, conditions in which such schooling that existed often took place came to light in the survey ordered by François Guizot, the French minister for education, in 1833 in response to concern about widespread illiteracy. This initiative, and the alarming statistics it uncovered, resulted in the Guizot Law of 1833, motivated by the perceived need to bring morality and enlightenment to the masses, which set out the conditions for a widespread, organised, and supervised elementary education with a school in every village or small group of villages. Underpinning the law was the view that 'universal elementary education shall henceforth be the guarantee of order and social stability'. What was envisaged for the primary schools was a very basic education for the masses, consisting of instruction on religion and morality, general social duties, and useful elementary knowledge.[3]

There resulted a gradual process of unification of schools from the July Monarchy and the Guizot Law onwards that helped to improve standards of literacy amongst the young. However, since schooling was still not compulsory nor free except for the very poor, attendance remained low and sporadic in the summer months in rural areas where children were required to assist with farming activities. This situation was exacerbated by parental resistance to change amongst the rural poor, where schooling and books were sometimes seen as endangering peasant culture.[4] In 1850, when, according to statistics, only 73 percent of children ages six to thirteen were enrolled in schools, the Falloux Law reaffirmed the Guizot Law with some significant changes—requiring, for example, that all communities with a population of over eight hundred should have a school for girls, and laid the foundation for elementary education for the next twenty years.[5]

Enrolment at elementary school did not, of course, necessarily mean a high level of literacy, and the subject matter and mode of address of the vast majority of books written for leisure reading in the first half of the century and beyond suggest a targeted readership primarily amongst the young of the bourgeoisie and the upper classes. The former, in particular, saw education as the means to social and financial success in life and the kind of secondary education on offer in the lycées or in schools run by religious orders was designed to groom those who would play an important role in society in the future. Private education for those who could afford tutors and governesses was still often a preferred alternative, especially for girls. Thus, demographic expansion, a prospering bourgeoisie, and developments in educational practice encouraged by legislation resulted in an increase in the numbers of literate children whom teachers and parents wanted to encourage with well-written reading material that would both entertain and instruct.

Despite the efforts to move towards unified and universal standards in schools, control of education remained a sensitive issue and there was an ongoing struggle between the church and the state. Even in state schools after the Guizot Law, religion continued to permeate all teaching at every level.[6] The Falloux Law of 1850 encouraged communes to entrust their schools to religious orders once more and Catholic education enjoyed the support of the established classes who saw it as a bulwark against socialism and revolution.[7] As will be seen in chapter 2, a strong religious influence continued to play an important part in the approach to writing for young readers.

THE BOOK TRADE

The book trade in the second quarter of the century was a very successful industry, with technological advances in papermaking and printing leading to better quality and cheaper and more widely available products at the same time as the demand for reading material increased amongst the now established bourgeoisie. Publishers employed new advertising and marketing strategies in selling their books and magazines. The period of the July Monarchy was important, in particular, for the rise of the illustrated book, with the introduction, inspired by the Romantic movement, of large numbers of small vignettes within the text as well as full page plates.[8] A lavishly illustrated two-volume edition of La Fontaine's fables, with 120 vignettes and 150 other decorations by the renowned illustrator Grandville (Jean-Ignace-Isidore Gérard), appeared in 1838 (having been published in *livraisons* between January and November 1837) and was a best-seller. A subsequent edition of Daniel Defoe's *Les Aventures de Robinson Crusoë* (1840), also illustrated by Grandville, appeared in 1838 and was certainly a popular gift book for the young.[9] Other popular illustrated books of this time were editions of Miguel de Cervantes's *Don Quixote* and Jonathan Swift *Gulliver's Travels.* Of course, these were expensive books aimed at an elite audience, but the increasing sophistication of printing techniques allowed for more and more children's books also to carry images on a less opulent scale.

Publishing for the young was now big business, with an unprecedented market for children's books of all kinds. The production of illustrated *abécédaires* was flourishing, and there was a huge demand for well-designed prize books designed to promote reading as a leisure activity.[10] In Martyn Lyons's analysis of the best-selling works in the first half of the nineteenth century, it is significant that works for young readers are at the top of the lists in terms of copies printed.[11] This can partly be explained by the appropriation of some works for use in schools and by a succession of adaptations of best-selling works for children. It is also noteworthy that books that had enjoyed publishing success in the previous century continued to be widely purchased. Lyons's table of best-sellers for the period 1811–1815 is headed by La Fontaine's *Fables,* François Fénelon's *Les Aventures de Télémaque,* and Claude Fleury's *Catéchisme historique,* and this remains the case in successive tables of assessment representing periods of five years up to 1850. More than half a million copies of each of these were printed in the first half of the century, and some editions were profusely illustrated. These three are followed in the 1811–1815 list by Charles Perrault's *Contes,* the fables of Jean-Pierre Claris de Florian, Laurent Pierre Bérenger's *La Morale en action,* the Abbé Barthélemy's *Voyage du jeune Anarcharsis,* and *Petit Buffon des enfants,* which all continue to figure in the later lists. These are joined after 1816 by Sophie Cottin's *Elisabeth, ou les exilés de Sibérie* and, briefly, *Claire d'Albe;* adaptations of Defoe's *Robinson Crusoe* after 1821; the large printings of Mme Jeanne-Mathurine de Saint-Ouen's *Histoire de France* in the next decade; and, after 1836, by the moral tales of Chanoine Schmid that were translated from German.

A PERIOD OF TRANSITION

By 1830, Berquin and Mme de Genlis, the two most popular and pro-lific writers for the young at the turn of the century, were dead. So also was Pauline Guizot, and Jean-Nicolas Bouilly was to die in 1842. However, their books were still in demand and new editions with illustrations revived texts popular in preceding decades. Berquin's short tales and playlets, in particular, retained their popularity and were repeatedly published in different compilations. A selection of his tales, now profusely illustrated and titled *L'Ami de la jeunesse* appeared in eight volumes between 1830 and 1834. Hachette published another, titled *Choix de petits drames et de contes tirés de Berquin*, in 1853 in the Bibliothèque des chemins de fer series, and again in 1861 in the hugely successful Bibliothèque rose illustrée, a volume that was still in print in 1888. Bouilly's *Contes à ma fille* saw a new edition published by Janet in 1830, and Cottin's *Elisabeth, ou les exilés de Sibérie* (1806) appeared in illustrated editions in 1849 and 1850. Julie Delafaye-Bréhier was still publishing in 1834 (*Marguerite ou la puissance des affections domestiques*); a sequel to her *Le Collège incendié* of 1821, titled *Le Verger des écoliers* (and described by Marie-Thérèse Latzarus as 'capable de donner aux enfants l'horreur de la lecture') appeared in 1841, and *Les Aventures de Roger, ou les dangers des mauvaises compagnies* appeared in 1844.[12] The new editions of a number of Sophie Renneville's edifying works, including the framed moral tales *Adèle et Justine, ou histoires d'une grand'tante* (1834) and *Eléonore ou la médisante, contes moraux et instructifs* (1834), indicate that there was still a strongly held belief in the value of such wholesome reading material.

The publishing successes of Berquin, Bouilly, and Mme de Genlis continued to spawn many imitators as they had done in the first three decades. The formula of the moral tale lingered on with similar titles and employing similar narrative strategies to promote normative patterns of conduct appropriate to the new bourgeois-dominated society. Ganna Ottevaere–van Praag claims that in the early nineteenth century the inspiration behind French children's books was more 'freinée par les exigences mutilantes des autorités pédagogiques' than in their English conterparts.[13] Moral tales were also extended into full-length narratives, often consisting of loosely strung together episodes with a thin linking plot, with titles such as *Les Vacances, ou l'application récompensée* (Amélie Courval, c. 1830), *Le Miroir de la jeunesse, ou le jeune âge instruit par ses propres erreurs et ses propres vertus* (Mme de Spérat, 1832) and *Zélie, ou le modèle des jeunes filles* (Julie Carroy, 1833) that clearly indicated the moral agenda. Often dismissed by critics as insipid and dull, these works continued to find favour with the parents who bought the books but also found an important niche as *livres de prix*.

NEW PUBLISHING VENTURES

Publishers who had the foresight to appreciate and exploit the potential of the expanding market for children's books were to play an important part in the directions in which children's books developed, both in keeping alive the conventional moral tale and in encouraging new departures and initiatives. Major players now appeared on the scene.

The publisher Alfred Mame in Tours specialised from the mid-1840s onward in books for school prizes, a practice initiated in the *collèges* in the early seventeenth century that had survived and been extended to elementary schools in the 1820s.[14] As the church once more played an important role in education, the demand was for texts that actively promoted a Catholic ethos. Mame, himself a fervent Catholic, recognised the business opportunities of such a demand and the need for a high-quality, dedicated product. His books, approved by the ecclesiastical authorities, soon became cherished for their clear typeface, elegant steel engravings, and colourful bindings that imitated silk or velvet and were often embossed with the name of the school in gold. The quality of his publications both enhanced the status of the institutions that bought them to present to their pupils and ensured the success of Mame's huge enterprise, which soon became the largest purveyor of prize books in France. His Bibliothèque illustrée de la jeunesse won a gold medal at the Paris Exposition of 1855.[15] Books were grouped in *Bibliothèques* corresponding to different age groups: the Bibliothèque illustrée de la jeunesse, the Bibliothèque de la jeunesse chrétienne, the Bibliothèque illustrée des petits enfants, and the Bibliothèque pieuse des maisons d'éducation, each of which had its own subset of series and a distinctive format. Mame employed his own stable of authors, many writing anonymously or under pseudonyms, whose mission was to defend religion and morality, inspire respect for the régime of the day and promote an ethos of diligence and piety in unexceptionable texts. As the books were awarded to diligent scholars in elementary schools, they reached a wide readership, including those children who would not, under normal circumstances, have had access to such quality books. Mame's output included, among the fictional narratives deemed suitable for children of eight to ten, such titles as *Les Braconniers ou les dangereux effets de la colère* and *Elisabeth ou la charité du pauvre récompensée*, which echoed the same sentiments as the moral tales of earlier decades. For children over twelve, Mame recommended historical works, and for older adolescents a series of works on history, science, travel, and literature, including *Oeuvres choisies de Buffon*, *Entretiens sur la chimie*, and *Nouveau choix des lettres de Madame de Sévigné*.[16] By 1850, the production of livres de prix was dominated by large provincial publishers, of which, after Mame, the most important were Ardant and Barbou in Limoges, Mégard in Rouen, and Lefort in Lille, and their publications were remarkably similar in terms of content, presentation, and cost. Like the tales of Berquin and Mme de Genlis, these stories privileged domestic realism, portraying family life in a recognisable contemporary world. It is noticeable, however, that—as in most children's books of the time—the upheavals and uncertainties of the age are ignored in favour of a sanitised and comforting depiction of reality that often suffers from sentimental overload. In many such works, the characters are cold and lifeless, the loosely linked episodes of the plot farfetched, and the language old-fashioned. Later commentators have been harsh on these authors ('témoins attardés d'une civilisation disparue') and their works, or ignore them completely.[17] Copies of many of these texts are now extremely difficult to locate.

Publishers like Blanchard, Didier, Janet, Lehuby, and Magnin recognised the possibilities of the market for gift books and produced special catalogues at Christmas and the New Year of *livres d'étrennes*—beautifully produced, copiously illustrated, and often expensive works by well-known authors and artists. In terms of content, however, these works differed little from the products of the livres de prix industry.[18] There continued to be firm control over the social and moral values imparted to the young reader, who was expected to share them unquestioningly. Works by Bouilly and Guizot were among those featured in these collections, as well as by Mme Delafaye-Bréhier, Amable Tastu, Mme Ulliac-Trémadeure, and Mlle Elise Voïart. Such prestigious publications were, of course, restricted to the fortunate children of aristocratic or bourgeois parents who could afford to invest in their offspring in this way.

Eugénie Foa is one of the more interesting and versatile witers of this period. An author of novels for adults promoting concern for the position of women, she founded the *Journal des enfants*, one of the earliest and longest-lasting magazines for young readers, in 1832 and contributed to *Le Dimanche des enfants. Journal des récréations*. She also wrote a number of works for young readers, including *Les Mémoires d'un Polichinelle* (1840) and *Le Petit Robinson de Paris* (1840). In response to the contemporary interest in historical themes, Foa specialised in tales that presented aspects of the lives of historical persons that would appeal to young readers and give them a sense of identification with the past and an introduction to culture. Hence her *Contes historiques pour la jeunesse* (c. 1843), which recounted the childhood of kings, artists, and other notable persons such as Napoleon Bonaparte, Captain James Cook, Wolfgang Amadeus Mozart, and Jean-Jacques Rousseau; *Les enfants illustres, contes historiques* (1858); *Les petits artistes, peintres et musiciens, contes historiques dédiés à la jeunesse* (posthumous edition, 1863); and *Les Petits savants, contes historiques dédiés à la jeunesse* (posthumous edition, 1868). Her story of the boyhood of Napoleon, which presented an image of the emperor as a marginalised and unhappy child consumed with the desire to make something of himself, was well known in translation. It details minor episodes from his childhood (probably of dubious accuracy), including loneliness at school, a snowball fight, and his early longings to be noticed. Like the exemplary lives narratives popular during the Revolution, such texts were intended to bring history to life and relate it to the present day but also to instil a sense of national pride in the readers and, like other moral tales, to furnish role models for the future leaders of society.[19]

In 1835, the young publisher Louis Hachette, whose publishing house was founded in 1826, secured a government contract to supply 500,000 copies of an *Alphabet des écoles*, 100,000 copies of a *Livret élémentaire de lecture*, and 40,000 copies each of geography, history, and arithmetic textbooks.[20] Hachette had identified the opportunities for producing school textbooks even before the promulgation of the Guizot Law and had begun to acquire existing titles and to publish guides for elementary schoolteachers. By the early 1860s, Hachette was one of the most important publishing houses specialising in schoolbooks and other books for the young.[21] One of Hachette's most successful acquisitions was the *Petite Histoire de France* of Mme de Saint-Ouen, a simplified chronology of royal births and deaths, battles, and treaties illustrated with portraits of sovereigns. This text, despite its dry approach, achieved enormous success in Hachette's first edition of 1834 and saw eighty revised editions up to 1880, selling in total over two and a quarter million copies.[22] In 1844 a contract was signed for an ambitious collection of some nineteen works on world history, from scriptural history to contemporary times. In the 1840s Hachette also advertised a new collection of revised textbooks of all kinds and began an innovative series of dual-language texts: the catalogue of 1849 contained fifty-four volumes of texts in Greek and Latin, with French translations on the facing pages. However, Hachette's most lasting contribution to the development of children's literature came with his exploitation of one of the technological advances of the age, the arrival of the railways. His innovative series, the Bibliothèque des chemins de fer, founded in 1852 and divided into a number of subsections, were small-format, elegantly produced texts (the forerunners of the pocket-size paperback) that were designed to be sold in the Hachette shops in the great railway stations to a new and eager market of travellers. At its inception, the Bibliothèque des chemins de fer promised 'à chaque voyager, selon son âge, ses goûts, sa profession, un ensemble d'ouvrages amusants, curieux, utiles et toujours moraux'.[23] As will be seen in chapter 2, the Bibliothèque rose illustrée, a collection devoted to books for young readers of all ages, became a dominant force in children's literature in the second half of the century.

Not all publishers perceived the significance of children's literature and their own role in its development in the same way, however. Pierre-Jules Hetzel, who was to become perhaps the most prolific and influential publisher of books for children in the nineteenth century, spoke scathingly of contemporary children's literature: 'J'ai eu l'horreur des livres bêtes qu'on donnait à notre enfance. Mon idée fixe a été de remplacer la littérature de gouvernante et de fruit sec qui nous suffisait autrefois par quelque chose de sain et de simple, qui pût tout au moins donner le goût du meilleur.'[24] To fulfil this aim of providing simple and wholesome literary fare he both drew on genres of the past and initiated innovative ideas throughout his career, which was marked by two highly productive and significant stages. In 1843, as well as publishing the works of Honoré de Balzac and Victor Hugo, he founded his *Nouveau magasin des enfants*, a collection that paid homage to Mme Le Prince de Beaumont in its title and contained a substantial catalogue of eighteen titles designed to appeal to both the mind and the eye of the young reader. Recognising the need for reading material that was more entertaining and stimulating to the imagination than the traditional moral tale, he aimed to revitalise children's literature by galvanising renowned writers of the time to adapt or produce suitable material for young readers and persuading established illustrators to collaborate in the enterprise. His first volume in the series was *Le Livre des petits enfants* (1843), a collection of extracts from Fénelon, Florian, La Fontaine, and other writers, illustrated by Grandville and Ernest Meissonier, which established a firm link between Hetzel's new project and the classics of the past. This was followed by several volumes of new and revised fairy tales by contemporary writers (see below); an edition of Perrault's *Contes* (1851), illustrated by, amongst others, Bertall (Albert d'Arnoux), Gavarni (Sulpice-Guillaume Chevalier), and Grandville; a *Mythologie de la jeunesse* by Louis Baudet (1845); and works of fantasy with inviting titles like *Le Prince Coqueluche* by Edouard Ourliac, *Vie de Polichinelle et ses nombreuses aventures* by Octave Feuillet, and *Histoire de la Mère Michel et de son chat* by Emile La Bédollière (all in 1846).[25] Hetzel himself contributed an imitation of an English tale, *Nouvelles et seules véritables aventures de Tom Pouce* (1844), using the pseudonym of P.-J. Stahl, under which he went on to write many stories for children in the second half of the century. He had clear views on the requirements of writing for children that refuted any notion that it was an easy task open to anyone who could churn out mediocre stories: 'Ce qu'il faut pour qu'un livre convienne à la jeunesse, c'est qu'il soit simple; c'est, ensuite, que dans ce livre il n'y ait point de confusion entre le bien et le mal et que l'un y soit séparé de l'autre assez scrupuleusement pour qu'un méchant esprit n'y puisse trouver sa justification. Or, pour faire un tel livre, il faut être à la fois un grand esprit et surtout un très honnête homme.'[26] After a period of exile abroad between 1851 and 1860, to which he was condemned for his political views and activities in 1848, he embarked on his return upon a long-term mission to provide a high-quality, wide-ranging series of books for the young including instructive works, adventure stories, poetry, and novels of domestic realism. His association with Jean Macé and the founding of the *Magasin d'éducation et de récréation*, which was to play a fundamental role in the golden age of children's literature, will be discussed in a later chapter.

Consideration will now be given to new departures and revivals that signalled the beginnings of a move away from the conventional moral tale that had dominated the market for so long and which laid the foundations for the future of children's literature in France.

FAIRY TALES

Hetzel was responsible, with his *Nouveau magasin des enfants*, for the brief renaissance enjoyed by fairy tales in the middle of the century. He later stated unequivocally his belief in the value of the *merveilleux* in terms that turn back on its exponents the argument that fairy tales are pernicious and corruptive for the young:

> Rien, vous ne pourrez rien découvrir aux enfants, si vous prétendez leur cacher le merveilleux, l'inexpliqué, l'inexplicable, l'impossible qui se trouvent dans le vrai tout aussi bien que dans l'imaginaire .... Le réel est un abîme tout rempli d'inconnu; demandez-le aux vrais savants .... Ah! revenez, revenons aux contes des fées pour les enfants, si, plus difficiles que La Fontaine, nous ne sommes pas assez bons pour y revenir pour nous-mêmes.[27]

The time was right for such a venture. The fairy tales of the Brothers Grimm had appeared in French in 1830 as *Contes populaires ou chroniques allemandes par l'amusement de la jeunesse. Vieux contes pour l'amusement des grands et des petits enfants*, a title that sought to reinstate the appropriateness of such narratives for all ages. Among the writers whom Hetzel persuaded to assist in restoring the merveilleux to children's books and who had worked with him on his highly successful publications *Scènes de la Vie publique et privée des animaux* (1840–42) and *Le Diable à Paris* (1844–46) were Alexandre Dumas, Paul de Musset, Charles Nodier, and George Sand (Amantine-Aurore-Lucile Dupin). They were all associated with the Romantic movement, which idealised the notion of childhood, seeing the child as the embodiment of innocence and spontaneity and a symbol of a lost golden age of purity and joy.[28] They were easily persuaded by the potency of the Romantic myth of the specialness of childhood to write for the young, and, encouraged by Hetzel, attempted to take children's literature back to its roots by exploiting the potential of the folk tale and fairy tale for imaginative and fantastical creation. This initiative also reflected the contemporary enthusiasm amongst adult readers for the *conte fantastique*, a short story of supernatural happenings that intrude into the real world in a disconcerting slippage between dream, hallucination, and reality. The fairy tales of E. T. A Hoffmann, like *Nussknacker und Mausekönig* (1816), can be seen as precursors of those of the French Romantics, who shared the interest in highly imaginative scenarios, grotesque characters, and metamorphoses and were inspired by a similar desire to reject dogmatism and conformity although, in their children's tales, they tended to avoid some of the more terrifying scenarios.[29] Their newly crafted fairy tales are pure escapism, firmly set in the world of the merveilleux rather than the banal and mediocre real world and, like many earlier fairy tales, feature humble peasant folk in rural settings. They were published in a small format (*in octavo*), attractively bound, and included a large number of illustrations. The Romantic penchant for vignettes, free-floating images without a frame used either as headpieces, tailpieces, or incorporated within the text, linked word and image more closely than ever before.[30] In this collection were Alexandre Dumas's *Histoire d'un casse-noisette* (1845), a reworking of Hoffmann's tale, which had 220 vignettes by Bertall; Musset's *Monsieur le Vent et Madame la Pluie* (1845); Nodier's *Trésor des Fèves et Fleur des Pois* (1844), with 100 vignettes by Tony Johannot; and George Sand's *Histoire du véritable Gribouille* (1851), illustrated by her son Maurice Sand.

Nodier asserted his admiration for Mme d'Aulnoy, Perrault, and even Berquin, claiming that he would wish his own works to be placed on a library shelf marked *ad usum adulescentulorum*.[31] The popular *Trésor des Fèves et Fleur de Pois*, subtitled explicitly 'conte des fées', employs almost parodically many of the devices of the more extravagant eighteenth-century fairy tale to create a bizarre initiation narrative in a world in which time and space are destabilised. A poor elderly peasant couple who have no children find a baby boy amongst their bean plants and name him Trésor des Fèves. As he grows up, their bean fields expand and flourish until it is decided to send him, at the age of twelve, to see something of the wider world and make his fortune. After encounters with a series of talking animals (including an entertaining fake philanthropic wolf) who do not play the traditional animal helper roles but exploit his generosity, the boy rescues the beautiful princess Fleur des Pois who is trapped in her tiny but strangely capacious chickpea carriage and is sent on a vertiginous journey lasting six years. He is rewarded, in the traditional manner, with a purse shaped like a pea pod containing magical objects that will help him achieve his every wish. His modest requests for shelter and food produce a sumptuous pavilion, a mouthwatering feast based on sugared puréed peas, and a wondrous palace containing, amongst other essentials for the wealthy gentleman, a picture gallery, a cabinet for antiquities, and a library of all the books that might be considered the most entertaining and useful for a young reader: *Don Quixote, Robinson Crusoe,* and *Gulliver's Travels*; almanacs; the works of the Bibliothèque bleue (the Oudot edition, naturally); books on agriculture, gardening, and fishing; and, of course, fairy tales. Contrary to the endings of traditional rags-to-riches tales, however, the novelty of wealth soon palls and when eventually he longs for his simple childhood amongst the bean fields and throws away his peapod purse in despair, a final narrative sleight of hand reunites him with his parents and his bride to be, the princess. The happy couple are to live with the aged parents in the palace, which is 'un pays d'âme et d'imagination où l'on ne vieillit plus et où l'on ne meurt pas', for, the narrator adds smoothly, 'C'est ainsi que finissent les contes de fées.'[32] In the close adherence to the fairy-tale model there is a tongue-in-cheek mood throughout the text, manifest in occasional asides from the narrator and in the relentless and ingenious variations on the use of peas, beans, and pea pods as both setting and agents of magic.

The Romantic fairy tale is perhaps most fully exemplified by George Sand's *Histoire du véritable Gribouille* (1850) with its idealised vision of nature and childhood and its exalted noble sentiments of heroism and self-sacrifice cast in a fantastic mould. Hetzel had already published Sand's *François le champi* and *La Petite Fadette* in 1848 and 1849, respectively, and requested a new tale for children based on the character of Gribouille, a gentle and wise simpleton figure of proverbial fame. The story of the struggle of a simple, naïve child's message of love against the forces of darkness is divided into two parts with the enticingly paradoxical titles 'Comment Gribouille se jeta dans la rivière par crainte de se mouiller' and 'Comment Gribouille se jeta dans le feu par crainte d'être brûlé'. The plot gestures initially towards Perrault's *Le Petit Poucet* in its portrayal of the disadvantaged youngest of seven children, but this narrative soon reveals a darker, more violent side. Gribouille's parents are greedy and dishonest, and the child is not only unloved for his difference from his uncouth siblings and misunderstood for his gentle docility but viciously beaten for his failure to conform to their ways. He is deemed to be a cowardly simpleton but is, in effect, a wise child whose common sense, diligence, and kind, self-sacrificing nature make his plight and his longing to be loved all the more pitiful. The tale is one of multiple metamorphoses and a constant slippage between dream and reality. The Romantic origins of the tale are manifest in the portrayal of the magical elements as spirits of nature that can take human form at will. Gribouille is confronted with the forces of good and evil when he accidentally releases the shape-shifting M. Bourdon from his imprisonment in a tree. He is adopted, with his parents' enthusiastic support, by M. Bourdon, but flees from his attempts to educate him as a wicked magician and is rescued by a good spirit in the shape of a beautiful maiden with blue wings who encourages him to leap into the river, where he is swept away. This suspenseful moment ends the first part, which echoes with his uncaring siblings' taunting proverbial refrain 'Fin comme Gribouille, qui se jette dans l'eau par crainte de la pluie'.[33]

Transformed into a branch of a tree, Gribouille is transported to an island paradise, where he enjoys a century of innocent frolic with the flower nymphs. The Romantic privileging of childlike simplicity is embedded in the narrative as his old world—now under the sway of M. Bourdon and slowly destroying itself through greed, corruption, and cynicism—can only be saved by Gribouille's special gift of love. In a monumental battle between M. Bourdon's insects and the birds led by the queen of the meadows, Gribouille saves the day, confounding M. Bourdon's threat to use him as a hostage and place him on a pyre by leaping into the flames himself. The naïve child thus becomes a Christlike figure, as with his death the forces of good triumph, humanity is restored to a state of fraternal happiness, and Gribouille becomes a martyr in the human world. Transformed once more into a forget-me-not, he is once again removed to the island paradise where he lives alternately as a flower and as a nymph for eternity. His actions thus speak not of his absurdity, but of the redemptive power of love. Sand's allegorical tale carries a clear moral message not unlike that found in more conventional contemporary children's literature, but the use of the fantastic elevates it to a more universal level of significance. It is saved from the maudlin by the breathtaking speed of events, worthy of the most baroque fairy tale, and by the constant shifting between idyllic and distopic scenarios. The strife between the insects and birds mirrors that between humans, and Sand does not spare the young readers' sensibilities in the vivid and cruel descriptions of the battles and man's inhumanity to man. Maurice Sand's vignettes capture the metaphorical role of the natural world in the text with strange, sombre landscapes swarming with even stranger and disconcerting creatures that are half human, half insect.

It is tempting to see Sand's depiction of a harsh, materialistic, and egoistic society as a comment on that of mid-nineteenth-century France after the revolution of 1848 in which she had been intimately involved in an unofficial political capacity as a writer of propaganda for the provisional government. Her contemporary pastoral novel, *La Petite Fadette* (1849), is dedicated to the prisoners of the revolution (among them her friend, the poet Alphonse de Lamartine) and similarly promotes a message of the transformative power of love and mutual understanding. M. Bourdon's realm is one in which greed and plundering have stifled goodness and compassion, and both humans and the dominating swarms of bees, hornets, and ants are in constant bloody competition for survival. The evil genius's credo, rejected by Gribouille, is that 'dans ce monde, il faut être voleur ou volé, meurtrier ou meurtri, tyran ou esclave … . Le plus sûr, selon moi, est de laisser travailler les autres et de prendre; prendre, prendre, mon garçon, par force ou par adresse.'[34] The vision of a society based on mutual love and respect reflects Sand's own particular political stance based on a utopian Christian socialism.

Hetzel returned to fairy tales later with one of the best-known of his publications, the expensive folio edition of *Contes de Perrault* (1861), with its exquisite and sensual illustrations by Gustave Doré, who was to illustrate many of the literary classics of Europe. His partly disturbing and partly seductive image of Le Petit Chaperon Rouge and the wolf in bed together, their heads turned towards each other on the pillow, exactly captured the spirit of Perrault's gloss on the tale in his *Moralité* (that young girls should beware of sweet-talking wolves who try to enter their bedchambers) and encapsulated the mood of the story for generations to come. Doré's detailed and atmospheric images of vast gloomy forests and exotic palaces have continued to delight child and adult readers alike, and still accompany the Livre de Poche edition today. Hetzel's lengthy and anecdotic preface, signed as P.-J. Stahl, offers a passionate defence of the merveilleux and its suitability for children.

On the question of morality to which is owed the 'milliers de livres en plomb dont on écrase le premier âge dans notre soi-disant frivole pays de France', he argues that for children moral teaching should be 'légère, aimable et gaie comme eux-mêmes. Elle ne doit donc grandir qu'à mesure qu'ils grandissent, et s'élever qu'à mesure qu'ils s'élèvent.'[35] Fairy tales resurfaced briefly with the Comtesse de Ségur's *Nouveaux contes de fées* (1857, see chapter 2) and Jacques Porchat's *Contes merveilleux* (1858) and briefly enjoyed new life in collaboration with the quest for knowledge in George Sand's *Contes d'une grand'mère* (1873 and 1876, discussed in chapter 3). However, the second half of the nineteenth century had other interests, and fairy tales were ousted by a different form of magic, that of science, and a different kind of adventure narrative. Nevertheless, as will become apparent, their structure and concern with the themes of initiation and maturation and of good versus evil continued to be exploited in different ways.

ADVENTURE STORIES

Although writers of fiction for the young were coming to appreciate the need to cater for the capabilities and interests of different age ranges, they generally focussed their efforts on the younger child reader. For young people of, say, twelve to fifteen, the contemporary moral stories and fairy tales must have held little interest. It must be recognised, of course that, as in previous centuries, young readers were not limited to the books written especially for them, but also had access to the books their parents read. In the first half of the nineteenth century, the immense popularity of novels by Balzac and Hugo, the popular works of Eugène Sue and the historical novels of Sir Walter Scott (whose reputation was high in France) and Alexandre Dumas père, many of which were serialised in *feuilleton* form, assured their availability to any young readers who had the opportunity and ability to tackle them. The popularity of Scott and Dumas, in particular, marked the beginnings of a genre that was to become a dominant feature of books for the young in the second half of the century: the adventure story. The development of this genre also signalled the sharper division between targeted readerships on the basis of gender. As will be seen in later chapters, the adventure stories in their glorification of male heroism were targeted at young male readers (although they also certainly had female readers) while books for girls went in a different direction.

Alexandre Dumas père's vast output of some five hundred works that brought history alive, mixing historical fact (for which he was indebted to an army of collaborators) with imaginative fiction and creating romantic heroes of minor historical personages, brought him considerable popular success with readers of all ages. Like many historical novelists, Dumas took liberties with chronology and often assigned his characters roles in historical events in which they did not in fact take part, but the background is meticulously and colourfully detailed, immersing the reader in the relevant period with exceptional vividness. Although not specifically targeted at young readers, these swashbuckling romances with their escapist, action-packed adventures of a bygone era and their picturesque descriptions of people and places certainly found a ready audience amongst older children and young adults. His most lastingly popular novel was, arguably, *Les Trois Mousquetaires* (1844), set in the reign of Louis XIII. The young protagonist D'Artagnan, who comes to Paris from Gascony in the hopes of becoming a member of the elite musketeers, becomes involved in averting a royal scandal, fighting against corruption, and defeating the villains alongside his glamorous associates Arthos, Porthos, and Aramis. The ingredients of this text have all the potential to hold the attention as well as delight a young readership avid for stimulating fare: the trajectory of the youthful idealistic hero from inexperienced adolescent to the attainment of his dream, the importance of solidarity among friends, the themes of glory and risking all for a noble cause, a large cast of memorable larger-than-life characters, the dominance of dialogue and action, the regular deployment of comic relief, and the devices of melodrama (coincidences, revelations, surprises, and suspense). This text and *Le Comte de Monte-Cristo* (1844), set in the early years of the century, in which Edmond Dantès, having discovered a fabulous treasure on the island of Monte-Cristo, assumes the persona of count in order to destroy the enemies responsible for having him imprisoned and falsely accused of being a Bonapartist spy, have remained the most popular of Dumas's works and continue to be available in abridged editions for young readers both in French and in translation today.

Imports of translations from English, many mediated to a French audience through the *Collection des romans étrangers*, the fourth section of Hachette's Bibliothèque des chemins de fer, strengthened the status of adventure stories and their popularity with adolescent readers. The novels of the American writer and traveller James Fenimore Cooper, in particular, which depicted a completely different cultural context and focussed on fast-moving action above all, achieved enormous success in France between 1820 and 1830. Most successful were his stories of heroism on the high seas and his stories of the Wild West, with struggles between the pioneers and the American Indians that offered a seductive concept of individual freedom and heroism in exotic surroundings.

His best-known work, *The Last of the Mohicans*, published in 1826, was quickly translated into French (*Le Dernier des Mohicans,* 1826), followed by *The Prairie* (*La Prairie,* 1828) and *The Deerslayer* (*Le Tuer de daims,* 1842) amongst others. Long before this genre was to have an incalculable impact on popular culture when it found its way to the medium of cinema, the picture of frontier life and of the solitude and dangers endured by the pioneers, the often bloodthirsty plots, and the descriptions of the wilderness offered an entirely new reading experience to young readers in France more accustomed to the often insipid moral tales.

The Western adventure story was taken up by French writers who had themselves experienced life in exotic climes firsthand. The novels of Gabriel Ferry (pseudonym of Louis de Bellemare) and Gustave Aimard (pseudonym of Olivier Gloux) are regarded as the principal exemplars of this genre, creating stereotypes of characters, settings, and plots that became integral to the vision of the American West in France.[36] Once again, these were novels aimed at an adult readership that also found an enthusiastic adolescent audience. Ferry's travel writing in the *Revue de deux mondes* and his later novels *Le Coureur des bois* (1850) and *Costal l'Indien, roman historique* (1852) created a mythology of the southern United States that became a favourite model for French writers. He had spent ten years, between 1830 and 1840, in Mexico, and his interest, like that of Carson McCulley, the creator of Zorro, lay in the period that followed the Mexican War of Independence. Ferry represents an earlier West than the more familiar one populated by gun-toting cowboys, sheriffs, and saloon girls. His favourite hero, a half-Canadian, half-Indian trapper (the *coureur des bois*) who is taciturn, courageous, and occasionally cruel, acts as guide through the wilderness and always fights on the side of justice, is the precursor of many outsider peripatetic heroes. The relationship between the coureur de bois and the other characters mirrors in effect that between author and reader, for he acts as guide, mediator of information, and leader in adventures. Ferry's works were full of dramatic incident but also detailed in terms of the description of the wide open spaces of his settings and of the historical background of revolution and bitter power struggles. His work influenced that of Gustave Aimard, who had a glamorous career as ship's boy, panhandler, and trapper in America and produced novels of pioneer life with titles like *Les Trappeurs d'Arkansas* (1858), *Les Pirates des prairies* (1859), *La Loi de lynch* (1859), *La Fièvre d'or* (1860), and *Les Outlaws de Missouri* (1868). As well as simplifying and further popularising the myth of the Wild West, Aimard wrote stories of the high seas and piracy often set in the seventeenth century. (*Les Titans de la mer* [1873] features both pirates *and* Indians.) As might be expected from his huge and rapid output, the plots of Aimard's novels are formulaic and repetitive and proceed at a breathless pace, depending, like the popular *roman-feuilleton*, on constant thrills, suspense, and a great deal of violence. Unlike Ferry, Aimard is less interested in instructing the reader in local colour and accurate historical recreation. His characters are recurrent stereotypes and the settings abstract rather than realistically described: the prairies and deserts are merely backdrops for action rather than places of interest in themselves. With the rise of the realist novel, however, such works fell from favour with the literary élite in the second half of the century, and became almost exclusively associated with popular culture and a juvenile readership.

Because these adventure stories were initially targeting adult readers, the didactic imperative was less overt and subordinated to description and incident, although the qualities of the heroes (tenacity, courage, decency and determination) and their actions in the cause of righting wrongs and defending the weak lend a moral dimension to the texts. In novels of adventure that specifically targeted a young readership, however, the traditional didactic agenda usually remained more visible. The novels of Robert Michael Ballantyne and Captain Frederick Marryat might be cited as examples from the English-speaking world in which the author feels obliged to present his readership with a clear moral and religious message while entertaining with action-packed adventures in unfamilar and dangerous environments. Marryat's *Masterman Ready or the Wreck of the Pacific* (1841–42) was popular in France and a number of Ballantyne's works, including *The Coral Island: A Tale of the Pacific Ocean* (1858) were quickly translated. Hachette published sixteen novels by Captain Thomas Mayne Reid in the Bibliothèque rose, including *Les Chasseurs de girafes* (c. 1879), *Bruin ou les chasseurs d'ours* (c. 1876), and *La Chasse au Léviathan* (1782). In these novels, Reid, who had lived in America and served in the war against Mexico, privileged educational descriptions of flora and fauna over overt moralising and piety. In France, the dichotomy of instruction and entertainment can best be seen in the enduring popularity of the Robinsonnade.

THE NINETEENTH-CENTURY ROBINSONNADE

The most influential novel in the history of French children's literature was an English work, Defoe's *Robinson Crusoe* (1719). The status of this text in France was established irrevocably when it was identified by Rousseau in his hugely influential *Emile, ou de l'éducation* (1762) as the only work of fiction that he would place in the hands of a young reader. Rousseau praises it for the depiction of survival in an alien environment far from civilisation and for its promotion of industry, determination, and initiative, Robinson Crusoe becoming the archetypal self-made man. Defoe's book spawned hundreds of adaptations and revised versions for readers of different ages in France alone, as well as imitations that themselves constituted a genre, the *Robinsonnade*.[37] The potential of Defoe's plot for adaptation to suit a wide range of differing agenda was quickly identified by writers seeking a more exciting vehicle through which to mediate moral values, and Robinsonnades continued to proliferate in France in every decade of the nineteenth century. They in fact remained a seductive scenario for novelists well into the twentieth century, as Michel Tournier's *Vendredi ou la vie sauvage* of 1971 demonstrates.

The popularity of this model in France was increased by the translation in 1785 of Joachim Heinrich Campe's *Robinson der Jungere* (as *Le Nouveau Robinson*; discussed in volume 1 of this study) and that of Johann David Wyss's highly successful *Der Schweizerische Robinson* (as *Le Robinson suisse, ou Journal d'un père de famille, naufragé avec ses enfans*) in 1814 by Mme de Montolieu. In Wyss's lengthy book of 1813, the adventures undergone by the family of six—father, mother, and four sons—shipwrecked on a desert island somewhere near New Guinea for over ten years serve as the basis for lessons on natural history, the physical sciences, agricultural methods, and artisan skills and in this respect it resembles many educational books of the period. Through endeavour, resilience, and resourcefulness, the family succeed in creating their own version of European civilization by managing the plant and animal life on their island and drawing on the inexhaustible supply of scientific knowledge they seem to have at their disposal. The text is heavily imbued with explicit Christian sentiment, promoting an idealised image of family unity, love of fellow humankind, an unwavering trust in God's providence, and the rewards of Christan virtue. To modern readers, the novel may seem both an overly optimistic belief in human nature and capabilities and ecologically insensitive in its approach to the utilisation and destruction of the island's resources. It also famously stretches the reader's credulity in its eclectic portrayal of the wildlife on the island, for creatures from every continent appear to coexist: lions and elephants, penguins, kangeroos, walruses, bears, wolves, whales, and boa constrictors all make their appearance. Like Defoe's text, Wyss's book underwent many revisions, abridgements, contractions, and, indeed, expansions, in translation. Mme Montolieu, a friend of Mme de Genlis and a confirmed disciple of

Rousseau, incorporated additions of her own that subsequently found their way into other versions. In 1824, she published another continuation titled *Suite du Robinson suisse. La famille naufragée*. A further translation of Wyss's book by Elise Voïart was published in 1837, in the introduction to the 1841 edition of which Nodier accords Wyss's text the premier position amongst the élite of children's books and acclaims the complete course in education that it offers.

The Robinsonnades published in the nineteenth century exemplify a range of what Gérard Genette calls 'diagetic transpositions'—that is, the rewriting of a text to make it appropriate to different audiences in temporal, geographical, or social terms—and they are fascinating for the cultural, political, social, and moral assumptions they reveal.[38] One of the most obvious tendencies was to introduce a youthful protagonist faced with analogous circumstances and dilemmas. A few examples are the acculturated *Le Robinson de douze ans* (1818) by Mme Malles de Beaulieu, the story of a French ship's boy abandoned on a desert island; Julie Delafaye-Bréhier's *Le Robinson français ou le petit naufragé* (1827); and Eugénie Foa's *Les Nouveaux Robinsons, aventure extraordinaire de deux enfants qui cherchent leur mère* (1865), all of which serve to promote the virtues of hard work and initiative in a more dynamic context than the conventional moral tale that in many ways they resemble. The setting of the archetypal narrative of survival was relocated from the desert island to other exotic climes that offered the reader information on landscape, flora, and fauna, thus producing Ernest Fouinet's *Le Robinson des glaces* (1851), Gustave Aimard's *Le Robinson des Alpes* (1888), and Louis Boussenard's *Les Robinsons de Guyane*, 1892). This approach culminated a century later, inevitably, in Jacques Hoven's *Robinson Crusoë sur Mars* (1896).

The strategy of targeting readers of different sexes, already well developed by the second quarter of the nineteenth century, also impacted upon the appropriation of the Crusoe model. In order to appeal to female readers, the protagonist's gender was reassigned, as in Mme Woillez's *Le Petit Robinson des demoiselles* (1835). In this novel, which is a heady mixture of exciting adventures and sentimentality, Emma, aged thirteen, is shipwrecked on an island with her faithful dog and learns to survive in much the same way as her male counterparts do. However, the concern with cultural norms and gender roles betrays itself in a number of ways. Emma is spared terrifying encounters with unfriendly natives, and the discovery of a cave in which she sets up home obviates the question of her ability to handle hammer and nails and allows her to focus on the domestic arrangements instead, making cooking pots and clothes. The introduction of Henriette, an orphan child younger than Emma for whom she must care, affords her not just companionship but the opportunity to develop her maternal and domestic instincts. The text is accompanied by attractive engravings showing Emma's progress and reflect this dualism. In one, Emma is shown in a traditional Robinsonian outfit (fur jacket, straw hat, and woven sandals) and carrying a bow. Her hair is neatly arranged and she appears both serene and well turned out. At her feet lie cooking pots and carpenter's tools, and she is surrounded by clearly domesticated animals: a parrot sits on her shoulder and a goat gazes up at her face. Beside her stands her dog, carrying a basket in his mouth. Despite the strangeness of the setting and the clothes, this image has the irresistible air of a well brought-up young girl setting out on a shopping expedition to the local market. The ending is a happy, if rather implausible, one: Emma is reunited with her father and they return with Henriette to live happily ever after in their château. In terms of the lessons they aim to convey, such Robinsonnades shared the agenda of the moral tales of the day, but a significant departure was the recognition that arousing the reader's interest and wonder by exposing their protagonists to dangerous adventures in exotic climes was a potent vehicle for the didactic element. The nineteenth century was to become the great age of the adventure story and Robinsonnades played a significant part in the development of this long-lasting genre.

LOUIS DESNOYERS: REALISM ON THE ROAD

Louis Desnoyers's *Les Mésaventures de Jean-Paul Choppart*, first published in serial form in the *Journal des Enfants* in 1833 under the title *Les Illusions maternelles* and in book form in 1836, is perhaps the most celebrated children's book from the first half of the century and one of the most revised and abridged. It was substantially revised in collaboration with Hetzel for publication in 1864 and achieved a second, wide and appreciative, readership. Desnoyers had contributed to a number of both adult and juvenile journals and had initiated in *Le Siècle* the system of the roman-feuilleton, the publication of novels in instalments. He was thus well aware of the potency of a mixture of suspenseful episodes, mysteries, and humour.

In his preface, Desnoyers deplores the state of children's literature, condemning works targeting children hitherto as 'niaises, ou barbares, ou inutiles, ou dangereuses', including fairy tales in the latter.[39] He goes further in the 1843 preface to his later novel, *Les Aventures de Robert-Robert* (1840), attacking the kind of virtue peddled by children's books as banal, exaggerated, false, and outmoded and riven with superstition and prejudice. He then praises the (unspecified) 'hommes d'un vrai talent' who have written not specially designed children's books but good books 'd'un certain genre', addressing the young reader with the same sensibility as they would their adult readers. (In the absence of specific references, it is tempting to wonder whether Desnoyers is simply contrasting the efforts of the many women writers of the period who were specifically children's authors with those of his male contemporaries, who occasionally produced works for the young.) One of his main objections to children's literature of the time was that it often lacked realism and relevance to the real world, 'comme si l'erreur était plus facile à comprendre que la vérité'.[40]

The plot and the protagonist of *Les Mésaventures de Jean-Paul Choppart*, the first of a number of nineteenth-century 'on the road' narratives, could not be more different from those of other contemporary works although it employs some of the conventional narrative strategies of the moral tale and contains echoes of Romanticism. It recounts the adventures of a runaway delinquent boy of age nine and a half and his naïve, reluctant, but easily led younger companion Petit-Jacques. This is only superficially a traditional pairing of opposing types (bad child/good child), since Petit-Jacques is soon seduced by the picture Jean-Paul paints of freedom from parental and social constraints and his role is never that of moral example or instrument of redemption for the transgressor. Despite the desire to escape from their everyday lives, they are not the romanticised wanderers of the contemporary fairy tales nor the innocents of traditional initiation narratives. It is not a longing for adventure that drives the protagonist to leave home initially—as is the case in Carlo Collodi's *Pinocchio* (1881), a text with which this is sometimes compared—but a desire to avoid punishment. The novel has more in common with another genre, the picaresque or rogue novel, one not normally associated with a juvenile audience. It differs, however, in that Jean-Paul Choppart, the son of a respectable bourgeois family, is already a delinquent, a scruffy, rude, and incorrigibly malicious child who torments his sisters, the family servants, and other children and drives his parents to despair. The reader is advised at the start, however, that this unsympathetic protagonist is not totally bad at heart and that he will only come to a recognition of his waywardness through time and adversity, and indeed he becomes less loathsome and more pitiable as the narrative progresses. With its extended plot and increased interest in individual psychology, Desnoyers's novel thus anticipated the Bildungsroman, or novel of individual development, that was to become a popular genre for both adult and young readers.

When domestic mischief escalates into a violent confrontation with his father, Jean-Paul flees and, after stealing some cherries, is taken to prison. Bravado pushes him to persuade the jailor's son, Petit-Jacques, to help him escape and accompany him on a journey of adventure. Yet Jean-Paul's adventures are not really adventures, nor are they heroic in any way. In many respects, the boys are victims of circumstances, for they end up working in a flour mill, and, after running away yet again, are taken up by a travelling show where beneath the superficial glamour they encounter cruelty, hunger, and exploitation such as they have never known. Nor are they truly as independent and free as they imagine, for they are watched over by a mysterious 'Géant' who repeatedly intervenes to save them and whose identity is only revealed on the last page of the text. The boys' sojourn with the travelling show is the opportunity for an extended satire on the bizarre company of caricatured street entertainers. They are not the strange fantastical creatures they seem at first, but shabby con artists. The *chef de troupe*, the Marquis de la Galoche, a charlatan and cheat with a quick wit and a ready, seductive line in plausible patter, and his wife, the self-styled 'Reine des îles Salmigondis', sword-swallower and mistress of the menagerie, lead a hand-to-mouth existence, quarrelling and abusing each other and their miserable troupe of performing animals and children. There is much humour and suspense in the descriptions of the boys' discomfiture as they learn to perform—disguised as savages, animals, and freaks of nature—in front of an audience. Their efforts always end in disaster: Jean-Paul falls into a tub of eggs and ripe cheeses, is forced to eat raw chickens, and, together with Petit-Jacques, causes havoc in the neighbourhood when they try to flee, dressed as bears, from a bear-baiting scene arranged by the Marquis. The text is by no means anarchic in its apparent relish of these disasters, however, for the scenes are punctuated by moral reflections on the part of the narrator, who maintains a constant dialogue with the reader, warning against the consequences of greed, gambling, dishonesty, and gullibility and railing against the exploitation of the weak and vulnerable.

Just as nothing is ever what it seems in the show, so the status of the boys as runaways is not what it appears, even to them. During a final show put on in a large country house, it transpires that their 'grand voyage autour du monde', which in effect has lasted only a fortnight and has taken them no farther than ten leagues from home, has been masterminded from afar as a plan of correction by Jean-Paul's father. Their oppressors have all colluded with instructions to punish the boys as much as possible and make life so uncomfortable for them that they repent of their actions and come to recognise the value of a repectable, loving home. The mystery of the tall stranger 'Géant' whose constant appearances at critical moments have unnerved Jean-Paul and tantalised the reader is revealed in a rather lame and unbelievable explanation: he is the concierge of the new house bought by M. Choppart, and has been recruited to act as overseer of the plan. In a dénouement worthy of a more traditional moral tale, Jean-Paul not only repents in tears but thanks his tormentors for their profitable chastisements.

Ultimately, this text, which is clearly addressed to a privileged child audience, presents a conventional message. The boys' misadventures prove that home is best and that the desire for freedom from social constraint is a dire mistake. Parental affection and filial gratitude and obedience are endorsed, although it could be objected that M. Choppart's plan raises moral questions about the validity of his method in the light of the suffering the boys endure in learning their lesson. The prejudices of the day emerge in the portrayal of characters, too: the Marquis, although also a collaborator in the plan, is excluded from the family reunion because, the narrator informs us, people of that sort are paid, not thanked. In the final summary of the fortunes of all the characters we are told that the irrepressible Marquis enjoys a brief moment of success when he persuades people to invest in his new scheme of piping music into their homes—in effect, he invents Muzak! The depiction of the poorer members of society, when not satirical and farcical, is cursory and conventional, for this is not where the author's interest lies. The novel is innovative in a number of respects, however. The reader is given access to a world very different from that inhabited by the majority of literary children at the time and is exposed to the cynicism, cruelty, and corruption encountered in real life. There are clear references to contemporary times in comments on the law, the fashion for fortunetellers, the cholera outbreak in the capital, and the financial exploitation of the gullible by scam mongers. The dangers to which vulnerable children are exposed are depicted in a grim manner in the interpolated life story of the clown Panouille, whose backwardness and lack of self-discipline result in him being stolen from his working-class parents by a fake beggar and enrolled in a begging fraternity. This truly picaresque tale of life on the streets amongst rogues that completes the perversion of the child's character is a mirror image, without the humour, of the fate that might have befallen Jean-Paul and Petit-Jacques and stands as a warning to the reader of the worst possible consequences of turning one's back on the security of home. Just as the boys are ultimately protected from too much harm, however, so the humour of the text protects the reader to some extent from the implications of this portrayal. The 'Géant' can thus be seen as the alter ego of the author, in that they both allow exposure to the harshness of life and the evil in society to a certain point, but also control that exposure and ultimately restore the child to a reassuring bourgeois environment of love and support.

Hetzel described the moral of the book thus, 'que la sagesse vaut décidement mieux que la folie et qu'il est mille fois plus fatigant de ne rien faire ou de faire des sottises que de travailler et de se bien conduire'.[41] Jean-Paul and Petit-Jacques are finally set on the road to being useful citizens: Jean-Paul becomes a model student and Petit-Jacques, whose social status as the son of a jailer prevents him from attending college, becomes an apprentice to a confectioner. In later versions, passages like the reflection on the treatment of child acrobats were removed as were some of the lengthy satirical descriptions and social commentaries that detract from the narrative of the boys' adventures and might, in any case, have gone over the heads of younger readers. Generally, however, the style is full of colour, humour, and verve, and the twists and turns in the fortunes of the boys hold the reader's attention. The foregrounding of an egoistic and rebellious child character and the colourful descriptions of the boys' misadventures in the mill and the fairground must have been exhilarating reading for a child of the 1830s. This is confirmed by Hetzel in his 1864 preface, where he claims that 'Jean-Paul Choppart a fait la joie, je devrais dire la jubilation, de tout ce qui était enfant il y a trente ans.'[42]

JOURNALS

The 1830s also saw the beginnings of an explosion in the publication of journals for young readers. The recognition of the child as an important entity in her own right, and by implication, of the potential of the child as consumer, was articulated in an editorial in *L'Abeille* in 1839: 'Enfants, vous devez être fiers, car vous êtes devenus une puissance! Vous aussi, vous avez votre presse et vos écrivains. Vous avez vos journaux, qui cherchent à vous instruire, vos écrivains, qui veulent vous plaire et vous intéresser.'[43] The increasing numbers of literate young and of newly literate adults after 1833 presented a huge new market to publishers for specially targeted magazines. The brief discussion here is no more than a broad-brush account of the development of magazines for young readers in the middle decades of the century. Between 1832 and 1856 some fifty-five new journals, albeit mostly short-lived, appeared, some for a mixed readership and many specifically for girls. The longest surviving titles from this period were Eugénie Foa's *Journal des enfants* (1832–97); the *Journal des demoiselles* (1833–1922); the *Journal des jeunes personnes* (1833–94), edited by Mme Ulliac-Trémadeure; and the *Magasin des demoiselles* (1844–81); their success was due to their ability to adapt to changing tastes and commercial methods.[44] Illustrations, including images by renowned illustrators and, after 1846, images in colour, were increasingly included. These magazines were largely for adolescents rather than for the very young and those addressed to young girls had a strong focus on fashion advice and news. They were not cheap products, and consequently were accessible only to the children of parents who could afford a subscription.

The writer Jules Janin set out in his editorial to the first issue of the *Journal des enfants* his desire to produce a quality paper for young readers and, like Hetzel, persuaded established writers to contribute both fiction and articles. Among them were the Vicomte de Chateaubriand, Judith Gautier, Victor Hugo, Alphonse de Lamartine, and Jules Michelet as well as those already associated with writing for children, like Desnoyers, Foa, and Tastu. The three main objectives of journals of this period were, like most children's literature of the time, to instruct, to entertain, and to inculcate morals. The points of view and narrative strategies presented in their fiction and nonfiction articles were closely akin to those in other works for children. The fictional or real-life anecdotes that commonly featured child protagonists as heroes or victims were socially and morally conservative, with the social order restored and endorsed by the endings. Although Catholicism was no longer the state religion after 1830, journals for the young continued to adhere resolutely to Catholic doctrine in their general approach. 'La religion est notre appui, notre guide, notre boussole ici-bas' was the opinion of the *Journal des jeunes persones* in 1846.[45]

The intellectual formation of readers was also important, with travel tales and historical narratives preferred over sentimental novels or novels of manners, which, according to the *Revue des demoiselles* in January 1845, presented a danger to readers by distorting their perception of the world.[46] Many titles mirrored those of adult papers (*Courrier des enfants*, *Gazette de la jeunesse*) to underline their seriousness and desirability, and although the emphasis of the contents was on morality and religion, there was a progressive tendency to offer factual and topical information. A major concern was the popularisation of science and technology, and readers were introduced to the latest advances in medicine (Edward Jenner's discovery of vaccine in 1796) and physics, as well as articles on astronomy, zoology, and biology; developments in industry; and such marvels as the first railways in 1837 and the laying of the telegraph cables beneath the Mediterranean Sea in 1853. The presentation of such information gradually came to take a place of prime importance in the journals and the emphasis on moral and religious themes began to diminish. As Alain Fourment notes, 'Il faut se mettre au goût du jour. L'époque est à la science et à la technique.'[47]

A further significant innovation was the discussion of political and current affairs: the return of Napoleon's ashes to France in December 1840 and the visit to Normandy of Queen Victoria in September 1843, for example, were reported in detail. The upheavals of 1830 and 1848 were also discussed, although often some months after the events, and emphasis tended to be placed on the social aspects. Of the revolution of 1848, for example, an article in *La Mode des demoiselles* expressed the hope that 'de cette révolution, qui a été plutôt sociale que politique, il ressortira enfin une organisation qui laisse moins de misère', while the *Moniteur des demoiselles* even more outspokenly declared that 'un grand acte de justice vient de s'accomplir: le peuple a brisé ses chaines, il est libre!'[48] Such coverage was a noteworthy aspect of the contributions of journals to the education of the young, since fictional works they were offered mostly shied away from a totally realistic and unvarnished portrayal of social conditions. The picture conveyed of the misery of the underprivileged classes was far from the image of the stoic, grateful poor, the objects of charity so often featured in moral tales. There were also articles on other countries (with China a particular interest) and issues like colonialism and slavery. France's colonial exploits in Africa were stoutly defended and praised as an important civilising duty in some journals: 'Admirez les efforts de notre armée, qui depuis seize ans lutte contre la nature et les hommes pour faire de l'Algérie une nouvelle France', the editorial of *L'Image* shamelessly encouraged its readers in 1847.[49] Opinion on slavery varied from outright condemnation to a more hesitant reluctance to show the white planters in a poor light. (Slavery was abolished by French law in April 1848.) The editors of journals in this period thus began to seek to arm their targeted readers for the modern world with knowledge rather than moral sentiment, and demonstrated an awareness of the presence and needs of an adolescent readership that would benefit from material beyond what was deemed suitable for a child, if they were not yet ready for that addressed to adults.

2

THE NOVEL OF DOMESTIC REALISM, OR THE FAMILY NOVEL

During the years of the July Monarchy (1830-48) and influenced by Louis-Philippe's more informal lifestyle and the devotion of the royal parents for their children, the ideal of family life had taken a strong hold on the public imagination and become the keystone of bourgeois society. The care and education of children and the development of the infant personality became a matter of great interest. This preoccupation with the family and the child's role in it continued in the Second Empire under Napoleon III (1852–70), who with his wife, the Empress Eugénie, cultivated an image of family intimacy.[1] The same phenomenon occurred in Britain, of course, where prints of Queen Victoria and Prince Albert playing with their offspring adorned the walls of many homes. It is this period from 1850 onwards, a period noted for its economic prosperity, civic improvement, and bourgeois self-assurance, that can be regarded as the most fruitful in the development of children's literature in the nineteenth century.[2]

The novel of domestic realism, or the family novel, developed from the moral tale of the first half of the century and mirrored the development of the realist novel for adults. Just as the novels of Honoré de Balzac and Stendhal and, a little later, Gustave Flaubert and Émile Zola were to respond to the middle classes' desire—increasingly dominant and flourishing after the Restoration—to read about characters like themselves and their neighbours, and a world with which they were familiar, so children's literature followed suit. The stories were expanded into lengthier narratives, divided into chapters with more complex and less predictable plots and involving more characters, and were more sustained in interest and variety. The genre offered an opportunity for women writers to enter the public arena, and large numbers were able to capitalise on their own experience as mothers and grandmothers, as had the exponents of governess literature in the eighteenth century. As in the realist novel for adults, writers of children's fiction took their plots and settings from contemporary society, and were largely concerned with family relationships and dilemmas or the plight of orphaned children and their search for a home and a niche within society. Plots were frequently motivated by economic concerns that affected children of both sexes and of both middle- and lower-class backgrounds. The struggle for survival of a bourgeois family fallen on hard times, and the new cares and responsibilities that this imposes upon its children, was a common theme. Yet, the wider fundamental problems of social constraints, poverty, inequality between the classes, and social oppression were never or rarely dealt with openly and objectively.[3] Whole areas of contemporary life—for example, the condition of the urban proletariat or the hardships of working children in the factories, mills, or mines—were largely glossed over in children's books despite the debates surrounding the laws that sought to address the problems. The hardships experienced by the poor were still generally portrayed as easily remedied by a gesture of benevolence towards individuals and any overt criticism of a social system that permitted oppression of the vulnerable tended to be replaced by a condemnation of the perversion of values at the individual and local levels. Whereas the tastes, manners, and ambitions of the middle classes were not just reflected but often satirised and attacked by writers of books for adults, we find, perhaps not surprisingly, a far more conventional and optimistic image of society in children's novels. Up to the 1880s and even beyond, the purchasers of books were likely to be, or aspired to be, members of the more economically privileged strata of society, and although the novels of domestic realism were less overtly and remorselessly edifying in their approach than earlier didactic moral tales, they still aimed to offer to their readers an education in moral and social values. The agenda of constructing, through address and an assumption of shared values, an ideal reader who would absorb unquestioningly the social, moral, and religious conventions of the prevailing dominant culture remained essentially unchanged from that of the earlier moral tale. Indeed, it is possible to argue that children's literature throughout the nineteenth century failed to liberate the child from adult authority (including that of the author) and ready-made ideologies, and therefore did not offer images of child characters growing to self-determinacy and having autonomy and agency.

Critics are frequently harsh on most nineteenth-century novels of domestic realism, condemning their conventionality, blandness, uniformity of themes, monotony of types, and their contrived, closed endings.[4] It is true that in many novels the characters and settings tend to lack differentiation and depth, and that the predictable happy endings that endorse contemporary values might be seen to stifle the reader's capacity for critical reflection. However, this is to underestimate the extent to which the novel for young readers evolved in the second half of the century. In the best and most enduring works, the narratives offer a far greater amount of precise detail about the settings, conditions, and accessories of daily life that provides the modern reader with a fascinating insight into the period. Although still often implausible and contrived, the plots unfold in settings that would have been familiar to many readers of the time, and the dilemmas or dangers are those that a reader might well encounter in real life. They also appealed to and stimulated the young reader's interest in the family life of other people and, especially for those educated at home, in activities at school. The young protagonists, both male and female, became less one-dimensional and more complex than in fictional narratives hitherto, even if they still shared some of the characteristics of the conventional good or bad child of edifying tales. The reader can follow the psychological development of the characters and the personal and moral challenges that they encounter as the narrative unfolds, rather than simply being coerced into admiration of an unchanging stereotype. However, at this stage, the characters are still modelled ultimately on the adult writer's concept of the child and childhood, and there is little attempt as yet to portray the child's inner life or to see the world through a child's eyes. Because of the predominance of women writers in this genre, the novel of domestic realism became increasingly associated with female readers and 'girls' stories' (even though they often featured male protagonists), a factor that undoubtedly affected their negative reception by early critics and writers of manuals of literature.

A central figure in the development of this genre was Louis Hachette, whose Bibiothèque rose illustrée collection was founded in 1856 as part of the Bibliothèque des chemins de fer series, designed to be sold at book stalls in railway stations. The highly successful Bibliothèque rose illustrée collection was presented in two formats, either with pink paper covers at two francs, or bound in red percaline embossed in gold lettering for two francs, seventy-five centimes, and initally offered a series of books for readers of ages four to eight and a series for readers aged eight to fourteen.[5] By the 1880s Hachette was also advertising the series Nouvelle collection illustrée and Bibliothèque des petits enfants, whose books came in blue covers with large lettering. The Bibliothèque rose illustrée collection included foreign as well as French authors: the fairy tales of Hans Christian Andersen and the Brothers Grimm; the moral tales of Schmid and Maria Edgeworth; the adventure novels of Captain Mayne Reid; and, of course, Miguel de Cervantes, Daniel Defoe, and Jonathan Swift all featured in the early catalogues. The books were amply illustrated, some with as many as ninety black-and-white engraved illustrations including vignettes, full-page plates, and ornamented capital letters by noted artists such as Emile Bayard, Bertall (the pseudonym of Charles-Albert d'Arnoux), and Horace Castelli.

Hachette also initiated in 1857 a new journal for children, *La Semaine des enfants*, that contained eight pages in double columns with three sections (historical narratives, short stories and plays, and instructive articles) and initially cost ten centimes. Its agenda of entertaining and instructing through the medium of text and image is apparent in its subtitle (*Magasin d'images et de lectures amusantes et instructives*), and the quality of the fare offered is demonstrated by the commissioning of illustrations by Gustave Doré to accompany a collection of tales from the *Mille et une nuits*. The back page of each issue contained a story in the format of the comic strip, using images like those published in the Epinal series (see chapter 6). Many of the works later published in the Bibliothèque rose illustrée collection appeared first (and sometimes simultaneously) in serial form in *La Semaine des enfants*.[6]

SOPHIE ROSTOPCHINE, COMTESSE DE SÉGUR (1799–1874)

The most successful and enduring writer of novels of domestic realism for children is indisputably the Comtesse de Ségur. Her statue stands in the Luxembourg Gardens, all her novels are still in print, and it is rare to meet a French person who has not read at least *Les Malheurs de Sophie*. Her twenty books for children were published by Hachette in the Bibliothèque rose illustrée collection between 1857 and 1871, and she quickly became the principal and best-selling author in their list.[7] Ségur's father, as biographers are quick to note, was the Count Rostopchine who gave the orders to burn Moscow rather than have it fall into the hands of the invading Napoleon in 1812, and many of her works draw upon her memories of an aristocratic childhood on a large estate in Russia.[8] The family settled in France in 1817, and although an ardent Francophile, she always signed her works 'Comtesse de Ségur, née Rostopchine'. Ségur only began to write late in life, after she had become a grandmother, and her first published work, *Nouveaux contes de fées pour les petits enfants* (1857), had its origins in the tales she told to her grandchildren. The majority of her books are dedicated to one or more of them, often using their names and their personal traits for her characters, and it is her knowledge of children (based on observation and experience) and her sympathetic grandmotherly narrative voice that account, to a large extent, for the popularity of her work. Her novels were profusely illustrated by several of the well-known artists who worked for Hachette, and she was a demanding author, critical of those illustrators who appeared not to have read the texts. Her personal favourite was Horace Castelli, although she complained to Emile Templier, who had taken over at Hachette, on one occasion that Castelli tended to make the children's hair look like snakes.[9] Ségur's association with Hachette lasted until her death, and new editions of her novels in Gallimard's Folio Junior collection with the original illustrations are still sold in Hachette outlets on mainline stations in Paris today, although in paperback rather than the gorgeous red-and-gold livery of the Bibliothèque rose.

Ségur's novels depict a range of childhood characters and offer the modern reader a vivid picture of the times with an evocative depiction of the social milieu of the Second Empire, of both the prosperous *haute bourgeoisie* and the rural peasantry, and touching in her later works on the implications of industrialisation and city dwelling.[10] Her work can be compared with that of Balzac for its range and inclusiveness and its combination of realism and caricature. Although contextualising references to actual contemporary or historical events are not lacking (the Crimean War in *L'Auberge de l'Ange gardien*, 1863; the 1830 flight of Charles X in *Quel amour d'enfant!* from 1866; French intervention in Italy on behalf of the Pope in 1867 in *Après la pluie, le beau temps,* 1871), Ségur's focus is firmly fixed on the minutiae of daily life: the homes, clothes, food, methods of transportation, and daily activities of her characters. In the case of her working-class settings, Ségur feeds into her plots information about the wages, working hours, reponsibilities, and economic and personal difficulties of a gatekeeper (*Pauvre Blaise*, 1862), a seamstress (*La Soeur de Gribouille*, 1862), innkeepers (*L'Auberge de l'Ange gardien*, 1863), a waiter in a café and a grocer's boy, as well as a farmer (*Jean qui grogne et Jean qui rit*, 1865), a factory foreman (*La Fortune de Gaspard*, 1866), young workers in a slipper factory (*Diloy le chemineau*, 1868), and numerous domestic servants and peasants. This material realism in the portrayal of everyday life, combined with imaginative and occasionally breathtakingly implausible plots, may perhaps account for the continuing fascination of these texts for the modern young reader. Yet, this could also be said to be true of the work of many of her contemporaries; what sets Ségur apart is the humour, the memorable dramatic moments, the larger-than-life eccentric characters that fill her works—and, above all, her perceptive portrayal of childhood.

Ségur did not subscribe to the romantic idealised view of children that was found in the poetry of Marceline Desbordes-Valmore and Victor Hugo. Rather than angelic models of innocence and purity, her fictional children are frequently flawed, subject to both the consequences of their own faults and the miseries and injustices of the outside world. Their bad tendencies are confronted in the plots, and although in some cases these are seen as innate (although not so overtly as in English evangelical texts in which children's misdemeanours are seen explicitly as the product of original sin) or the result of childish self-absorption and inexperience they are also shown to be caused by parental over-indulgence, cruelty, or neglect, an interpretation daring in children's books of the time and challenging to the parent reading alongside the child. Because such tendencies in a child's personality are at an early stage, the key to redemption clearly lies in a well-regulated and pious upbringing and the early recognition and eradication of vice, an objective that the novels themselves promote to their largely bourgeois readership. Even apparently innate tendencies can be overcome by firm and sympathetic correction and personal effort, or confession and repentance, although, as will be seen, this conviction is modulated by Ségur's class consciousness, and not all her characters are capable of choosing the right path.[11]

The world of her fictional children is communicated through details of their clothes and food, their toys and games, and their imaginative play and interaction with the natural world. Her emphasis is on simplicity, moderation, and utility: even the children of wealthy families wear plain clothes while elaborate dress is mocked, and they entertain themselves best not with expensive and elaborate toys but by going for walks; collecting flowers, fruit, and nuts; fishing; reading; making things; and playing hide-and-seek. They are energetic, enthusiastic, and inventive. They squabble, get into mischief, and relish vigorous, rough-and-tumble play, unlike the passive and static paragons of earlier texts. Ségur excels in the perceptive rendering of children's conversation, their thought processes, and their interaction. A particular attraction of her works is the presentation of the dialogue as if in a play script, with linking passages of description and contextualisation—a strategy not new in children's books but extremely effectively used by Ségur—varying the pace and imparting a vivid and dramatic immediacy to the scenes. The child characters' language is lively and (with some exceptions) believable in its range and focus, and amongst her most significant innovations was the portrayal of the interaction of children in a group and of children on their own without the presence of adult figures. Moreover, she far exceeded the majority of her contemporaries in her ability to write for and address a child readership without patronising or lecturing. The narrative voice is far from the traditional teacherly one, and the reader is not subjected to lengthy exhortations or moral reflections. Her address is directly to the child reader rather than covertly to parents, providing children with their own narrative in which child protagonists are foregrounded and adults are often portrayed as deficient. Although still offering role models of good and bad behaviour, Ségur's chief protagonists are more rounded characters and they are allowed to learn their lessons about behaviour and attitudes not from adult sermonising or from stories narrated to them but, in Rousseauistic fashion, from firsthand and frequently painful or embarrassing experience. As in most children's literature, there is ultimately a clear distinction between good and evil in Ségur's moral universe, and the agents of disorder or disruption are suitably punished. There is, however, a tantalising ambiguity about behaviour at times, as the discussion below demonstrates, that nuances an overly Manichean view of the world and of human nature.

With the progression of her career and the growth of her grandchildren, the scope of Ségur's work broadened to address children of different ages. Her characters become older, and the world they move in and the dilemmas they encounter become broader in scope. While the novels for young children feature plots restricted to the domestic environment, those for older children move beyond the home and those for adolescents feature, in some cases, the world of work, courtship, and marriage. Ségur was conservative, monarchist, and deeply religious, and all her novels reflect the values of a society that she felt was increasingly under threat. Her preoccupations are more evident, however, in her novels for adolescent readers, where her dislike of contemporary social changes, her emphasis on piety, and her defence of Catholicism became more overt, as they did in her own life. Towards the end of her life she became increasingly devout and, depressed by the defeat of the French army in the Franco-Prussian War, burdened with anxieties about her many children and grandchildren, and distressed by the establishment of the Third Republic she entered a religious order for laypeople.

A central theme running through her oeuvre is the promotion of family values, and many of her plots are geared towards the restoration of fragmented families by the reunion or rehabilitation of their members or the forming of new, extended, families through the integration of orphans or outsiders. Both child and adult characters are spontaneously and informally adopted by others and the resulting happiness is seen to result from their having chosen, or been chosen, to belong to a family group. Indeed, the ideal families are often the unconventional ones (like that in *L'Auberge de l'Ange gardien*, which brings together a group of people of different ages, nationality, and social status) and natural families are equally often dysfunctional (like the miller's family in *Les Petites filles modèles*) or plagued with problems between parents and their offspring (like the unmanageable child in *Quel amour d'enfant!*). Ségur's own aristocratic background informs her preference in the early novels for locating her plots in a privileged social setting, and her attitude towards interaction between social classes has been seen as paternalistic and old-fashioned even for her own time.[12] Her portrayal of the peasantry and of working-class characters certainly resembles that of many of her contemporaries, often displaying a strong element of stereotyping. The children of the poor tend to be either exemplary in their goodness, humility, and diligence, like the son of a concierge in *Pauvre Blaise* who becomes the instrument of the salvation of the members of a noble family (a type also much beloved of Victorian writers) and the backward adolescent in *La Soeur de Gribouille* (1862), or irredeemably bad, like the thieving and lying Jeanette in *Les Petites filles modèles* (1858) or Alcide, the malign influence on other boys in *Le Mauvais génie* (1867) who is eventually executed as a criminal. Both types are seen as products of their family environment, which is marked by either a cheerful acceptance of their place in society and a commitment to a pious and hardworking life or by a deeply rooted tendency to dishonesty and violence.

The transgressive working-class characters tend to be seen as beyond redemption, but while the undesirable character traits and behaviour of socially privileged characters—children and adults alike—are also condemned and punished, the transgressors are more often portrayed as susceptible to improvement and thus redeemed. Exceptions to this are the well-to-do brothers in *François le bossu* (1864) who persistently mock the invalid protagonist and die as an indirect result of setting fire to a neighbouring château, and Georges in *Après la pluie, le beau temps* (1871) and Giselle in *Quel amour d'enfant!* whose delinquency in both cases is seen as the result of indulgence by besotted parents. Defective adult authority figures of any social class are ridiculed, punished, or removed by death. An original feature of Ségur's work is the often warm relationship between the deserving poor and the wealthy, their lives linked by circumstances that generate mutual gratitude and affection, a scenario that appears frequently in her novels, notably in *Pauvre Blaise* and the novels featuring the Général Dourakine (see below).

The conflict between classes is best portrayed in *Diloy le chemineau*, constructed around a shocking episode in which the proud aristocratic child Félicie insults the tramp Diloy and he responds by spanking her. Such a flouting of social boundaries and taboos by both parties remains a shameful secret that binds them until they recognise their fault and respond positively to the opportunity for redemption. Ségur reserves her greatest scorn in several works for the ambitious *parvenu(e)*, like Mme Fichini in *Les Petites filles modèles* or the whole Tourneboule family in *Les Vacances* (1859) whose vulgarity, arrogance, and lack of discrimination are castigated through ridicule, humiliation, physical discomfort, and, in the case of Fichini, sickness and death.

Despite the realism of her settings, Ségur has a penchant for melodramatic situations and devices. Her novels are full of surprises, coincidences, reversals of fortune, and larger-than-life, eccentric characters. The staple ingredients of popular fiction, such as coincidences, unforeseen disasters, moral dilemmas, patriotic gestures, and tear-jerking scenarios, are combined and exploited according to the moral or literary demands of each text.[13] In effect, she appropriated elements from many different genres—notably, fairy tales, the picaresque novel, the memoir, the social problem novel, the comic novel and the *Robinsonnade*, incorporating farce, terror, satirical caricature, tragedy, sentimentality, high drama, and pathos. Such borrowing from adult literature blurs the boundaries between literature for the young and old in an intriguing way. Occasionally there is an explicit intertextual gesture: in *Un Bon petit diable* (1865), Charles Dickens's *Nicholas Nickleby* is not only read by the protagonist Charles, but the school he attends run by Monsieur Old Nick is very reminiscent of that portrayed by Dickens, whose works, also published by Hachette, were well known in France at the time. Aside from her many innovations, Ségur also exploited the conventions of contemporary children's literature in ways amounting to pastiche and even parody, breathing new life, for example, into such devices as the traditional pairing of exemplary and wicked characters and the use of symbolic names, and satisfying the reader's expectations by portraying the arrogant humilated, the bad punished in comic or violent ways, and the good rewarded in extravagantly happy endings. In *Les Bons enfants* (1862), a collage of short episodes of boisterous activity involving characters based on no fewer than sixteen of her grandchildren, Ségur gives the reader an insight into her eclecticism and her views on the indispensable elements of narrative as the children take it in turn to relate a story that is then subject to the comments of the others. The tales range from Camille's lengthy fairy tale, which is nevertheless criticised for its lack of explanation, Sophie's stilted and repetitive account of the supposed nefarious habits of the Chinese, and Jacques's moral tale (taken directly from Arnaud Berquin) of the trapping of a thief to Pierre's tragicomic tale of a drunken pig, Elisabeth's story of seeing a child-stealer attacked by bears at the Jardin des Plantes, and Léonce's two adventure tales set in foreign climes (one an account of an attack by wolves on a journey through a forest and the other a suspenseful tale of mysterous happenings in an inn). These storytelling sessions are also lessons in listening and reacting: Sophie's halting presentation results in feigned snores from the other children while she constantly interrupts other people's narratives with irrelevant questions, and when Henriette's tale of Poucette (based on the model of Charles Perrault's *Le Petit Poucet*) is criticised for its nonsequiturs and arbitrariness, there follows a discussion on the ethics of tact in criticism. Ségur's own versatility is apparent in her oeuvre, which apart from the novels includes an early text of advice on childcare and health (*La Santé des enfants*, 1855); three religious works (*Evangile d'une grand-mère*, 1865 and 1869; *Les Actes des Apôtres*, 1866; and *La Bible d'une grand-mère*, 1869); and a volume of *Comédies et Proverbes* (1865), lively plays for children including a dramatised version of her story of the sad fate of a spoilt child, *Quel amour d'enfant!*

A number of her plots are based on the fairy-tale model of initiation and the overcoming of adversity before maturation and successful integration into society, but they are brought firmly into the modern world and feature updated versions of fairy-tale characters and topoi. The transformations the young protagonists undergo in transcending their difficulties are social and psychological ones—the achievement of self-mastery, reason, and virtue—in which they are aided not by magic but by kindly benefactors in the shape of wealthy patrons or adoptive parents. Their adversaries are often their own failings, no longer externalised as dragons and monsters but clearly identified as greed, pride, vanity, indolence, and the like. They are further persecuted or oppressed not by wicked fairies but by more contemporary villains, offering a critique, fairly radical in children's literature for its time, of adults who abuse their socially sanctioned position of authority as parent, guardian, schoolmaster, or employer. Ségur's works display a degree of xenophobia and anti-Semitism repellent to today's reader (although not uncharacteristic of her time), as many of her most irredeemably unpleasant characters are foreign, like Mme Fichini in *Les Petites filles modèles* and Mme Mac'Miche in *Un Bon petit diable*, both vicious guardians of unhappy children; Mme Juivet, the exploitative shopkeeper in *Mémoires d'un âne* (1860); and M. Frölichein, the brutal German industrialist in *La Fortune de Gaspard*.[14] Her dislike of the

English is apparent in *Les Bons enfants* in a scene where a group of children discuss the English fear of the French, prompting one to say with chauvinistic enthusiasm, "'Quand je serai grand, je me ferai marin, pour me battre contre les anglais." "Moi aussi! moi aussi!" dirent tous les garçons.'[15] However, many of the eccentric benefactors who take an interest in poor or ill-treated children are also foreign, their behaviour marked by a comic appearance, volubility, violent outbursts of emotion, and a prodigious appetite, like the volcanic tempered Général Dourakine; the caricatured Englishman M. Georgey, in *Le Mauvais génie* (1867), who is obsessed with eating turkey; the talkative, hyperactive Italian doctor Paolo who cures François in *François le bossu* (1864); and the two clownish Polish refugee soldiers, Boginski and Cozrgbrlewski (known as 'Coz' because nobody can pronounce his name) who act as guardian angels to the two country children Innocent and Simplicie in Paris in *Les Deux nigauds* (1862). The comic element is enhanced by the reproduction of the thickly accented French they speak and their frequent picturesque oaths and expressions ('Sac à papier!' 'Oh, my dear!'). Their very status as foreigners and outsiders adds to the unconventional nature of their intervention in the plots, their unpredictability and temperamental instability inspiring both affection and alarm in characters and readers alike. This strategy creates an intriguing 'doubling' of good and bad characters in Ségur's works that both draws attention to, and destabilises, the polarised roles they play.

Ségur's first published work was, in fact, a collection of fairy tales for young readers. The *Nouveaux contes de fées pour les petits enfants,* a collection of five tales, first appeared separately in Hachette's journal *La Semaine des enfants* and simultaneously in book form in 1857, with a dedication to her granddaughters, Camille and Madeleine de Malaret. The least known and commented upon of Ségur's works, the *Nouveaux contes de fées* enjoyed the status of being illustrated by Doré, the last of the great Romantic illustrators.[16] In fact, the tales are not as original as the title suggests, for there are several echoes of Mme d'Aulnoy's extravagant tales; 'Histoire d'Ourson', the story of a boy born covered in bearlike hair, has similarities to traditional Russian tales; and 'La Petite souris grise' is taken directly from a collection of fairy tales by Ducray Duminil published in 1798–99. Although they draw on the plots and topoi of traditional fairy tales, these stories also reflect Segur's later works in that they foreground child protagonists and contain many of her major themes.[17] They also exhibit a greater degree of external and psychological realism characteristic of Ségur's later works, with the descriptions of settings—whether cottage, palace, or forest—evoking the physical presence of a concrete world. Besides being beset by evil fairies or enchanters, the young protagonists are faced with dilemmas analogous to those in real life in which they must learn to embrace virtue and act correctly in order to become model adults. Three represent exemplary types while two have character flaws (vanity, curiosity, disobedience) that lead to their exploitation by the forces of evil and to perilous situations for themselves and others.

An essential part of their development is the recognition of their personal power to destroy or restore order in their world rather than a reliance on magic. The *merveilleux* is present in abundance but is clearly harnessed to a covertly didactic end consonant with the moral and socioeconomic values and the gender assumptions of the period. 'Le Bon petit Henri' features the quest of a poor cottage boy to obtain a magic herb growing on a remote mountaintop that will cure his mother of her life-threatening illness. His diligence and effort in acquiring manly skills are rewarded by various magical agents in not only the restoration of his mother's health, but with a new home and the wherewithal to earn a living. Contrary to the traditional rags-to-riches scenario of fairy tales, Henri's resolution not to wish to obtain by magic more than they need to lead a modest and virtuous life (clothes, food, two horses, and two cows) suggests the desirability of humility, moderation, and the acceptance of one's social status. The 'Histoire d'Ourson', like Charles Perrault's 'Riquet à la Houppe', is a story of the power of love to conquer suffering and prejudice. A remedy offered by a good fairy, that Ourson may exchange his skin with someone in whom he inspires love enough to agree to help, places the responsibility on Ourson to earn his reward. The opportunity to free Ourson from his curse is willingly embraced by his self-sacrificing cousin and childhood friend Violette, and after a monumental battle between good and wicked fairies worthy of a Mme d'Aulnoy tale, both Ourson and Violette are restored to their rightful inheritance of beauty and royal status.[18] This portrayal of the plight of the physically disadvantaged child and the theme of redemption through love was reworked by Ségur in a realistic context in *François le bossu*, in which a boy afflicted with a twisted spine and feeble health has the same power of inspiring empathy as Ourson and is eventually cured not by a magic spell but by a flamboyant Italian doctor and finds happiness with his childhood sweetheart. The 'Histoire de Blondine, de Bonne-Biche et de Beau-Minon', which also draws on the motif of metamorphosis, exemplifies the consequences of personal choices and actions. Rescued from the wickedness of a stepmother and an evil enchanter by a doe and a white cat (the forms that a fairy and her son, the prince Parfait, have been cursed to inhabit) and transformed by a period of sleep into an adolescent, the little princess Bondine has to learn whom to trust, and to resist temptation. Her vanity and lack of experience put Bonne-Biche and Beau-Minon in danger as well as herself, and it is only through recognition of her fault and repentance that she can begin her journey towards redemption for all. Once more personal effort is essential, for Blondine must cultivate all the female and domestic virtues (patience, endurance, submission, and hard work) surviving alone in a cabin in the forest—rather like the heroine of Mme Woillez's *Le Robinson des demoiselles* (see chapter 1).

Ségur later submitted a belief in fairies to comic treatment in *Un Bon petit diable* (1865), in which the mischievous boy Charles, mistreated by his violent and unscrupulous Scottish aunt Mme Mac'Miche, who intends to cheat her ward of his inheritance, gets back at her by exploiting her fear of magic. This novel is one of extremes, encompassing both Mme Mac'Miche's cruelty, Charles's inventive tricks that cause mayhem at home and at school (including an episode in which he ties cardboard demons' heads to his backside and terrifies his aunt by dropping his trousers in a haze of sulphurous smoke), a cast of bizarre characters, and a graphic description of the eventual undignified death of Mme Mac'Miche. In this text, despite the farcical element, the young protagonist—and by implication the reader—is empowered by the possibility of a reversal of the balance of power between adult and child and the assertion and reinstatement of the child's rights.

The three 'Sophie' books are worth considering in some detail because, although having much in common with earlier children's books (the privileged social settings are reminiscent of that in Mme de Genlis's *Les veillées du château*, 1784) they exemplify the advances in narrative techniques with which Ségur can be credited. *Les Malheurs de Sophie* (1859), illustrated by Castelli, presents a series of adventures in miniature within a secure family environment of a naughty child who learns to confront her tendencies towards greed, impatience, disobedience, and unthinking cruelty through frequently painful experience. The dedication, to Ségur's granddaughter Elisabeth Fresneau, suggests a close link between Sophie, the author as both child and grandmother, the dedicatee, and the reader:

> Grand'mère n'a toujours été bonne, et il y a bien des enfants qui ont été méchants comme elle et qui se sont corrigés comme elle. Voici des histoires vraies d'une petite fille que grand'mère a beaucoup connue dans son enfance.

The dedication goes on to list Sophie's faults in the manner of a traditional moral tale ('elle était gourmande, elle est devenue sobre; elle était menteuse, elle est devenue sincère; elle était voleuse, elle est devenue honnête …'),[19] but herein lies the intriguing ambiguity of the text, for Sophie is, in effect, never cured of her faults, remaining incorrigible at the end despite her intentions to reform. This lends a potentially subversive feel to the book that is misleading, suggesting that Ségur is not in fact promoting conventional virtues as represented by Sophie's mother, Mme de Réan, and is privileging transgressive behaviour. Such an interpretation may inform modern readers' enjoyment of the text but may have been unsettling (or, arguably, liberating) to Ségur's contemporary readers and is totally inconsistent with the conservative and traditionalist moral stance underpinning Ségur's other works. There is a practical reason for this apparent anomaly, however: *Les Malheurs de Sophie* is in fact a 'prequel' capitalising upon the sucess of 1858's *Les Petites filles modèles*, which portrays the taming of an older, orphaned Sophie in a family of three well-adjusted, gentle, and obedient daughters. *Les Malheurs de Sophie*, in portraying the life of Sophie before the loss of her mother in a shipwreck and her father's remarriage to a cruel stepmother, thus inevitably has to close with Sophie still uncorrected of her faults.

The text is divided into short chapters depicting discrete episodes that repeat the pattern of a basic storyline (bright idea or temptation leading to disaster, leading to a lesson learnt, albeit temporarily) and illustrate one or more character flaws. The brevity of the chapters and the predictable nature of the treadmill plot indicate that this is envisaged as a text for younger children, as do the episodes themselves. Sophie's misadventures take place in the home, garden, or park, drawing on the hazardous potential of a familiar world, and are the consequences of her egocentric and impetuous nature to varying degrees of severity: she is almost burnt by stepping into builder's lime, which she has been forbidden to approach; is ill after gorging on warm bread and cream; ruins her favourite doll by warming it in the sun and curling its hair with hot tongs; and inadvertently causes the death of several animals through her fascination with experimentation (cutting up live fish, drowning a tortoise, using holly to whip a donkey). Like most young female fictional children of this period, she is most severely punished for indulging her passions and instincts, but Ségur introduces a note of ambiguity into the portrayal of female upbringing. The first chapter reveals the anomaly in the function of a doll as an educational tool, for while the child is encouraged to practise her maternal skills on it, she must also recognise the limitations of its potential for being treated as a real live baby. Sophie's rejection of the mutilated doll can in fact be read as an impatience with the maternal role.[20] Furthermore, when Sophie, wishing to emulate her friend whom she has heard praised for her prettiness, cuts off her eyebrows and stands in the rain to make her hair curl, she is humiliated and criticised for her coquetry by the very forces of patriarchy (her father and cousin Paul) whom she has sought to impress.

Although Sophie is repeatedly forgiven when she owns up and repents of her misdeeds, she also incurs physical discomfort, ridicule, exclusion, and deprivation; and on one occasion when she perpetrates that most heinous of childhood sins, a lie, she is whipped by Mme de Réan, who is otherwise portrayed as wise, kind, and patient.[21] Mostly, the unfortunate consequences of Sophie's bright ideas are seen as punishment in themselves. Indeed, the use of the word *idée* becomes synonymous with misfortune, a link that is reintroduced in the case of another Sophie in *Les Bons Enfants* and yet another in *Mémoires d'un âne*, whose ideas also lead to trouble. Despite these consequences for herself and others, and her failed attempts at self-policing, Sophie must have been an attractive figure for young readers of the time for her sheer irrepressibility. Her faults, moreover, are linked to qualities that have positive connotations (self-confidence, boundless energy, determination, initiative, a lively curiosity and inventiveness) that have continued to endear her to modern readers. Sophie, who is only four, is contrasted with her sensible, obedient, and thoroughly socialised cousin Paul, age five, but Paul is by no means the paragon of goodness of conventional moral tales. He is frequently Sophie's partner in crime, persuaded into misconduct by her false reasoning and periodic sulks, and the sheer dynamic force of her personality. Even when not directly involved, his chivalrousness prompts him to defend Sophie (as when he rolls in holly bushes to cover up the fact that she has scratched his face, a generous act that eventually shames Sophie into a confession), or to come to her aid. In a frightening scene clearly evoking *Le Petit Chaperon rouge*, Sophie's disobedience and greed cause her to be attacked by a wolf as she lingers behind her mother on a walk through the woods, and she is rescued just in time by the family dogs and Paul's bravery.

The misadventures are played out in scenes in which the children are alone, a strategy that allows the interaction between them to be developed. Here Ségur's insight into children's apprehensions, desires, and language becomes apparent. The arguments that break out between Sophie and Paul (who is also capable of losing his temper) are energetic, spontaneous, and, to a large extent, believable although at times their articulacy and capacity for self-analysis seem implausible for their ages. Here the effect of the dialogue as script, alternating with third-person narrative and description, is particularly striking and aids reader identification with the characters in the reading process, particularly if a child is being read to aloud. The light touch with which Ségur evokes the material world of Sophie and Paul—with their toys, clothes, food, pastimes, and pets—is immensely attractive, although her portrayal of relationships with servants reveals a condescending and paternalistic attitude. The servants, too, are invariably depicted as slightly comic or in need of discipline, like Lambert the gardener, who relishes describing the gruesome demise of the donkey, or Sophie's maid, who loses her post for disobeying Mme de Réan and indulging the child's greed.

While in *Les Malheurs de Sophie* the father makes sporadic appearances in the text, in *Les Petites filles modèles* (1858), illustrated by Bertall, the domestic context is a totally female one, with two widowed mothers living together with their daughters in a large country house. The model young girls, Camille and Madeleine de Fleurville (who are based on two of Ségur's granddaughters) display all the desirable feminine attributes of kindness, gentleness, and amiability, and are put in charge of the younger Marguerite de Rosbourg, thus allowing them to prepare for their future role in life by developing self-confidence, judgement, and a sense of responsibility. In effect, this text is virtually a guide to an ideal female upbringing. Disruption is introduced into their lives by the arrival of Sophie, who has been living unhappily after the death of her parents with her cruel stepmother, Mme Fichini. Constantly subjected to mental and physical abuse and denied love or teaching, Sophie has not only not acquired the good habits of the other girls, but her undesirable characteristics have been exacerbated. After a number of incidents manifesting her usual defects (she falls in a pond, steals pears, leads Marguerite astray, taunts and fights with Camille and Madeleine), she is cured of her temper and waywardness by sympathetic correction administered by Mme de Fleurville, her new surrogate mother, whose reason, sensitivity, and firm kindness effect the transformation of Sophie into another model girl. Ultimately, contemporary gender norms are reinforced as she becomes 'non pas la Sophie d'avant-hier, colère, menteuse, gourmande et méchante; mais une Sophie douce, sage, raisonnable'.[22] The acquisition of adopted sisters allows for a range of emotions and family relationships to be explored and, as in *Les Malheurs de Sophie*, the dialogue is lively and the narrative voice informal and optimistic.

Although there is still no concerted attempt to portray the world through the child's eyes, Ségur's focus allows for a far greater possibility of identification between the reader and the protagonists than in earlier moral tales, and the depiction of the contrast between desirable and undesirable role models is more nuanced and interesting. Nevertheless, contemporary class assumptions are embedded in the contrast between

Sophie, who is forgiven for stealing pears when she admits her guilt, and the miller's daughter Jeanette, who is portrayed as an incorrigible liar and thief, and emphasised by the fact that Jeanette is regularly beaten by her equally dishonest parents not for stealing but for being found out. Ségur is frequently criticised for an apparent obsession with physical violence, but it is clear in her novels that beating or whipping are condoned only for grave misdeeds, and those adults who abuse their position, like Mme Fichini, are roundly condemned and often made to suffer the same fate. The distancing effect of her foreignness and the obvious allusion to the stereotypical ambitious stepmother of fairy tale perhaps serves to make less uncomfortable for the child reader the real evil that Mme Fichini represents. Nevertheless, the incident, reported by the child herself, in which Sophie's late father whipped Mme Fichini to within an inch of her life for hitting Sophie, is a troubling one for it is apparently condoned by the author, even if it might appeal to a child reader's sense of justice. It is noticeable that here, as in the other novels, there seems to be no question of any official sanction being invoked against the abuse of children by members of the upper classes.

The third, longer book in the trilogy, *Les Vacances* (1859), also illustrated by Bertall, is a conflation of different genres, framing a Robinsonnade, a ghost story, and a chapter of gleeful social satire within a family story. It is above all a novel of reunion and reconciliation, in which families fractured by the presumed loss at sea of some of their members see the return of their loved ones. It features the same inhabitants of the Fleurville château together with three boy cousins, Léon and Jean de Rugès and Jacques de Traypi, and their parents, and reintroduces Sophie's cousin Paul, who has unexpectedly survived the shipwreck in which his parents and Mme de Réan died.[23] The crowded household allows for much lively description of the activities of its members, and Ségur's talent for portraying the interaction between a group of children is seen at its best. The structure includes both dialogue and longer stretches of narrative as Sophie tells of her life with her stepmother and Paul recounts his adventures amongst the *Peaux rouges*, and the varied content is designed to appeal to readers of both sexes. The development of the plot depends upon a series of farfetched contrivances: the appearance of a sailor from the wrecked ship who has a wife and child in the neighbourhood heralds the return of Paul and the ship's captain, none other than the husband of Mme de Rosbourg and now Paul's surrogate parent, after they have been believed dead for six years. M. de Rosbourg is one of the few effective father figures in Ségur's works, and his more dynamic role in family affairs is linked with his status as a hero rather than just as a representative of patriarchy. Paul's account of their life in an unknown land owes much to the traditional Robinsonnade, although dangers and discomfort are minimised, and the experience has made him strong, independent, and courageous. This tale of survival in an alien environment mirrors and transposes into an exotic climate the narrative of the other children's games of building and furnishing wooden huts in the garden, and chasing butterflies, and their encounter with some of the more unsavoury members of the community—the thieving miller's family and the local boys who attack a helpless simpleton. The tense relationship between the savages and the initially wary shipwrecked companions that develops into friendship and understanding is also mirrored in the family plot, as Léon, whose cowardice makes him spiteful, resentful of Paul, and disliked by the other cousins is helped by Paul to overcome his fears and behave manfully, earning universal respect and affection.

The brief introduction of the Tourne-boules, a neighbouring nouveau riche family, is a highly comic scene demonstrating Ségur's dislike of ostentation, extravagance, and unwarranted social snobbery. The Tourne-boules are both keen to flaunt their wealth and just as avidly enthusiastic to try to sell their possessions to pay off their debts, and the snobbish and boastful daughter is firmly put in her place by the children of the château, whose genuine social superiority manifests itself in their modest, sensible behaviour. The reunion of husbands and wives, fathers and children, and Sophie and Paul, played out before the extended family of cousins, testifies to the enduring nature of family feeling and the power of prayer. In *Les Vacances*, Ségur's strong religious beliefs come to the fore more overtly, especially when Sophie is taken to visit the dying and repentant Mme Fichini, now miserable after marrying a scoundrel, and gladly accedes to her desire for forgiveness. The refusal of M. de Rosbourg to help Mme Fichini's sick child because of her parentage and the unlikelihood of her survival seems inconsistent with this pious sentiment, however, and is shocking to the modern reader. Ségur clearly envisaged that she would write no more about this group of characters, for an epilogue tells briefly of their later lives in which they intermarry and, as in a fairy tale, live happily ever after in close proximity to one another.[24]

While *Les Malheurs de Sophie* is generally considered to be based on Ségur's own childhood, autobiographical and contemporary elements can also be found in the two novels that feature one of the favourite characters of her oeuvre, Général Dourakine. In *L'Auberge de l'ange gardien*, illustrated by Valentin Foulquier, and its sequel, *Le Général Dourakine*, illustrated by Emile Bayard (both published in 1863), the exploits of the irascible, impulsive, vain, and childlike Russian aristocrat are played out first in the French countryside, where he is a prisoner after being captured during the Crimean war, and subsequently on his estate in Russia.[25] The plot of *L'Auberge de l'ange gardien*, which begins with a babes-in-the-woods scenario, involves the creation of a new family at the inn via the informal adoption of Jacques and Paul Dérigny (based on Ségur's grandsons Jacques and Paul de Pitray) by the innkeeper Mme Blidot and her sister Elfy, one of Ségur's most attractive female characters, and two marriages, under the patronage of Dourakine. He is perhaps the most extreme of Ségur's eccentric benefactors, combining the qualities of both ogre and fairy godmother. Dourakine is, moreover, a kind of dispossessed orphan himself, desperately searching for the security and unconditional love of a family. His greed, unreasonableness, and extravagant outbursts of temper make him an object of both terror and good-natured ridicule to the family at the inn, and his boundless kindness, generosity, and mania for intervening in the lives of others, arranging marriages and solving their financial problems with dowries and gifts, earn both respect and affection as well as gratitude.[26] His personality, which manifests all the faults of Sophie writ large and affects others more dramatically, poses a paradox in the moral scheme of Ségur's oeuvre because he is indulged and not punished for his lapses, which are explained by the fact that he is Russian and compensated for by his largesse. It is true that he is made to feel ashamed when he thrashes a thieving child with his *knout* (a long whip), but he is allowed to redeem himself through an act of generosity toward the boy that exculpates him in the eyes of the other characters. He seems temporarily cured at the end of *L'auberge de l'ange gardien* by integration into the calm happiness of the family at the inn, but readers of the sequel learn that he remains as violent tempered and impatient as ever. The reader is left with an uneasy sense that his actions, though more reprehensible than Sophie's, are seen as less pernicious because of his gender and status.[27]

In *Le Général Dourakine,* the general returns to Russia with his newfound family in tow in order to settle his affairs before returning to France to die. It is a return for Ségur, too, and an opportunity to condemn all that she detests about the country of her birth, as she presents a very bleak image of a barbarous country still sunk in feudalism where violence, corruption, and persecution are rife.[28] This view is mediated through the eyes of the Dérigny family, who represent the reader in their initiation into the strange manners and habits of Russia, and the story of the escaped political prisoner and persecuted Catholic, the Polish prince Romane.[29] His account—based on a true story—of his incarceration in a rat-infested dungeon as a result of being wrongfully accused as a conspirator against the Russian rule of Poland, and his escape across the Siberian steppes in the snow, give the reader an insight into the grim reality of the life of a condemned man.[30] In including this story, Ségur addresses the two highly topical subjects of the independence of Poland from Russia and the conflict in Russia between the Catholic Church and the Russian Orthodox Church. For Dourakine, the visit is also the opportunity to confront and leave behind the habits of the Russian landowner, including the right to whip his inferiors. The two Dourakine novels thus represent a civilising process not dissimilar to that undergone by numerous fictional transgressive children, a process made more critical, in Dourakine's case, because of his age and responsibilities. He eventually recognises that he is perceived by his French friends as an ogre to be placated with food and soothing words like a child, and is appalled by this demeaning image. At his estate of Gromeline, his violent tendencies are gradually displaced onto his niece, the grasping, treacherous, and sadistic Mme Papofski, who seeks to usurp Dourakine's wealth and disinherit his other niece and her family, the Dabrovines, in favour of her own unruly brood. Mme Papofski is eventually routed in a bizarre scenario in which, when she tries to blackmail the corrupt local chief of police, she is caused to fall partially through a trapdoor and is mercilessly whipped on the lower half of her body by unseen hands. This extraordinarily cruel yet comic (and potentially sadoerotic) moment provokes a tension in the reader between condemnation of the chief of police's actions and pleasure at the humiliation of Mme Papofski, for whose own viciousness with the knout this is an appropriate punishment.[31] Ségur clearly disapproves of the inhuman abuse of privilege by the nobility and the events of this novel indicate how she, and Dourakine, turn their backs on the past of the country of their birth. In marrying his niece's daughter, Nathalie Dabrovine, to the prince Romane, Dourakine creates a second new family, thus becoming the founder of a dynasty, and his return to France at the end of the novel, having given freedom to his serfs, represents a return from the past to a new and stable life in a more modern and civilised country.[32]

The success of one of Ségur's most amusing novels, *Les Mémoires d'un âne* (1860), possibly influenced by Apuleius's *The Golden Ass* and illustrated by Castelli, derived largely from the personality of the narrator, the brave and frequently malicious donkey Cadichon. Her approach to this conceit is a gently ironic one, for embedded in the narrative is a discussion of the plausibility of just such an achievement. When his child owners wish that Cadichon could talk and tell them stories about his life, a novel by Julie Gouraud, *Mémoires d'une poupée*, is invoked as a precedent. While little Elisabeth firmly believes that the doll was the author, her older siblings mockingly disabuse her, explaining the pretence as just an amusing literary strategy, a situation that is doubly entertaining since it is presented to us through the 'voice' of Cadichon himself. On the last page Cadichon tells the reader that his decision to write his memoirs was in response to a dispute between the children about whether he was capable of understanding his actions and motivations, and is therefore, since he lacks the power of human speech, an attempt at self-analysis. He is also a very literate donkey, since his story is constructed as a picaresque tale, complete with many of the characteristics of the genre, including an initial exile from home, the corruption of the protagonist by his environment, and an eventual recognition of personal responsibility that leads to repentance, expiation, and a reconciliation with society. He is an alert and entertaining narrator, capable of understanding human speech (and relating, with total recall, conversations he has overheard) and of experiencing a full range of human emotions.

Cadichon's story offers a wide-ranging reading experience, manipulating the sentimental and the comic, suspense and high drama, the violent and the poignant, within the overarching narrative of self-development. It begins with his running away from his master's farm where he has been overloaded, beaten, and starved, and narrates the vicissitudes of his life with a series of good and bad masters. Cadichon's indignation at the way he and other animals are treated breeds resentment and a desire for revenge that in turn make him rebellious, ill-natured, and vicious. He responds both in kind by kicking out at his tormentors, and, because he prides himself on being cleverer and more rational than humans, by playing tricks on them (such as dragging clean washing into a dung heap and hiding in a ditch to avoid work); such tricks provide much of the humour of the text. Like the picaro, he learns to outwit his masters and becomes lazy, arrogant, and overconfident. His retrospective self-examination accurately identifies the way in which cruelty can corrupt the victim, a condition from which he is eventually saved when he is sold to a wealthy family to amuse their sick daughter, whose vulnerability brings out his chivalrous side and demonstrates his fundamentally good heart. Fiction is eventually elided with reality when, distraught after her death, he is rescued by a group of children who bear the names of Ségur's granchildren and he embarks upon what seems to be the most stable and happy period of his life, becoming something of a local celebrity. In an episode strongly reminiscent of a scene in Alain-René Lesage's picaresque novel *Histoire de Gil Blas de Santillane*, he overhears robbers in a cave in the forest and helps to flush out the villains by luring them with his braying.[33] A further gesture towards the picaresque novel is the interpolated life history of Cadichon's old friend, the dog Médor, with whom he has shared both happy and miserable times, and whose accidental death at the hands of an inexperienced boy during a partridge shoot leads to Cadichon's eventual conversion. Recognising that his instinctive vengeful retaliation is inappropriate, corrupting his character, and alienating the family that loved him, he is able, in a final test of character, to prove himself loyal and trustworthy, demonstrate his repentance, and achieve reconciliation through good deeds.[34] Like the reformed picaro, Cadichon anticipates ending his days in a comfortable home, surrounded by his loved ones and indulging in the luxury of writing his memoirs.

The two novels that take place in Paris, *Les Deux nigauds* (1862) and *Jean qui grogne et Jean qui rit* (1865), both illustrated by Castelli, also have a touch of the picaresque about them and present a satirical view of urban life. The former, one of Ségur's most comic works, is an 'up from the country' tale of two children, Innocent and Simplicie, from a rural bourgeois family in Brittany, whose longing to experience life in Paris is manipulated by their father as a cure for their constant whining and sulking. They are sent to stay with a sadistic aunt, and their naïve enthusiasm for the city is soon diminished. The novel begins with a coach and train journey in which different social types are crammed together, an occasion for an amusing episode involving the sharing and stealing of food, violent discomfiture, and embarrassment. (Did Guy de Maupassant perhaps have this scene in mind when he wrote *Boule de suif* in 1880?) The youngsters soon regret leaving home when the glamour they craved turns out to be for Innocent the harsh life as a *pensionnat* in a school full of delinquents and for Simplicie the rigours of high society, where her lack of social graces and knowledge of fashion lead to ridicule in both the street and the drawing room.

The title *Jean qui grogne et Jean qui rit* suggests a parodic gloss on traditional moral tales, but is in fact a sombre and sad story of the induction of two Breton cousins of dissimilar temperaments into the world of work in Paris. It is also one of the most sentimental, religious, and lachrymose of Ségur's novels, exploiting to the full the pathos of a preternaturally pious dying child. Initially, there are similarities with *Les Mésaventures de Jean-Paul Choppart*, as the boys encounter adventures on the road, but once they arrive in Paris the narrative traces their parallel but radically different careers. While Jean and his brother Simon, who work as waiters in a café, thrive through their diligence and thriftiness, the reader witnesses the descent of Jeannot—an assistant in a grocer's shop whose constant snivelling and sulky complaints alienate everyone around him—into idleness, lying, and thieving and, eventually, prison. His sense of being discriminated against is exacerbated by the preferential treatment given to his cousin by a series of helpers who prefer Jean's open, cheerful, eager manner, but he fails to grasp his own responsibility in this and allows himself to be easily corrupted by a dishonest fellow servant in his second post. Ségur's satirical depiction of the world of urban tradesmen, their striving after elegance and aping the nobility with their formal balls and musical soirées, and the description of their overdressed vulgarity and conspicuous consumption on these occasions leaves the reader in no doubt about her view of the pretensions of the 'fumistes, bouchers, serruriers, épiciers, fleurs artificielles, papetiers, modistes, lingères, cordonniers, etc.' of the capital.[35] This novel also features a mysterious benefactor, M. Abel, a successful painter and inveterate practical joker who takes an interest in the boys' lives and manipulates events, arranging jobs and Simon's marriage and providing money, furniture, and clothes to ensure his favourites a stable future. Like Dourakine, M. Abel is an ambiguous figure, for he is also used by Ségur as a tool to ridicule the tradesmen, although his deliberate disruption of their social occasions with his rowdy jokes could be interpreted as discourtesy to his hosts and a lack of social decorum on the part of one who should know better. Moreover, the plot in the second half of the novel is top-heavy with lengthy tearful expressions of gratitude and affection on the part of Jean and Simon, who unquestioningly accept M. Abel's organisation of their lives without any suggestion that they might see themselves as puppets of a rich man's ego. In novels of this period, if the role of the rich is to be charitable, the role of the poor is to be endlessly grateful—even, it would seem, when this involves surrendering control over their own lives.

Two of Ségur's novels for adolescents, written towards the end of her life, are amongst the most pessimistic and have clear relevance to contemporary social issues. When Ségur dedicated *La Fortune de Gaspard* (1866) to her grandson Paul de Pitray, she was addressing a future reader: 'Cher petit, quand tu seras plus grand, tu verras, en lisant l'histoire de Gaspard, combien il est utile de bien travailler.'[36] She is clearly alluding not just to the content of the narrative, a story of a boy's rise from peasant to factory manager, but to the need to progress in his studies. In its topical portrayal of industrial expansion in the Second Empire and the value of education for the peasantry (a subject tackled at the request of her friend Emile Templier) the didactic message of this novel is, however, an ambiguous one.[37] The different attitudes towards education embodied in the characters reflect the contemporary debate about literacy in the 1860s. The questionnaires ordered in 1864 by the minister for education, Victor Duruy, revealed that the anxieties and prejudices exposed by the Falloux Law of 1850 (see chapter 1) were still widespread amongst both the conservative faction (who feared that education for the masses might encourage rather than prevent immorality, discontent, and insurgency) and the peasantry (who were suspicious of the ideas promoted in school textbooks as a threat to their own values and to the tradition of practical education in the home). It would seem that Ségur, too, disliked the implications of the Falloux Law because of the harmful and disruptive effects that instruction might have on the lower classes.[38] The census of 1866 revealed that 39 percent of the total population of France were still illiterate, and the reforms of the Duruy administration attempted to extend and improve conditions in primary education.[39] *La Fortune de Gaspard* accurately reflects the situation still prevailing in many rural areas: the sporadic attendance of the children at school, the poor quality of education offered by untrained and harassed masters, and the indifference or resentment of peasant families. Indeed, the depiction of schools in city and country in *Les Deux nigauds* and *Les Fortunes de Gaspard* indicate that the standards and conditions of education in elementary schools had changed relatively little since the eighteenth century.[40]

The portrayal of the development of Gaspard, who wishes to maximise his opportunities in life through education, is far from a straightforward endorsement of his aims. The reader is initially encouraged to applaud Gaspard's determination and deplore the hostility of his brother Lucas, who prefers working in the fields to poring over books, and his father, who is not convinced of the value of education and prioritises farm work over his sons' attendance at school. However, book learning is seen as harmful to Gaspard's physical and moral well-being, for his fantasies of becoming a successful industrialist begin to alienate him from his family and pervert his sense of values. Despite the warnings of his family and even the schoolmaster, who tells him, 'Songe bien qu'il ne suffit pas de parvenir à la fortune, il faut avant tout marcher droit son chemin', the blessing of education becomes a curse.[41] His pursuit of false objectives blind him to the nature of happiness, and when he is taken under the wing of the industrialist M. Féréor, his success derives not from his technical knowledge but from acting as a spy on his fellow workers. His 'adoption' symbolises his entry into the world of industry and a move away from his roots in accepting to serve the interests and values of a new father figure.[42] Gaspard's redemption can only take place when he has learnt, under the influence of his wife Mina, the duties of a good son, husband, master, and Christian, a dénouement flagged up by Ségur in the second half of the dedication: 'Et tu sauras, ce que Gaspard n'a appris que bien tard, combien il est nécessaire d'être bon, charitable et pieux, pour profiter de tous les avantages du travail et devenir réellement heureux.'[43] After his own transformation, he can begin to transform his world by the means of education and charitable acts. Ségur's agenda here is to satisfy her publisher's request to show that a basic education is of value to all (Gaspard's brother Lucas gets into many practical difficulties because he lacks basic reading and writing skills), but at the same time she voices her own opinion that more advanced instruction risks creating a moral trap—especially, it would seem, for the lower classes—if not linked with a virtuous and pious existence.

Ségur's last novel, *Après la pluie, le beau temps* (1871), with illustrations by Bayard, covers both the childhood and young adulthood of her protagonists and portrays the vulnerability of young girls who are both orphaned and wealthy. The first half of the novel is a familiar account of a distressed childhood, with the kind, patient Geneviève constantly blamed for acts committed by her cousin, Georges, by her guardian, and his besotted father, M. Dormère. The eccentric benefactor in this case is a woman—the energetic, independent, and garrulous spinster Mlle Cunégonde Primerose, who takes Geneviève under her wing, removing her from the home in which she is oppressed and taking responsibility for her education. Mlle Primerose uses her knowledge of the law to thwart M. Dormère's plans of marrying Geneviève to his son by getting his guardianship revoked, threatening to expose Georges's theft of money from his father and drag the family's reputation through the courts. She also masterminds the marriage of Geneviève to her alternative suitor, Georges's exemplary cousin Jacques. Georges is an extreme example of how the indulgence of childhood misbehaviour perverts the character, for he becomes a dissipated youth, a consummate liar, and a cynical fortune hunter. Ségur makes it clear that he is the product of his upbringing, and even Georges comes to despise his father for his misplaced favouritism, and eventually dies repentant. Two interesting aspects of this novel are the introduction of a black character, Geneviève's servant Rame, and the deployment in the plot of contemporary events. Although the ebullient nature and fractured French of Rame furnish much of the comic element in the text, the portrayal of the transformation of the prejudice, born of ignorance, that he experiences into a warm appreciation of his qualities is well achieved and the moral standing of the other characters is, in effect, measured by their attitude towards him. Rame is responsible for the main heroic act in the book, risking his own life to save Jacques, now a Zouave fighting for the pope against the forces of Giuseppe Garibaldi, from a rebel bullet. The last chapters exemplify Ségur's horror at events in Italy in 1861 and 1867, and her patriotism is evident in the assertion that the victory of the papal troops was due to the courage of the French soldiers 'débarqués à temps pour compléter la déroute honteuse des misérables bandits'.[44] Her fervent Catholicism is further noticeable in the fact that when Geneviève and her friends arrive in Rome and visit all the holy sites, no mention is made of the monuments of the city's great pagan legacy.

Despite Marc Soriano's view of Ségur as racist and reactionary, there are many testimonies in personal memoirs to the pleasure with which young people have read her works.[45] François Mauriac, for example, speaks of *Les Malheurs de Sophie* as a 'livre de chevet', claiming that 'le cortège des petites filles modèles et des bons petits diables me suivait dans ma chambre et peuplait mon sommeil'.[46] The website of the Musée de la comtesse de Ségur at Aube has a link to sites where schoolchildren enthusiastically discuss their reading of her works, proving that, despite the wealth of reading material available to young readers today, interest in her works continues.[47]

SÉGUR'S CONTEMPORARIES AND SUCCESSORS IN THE BIBLIOTHÈQUE ROSE ILLUSTRÉE

While the catalogues of Hachette's works for young readers that appeared in the back of many of their publications reveal the large number of predominantly women writers in this field, many of them have been almost entirely forgotten. Their works have not, for the most part, been reissued, and copies are often difficult to locate. A list of 1889, chosen at random, lists in the Bibliothèque rose illustrée works by Mlle Carpentier (six titles), Mme Carraud (three titles), Mme Cazin (nine titles), Mme Colomb (one title), Mlle Fleuriot (ten titles), Mme Fresneau (Ségur's daughter; four titles), Mlle Gouraud (twenty-one titles), Mme de Pitray (eight titles), Mme de Ségur (nineteen titles), Mme de Stolz (sixteen titles), and Mme de Witt (three titles), amongst others. A large number of these titles refer explicitly to a family relationship or situation. There is space here to consider only a few of these writers in order to identify differences in approach and to give a flavour of the development of the genre in the second half of the century.

Zulma Carraud (1796–1889) and a New Project

While most of the writers of the Bibliothèque rose were addressing a bourgeois or upper-class readership, Zulma Carraud directed her works to the children of the rural poor and their parents. She was interested in elementary educational projects, her experience as a teacher at a rural school in Nohant having revealed the lack of appropriate books for her pupils, and, as she wrote to her close friend, Honoré de Balzac, her experience with her own two sons had taught her the importance of the early years of life in educating children.[48] Carraud went on to produce a series of simple texts for use in the teaching of reading at an elementary level, one of which, *Historiettes à l'usage des jeunes enfants qui commencent à savoir lire* (1853), first appeared in Hachette's *Semaine des enfants* before going through twenty-four editions in the Bibliothèque rose illustrée.[49] This consisted of very brief narratives on topics related to everyday life similar to those that informed Berquin's work. Thus, a disobedient boy falls in a river while another, ill with measles, disobeys his doctor and opens his window, causing lasting damage to his eyesight, and a calm, passive boy who never rises to the taunts of his playmates springs instantly to the defence of his younger brother when under attack. Carraud also wrote *Les Métamorphoses d'une goutte d'eau* (1864), an early foray into the fashionable area of the popularisation of science for children. Listed in the Bibliothèque rose collection for children ages eight to fourteen, this work exploits the convention of a dialogue between an adult and a child that ranges through explanations of natural phenomena and of the uses of natural products. Her first published work, *La Petite Jeanne, ou le devoir* (1852), subtitled *Livre de lecture courante à l'usage des écoles primaires de filles*, had been written for the pupils of a village girls' school and published as one of Hachette's *livres élémentaires*. This instructional narrative depicts the four stages of life of the very poor child Jeanne, first seen begging with her ailing mother, who survives and prospers as an adolescent, wife, mother, and subsequently widow by dint of hard work, honesty, and perseverance. The novel encompasses a variety of setbacks and troubles that Jeanne must surmount and, like its companion text for boys, *Maurice ou le travail* (1853), offers a model of industriousness and hope to the poorest in society. *La Petite Jeanne* was later reissued in the Bibliothèque rose illustrée, where it was a best-seller for decades.

Both texts endorse very clearly demarcated gender roles. In *La Petite Jeanne* there is a network of female characters and influence in a pattern repeated over two generations. After demonstrating her honesty by returning a bracelet found by the wayside, the child Jeanne earns the patronage of a well-to-do woman whose daughter teaches her the basic skills of reading, writing, sewing, and knitting that enable her to meet her own needs and which she in turn later teaches to the daughter of a farming family for whom she goes to work. When her mother dies, Jeanne continues to live with the neighbour who took them in and whom she, in return, cares for in her old age. Jeanne commands respect and admiration everywhere for her goodness, cleanliness, diligence, and dutifulness to her employers and, when she marries, impresses all the villagers with her well-planned house and clean, well-fed, and healthy children. Carraud essentially presents to her readers a model based on middle-class values that involves adopting, to a suitably limited extent, new ideas and approaches to work, child rearing and healthcare as well as a capacity for planning, thriftiness, and perseverance, but one still based firmly within the context of their own class.[50] The family structure depicted, for example, is not that of the ideal nuclear family, but an extended one in which outsiders play a part. Any suggestion of *déclassement* is resisted by the endorsement of a strong preference for rural life, and Jeanne's success in life is predicated upon being useful, caring for and earning the affection of others within a modest domestic context. Her daughter's life repeats the same pattern, promoting the view that women should perpetuate these values in succeeding generations in order to create a happy and stable community.

The protagonist of *Maurice ou le travail* devotes his life to hard work and providing for others from the moment his father is paralysed in an accident when Maurice is only eight and he begs the local blacksmith to let him assist in the forge. Although he learns reading, writing, and arithmetic in the evenings with the local teacher, he refuses the opportunity to go to a school, where he could learn to develop his artisan skills, preferring to stay with his father and work locally, a decision praised by all. As in Ségur's *Pauvre Blaise*, education is seen as vital to self-improvement for the poor within the individual's allotted social status, not as a passport to a higher social class. After his father's death, Maurice embarks on the typical apprentice's *tour de France*, visiting various workshops to develop new skills, and returns eventually to set up his own blacksmith's shop. His departure is approved as a means of shedding the ignorance that provincialism can breed, but his desire to remain faithful to his background and return to his roots is thoroughly endorsed. The brief sojourn in Paris, where he risks being led astray by acquaintances, reinforces the notion of the city as a site of danger and corruption, and the countryside as the place of opportunity and happiness. After acquitting himself well as both apprentice and in military service, he marries and creates a comfortable life for his family, building his own house and shop and generating business through his willingness to work long hours. In this text the network of male duty and responsibility is depicted through Maurice's devotion to the priest and teacher and his own teaching of his son and an unemployed friend who benefits from both Maurice's example and their discussions on the importance of work. Maurice becomes a successful self-made man in a modest way, and, like Jeanne, is seen to be willing to embrace new ways in the name of progress. His family's health, as well as their economic well-being, derives from his thoughtfulness and the careful planning of their home. As an elderly man he becomes the assistant mayor of the village and is involved in many improvements to local roads and amenities, thus performing a service to the wider community. Here, too, the values are handed down to the next generation as his son Charles, rejecting the opportunity to make a career in the army, returns to work at his father's forge and is charged with conserving the family's financial status through his own efforts.

Victorine Monniot's Best-Seller

Published the same year as Ségur's *Les Petite filles modèles*, the *Journal de Marguerite ou deux années préparatoires à la première communion* (1858) by Victorine Monniot (1825–1880) was also a best-seller, running into more than a hundred editions. Based on Monniot's diary of her own experiences as a child and adolescent on the Ile Bourbon (now La Réunion) with her widowed mother and siblings between 1835 and 1845, the book appealed to the contemporary taste for exoticism stimulated by the colonial activities of the Second Empire. Dedicated to 'les enfants de l'île Bourbon', the *Journal de Marguerite* introduced the island to young French readers with its detailed descriptions of its flora and fauna and the lives and traditions of its inhabitants. Monniot's sojourn there was before the abolition of slavery in 1848, and her account depicts the paternalism and prejudices of that period as well as the good intentions of some of the masters and her own hatred of the evils of the system. Monniot's work reveals her to be a profoundly Catholic writer, and in the persona of Marguerite she portrays the advantages for a young girl of a strict religious upbringing. Events in the book closely follow her own experiences, including the deaths of two younger sisters, one on the island and one on board the ship that was bringing the family back to France, and are imbued with a strong sense of pious resignation and sacrifice. Nevertheless, the frequently boisterous activities of Marguerite and her brothers and sisters, and their reactions to their journeys to and from the Ile Bourbon and their life there, reveal, as with Ségur's fictional children, a more plausible image of children's thoughts and feelings and their way of expressing themselves, than in many edifying texts hitherto. A sequel, *Marguerite à vingt ans* (1861), the lengthy religious passages of which were abridged in later editions, depicts Marguerite's decision to enter a convent.

Julie Gouraud

The writing career of Julie Gouraud (1810–1891) spanned both halves of the nineteenth century and lasted some fifty years. She was involved in the founding of the *Journal des jeunes personnes* in 1832, contributing two articles to each monthly issue up until 1870, and was one of the most prolific writers in the Bibliothèque rose illustrée series, although she has not achieved the lasting status of Ségur. Her writings are imbued with what Marie-Thérèse Latzarus calls a 'moralité souriante', and promote desirable social attributes like kindness, simplicity, good humour, and gratitude.[51] Many signal the family setting explicitly in the title: *Cécile ou la petite soeur* (1862), *La Famille Harel* (1878), *Chez Grand'mère* (1882), and *Quand je serai grand* (1888). Gouraud also responded to the current interest in travel narratives by sending her protagonists on journeys (such as that in the Dauphiné in *Les Vacances d'Yvonne*, 1859) that allow for the introduction of informative picturesque detail about the countryside, the local people, and customs. Less overtly moralising than many of her contemporaries, Gouraud's works for the Bibliothèque rose illustrée are simple stories of good, modest, and diligent children of different social classes who act as examples to others and find happiness themselves in overcoming disadvantages and achieving their goals. Thus, the protagonist of *Le Petit colporteur* (1867) seeks to earn a living after his father's death by becoming a travelling pedlar with the help of the local schoolmaster and nobleman. After recognising reluctantly that he will have to change his wares from useful objects like needles, scissors, woollen stockings, and cotton nightcaps to items like cheap jewellery more in line with the wants of the well-to-do visitors in the spa towns he frequents in search of customers, he prospers and eventually acquires his own shop. Pierre is not corrupted by his travels but retains his integrity even in an environment that encourages pleasure seeking and improvidence. He is tempted to gamble in a casino only once, then turns his back on it forever. Honesty, diligence, and saving rather than squandering one's earnings are seen to be the key to happiness and economic success for the children of the poor in a society in which money rules.[52]

In some of her most successful works, Gouraud exploits the potential of an unconventional narrator or protagonist. In *Mémoires d'un caniche* (1866), illustrated by Bayard, a text that, like Ségur's *Mémoirs d'un âne,* recalls the picaresque genre, she adopts the strategy of foregrounding an animal hero, recounting the adventures of a poodle from a well-to-do background who rescues a drowning child, gets lost in a forest, and experiences life in the slums before being restored to his home and settling down to write his memoirs. Kindness to animals, whether domesticated or in the wild, had long been a popular theme in children's books, exploiting the affinity of children with animals to encourage the development of the humane qualities of compassion and charitableness, and a fictional character's morals were often illustrated through the way they treated their pets. The Grammont Law of 1850, which gave protection to animals and set out penalties for their ill treatment, prompted an increase of interest in animal stories. Also published in the Bibliothèque rose illustrée was Mlle Fleuriot's *Bigarette* (1875), the main character in which is a chicken, and Judith Gautier's *Mémoires d'un éléphant blanc* (1893), in which an elephant helps the education of an Indian princess.

Gouraud's *Lettres de deux poupées, recueillies et publiées par Mme Julie Gouraud* (1864) was her first work for the Bibliothèque rose illustrée and demonstrates that the 'doll story' genre, initiated at the beginning of the century, was still going strong. Examples like Sophie Senneterre de Renneville's *Conversations d'une jeune fille avec sa poupée* (c. 1822), which mirrored the popular eighteenth-century texts based on conversations between a mother and child, portrayed the 'education' of a doll in which the child owner is encouraged to act as mother and teacher, replicating her own educational experience, enacting with the doll the stages in a girl's development and rehearsing her future role as wife and mother. Others, like Gouraud's earlier *Mémoires d'une poupée, contes dédiés aux petites filles* (1839) portrayed an autobiography of a doll that offered a model of self-development and allowed for objective comment on the world of humans. This text also has its picaresque elements, for the plot is predicated upon the change of owners in whose hands the doll, Vermeille, finds herself. Different manifestations of female behaviour are evoked as Vermeille is offered as a prize in a lottery and belongs successively to owners of different social classes and temperament. She is ill-treated and neglected by the rich child who wins her, and eventually the reader learns, in a chapter written by the hand of another, that she is the victim of the well-meant intentions of another child who, like Ségur's Sophie, attempts to treat her as human, warming her feet near a fire of wood shavings.[53]

In Gouraud's *Lettres de deux poupées*, the format is that of the traditional novel of letters, based on the conceit that the correspondents are able to communicate with each other in this way although they lack the power of speech. From their origins in a shop in Paris the dolls go to different homes: Charmante to the daughter of a rich businessman in Bordeaux, the other, Merveille, to a wealthy family who spend the winter in a château in Alsace. Their lives are the starting point for reflections on the relative merits for a doll of city and country life, of an existence in high society, or as a 'bonne bourgeoise de poupée'.[54] The content is similar to that of the compilations popular in the ancien régime, for the dolls regale each other with edifying stories, informative discourses on topics from the Seven Wonders of the World to pearl fishing and the uses of tortoiseshell, and descriptions of the activities (including an encounter with an elephant) that they share with the children of their families. The text also presents the history of dolls and their important educative role in the upbringing of girls, serving to discourage idleness, foster an interest in sewing and domesticity, and act as facilitators of discussion between mother or governess and child. It also touches upon the cruelties inflicted on their dolls by unthinking or unkind children.

The dolls themselves are not static personalities, and represent the potential problems of growing up female. Merveille is initially the more confident and dominant personality, chiding Charmante for her disgruntlement at being removed to the provinces and praising the pleasures of a simple life in the country, but she is also more impressionable than her friend and has to develop self-awareness. When she is in danger of being seduced by the vacation pleasures of the wealthy, revelling in the excursions and basking in the glory of performing as a dancer on a high wire, she receives a warning against a life of pleasure from Charmante who now prefers study and a quieter life. Class consciousness and a paternalistic attitude towards the poor remain much like those of ancien régime texts and extend to the dolls as well. Merveille castigates her own reluctance at being left for a night at the gardener's cottage to soothe a sick child, but because of her privileged glimpse into the life of the family is able to reassure her young owner that poor children are as cherished by their virtuous and uncomplaining parents as the wealthy. Moreover, the conventions of class difference are preserved intact in this episode, for the 'rich' doll is carefully placed in a cupboard by the gardener's wife who tells her child that 'une poupée en robe de soie, ça n'est pas pour nous, ma mignonne', and the gift of a doll dressed as a traditional Alsacienne is provided by Merveille's family instead. The difficulty of finding an appropriate ending to a text of this sort is not resolved very satisfactorily by Gouraud. Charmante's joy at the prospect of a projected trip to Paris and a possible chance reunion with Merveille is tempered by the news that, to satisfy a whim of her owner, her eyes are to be replaced in a doll factory thus bringing their correspondence temporarily to a halt. This reminder that the dolls are not human is perhaps only intended as a convenient form of closure, but strikes a rather chilling note and reminds the reader that, even for dolls, life may hold unpleasant surprises.

Zénaïde Fleuriot

Another prolific writer, and one whose works have been deemed to have more literary merit than most, was Zénaïde Fleuriot (1829–1890), many of whose novels were published by Hachette in different collections. She contributed to Hachette's *Journal de la Jeunesse* along with writers like Alfred Assollant, Julie Colomb, Julie Gouraud, and the English writer Ouida (Marie Louise de la Ramée) and wrote mainly for adolescent girls, with some texts for younger children. Like that of her contemporaries, her work is socially conservative, traditionalist, and Catholic, her main inspiration being 'la foi, la famille et la nature'.[55] Titles amongst her eighty or so publications in just under thirty years include *Sans beauté* (1862), *Un coeur de mère* (1863), *Miss Idéal* (1869), *Le Petit chef de famille* (1874), *Bigarette* (1875), *La Petite duchesse* (1876), *Un enfant gâté* (1877), *Tranquille et Tourbillon* (1880), *Gildas l'intraitable* (1886), and *Parisiens et montagnards* (1888). Her focus is mainly on the bourgeois family and her novels, also like those of Ségur, are imbued with a strong sense of family values grounded in traditional Christian morality, which her characters strive to maintain or recapture if they are isolated or mistreated. She has a penchant for the idealistic image of the child as redeemer of an erring adult, and her orphaned or abandoned children are capable of great acts of self-sacrifice and heroism. Many have to assume responsibilities beyond their years, looking after siblings or learning to cope alone. The long-suffering patience and gentleness of the unhappy protagonists of *Tombée du nid* (1881) and *De trop* (1888), for example, eventually soften the hard hearts of the adults around them.

Fleuriot's novels are less maudlin and sentimental than those of most of her contemporaries, however, and despite her conservative, even reactionary views, convey a strong sense of realism. She has, like Ségur, been seen as a follower of Balzac in her use of detailed description of her characters' homes, apparel, and belongings to indicate their personality and in her portrayal of social structures and mechanisms.[56] The implications of economic prosperity or disaster are frequent themes, and the consequences of the latter are often the starting point of her plots. (Fleuriot herself had worked as a governess after her family fell on hard times.) Her views on class difference, while still of their time, are less patronising or contemptuous than in many contemporary juvenile novels, for her peasant and working-class characters are not invariably stereotyped as either stoic victims or vicious brutes. As in most fiction of this period, however, it is the respectable, hardworking, and grateful poor who succeed in life and then only within certain social limits. Fleuriot is not blinkered to the foibles and faults of her prosperous society, and the arrogant, materialistic, and hard-hearted are clearly castigated and the narrow-minded and ostentatious satirised. Her later novels reflect post-1870 life under the Third Republic and the less rosy side of reality is not ignored: *Aigle et Colombe* (1873) and *Monsieur Nostradamus* (1875), which feature an indictment of the Paris Commune and the siege of Paris, respectively, represent a rare intrusion of current or recent social upheavals in children's books; and in *Papillonne: souvenirs de jeunesse d'un vieux campagnard* (1892) she deplores the influences to which girls are exposed in the workshops of Paris, especially the corruptive power of unsuitable reading matter. The resolutions to her plots are, however, cheering and salutary, and leave the reader with a generally optimistic view of contemporary society and human nature.

Three examples will illustrate the themes and narrative strategies that characterise Fleuriot's work. In *Parisiens et montagnards* (1888), a novel for adolescents, a slender plot involving a sick boy of fifteen, grief-stricken after the death of his twin sister, who is taken to Switzerland by his family, is the vehicle for much picturesque detail about the lakes, mountains, and way of life around Lucerne. The novel provides interesting insight into nineteenth-century tourism through the experiences of the family (consisting of Alfred, his engineer father, his sister Camille, and his aunt) in a hotel and a rented chalet in the mountains, and their excursions by boat and mountain railway. There is some attempt to explore the psychology of the boy whose internalisation of sorrow coinciding with the growth of adolescence has seriously affected his physical well-being but whose energies and enthusiasm for life are speedily restored by exercise, fresh air, and the distraction of new sights and activities. He is a far more robust and believable figure than the saintly, romanticised invalids so frequently depicted in children's books in the nineteenth century. Fleuriot's novels abound in nicely observed portraits of adults that reveal some of the preoccupations, interests, and attitudes of contemporary society. Here, the character of Tante Eugénie is an affectionately humorous portrait of a fussy middle-aged maiden aunt, a reluctant tourist for whom every mode of transport is a torture and every natural feature a threat and whose main preoccupations on the journey are her medicines, her luggage, and predictions of disaster. Her self-immobilising nervousness both amuses and exasperates the younger members of the group, and acts as a strong contrast to the increasing resilience of the invalid who refuses to be restricted by her well-meaning efforts to curtail his exploits. The family's sojourn in a mountain chalet introduces a poor Swiss family who form the subject of the central part of the plot, a story of middle-class benevolence and working-class gratitude and self-help. The bright and eager twelve-year-old Arnold who acts as their mountain guide is taught to write and procures a job as a waiter at the hotel where he flourishes while an interesting twist to this otherwise conventional plot is provided by the plight of his brother, Heinrich, who is also given employment at the hotel but who is unhappy away from his family and his mountain activities. The admission that happiness does not always depend on integration into society is rendered a shade patronising, however, by the fact that Heinrich is portrayed as unintelligent and gauche. In an epilogue that reveals a happy ending for all (a popular strategy in the novel of domestic realism), Alfred and Camille, now a married woman, return to their old haunts seven years later and find all of Arnold's family happily employed and prospering in their chosen métiers.

Tranquille et Tourbillon (1880) might appear from the title to be structured upon a conventional contrasting of types, but Fleuriot manipulates this narrative contrivance in an interesting way. The plot does indeed contrast the young Béatrix—nicknamed Mlle Tranquille by her guardian aunt, a wealthy baronne, for her calm, passive, obedient nature—with her cousin Tancrède (Tourbillon), a hyperactive and uncontrollable boy. However, Fleuriot undermines and confuses the reader's expectations by opening the text with the baronne's irritation at Tranquille's quiet goodness, which she finds monotonous and tiresome, relishing the prospect of having a noisy, active child at her château. The reader is initially disorientated by this change of perspective, although the servants' love and pity for Tranquille, and the universal approval of her character, discourage the temptation to share the baronne's view. Tourbillon, despite his thoughtless (and often deliberate) misdemeanours and his rude and abusive behaviour to all, immediately displaces Tranquille in the thoughts of the baronne with his self-interested sycophancy. The critique of the baronne, who is vain, self-obsessed, and constitutionally unable to keep still, craving travel and constant amusement, soon becomes clear. Her tolerance of Torbillon's behaviour is partly motivated by snobbery, for he bears the family name while Tranquille is a poor relation, and she remains blind to the relative merits of the children until, on her sickbed, she glimpses Tourbillon's cynical selfishness for herself.

Fleuriot provides an evocative picture of life in a great house and park, detailing the interminable evening card games and dinner parties, the walks and carriage rides. The portrayal of the idle rich is revealing: apart from the baronne's misplaced energies, the visiting neighbours (a colonel and his diminutive wife) are satirised for their shallowness and disinterest in politics or events outside their immediate lifestyle. They are counterbalanced by the figure of an elderly archaeologist who approves warmly of Tranquille, admiring her intelligence, drawing ability, and genuine enthusiasm for architecture and archaeology, which contrasts with her aunt's view of her collection of antiques and fossils as merely decorative possessions. When Tourbillon is sent to school to make a man of him, the baronne comes to realise Tranquille's worth ('Il y a une monotonie dont on ne se lasse jamais: c'est celle de la bonté'), while Tourbillon's profoundly egoistic characteristics are seen as a bad omen for his future ('le désespoir des familles et souvent la honte des nations').[57] Tourbillon's exile from access to the wealthy, leisured life of the great house is symbolised by his assumption of his old clothes, while the baronne, for all her social privileges and role as lady bountiful, must learn moral discrimination.

One of Fleuriot's favourite types appears in *Le Petit chef de famille* (1874) in the person of a twelve-year-old boy, Raoul, who is left as the head of the family after the death of their father and the grave illness of their stepmother. An indication of the effect of contemporary events on children surfaces at the beginning of the novel, where Raoul is seen commanding a group of boys playing as soldiers, carrying out military exercises in their makeshift uniforms and with wooden weapons. His valiant efforts to keep up morale when disaster strikes are pitted against the tantrums of his spoilt younger sister Charlotte, who refuses to accept that their situation has changed and acts like a selfish and demanding brat. The child characters are not as one-dimensional as they might first appear, however, for Charlotte also displays flashes of impulsive kindness and sensitivity and her rages are seen to stem from her failure to grasp the economic implications of their situation. Her babyish egotism is softened by her close relationship with the old grandfather, who takes the children into his home, and her imitation of his mannerisms and language ('Mille tonnerres!') and her self-assured prattle and opinions ('je suis fâchée contre le bon dieu') are the source of much of the humour in the text.[58] Fleuriot's portrayal of the different environments in which the children find themselves and of their relationships with each other and with adults creates a compelling picture of the period. In the depressing portrayal of the village school where Raoul encounters the haphazard system of teaching boys of different ages in the same room, Fleuriot's satirical depiction of the incompetence and lack of interest of the assistant master who takes every opportunity to leave the classroom and drink and talk politics with his friends, and the idleness and cruelty of some of the pupils, are an indictment of educational standards before Jules Ferry's laws on education in the 1880s. The greatest danger to Raoul's character, however, comes from his dilettante cousin Gustave, who encourages him to play truant and go on fishing expeditions. Gustave represents a model of what Raoul might become if he fails to learn to take his responsibilities seriously, and is an example of Fleuriot's condemnation of the self-centred idle rich. Raoul is saved by his conscience before too much damage is done, and, having passed the examination for entrance to a college in Nantes, is set to work hard at his studies and fulfil his role as head of the family.[59]

Despite the interest of the realistic depiction of the period, Fleuriot's books have not lasted like those of Ségur, in part, perhaps, because she is less successful at capturing the child's voice and lacks Ségur's ability to locate her narrative at the linguistic level of the young reader.[60] Nevertheless, she deserves to be better known than she is at present.

Olga de Pitray (1835–1909)

Ségur's daughter Olga de Pitray similarly never achieved the same degree of fame as her mother, although her novels are not without literary merit. Among her more commercially successful works were *Le Château de la Pétaudière* (1876), a realistic story about contemporary children, and *Voyages abracadabrants du gros Philéas* (1890), a fictional autobiography of the fantastic adventures of a descendent of the Baron von Munchausen. *Robin des bois* (c. 1889) is interesting for its portrayal of the psychology of a young boy torn by conflicting desires about his future. Robert, the weaker of the twin baby sons of a peasant farmer, is spoilt by his mother and grows up imperious and dominating, commanding the village boys in their forays into the woods. His life is changed by a meeting with a poacher, whose romantic description of himself as 'le roi du forêt' seduces Robert and increases his natural inclinations for hunting. Their friendship perverts the boy's sense of honour and duty as he becomes drawn more and more deeply into the poacher's illicit activities, a corruption exacerbated when he acquires his first gun and a book about Robin Hood. His reading is shown to have an equally pernicious effect on him as his fantasies of emulating his hero and becoming the leader of a band of adventurous forest dwellers drive him to embark on a double life as model schoolboy by day and apprentice poacher by night. The question of education for the masses raised by Ségur in *La Fortune de Gaspard* is addressed by Pitray through the attitude of the twins' father, who, himself a former star pupil of the village school, is proud of the boys' academic prowess but also clearly endorses the widespread view amongst the ruling classes when he asserts, 'Si j'ai donné de l'instruction à mes fils, après en avoir reçu moi-mème, c'est pour mieux cultiver la terre. Notre pays aime mieux les laboureurs que les déclassés.'[61]

The portrayal of Robert's pain as he wrestles with his conscience is well delineated. Bound to the old poacher by complex feelings, he cannot break free, and eventually does indeed become an outlaw like his literary hero, except that in reality it is a life of shame, fear, and regret that alienates him from his gentle brother, his family, and society. After a series of bloody confrontations with the gamekeeper and the gendarmes, Robert is captured and both twins are brought close to death through suffering. Even when he is released through the intervention of the local landowner, redemption is not immediate. His character must be tested and Robert must restore harmony to the family through his own actions. They suffer ostracism in the community until his fortunes are dramatically reversed when in a melodramatic narrative coup he rescues the gamekeeper's two daughters from a rabid dog. A new friendship ensues, as a result of which Robert is able to pursue his activities on the right side of the law. Unable to adapt to the quiet of everyday life, he becomes a soldier, channelling his energies into serving his country and winning the Croix d'honneur for bravery. On his return home, his fortunes come full circle when he is nominated the gamekeeper's successor. Pitray's novel, which is more characteristic of the realistic and psychological novel of her time than those of her mother and contains much vivid detail about the lives of country dwellers, thus offers a lesson in making one's talents serve society and a grim picture of the consequences to self and family of choosing to live outside its bounds.

The second half of the nineteenth century also saw the flowering of a genre that, unlike the closed and predictable world of the novel of domestic realism, opened up horizons of possibilities and involvement for young readers in environments and situations beyond the world and the experience of their parents. The next two chapters consider the ways in which the didactic impulse was turned away from questions of everyday morality and domestic socialisation and, in the novel of adventure, was channelled into new avenues of experience and enquiry.

3

PIERRE-JULES HETZEL, JULES VERNE,
AND THE ADVENTURE OF SCIENCE

A significant step in the evolution of French books for the young came with the return to France in 1860 of Pierre-Jules Hetzel after nine years of exile in Brussels, when he installed his publishing business at 18 rue Jacob in Paris and devoted himself to developing his project of publishing for the young.[1] Books, for Hetzel, played a vital part in the development of the child: 'la santé morale et intellectuelle d'un enfant est tout entière dans le choix et dans la qualité des lectures qu'on lui fait faire'.[2] Together with Jean Macé and, subsequently, Jules Verne, he founded in 1864 the influential *Magasin d'éducation et de récréation,* an illustrated magazine dedicated to young readers, and then the Bibliothèque d'éducation et de récréation series which published in volume form many of the serialised novels and other pieces that had appeared in the *Magasin.* The volumes of this collection, originally called the Bibliothèque illustrée des familles, were highly desirable products, with their trademark red, black, and gold illustrated covers, and were often chosen as prizes by the French Ministry of Education; they are still much sought after by collectors today.[3] Hetzel was remarkably adept at advertising and marketing his product. The elaborate posters publicising the new volumes of *livres d'étrennes* alerted parents to new publications and catalogues for all the different collections were appended to each volume of the Bibliothèque. In one such catalogue from 1887–88, published twenty years after the beginning of Hetzel's project, we find the following celebratory promotional blurb: 'Quels souvenirs agréables et charmants ce titre général ne rappelle-t-il pas aux hommes jeuncs d'aujourd'hui, ceux qui entrent dans la vie au moment même où une révolution complète s'opérait, en leur faveur, dans la littérature!'[4]

THE *MAGASIN D'ÉDUCATION ET DE RÉCRÉATION*

The *Magasin* was a fortnightly publication of thirty-two pages, beginning 20 March 1864 and costing sixty centimes in Paris, with each twelve issues collected in a *volume semestriel*.[5] It was printed in double columns of clear, elegant typeface on good-quality paper with a large number of illustrations by well-regarded artists like Emile Bayard, Lorenz Froëlich, and Jean Geoffroy and was the first such publication to be *couronné* (awarded a prize) by the Académie française. Inevitably, there was rivalry between Hetzel's paper and the *Semaine des enfants* published by Hachette, which ended when the latter was acquired by Hetzel and subsumed in the *Magasin d'éducation et de récréation* in 1876. The *Magasin* was conceived as a publication that would bring together the whole family (indeed, from 1869 on it carried the subtitle *Journal de toute la famille*) and its mixture of tales for the very young, poems, short stories, instructive articles, and serialised novels attempted the daunting task of appealing to all ages and all tastes. In an editorial address to the readers in the first issue of the *Magasin* Hetzel outlined his mission thus:

> Il s'agit pour nous de constituer un enseignement de famille dans le vrai sens du mot, un enseignement sérieux et attrayant, qui plaise aux parents et profite aux enfants. Education, récréation, sont à nos yeux, deux termes qui se rejoignent. L'instructif doit se présenter sous une forme qui provoque l'intérêt: sans cela il rebute et dégoûte de l'instruction; l'amusement doit cacher une réalité morale, c'est-à-dire utile: sans cela il passe au futile, et vide les têtes au lieu de les remplir.[6]

This editorial policy emphasised the mutual dependency, in Hetzel's view, of instruction and entertainment, although it also reveals that 'entertainment' was, in effect, understood as a means of influencing young readers through the mediation, in an attractive manner, of socially sanctioned knowledge and morals.[7]

Hetzel's desire to supply quality reading material of wide interest and unimpeachable morality that would introduce the young to the pleasures of reading and encourage the process of insertion into culture has already been seen. His view that writing for children was a highly responsible and demanding task rather than a soft option is demonstrated in his fulminations in the preface to Louis Ratisbonne's collection of poems about childhood, *La Comédie enfantine* (1860–61) against

> ces plumes mercenaires qui font métier d'écrire à la douzaine ces livres sans goût ni parfum, ces livres plats et sans relief, ces livres bêtes auxquels semble réservé le privilège immérité de parler les premiers à ce qu'il y a de plus fin, de plus subtil et de plus délicat au monde, à l'imagination et au coeur des enfants.[8]

The young reader was not only deserving of the very best in both the material aspect and the content of the paper but was also to be respected by means of a simple but intelligent style of writing that would inspire interest and reflection rather than patronised by a puerile or condescending approach. This agenda promoted an attempt at a less constrained and unequal author-reader relationship, one founded more on honesty, affection, and regard. Lessons on behaviour and attitudes and the castigation of undesirable attributes would still be included, but in less overtly presciptive and more entertaining narratives. He rejected the notion that such teaching should necessarily have to be overly serious and tedious, noting, 'La morale n'est exclusive ni de la bonne humeur, ni même de la gaieté. Les vérités n'ont pas besoin d'être empesées pour être respectables.'[9] The end result, nonetheless, would still be one determined by the adult writer, and therefore the balance of power remained essentially unchanged.

Both the title of the paper itself, which gestures towards Mme Le Prince de Beaumont's *Magasin des enfants* of 1756, and the aim to create a kind of family encyclopedia suggest a link between Hetzel's objectives and the didactic agenda of the Enlightenment. The desired role of the paper in the personal and intellectual development of its readers is succinctly expressed in the editorial address of the first issue: the mixture of genres in its contents would 'contribuer à augmenter la masse de connaissances et d'idées saines, la masse de bons sentiments, d'esprit, de raison et de goût qui forme ce qu'on pourrait appeler le capital moral de la jeunesse intellectuelle de la France'.[10] The distinction between education and instruction was a significant one: the former concerned morality while the latter concerned the transmission of knowledge, and the two were indissolubly linked. The moral principles underpinning Hetzel's ethos were essentially universal ones based on individual conduct that suited very well the emerging republican outlook. At a time when the conflict about the role of religion in education was raging, and despite the fact that he supported Jules Ferry's views on an *école laïque*, Hetzel avoided making this a problematic issue for his young readers.[11] God is still frequently mentioned in the *Magasin*—indeed,

Hetzel invoked in the third issue the 'trois préceptes' of loving God, loving one's neighbour as oneself, and of not doing to others what one would not wish to have done to oneself—but this can be seen as a strategy of reassurance to all his readers, and was a common universalist approach amongst supporters of a lay morality.[12] The aim throughout the *Magasin* was to stimulate the individual conscience rather than to lay down prescriptive rules of conduct, praising a model of individual effort and self-policing based on common sense, moderation, respect for oneself, and solidarity with others. Education and hard work were perceived as the key to personal success and happiness and vital to the process of shaping the future of the nation, a collective enterprise for which children were enjoined to prepare by taking their studies seriously. The two most important spaces of the social cohesion that ideally would result from individual endeavour were the family and the *patrie*, concepts that encapsulated the values of the Third Republic and are constantly celebrated in the *Magasin*. The articles on a wide range of topical issues relating to the natural sciences, physics, chemistry, history, geography, and economics commissioned for the *Magasin* were intended to complement the teaching that children received at school and to impart information more widely within the family context. A not unimportant objective was that they would prompt discussion and debate between parents and children from which all might benefit.

A typical issue of the *Magasin* contained a lengthy episode of a novel by Jules Verne; an episode of another novel or a work of a lightly fictionalised scientific nature; an episode from a moral tale or a short story about childhood; factual or biographical pieces or short articles on science or grammar (by Ernest Legouvé, a member of the Académie française); fables or poems (by Louis Ratisbonne or Victor de Laprade whose favourite themes were the family, love, friendship, and patriotism); and a simple illustrated tale for the very young. Among the novels published for the first time or revived in the pages of the *Magasin* and subsequently in volume form in the Bibliothèque were Jules Sandeau's *La Roche aux mouettes* (1871), a story of maternal devotion, and Louis Desnoyers's *Les Mésaventures de Jean-Paul Choppart* (1868). André Laurie, a former Communard, produced a series of fourteen works titled *La Vie de collège dans tous les pays* (1881–1905) through which he mediated his own progressive ideas and aimed to promote greater understanding of other nations by depicting a social aspect that would appeal to young readers. The daily lives of schoolchildren in many different countries (England, Germany, Italy, Japan, Russia, Spain, and Switzerland) as well as in different parts of France were portrayed in a lightly fictionalised, entertaining style, with much detail and amusing anedotes about lessons, teachers, homework, examinations, punishments, recreational activities, food, and the like.

Many of the short stories and serialised texts in the *Magasin* were written or adapted by Hetzel himself, under the name of P.-J. (or 'Papa') Stahl. He was responsible for numerous short pieces on the ethics of conduct in different everyday situations, and tales portraying children's relationships and experiences with a clear moral message and titles like *Le Petit tyran* (1869), *Révolte punie* (1872), or *Les caprices de Manette* (1874). Often animals are foregrounded in short stories for the very young or in lengthier narratives, as in *Histoire de la famille Chester et de deux petits orphelins* (1873, adapted from English), which features a litter of mice; *Histoire d'un âne et de deux jeunes filles* (1874), one of Stahl's best-known narratives, which featured the hardships of the proletariat and may have capitalised upon the success of the comtesse de Ségur's *Mémoires d'un âne* of 1860; *Odyssée de Pataud et de son chien Fricot* (1877), and *Histoire d'un perroquet* (1878). Writing to a friend about *Histoire d'un âne et de deux jeunes filles*, which he describes as a fable, Hetzel echoes Charles Perrault's prescription for making a lesson palatable to young readers by concealing it beneath an entertaining narrative: 'La petite médecine est absorbée, qu'il aurait refusée peut-être si elle lui eût été offerte dans la tasse ordinaire.'[13] The *Histoire d'un âne* was, in fact, extremely successful, as Hetzel remarked with delight, if also with a momentary lapse of taste ('cinq mille ânes sont déjà dévorés, c'est pire que sous le Siège').[14] He also produced rewritten versions of successful novels in other languages, most notably *Les Quatre filles du Docteur March* (1880, from Louisa May Allcott's *Little Women*), *Les Patins d'argent*, (1875, from Mary Dodge's *The Silver Skates*), and *Les Contes de Tante Judith* (1890, from Margaret Gatty's *Aunt Judy's Magazine*). These were recast to fit the overall agenda of the *Magasin* and to make them appropriate to a French readership. His adaptation of Johann David Wyss's *Le Robinson suisse*, for example, sought to modernise and simplify the original's interminable passages on natural history and science, recast the passages of Protestant morality of the original, and modify the more gratuitously brutal episodes that distressed the readers he had consulted.[15] His description in his preface of Wyss's concept of imitating Daniel Defoe's *Robinson Crusoe* with a family as protagonists as that of 'confisquer, à l'usage du jeune âge, une idée de génie' reflects upon his own action in choosing to update and render the novel more palatable to the readers of his day, and, more generally, upon his strategy of appropriating the works of other writers and adapting them to his own ends.[16]

THE ALBUMS STAHL

Hetzel furthered his commitment to catering even for very young children with the introduction of the Bibliothèque blanche series in 1871, which featured most of the fairy tales originally published in *Nouveau magasin des enfants* in the 1840s and short tales of family life. For this young audience, Hetzel produced the Albums Stahl, an innovative series containing large illustrations accompanied by a few brief lines of text, the forerunners of the picture book and the *bande dessinée*. The best known are the stories based on the character of a little girl, Mlle Lili, that were illustrated by Froëlich and presented by 'un papa'. They were amusing and unexceptionable little tales, extracted from the *Magasin*, of the exploits at home and abroad of a small child, her cousin Lucien, and her friends. Other albums feature M. Jujules, M. Toto, and a pair of twins. The illustrations depict chubby little toddlers in a well-to-do environment, not unlike the rosy-cheeked, angelic scamps of late-Victorian literature. Their daily activities, however ordinary, are imbued with significance and dignity as they, too, are dignified in a gently humorous manner via the juxtaposition of the formal and the childish in their names. In *Le Premier cheval et la première voiture* (1874), for example, a serious-faced toddler is shown being bounced on the knees of another child scarcely bigger than herself. Even here there is an underlying didactic dimension that mirrors that of the stories and articles for older children. Mlle Lili is often shown looking at a book, and provides a model of early learning in the *Alphabet de Mlle Lili* (1865); in *La Poupée de Mlle Lili* (1886) she is shown teaching the alphabet to her doll. She was also allowed to undertake several miniature voyages of discovery: in *Voyage de découvertes de Mlle Lili et de son cousin Lucien* (1866–67), the two children and the reader are introduced to mountains, forests, and rivers, and her travels were extended in *Voyage de Mlle Lili autour du monde* (1868), *Mlle Lili en Suisse* (1885), *Mlle Lili à Paris* (1890), and *Mlle Lili au Jardin des Plantes* (1899). A parallel series involving M. Jujules, which portrayed activities more likely to appeal to boys and including *M. Jujules à l'école* (1880) and *Le Jardin de M. Jujules* (1882), were in the same vein. Many depict a first experience of life beyond babyhood, like *Le Premier chien et le premier pantalon* and *La Première chasse de M. Jujules et son lendemain* (1890). The interaction between siblings or playmates in the family context is depicted with warmth and humour, presenting an image of harmony and happiness to the reader in such albums as *Mon petit frère, ou une visite à la nourrice* (1878) and *La Fête de Mlle Lili* (1882). Also listed amongst the *Albums Stahl* in the

1885–86 catalogue were collections of songs and nursery rhymes, again illustrated by Froëlich, but this time in colour.

THE WONDERS OF SCIENCE

The most important of Hetzel's projects was the communication of scientific information, since—at a time when the Industrial Revolution was well underway and scientific discoveries and feats of engineering were advancing apace—science was perceived as a vital key to national progress. In his preface to the 1867 edition of Jules Verne's *Voyages et Aventures du capitaine Hatteras*, Hetzel established the importance of this agenda in his overall project with the assertion that 'il faut bien se dire que l'art pour l'art ne suffit plus à notre époque et que l'heure est venue où la science a sa place faite dans le domaine de la littérature.'[17] While Hetzel looked after the recreation, the literary aspect of the *Magasin*, his co-founder Jean Macé was placed in charge of overseeing the education side—in particular, the popularising of science. Macé, a confirmed republican who like his old school friend Hetzel had been in exile after the coup of 1851 that led to Louis Napoleon becoming emperor, was a journalist and a teacher in a girls' school. Totally committed to the idea of a sound education for both sexes and all classes, which he saw as the sine qua non of emancipation and equality, he founded, in 1863, the Société des bibliothèques populaires du Haut-Rhin in order to make available to the working classes the means to acquire an education. In 1866 he launched the Ligue française de l'enseignement, which saw the school as the instrument of social and political progress and campaigned actively for a system of secular education that would be obligatory (and free) for everyone, a system that would only fully come into being with the Ferry laws and the *école laïque* of the Third Republic in the 1880s.[18] Even before his association with the *Magasin*, Macé had produced a book for children that aimed to make scientific information accessible and interesting to young readers. Hetzel, to whom he submitted the manuscript, was so delighted with *L'Histoire d'une bouchée de pain* (1861), which explained the processes of digestion to young girls in an entertaining manner, that he recommended it to Charles Augustin Sainte-Beuve, a major figure in the selection of books to be awarded a prize by the Académie française, describing Macé as 'une vraie plume au service de la science, une plume savante et aimable' and the book as 'ce frais et solide breuvage', contrasted with the 'si triste tisane' of 'la littérature de gouvernante qu'on leur sert d'ordinaire'.[19] The work was indeed recommended by the Académie and was a huge success, with new editions appearing constantly for some forty years.

The commitment of Hetzel and Macé to popularising science and technology for the young in the *Magasin* involved bringing in as collaborators some of the eminent names in the different branches of science, including the entomologist Jean-Henri Fabre, the astronomer Camille Flammarion, the architect Eugène-Emmanuel Viollet-le-Duc, and the economist Maurice Block, who contributed occasional short pieces. Macé himself continued to write imaginative narratives based on scientific fact: the sequel to *Histoire d'une bouchée de pain*, titled *Les Serviteurs de l'estomac*, a fable based on parts of the body, appeared in the first issue of the *Magasin* and was followed in 1864–65 by *Histoire d'une goutte d'eau* and *Histoire d'un grain de blé*. He also contributed historical pieces, notably *L'Anniversaire de Waterloo* (1864) and *La France avant les Francs* (1879), and a curious allegorical tale titled *Voyage au pays de la grammaire* (1866–67) in which a little boy visits the homes of the different parts of speech, who introduce themselves and explain their functions and relationships. Paul Gouzy's *Promenade d'une fillette autour d'un laboratoire* (1887) is an introduction to chemistry that deploys a humorous approach in order to demystify the subject. Articles and short stories about the natural sciences describing the life cycle and habits of plants and animals were predominant, with titles such as *Aventures d'un jeune naturaliste* (1869) and *Aventures de deux enfants dans un parc* (1883) by Lucien Biart, and Ernest Candèze's *Aventures d'un grillon* (1877) and *Périnette. Histoire surprenante de cinq moineaux* (1886). The latter, in particular, introduced an allegorical and moral dimension to Candèze's narratives that could be seen to be of universal application, as Sarah Trimmer had done in her *Fabulous Histories* (1786), later known as *The History of the Robins*, a book that was popular in France. Such texts also encouraged children to look closely at, and appreciate as fellow living beings, the small creatures that all too often were tormented or killed in their games. A common strategy employed to make the information more accessible was to feature a child protagonist or addressee within the text, encouraging reflection and inviting the reader to concur with the point being made. Of course, this was not a new approach, as the many texts popularising science in the previous hundred years demonstrate, but more imaginative attempts were now being made to involve the young reader through the inclusion of humour and, above all, of ample and enticing illustrations. The appropriation in the titles of the words *histoire, aventure*, or *voyage*, associated increasingly at this time with dramatic tales of adventure and exploration, could be seen as a marketing ploy, a hook to attract the reader and disguise the didactic nature of the text. Indeed, the use of such grand titles to describe what were effectively narratives analogous to the *leçons des choses* of the eighteenth century, describing existing phenomena and lacking in dramatic action and surprises, has been seen as a degradation and emasculation of the vocabulary and the spirit of the novel of adventure.[20] However, for Hetzel and his contributors, the quest for knowledge *was* the great adventure, and the appearance of such scientific fables and tales alongside episodes of the novels of Jules Verne underlined the *Magasin*'s agenda of offering young readers a voyage of discovery through their reading by evoking the marvels of the universe and the wonders of science.

The *Magasin d'éducation et de récréation* was not the only vehicle for presenting science to a young audience, for similar works appeared in Hachette's *Bibliothèque des merveilles* from 1860. However, apart from the more imaginative works of A. Castillon, such as *Récréations physiques* (1861) and *Récréations chimiques* (1866), which attempted to situate the scientific information in a domestic context and in language to which children could relate, this series was more conventionally didactic in its approach. The greater popularity of the *Magasin* and the Bibliothèque d'éducation et de récréation can also be attributed to Hetzel's coup in signing up the writer whose name has become synonymous with what can be termed, in the broadest sense, 'science fiction'.

JULES VERNE

If the jewel in the crown of Hachette's Bibliothèque rose was the Comtesse de Ségur, the star author for Hetzel was undoubtedly Jules Verne (1828–1905). After the fairy tales of Charles Perrault, Verne's novels are the most widely known French works outside France and the most widely translated, abridged, imitated, and transfered to other media in the shape of adaptations for film, TV, and comic books. Just as Hachette's signing of Ségur is seen as a seminal moment in the history of French children's books, so the meeting between Hetzel and Verne in 1862 sparked an enterprise that lasted for decades and was to create a significant new direction in the provision of literature for young readers. Allegedly inspired by a Thomas Cook travel brochure for a trip around the world, Verne created a new version of the adventure story that both drew on and exceeded the format and devices of earlier works in the genre. Verne had read and admired James Fenimore Cooper, Daniel Defoe, Edgar Allan Poe, Sir Walter Scott, and Johann David Wyss in his youth and appropriated the basic formula of a strong hero who encounters and overcomes numerous hazards and dangers, including the machinations of a villainous enemy, in the accomplishment of a mission. This formula, the oldest of story types, which derives from myth and classical epics, underpins most adventure stories, but Verne's success lay in the manner in which he breathed new life into the stereotypical characters and situations. His versatility is evident in his incorporation of elements from many other genres. A clear link can be perceived with François Fénelon's *Les Aventures de Télémaque* and Jonathan Swift's *Gulliver's Travels* in Verne's mixing of reality and fantasy, for example, as well as with the Robinsonnade tradition in the privileging of the theme of survival in alien environments and with fairy tales in the battles between good and evil.

In accordance with Hetzel's agenda, this huge and varied output presented not just entertaining adventures but a bold and overt didactic dimension. Verne's novels offered both an escape from everyday reality and a pathway to knowledge, seeking to interrogate the relationship of human beings to the universe and to teach readers of all ages to understand and appreciate the wonders and potential of nature, science, and human endeavour. His first novel, *Cinq semaines en ballon*, the story of an unprecedented journey from Zanzibar to Senegal in search of the source of the Nile by three Englishmen in a hot air balloon, was published by Hetzel in 1862.[21] The success of this book led to the conception of a series of novels of amazing journeys (grouped under the generic series title Voyages extraordinaires after 1867) that was to amount to sixty-four works over a career of more than forty years. The majority of the novels are based on the initiation or quest narrative, opening with the protagonists setting out on a journey, with knowledge being sought and/or acquired by the protagonists in the course of their life-changing experiences.[22] The journey for the reader thus mirrors that of the protagonist through engagement with the text, and the pedagogical element is enhanced for the reader by the passages of extra historical, geographical, or scientific information fed into the novel by the author. Verne was contracted to produce two to three books a year, and this was no mean feat given the length of some of the novels, most of which appeared first in the *Magasin d'éducation et de récréation*. The first issue of the *Magasin* in March 1864 carried the first part of the *Aventures du capitaine Hatteras. Les Anglais au Pôle Nord*; in the magazine's preface Hetzel described Verne's aim as to 'refaire … . l'histoire de l'univers'.[23] In 1864, too, Verne became a co-director of the *Magasin* and was therefore intimately involved with Hetzel's project of revitalising books for young readers at every level.

With his creation of page-turning plots, stunning set-piece scenes, and memorable, dynamic, or eccentric characters, Verne was to create a new version of a winning formula that has influenced the work of many writers and filmmakers to the present day, although the didactic agenda has usually been jettisoned along the way. The subtitle of the Voyages extraordinaires series, 'Les mondes connus et inconnus', signals the range of the settings of Verne's novels. In using the adventure story as a medium for education, Verne opened up exciting new possibilities in extending the locus of the initiation or quest narrative to previously unimagined realms. His characters inhabit, visit, or explore virtually every spot on the globe, including the North and South Poles. With this truly international scope, the novels exploit the contemporary interest in travel and exploration and provide an unprecedented vicarious touristic experience for the reader with their depiction of unfamiliar and exotic places. The directions, coordinates, and travelling times are carefully documented, and maps or charts often included, so that the reader can complement the experience of reading the text by following the fictional journeys visually. One of his most enduringly popular novels, *Le Tour du monde en quatre-vingts jours* (1873), allegedly inspired by just such a journey made in 1870 by the wealthy American George Francis Train and by an autobiographical account of 1872 titled *Round the World* by William Perry Fogg (whose surname Verne appropriated for his phlegmatic protagonist) provides a thrilling whistlestop tour for the armchair traveller. But in Phileas Fogg the novel also satirises the blasé tourist who is not remotely interested in the scenery of the countries through which he passes (unlike his valet Passepartout), the narrator presenting this to the reader by the comic strategy of describing what Fogg does not notice.[24] Verne's novels also feature an imaginative portrayal of places that humans had never been, nor, in his time, envisaged ever being able to go, travelling vertically, to the bottom of oceans, down to the centre of the earth, and up into space, locations that are described in similar detail and with equal conviction. In the more fantastic novels, the marvellous travelling machines and superhuman feats of endurance exist side by side with aspects of a world familiar to the readers, and the characters move between the known and the unknown worlds. This slippage between known geographical fact and fantasy in his settings is characteristic of his embrace of both realism and the *merveilleux*, a strategy that admirably satisfied the dual imperatives of instruction and entertainment.

Location is only part of the story, however. The plots are set not in a legendary past nor an imaginary future but are firmly grounded in the nineteenth century, with specific dates and contemporary references. Woven into Verne's narratives is information on recent history that does not just serve an expository or contextualising function but plays an important part in the adventure plot, immersing the reader in vicarious experience of historical events. He tackles many of the international events and major social and political issues of his day, including capitalism, nationalism, colonisation, race relations, and of the role of the United States and the power of finance in world affairs.[25] Thus, to name but a few widely varied examples, the campaigns against the slave trade of the 1850s and 1860s and the explorations of David Livingstone and Sir Henry Morton Stanley in Africa feature in *Un capitaine de quinze ans* (1878), the American Civil War of 1860–65 in *Nord contre sud* (1887), the Indian Mutiny of 1857–59 in *La Maison à vapeur* (1880), the conflicts of the 1860s between Russia and the central Asian states in *Michel Strogoff* (1876), the Irish nationalist movement in *P'tit bonhomme* (1893), and the Greek war of independence in *L'Archipel en feu* (1884). His particular interest in questions of colonisation addresses a major aspect of world affairs in the nineteenth century, and reflects the period under Napoleon III of French intervention in Africa, China, Italy, and Mexico, and the Third Republic's expanding empire in Africa, Asia, and Australasia. Issues of conquest, domination, resistance, and insurrection are central to the novels. Indeed, Verne's oeuvre has been seen as both representing and—in its own aim to embrace a vast range of knowledge—to embody, the 'drama of empire'.[26] Specific French concerns are addressed in *Cinq semaines en ballon* (the resistance to French attempts to conquer Senegal), *Les Cinq cents millions de la Bégum* (1879, the Franco-Prussian War), and *Famille sans nom* (1889, the French Canadian insurrection of 1837). The historical referencing serves to add credibility to the fictional adventures and, through the involvement of the characters in these events, Verne's readers were able to imbibe an intimate, if not impartial, glimpse of the factors that shaped, and were still shaping, the world in which they lived. The suggestion that such a concern with the political evolution of the world was unexpected in a 'children's author' misconstrues the import of Hetzel's agenda and the move in the last third of the century towards generating an awareness of such matters in young readers in order to strengthen the future of the Third Republic.[27]

Verne's own political outlook has generated much debate amongst commentators on his works and indeed often seems ambiguous. On the one hand, his own comfortable bourgeois lifestyle, his horror at the events of the Paris Commune, and his opposition to Alfred Dreyfus in the famous case of 1894 are adduced as evidence of a bourgois conservatism.[28] His novels, however, it has been argued, can be read as conservative, radical, or both.[29] A conservatism is certainly apparent in his works in his concept of the hierarchy of social relationships: the majority of his protagonists are of bourgeois origins, and many of his texts feature a close association and interdependency between master and servant.

Members of the upper classes are often satirised, and, surprisingly, considering Verne's interest in the building and operating of machines, the working classes play a relatively minor role and, if oppressed, are shown to be the victims of a particular situation or individual rather than of a wider class system. He praises the virtues of commercial enterprise, although he is critical of a cynical and dehumanising capitalism in, for example, *L'Ile à hélice* (1895), which depicts the conflicts among a group of American millionaires on their artificial island. This suggests a political stance not so very different from that of some of the writers of the Bibliothèque rose. Yet, on the other hand, amongst Verne's most notable heroes are outsiders, rebels, freedom fighters, and visionaries who reject the social order, and his novels reveal a deep sympathy with enslaved people throughout the world. An unequivocal opposition to slavery, for example, is manifest in several works, notably in *Nord contre sud* and in *Un capitaine de quinze ans*, in which a group of American citizens, black and white, are captured in Angola by Portuguese slave traders. In this grim portrayal of the plight of the sick and dying slaves on a forced march through the jungle, the image of a pair of severed hands still manacled together is a striking statement of Verne's view of humankind's inhumanity in the name of profit. However, the racist prejudices of the day are also apparent in his works, particularly in the portrayal of Africans and South Sea islanders who are seen as ugly, animalistic, and given to cannibalism and piracy.[30] The Sioux Indians in *Le Tour du monde en quatre-vingts jours* and the Tartars in *Michel Strogoff* are also seen as vicious and inhumanly aggressive. The native inhabitants of distant lands often play a negative role in the narratives, representing a threat to the white explorers and engaged in bloodthirsty rituals, like the human sacrifices at the enthronement of the king of Dahomey in *Robur le conquérant* (1886) and the river burial of the king accompanied by fifty live slaves and a number of wives in *Un capitaine de quinze ans*. The perpetration of such extreme horrors is, however, generally presented as the perverted work of the despotic tribal rulers rather than of the people at large, a view that has been seen as typical of the kind of argument deployed in the Third Republic to justify military intervention abroad and the colonial project in general.[31] American blacks are, on the other hand, portrayed more sympathetically, like Nab in *L'Ile mystérieuse* (1874–75), although, like Frycollin in *Robur le conquérant* (1886) they are frequently depicted as comic or cowardly and are nearly always cast in a position of subservience. Whether Verne can therefore be accused of promoting racist views to adolescent readers is a moot point. The appearance that his novels create of telling a factual story arguably makes the unsophisticated reader more open to political suggestion.[32] However, his readers were, of course, products of the same cultural environment and such views were widespread in the novel of adventure, as a reading of R.M. [Robert Michael] Ballantyne or Sir Henry Rider Haggard will demonstrate.

Verne's attitude towards colonial expansion is a correspondingly ambiguous one. It has been argued that the geography of the novels can be read as a 'site of resistance'.[33] His attacks on the iniquities of colonial imperialism are, however, directed mainly at the British in, for example, his discussion of the massacres during the Indian Mutiny of 1857–59 in *La Maison à vapeur* (1880) and *L'Île mystérieuse*, and the genocide in the Maori rebellion in New Zealand of the 1860s in *Les Enfants du capitaine Grant* (1867–68), in which condemnation of the British attempts to annihilate the indigeneous populations in Oceania is mediated through Paganel, a French geographer. Anti-British feeling is deeply embedded in *Vingt mille lieues sous les mers* (1869–70) and became more virulent in the later novels, like *Mistress Branican* (1891), which refers to the murder of aborigines in Australia. In *Hector Servadec* (1877), an improbably fantastic novel in which a disparate group of people are carried off on a comet that has crashed into the earth, the British garrison from Gibraltar are the only ones who refuse to cooperate in the business of survival and are lost in space. It would seem that Verne's objection to colonisation and his sympathy for national liberation movements, while certainly humanitarian, are essentially chauvinistic, for little is said about French colonial enterprise. This stance contrasts with the jingoistic approach of many contemporary magazines for the young, in which French intervention in other countries is overtly celebrated as a brave and altruistic crusade of bringing enlightenment to benighted cultures (see later discussion). Verne's view of the exploitation and development of the earth's natural resources as essential to progress suggests, however, that he accepted colonisation as necessary while deploring the abuses of power to which it led.[34] In effect, the fundamental theme in his oeuvre of journeys of exploration of other lands that involve destruction and conquest entails an assumption of the right to do so.

A central concern in the majority of Verne's works was to satisfy Hetzel's desire to exploit public interest in scientific discovery and to communicate to young readers an awareness of the wonders and potential of science, the new merveilleux,[35] and his oeuvre represents a systematic coverage of all areas of scientific knowledge: the nature of his plots allow for the mediation of information about physics, chemistry, astronomy, marine biology, botany, minerology, and much more. In many of the novels, a scholar or teacher figure is featured (like the geographer

Paganel in *Les Enfants du capitaine Grant*, or Otto Lidenbrock in *Voyage au centre de la terre*, 1864) to act as mediator of knowledge to both the other characters and the reader, seizing the opportunities furnished by the plot to expound on such subjects. Verne's researches into scientific developments enabled him, through a mixture of existing knowledge, inspired guesswork, and a taste for fantasy, to push the frontiers of that knowledge to the extreme. Most striking to the modern reader is his apparently prophetic depiction of the possibilities of machines (submarines, flying machines, space capsules, great engines, and monstrous weapons) that allow human beings to overcome limitations of movement in space and time, to travel unimaginable distances over land, on and under water, or in the air, and to engage in acts of great heroism or great destruction. His novels exhibit shifting boundaries between reality and imagination, between known fact and the imagined infinite capabilities of science, a potent mix that earned him a reputation as the father of science fiction. However, it has now been convincingly shown that Verne drew extensively on existing written material on topical issues, recycling and expanding both information about recent scientific developments (submarines, the telephone, air balloons, electricity) and speculation in the press about technological innovation and was thus less an inventor than a meticulous gatherer of knowledge.[36]

The power of science to facilitate humankind's control over nature is a central preoccupation, but the power of nature to resist this mastery is portrayed in an equally compelling manner, as in *Voyage au centre de la terre* (1864) where the attempt to reach the earth's core comes to an end when the explorers are vomited out of a volcano after a storm in an underground sea. The battle between the two is often represented in the many illustrations in the original editions, and especially in those of Edouard Riou, which depict the protagonists dwarfed by the natural world and vulnerable to its forces. The reader is acquainted with comets, meteors, eclipses, tropical storms, hurricanes, snowstorms, and undersea volcanic eruptions. Yet the resources of nature, perceived (with no apparent ecological concerns by Verne at that time) as limitless, provide the means, when harnessed by science, to the fulfilment of dreams of the infinite potential of human ingenuity for good or evil. Many of the marvellous machines in Verne's work—like the submarine Nautilus in *Vingt mille lieues sous les mers*, or the Albatross, the galleon of the skies in *Robur le conquérant* (1886), or the great trainlike transporter shaped like a series of Hindu temples pulled by a metal elephant in *La Maison à vapeur*—depend on water, wind, or steam power, or his favourite and most venerated source of energy, electricity.[37] The technical specifications of these machines and his other inventions are profusely and convincingly detailed, but there always remains a fundamental secret of how exactly they operate and how their astonishing capabilities are enabled. The Nautilus, for example, performs manoeuvres that are scientifically plausible, but it is also capable of leaping from the waves like a dolphin. The Albatross, with its propeller-topped masts, can sail through the clouds for enormous distances without stopping. The power of many of these machines is ambivalent, for they can be used for humanitarian purposes but also as engines of death. In effect, Verne's later novels reflect his increasingly pessimistic view of the manipulation of science by those motivated only by greed, commercial interests, or the desire for conquest through annihilation.

The passages of scientific detail that pervade the novels undeniably interrupt the flow of the plot and are commonly abridged or omitted altogether in modern versions for young readers. While readers today are unlikely to be entranced by lengthy descriptions of the different classifications of fish in *Vingt mille lieues sous les mers*, for example (if experience with students is anything to go by), it is impossible to ascertain with any certainty how Verne's contemporary readers would have received such passages. Critical opinion varies on this: while Jean Chesneaux asserts that, despite allowing Verne to indulge his poetic fancy in strange-sounding names, the lengthy enumerations and descriptions of species and natural phemonena have 'absolutely nothing to do with children's literature', François Caradec considers that they respond to children's love of precision, lists, and collecting objects and that only adults would be tempted to skip them.[38] At the same time as it enlightens readers, the factual information has a function in the fantastic dimension of the novels offering, paradoxically, an escape for Verne's contemporary readers from the squalor and impersonality of the industrial age as well as a celebration of its uniqueness. Moreover, Verne's machines are not actually related to the everyday or industrial needs of the nineteenth century, but are created by their inventors for extraordinary purposes.[39] Although the majority of the novels are located in the real world, a number in fact deal with the viability of alternative communities or colonies within but separate from the familiar world, like the rival cities in *Les Cinq cents millions de la Bégum* (1879), the propeller-driven island in *L'Île à hélice*, or the city in the coal mine in *Les Indes noires* (1878).

Verne's novels expanded significantly the traditional gallery of literary types. Because of the focus on plot characteristic of the adventure story, there is relatively little character development as such, and a general tendency towards a Manichean view of human nature. In many cases his characters are driven by a single obsession or goal (to find a father or to reach the moon), are reduced to a single function (as mother figure, for example, or comic sidekick), or are part of a double act (master and servant, desirable and undesirable suitor, man of courage and coward).[40] The large majority of his protagonists are men, offering not characters with whom adolescent readers were intended to be able to identify immediately, but figures to inspire admiration, envy, or fear; performers of heroic deeds; or monomaniacs capable of treachery and evil on a grand scale. It has been argued that Verne seems for the most part to be positively resisting the possibility of reader identification and empathy through his use of exaggeration or simplification.[41] Herein lies a significant difference between Verne and writers of the adventure novel in English such as Ballantyne and George Alfred Henty, for whom the promotion of positive models of masculinity and 'muscular Christianity' to adolescent readers was a crucial element. (A few of Verne's novels have young protagonists, and they work to a rather different formula, as will be seen below.) Verne's strategy both expands the scope of the protagonists' activities and their investment in the adventures in terms of experience and expertise, and offer the reader an escape from the childhood world of most literature produced for the young into a sophisticated and spectacular adult world. The relative absence of women in the novels is very noticeable, famously inspiring William Golding's comment that Verne must be the only French writer to take a character (Phileas Fogg) around the world in eighty days without meeting more than one woman on the way.[42] Apart from a few rare exceptions, female characters play very conventional, secondary roles as daughters, sweethearts, mothers, or servants. Even those with less conventional attributes are relatively marginalised: in *Voyage au centre de la terre* (1864), Professor Lidenbrock's seventeen-year-old ward, Graüben, is also an accomplished minerologist, but stays at home while her guardian and his nephew Axel, her fiancé, go on their incredible journey, and acts only as an absent muse to sustain the young man in his quest. Female characters who are more foregrounded in the plots tend to be endowed with stereotypical attributes, like the ethereal Nell in *Les Indes noires*, the child brought up in the coal mine who has never seen daylight and is seen as a kind of beneficent spirit of the mine; the beautiful opera singer, La Stilla, in *Le Château des Carpathes* (1892), who is equally etherial and, moreover, dead; epitomes of motherhood like Mistress Weldon in *Un capitaine de quinze ans*; or loyal wives like Mistress Branican *(Mistress Branican*, 1891) who crosses continents in search of her husband. Jeanne de Kermor, in *Le Superbe Orénoque* (1898), who is also engaged in a quest for a lost relative—in this case her father—offers a more dynamic character to interest female readers, for she travels to South America disguised as a boy with a male companion whom she will eventually marry.

Verne's protagonists are, for the most part, gentlemen scholars, inventors, engineers, scientists, sea captains, and explorers, like the scientist Dr Ferguson in *Cinq semaines en ballon*, the marine biologist Pierre Arronax in *Vingt mille lieues sous les mers*, the professor of minerology Otto Lidenbrock in *Voyage au centre de la terre*, and the explorer Hatteras in *Les Aventures du capitaine Hatteras*. Not all are heroic by any means, or not always heroic in the same way. In his description of the engineer Cyrus Smith, one of the stranded refugees of *L'Île mystérieuse*, Verne presents what seem to be the essential qualities of all his most heroic protagonists. Highly intelligent and knowledgeable, practical and resourceful, Smith has in abundance 'ces trois conditions dont l'ensemble détermine l'énergie humaine: activité d'esprit et de corps, impetuosité des désirs, puissance de la volonté'.[43] These characters are frequently accompanied in their travels by a less experienced young person through whom newly acquired knowledge is mediated to the reader, the role played by Lidenbrock's nephew Axel, the narrator of *Voyage au centre de la terre*, or a comic servant figure to provide light relief like Fogg's manservant Passepartout. Verne's world is a very homosocial one, and the theme of companionship and brotherhood in adventures is a common feature. Many novels portray the interaction of a group in an unprecedented situation and an isolated environment, whether it is a trek through a jungle or across the tundra or trapped on an ice flow (*Le Pays des fourrures*, 1873) or carried away into space on a comet (*Hector Servadac*). The travel motif can be seen to satisfy the demands of the narrative of initiation even in the case of the adult characters, in that knowledge and experience are acquired that demonstrate the limitations of their existing expertise and lead to a better understanding of self, their profession, and the world. Their journeys are not always initially of their own choosing, however, and they can be reluctant travellers. Thus, Arronax is kidnapped aboard the Nautilus by its mysterious Captain Nemo, and only gradually comes to appreciate the exposure this affords him to wonders of the deep far beyond his knowledge and imagination; in *Robur le conquérant*, Uncle Prudent and Phil Evans, the president and secretary, respectively, of the Weldon Institute in Philadelphia, are abducted by Robur and taken around the world in the Albatross in order to prove to them its superiority to American inventions.

Verne's most notorious villains are also frequently scientists or inventors, evil geniuses driven by hatred or the desire to acquire great wealth and power through conquest and control. Such a narrative doubling suggests the tantalisingly fine line in these texts between the exceptional hero and the monstrous villain but also demonstrates Verne's awareness of both the potential of science for good and the dangers of its perversion in the wrong hands, a concept that itself brings into question a number of ideological assumptions.[44] In *Les Cinq cents millions de la Bégum* (1879), for example, a novel published after the Franco-Prussian War, the contrast between the French professor and philanthropist Sarrasin who sets up an ideal city in Oregon organised along utopian socialist lines and the power-crazed German Schultze who builds a rival city to manufacture gigantic canons is a portrait of French idealism and altruism pitted against a desire for universal domination explicitly constructed as the German mission to take over the world.[45] In a fantastic gesture of *revanchisme* on Verne's part, Schultze's megalomania is his own undoing, for eventually he is found dead, frozen, and mummified by the carbonic acid from one of his own giant torpedo shells, the supernatural sphinxlike giant seen through the convex window in his secret lair reduced to a shrivelled corpse. Thus, reassuringly, evil is seen to self-destruct and the missile fired at Sarrasin's city to destroy the French inhabitants overshoots and is doomed to circle the earth as a satellite forever. Despite its chauvinism, it has to be said that this novel can still generate a frisson in readers aware of the horrors of the twentieth century and the preoccupation with international terrorism in the twenty-first. In *Le Château des Carpathes*, a gothic tale of terror and superstition in which mysterious apparitions and noises emanating from a castle hold the local villagers in thrall, Verne depicts the manipulation of electricity in the service of evil. The wicked Rodolphe de Gortz, having stalked a beautiful opera singer in life, torments her grieving lover, who holds him responsible for her death, by 'resurrecting' her with the projection of a life-size image onto glass on his battlements, accompanied by a phonograph recording of her voice, thus foreshadowing both cinema and television and, arguably, their potentially corruptive power.

The most interesting characters are those exceptional and mysterious men like Nemo and Robur who seem to embody aspects of both the good and the monstrous and exemplify Verne's fascination with flamboyant individualism. In the course of his unsought voyage aboard the Nautilus in *Vingt mille lieues sous les mers*, Arronax is drawn to his enigmatic captor, Nemo, a man of indeterminate age and nationality who speaks a strange language and whose very name (that taken by Odysseus in his encounter with the cyclops in Homer's *Odyssey*) is a challenge to the conventions of society. Nemo in fact lives totally outside society by choice, alienated from his fellow humans and answerable to no one, traversing the world's oceans with a handful of crew members in his submarine. He remains a solitary figure, defiant and driven by an unexplained hatred and desire to dominate, striking terror into the world with his attacks on other vessels. When he plants his anarchist's black flag at the previously unexplored South Pole, he appears the embodiment of the urge to conquer the unknown and be master of all he surveys. Yet it is intimated that he has also known great suffering and he identifies with the poor and oppressed. He is also an intellectual and a cultured man: he plays the organ and the Nautilus has a library and gallery containing books, pictures, and artifacts that represent (not unlike Verne's oeuvre itself) the sum of human achievement. Like Arronax, who narrates the story, the reader is intrigued by the tantalising glimpses of his multifaceted character and torn between the conflicting views of Nemo as evil genius and misanthropist or great humanitarian. Although Arronax comes to see Nemo as heroic and sublime, the secret of Nemo's identity is never revealed in this text and his disappearance and presumed death in the maelstrom that swallows the Nautilus at the end are left ambiguous. Nemo reappears, however, in the later novel, *L'Île mystérieuse* (1875), living with the remnants of his power, the Nautilus and a fabulous treasure, in a cavern beneath a volcano. The secret of his identity is at last revealed and the events of the earlier novel contextualised: he is an Indian prince whose vengefulness stems from the massacre of his family and the destruction of his ideals in a failed revolt against the British, for whom he has an implacable hatred.

If Nemo is the master of the seas, then the equally mysterious Robur is the master of the air. There are no other conventional heroes in *Robur le conquérant* with whom the reader can identify, for the American men of science are seen as shortsighted fools faced with Robur's genius and his incredible flying machine. They refuse, rather than embrace, the opportunity for adventure he offers and, throughout their journey, remain fearful and disinterested. Like Nemo, Robur is of uncertain nationality and is proud, vengeful, hostile, and seemingly indestructible. Unlike Nemo, however, he wants fame and the acclaim of his fellow men for his scientific prowess. When the Albatross is blown up, he returns with a rebuilt machine to attack the new American hot air balloon built by his rivals, then disappears with the messianic proclamation that the world is not yet ready for his inventions. Robur's subsequent trajectory is the opposite of Nemo's, however: from potential hero and benefactor he becomes, in *Le Maître du monde* (1904), another of Verne's deranged megalomaniacs bent on commanding and terrorising all the elements with his new invention, a hybrid monster machine that is car, plane, and ship. After aspiring to challenge the heavens, he dies in an appropriately apocalyptic manner in an electrical storm. The enigmatic and elusive quality of these characters is manifested in a humorous way in the eccentric Phileas Fogg, who is obsessed with punctuality and order and appears phlegmatic and disengaged from everything but his timetable and his games of whist in the course of his journey against the clock. He remains unknowable to his companions and the reader alike (he is wrongly suspected of being a bank robber by Fix, the detective who pursues him), yet he displays great courage and unsuspected prowess as a sailor in the last stages of the journey. The ending of *Le Tour du monde en quatre-vingts jours* is a double *coup de théâtre*: Fogg thinks he has lost his bet until it is discovered by chance that he has gained a day by going from east to west around the world. Verne thus springs a scientific surprise on both characters and reader, and Fogg's proposal of marriage to the Indian princess they have rescued along the way is an uncharacteristic gesture that seems to turn on its head the portrayal of the confirmed bachelor but brings about a tongue-in-cheek 'happy ending'.

In his portrayal of survival in extraordinary places, Verne is obviously drawing on the model of the Robinsonnade. In his autobiographical *Souvenirs d'enfance et de jeunesse* (1890), he describes how he adored *Le Robinson suisse* as a child ('Que d'années j'ai passées sur leur île! Avec quelle ardeur je me suis associé à leurs découvertes! Combien j'ai envié leur sort!').[46] In *L'Ile mystérieuse*, the engineer Cyrus Smith and his comrades, refugees from the American Civil War stranded on an island after their hot air balloon crashes, have to make even the most elementary tools of survival from scratch and end up replaying all the technical achievements of mankind, from carving wood, making fire, and smelting metals to cultivating the land, building a house, making their own clothes and cooking vessels, and 'reinventing' amenities that Robinson Crusoe never dreamed of, including a lift and a telegraphing apparatus. They even train a large monkey to act as a servant, sweeping the floors of the abode and serving at table—a parodic comment, perhaps, on the educability of all human beings whatever their class or intellectual ability. If this text amounts to a subversion of the Robinson myth, the reworking of the castaway motif in *L'Ecole des Robinsons* (1882) can be seen as a parody of both *L'Ile mystérieuse* and the Robinsonnade tradition in general. The plot adheres superficially to the tradition: an idle wealthy young man undergoes a transformative educational experience, learning to support himself and cultivate his manual skills when he is shipwrecked on a desert island along with his tutor while on a cruise before choosing his career in life. But the island belongs to his millionaire uncle and the whole adventure is a staged illusion, a controlled experiment to test the young man's mettle. The wild animals are fake, and the Friday figure is no native islander. Through the multiple levels of intertextual reference, Verne thus presents an entertaining gloss on the influence of the Robinsonnade tradition as a didactic tool in literature, even in his own works. His sequel to Wyss's *Le Robinson suisse*, titled *Seconde Patrie* (1900) is, however, a self-conscious attempt to contribute to a genre that, according to his claim in the preface, had influenced him as a writer. This narrative takes up the plot and characters of Wyss's novel some twenty years later and the characters explicitly use their knowledge of Robinsonnades as a kind of route map for making sense of and controlling their own situation.[47]

It is in novels evoking the Robinsonnade tradition that Verne's younger protagonists come to the fore. Here the emphasis is more on the process of maturation and the development of mental and physical qualities in the business of survival rather than on outstanding heroic deeds, although there is heroism in the courage and energy with which they confront their situations. Verne's young characters are usually orphans, or separated from their families and, with some exceptions, between the ages of eleven and fifteen, thus highlighting the period of initiation into adulthood. All have the spontaneity, optimism, and energy of youth and inspire admiration and affection in those around them. In *Deux ans de vacances* (1888), for example, a group of fifteen schoolboys from New Zealand find themselves alone at sea when their cruise ship is set adrift. They are shipwrecked on a desert island that they quickly colonise, setting up home in a cave and giving names to the island's features. To some extent, the conventions of the Robinsonnade are subverted here, too, for one of the boys, Service, a fan of *Le Robinson suisse*, models himself on the character of Jack, but his attempts to mould reality to its fictional counterpart result in failure and disillusionment (a recalcitrant ostrich refuses to be tamed despite his confident efforts). This reminder that fiction cannot always be relied upon to offer models for real-life situations, although not new in books for adults, was a relatively unusual corrective to the aim of presenting exemplary lessons so common in children's literature. In this world without adults, the initiative, resourcefulness, and energy of the boys nevertheless make them attractive role models although Verne does not paint an idealised or nostalgic image of their situation or of childhood itself. Anyone who has read William Golding's *Lord of the Flies* (1954) will be surprised to find in Verne's novel a very similar scenario in the boys' attempts to continue the habits of their former civilised existence and the ugly consequences of the rivalry between two of the boys and their respective followers. The feud between the French boy Briant, and the New Zealander Doniphan, in which the latter sets up a rival camp of hunters, is resolved here, however, when each has the occasion to save the other's life. The character-building aspect of their experiences in terms of physical challenges and dangers (they are attacked by wild animals and a gang of mutineers) and the gradual development of fraternal collaboration are firmly established, and when the castaways eventually return to New Zealand, having commandeered and repaired the mutineers' ship, their adventures have prepared them fully for manhood. Although the younger boys are not very differentiated, the main characters, with their different attributes and talents and the relationships between them, are well delineated and the portrayal of the daily life and numerous adventures on the island is varied and exciting enough to sustain the reader's interest despite the novel's length.

A different model of maturation is offered in the depiction of the trials undergone by the protagonist of *Un capitaine de quinze ans*, Dick Sand, for circumstances force the novice sailor to assume responsibilities far beyond his years in an alien and sinister adult world. Finding himself left in charge of a vessel after the demise of the captain and crew in a whale hunt, Dick finds himself frustratingly helpless to protect the ship owner's wife Mistress Weldon and her child when they are deceived and captured by the treacherous Negoro and the slave-traders in the African jungle. The different type of heroism involved here is clearly signalled by Verne after Dick and his companions finally escape the murderous attempts of their enemies and reach safety in the statement that although 'des actions d'éclat' could not be attributed to him, his resolve, strength of character, loyalty, and courage 'avaient fait de lui une sorte de héros'. The importance of education is underlined in the last pages, for Dick throws himself into his studies to overcome his sense of inadequacy ('une sorte de remords, - celui de l' homme qui, faute de science, s'était trouvé au-dessous de sa tâche!'), and is soon qualified to be put in command of one of Mr Weldon's vessels as a full-fledged captain.[48]

In some cases the youthful character is under the wing of a mentor or father figure who acts as guide and teacher in the process of initiation and maturation. This is almost never the biological father, who is frequently absent, lost, or less effective as a role model, and the theme of adoption by a 'père spirituel' is repeatedly reworked.[49] The fifteen-year-old Habert Brown in *L'Ile mystérieuse*, who has been helped to escape from North America by a surrogate father figure, becomes the protégé of Cyrus Smith, who teaches him everything he knows. The two children in *Les Enfants du capitaine Grant* are accompanied and protected by Lord Glenarvan in their search for their own father, the legendary explorer who sought to establish a new Scotland in the Pacific. During their journey, which takes them across dangerous territories in South America and Australia, Robert Grant, age twelve, after narrowly escaping death in an earthquake following a volcanic eruption and being carried off by a giant condor, comes to see Glenarvan as a father figure. Like Dick Sand, Robert is initiated into manhood through his trials, eventually saving the others by an act of bravery and initiative, and although he becomes a sailor like his biological father, it is really Glenarvan who has been the greatest influence on his development. Dick Sand is also an orphan, adopted and educated by the shipowner he serves, while in *Hector Servadac*, the 'adoption' of the two small children Nina and Pablo by Servadac and his efforts in educating them during their journey on the comet effects a change as much in him as in his charges.

Harvey Darton asserts that the true originality of adventure stories and what distinguishes them from the moral tale is the absence of overt moralising or appeal to a particular code of conduct or dogmatic religious belief.[50] Unlike the novels of the Bibliothèque rose, Verne's works do not offer the readers conventional models of behaviour for everyday situations but are certainly concerned with good and evil on a much wider scale. Verne does not lecture the reader on manners and mores, but invites reflection on the consequences of actions through engagement with his characters, and on the moral implications of historical events through his plots. Nevertheless, the moral basis of his works is unexceptionable in contemporary terms: the personal attributes advocated are still fundamentally gendered in a traditional way and the view of history promoted, although humanitarian, is essentially a chauvinistic and ethnocentric one. There are conventional references to religion in the form of prayers, and affirmations of belief in providence by characters, but the development of events is generally seen more as the result of chance than as the intervention of a benign or disapproving deity. Such a lack of an overtly stated moral or religious agenda attracted criticism from some of his contemporaries, like Ségur's close friend Louis Veuillot, who could not envisage the separation of books for young readers from the traditional pedagogical parameters.[51]

Verne's novels integrate elements of fairy tale, legend, and myth that link them with earlier narrative forms with which young readers would be familiar, both in terms of references (Marcel's approach to Schultze's lair in *Les Cinq cents millions de la Bégum* is described in terms of seeking the Minotaur in his labyrinth; *La Belle au bois dormant* is evoked in Mistress Branican's long sleep) and, as has been seen, in fundamental story patterns (the quest fraught with dangers, the hero's initiation into adulthood, the battle between good and evil). They are also closely related to the conventions of popular *feuilleton* literature, which was widely accessible to adolescent readers, notably in their exotic settings and melodramatic events, the intrusion of the mysterious and gruesome, and the expected rewarding of the good and punishment of the wicked. They are both formulaic and full of surprises, with no shortage of catastrophic disasters and dramatic encounters that testify to the fertility of Verne's imagination and his sheer narrative audacity. He is an undoubted master of the dramatic set-piece scene. Thus, to select but four examples from so many, in *Voyage au centre de la terre* the reader is presented with the discovery of a vast underground sea complete with monsters and electrical storm and a herd of mastodons with their giant prehistoric shepherd, and in *Vingt mille lieues sous les mers*, a visit to the lost civilisation of Atlantis and the breathtaking incident in which the submarine is stuck beneath the Polar ice. As in popular melodrama, unexpected twists of plot, coincidences, implausibilities, and surprises assail characters and readers alike, and clues in the shape of arcane coded messages, cryptograms, runes, mysterious maps, ancient letters, or unexpected legacies are accumulated to intrigue and maintain suspense before a dramatic revelation that tests the readers' credulity to the limit. In *Un capitaine de quinze ans*, when the young leader of the shipwrecked travellers realises that the country through which they are trecking is not Bolivia, as they had been led to believe, but Africa, Verne's account of the outrageous attempt by their treacherous guide to reassure them that a herd of giraffes are actually South American ostriches is almost parodic of the genre. Characters reappear in extraordinary coincidences, like Nemo, and the traitor Ayrton from *Les Enfants du capitaine Grant,* who are both encountered in much reduced circumstances in *L'Ile mystérieuse.* The young reader's sensibilities are not spared the descriptions of torture, murder, and other bloody deeds that Verne defends as emanating from 'le souci de la réalité', demonstrating humankind's inhumanity through greed or the lust for power.[52] There is humour of a farcical kind that must have appealed to young readers, notably in the portrayal of the many larger-than-life or eccentric adult characters like the ridiculous Aristobulus Ursiclos in *Le Rayon vert* (1882), or the single-minded childlike entomologist, cousin Bénédict, in *Un capitaine de quinze ans,* whose vagaries illustrate that not all men of science are seen as heroic in Verne's literary universe. The figure of the comic servant is also deployed, as in popular theatre, for light relief and to vary the mood of tension, as in, for example, the frantic terrors of Frycollin in *Robur le conquérant* and the antics and mishaps of Passepartout in *Le Tour du monde en quatre-vingts jours.* There is pathos, too, as in the depiction of the plight of the sick child in *Un capitaine de quinze ans.* In this novel, Verne even takes the daring step, extremely problematic in children's books, of allowing an animal hero, the dog Dingo, to die after saving the lives of his temporary masters.

A significant respect in which Verne's oeuvre differs from the popular *roman-feuilleton* and signals that the aim of his work was family entertainment is the complete absence of any intimations of sexuality or sexual activity and the only rather perfunctory introduction of a love interest in some texts. In *Voyage au centre de la terre*, the relationship between Axel and Graüben is maintained at a cerebral level and, although they marry at the end, it otherwise plays little role in the text. As in fairy tales, marriage for the male hero seems to be in the nature of a reward for his endeavours or a convenient form of closure. This constraint was, in fact, the subject of a humorous remark by Verne who complained about the difficulty of writing to the formula agreed with Hetzel, and of trying to hold the reader's interest without resorting to scenes of passion and adultery. Verne appears in fact to have resented to some extent the control of Hetzel over his creativity ('le milieu assez restreint où je suis condamné à me mouvoir') and he certainly pushed those constraints as far as they could be stretched.[53]

After being marginalised for many decades by literary critics as a writer of popular novels or potboilers, Verne has more recently been recuperated as a writer who merits serious attention for his literary style as well as for what his novels reveal about the attitudes and issues of his day. His works have been subject to scrutiny by psychoanalyst, Marxist, and structuralist critics amongst others and have been seen as highly creative, complex, and inviting readings from a 'plurality of perspectives'.[54] Welcome though the revisiting of Verne is, most studies tend to downplay or ignore the significance of the juvenile readership that undoubtedly formed a large part of his targeted audience. Evidence suggests that his popularity with young readers may in effect have influenced negatively critical response to his works.[55] Émile Zola's dismissal of Verne certainly suggests that this was the case, as he explicitly links the huge sales of the *Voyages extraordinaires* with those of alphabet books ('Si les *Voyages extraordinaires* se vendent bien, les alphabets et les paroissiens se vendent bien aussi à des chiffres considérables … . [Ils sont] sans aucune importance dans le mouvement littéraire contemporain.'[56] Indeed, there is also evidence that Verne himself was reluctant to be seen just as a writer for the young and felt that the fact that he was never elected to the Académie française was because he was not seen as a serious writer.[57] However, his remark to Hetzel that 'Quand véritablement on n'écrit pas que pour les enfants, il ne faut pas être lu que par les enfants' should not be misconstrued as a repudiation of part of his audience, but rather as an awareness of the breadth of the targeted readership of the *Magasin d'éducation et de récréation*.[58] Verne can thus be seen as perhaps the first of those writers of what is known today as 'crossover' literature—that is, one that commands a dual readership of adult and child. Whereas in earlier children's books the role of the adult reader was to enhance or share the pedagogical aspect of the reading experience, Verne's works offered a thrilling narrative and instruction to readers of all ages, on equal footing. Indeed, it has been shown that analysing the novels from the specific perspective of a young readership can bring out illuminating and largely ignored aspects of the text, not least an introduction to literary and cultural codes past and present through the links with and echoes of other texts.[59] His works teem with references to other writers and other texts, contemporary and classical, scientific and fictional. Verne himself described his literary method as a 'cuisine littéraire' and he has now been established as a 'profoundly intertextual writer'.[60] This even extends to an internal referencing: texts are occasionally interlinked not just by the reappearance of some of the characters but by a recapitulation or filling in of events from earlier novels. In *L'Île mystérieuse*, the elderly Nemo is even informed, like Don Quixote, of the publication of his earlier exploits.

It should not be forgotten that an important contribution to the success of the *Voyages extraordinaires* series was the superb work of the illustrators, notably Riou, whose copious and varied full-plate images captured the spirit of the text in terms of both portraits of characters and machines and the depiction of seminal dramatic moments. The original Bibliothèque d'education et de récréation editions demonstrate the complicity of text and image at its best. The representation on the gilded covers of a scene or compilation of scenes from the text, besides making the book a beautiful object in itself, offer an immensely enticing advertisement for the contents. The very visual nature of Verne's novels lent them admirably to illustration, as the many comic-book versions testify. The present writer first encountered his works through the Children's Illustrated Classics series which, as the title indicates, presented great works of literature in brightly coloured comic-strip form and were extremely popular in the mid-twentieth century.

Verne achieved a considerable following in Britain as well as in France, largely due to the serialisation of many of his novels in the widely read *Boy's Own Paper*, acquiring, according to one commentator, 'a cultural significance in Victorian and Edwardian Britain second to none'.[61] His contribution to the development of books for the young was emphasised in the eulogy written by his friend and fellow contributor to the *Magasin d'éducation et de récréation*, André Laurie, which appeared in *Le Temps* after Verne's death in 1905. Commenting on the immense popularity of the novels in many different languages over a period of forty years, Laurie writes that 'ses livres sont naturellement la lecture de prédilection d'une jeunesse éprise d'au-delà dans le monde sensible et d'idéal dans le réel'. He praises the clarity of Verne's style, the immaculate structuring of his novels and the breathtaking scale of his canvas, and asserts that his literacy legacy was that 'il a fait penser, rêver, marcher l'humanité'.[62] Another eulogy, appearing anonymously in *L'Humanité*, also testifies to the contemporary perception of Verne's status as a writer for the young, claiming that his oeuvre 'a exercé, pendant quarante ans, sur les enfants de ce pays et de l'Europe entière, une influence qu'aucune autre oeuvre n'a certainement égalée. Elle a été, tout à la fois, un instrument d'éducation positive et de développement moral.'[63] A recent homage by J. M. G. Le Clézio (himself an author of books for young readers) in a special issue of *Geo* magazine devoted to Jules Verne describes his childhood experience of reading the Hetzel editions of Verne's novels belonging to his grandmother after World War II: 'Il est probable que c'est en eux que j'ai appris à lire, laissant flotter mon regard d'illustration en illustration, laissant errer mon esprit sur les listes de mots, les noms, les lieux, les cartes, toute cette magie.' He also testifies to an awareness of the contemporary relevance, for a child born in 1940, of Verne's inventions, which 'avec ce recul du temps, [elles] prenaient un sens prophétique, une sorte d'incongruité maléfique qui décuplait leur force', and hence 'un sentiment très étrange qui faisait avoisiner l'exploration de l'avenir et la connaissance du passé', an experience that can still be shared by a reader in the twenty-first century.[64]

GEORGE SAND'S *CONTES D'UNE GRAND-MÈRE*: FAIRY TALES MEET SCIENCE

The desire to communicate to young readers an awareness of the marvels of nature and an engagement with contemporary scientific debates also informed George Sand's *Contes d'une grand-mère*, a late flowering of the fairy tale in nineteenth-century France, based on bedtime stories she had told her own grandchildren and published in two groups in 1873 and 1876.[65] In her *Histoire de ma vie* (1855), George Sand (pseudonym of Amantine-Aurore-Lucile Dupin) articulated the conviction that fantasy was essential for the child's healthy development ('Retrancher le merveilleux de la vie de l'enfant, c'est procéder contre les lois mêmes de la nature'), and in the *Contes d'une grand-mère*, the *merveilleux* is used as a medium of education about nature and the relationship between humans and the natural world as well as exemplifying the traditional fairy-tale theme of maturation.[66] This pedagogical agenda is made explicit in the dedication of 'Le Château de Pictordu' which addresses her granddaughter, Aurore Sand, but also, implicitly, adult readers:

> La question est de savoir s'il y a des fées, ou s'il n'y en a pas. Tu es dans l'âge où l'on aime le merveilleux et je voudrais bien que le merveilleux fût dans la nature, que tu n'aimes pas moins .... Reste à savoir où sont ces êtres, dits surnaturels, les génies et les fées; d'où ils viennent et où ils vont, quel empire ils exercent sur nous et où ils nous conduisent.[67]

Like the earlier *Histoire du véritable Gribouille*, the tales in this collection draw extensively on traditional fairy-tale ingredients like metamorphosis and anthropomorphised animals and plants, and often contain sinister and frightening elements.

In some of the tales, the protagonist is a young person who has to undergo various trials to achieve self-knowledge and maturation, and elements of the natural world are deployed as metaphors for aspects of human self-development. In 'La Reine Coax', a tale full of menace, for example, the metamorphosis of humans into frog and swan is deployed to teach a young girl with froglike features that true wisdom and happiness lie in the recognition and acceptance of what one is. The dangers of trying to alter and constrain nature in the wider sense is seen in the destruction caused by attempts to create an artifical garden out of the profusion of nature in the château garden. In 'Le Nuage rose', the young peasant girl Catherine is taught by an elderly aunt that she must overcome her preoccupation with a pretty pink cloud (symbolising the fanciful illusions of youth), which soon turns into a destructive thunder cloud, before she can learn to become an independent and productive woman as a spinner of fine thread. After a dream in which she has to sweep up all the clouds, Catherine learns that she can acquire control over her life by seizing the passing clouds of temptation and rendering them powerless, channelling her energies into the profitable development of her talents rather than dissipating them in fruitless and dangerous dreams.

Local superstition merges with fantasy and reality in 'Le Géant Yéous', in which the son of a mountain man crippled by a fall of rock seeks revenge on the mountain and, in devoting himself to breaking up the giant piece of rock and putting it to good use on the glacier, learns to confront his demons and create his own future. In telling his story to the unnamed narrator who once knew and helped his father, the young man, a self-taught lover of adventure stories, constructs his labours as a prolonged and dangerous battle against the giant who stalks the mountain and now lies in harmless pieces. Superstition also informs 'Le Chêne parlant', for, despite its evil reputation amongst the peasants, the great oak tree in the forest gives shelter to the unhappy eleven-year-old orphan Emmi who runs away from the farm where he works. During the two seasons that he lives in its branches, he learns not only to love and respect trees, but also self-sufficiency in feeding himself and making tools and other necessities. This tale also gives the reader an insight into the plight of children drawn into a life of begging and thieving when Emmi befriends an old woman in a village of false beggars and is rescued from being sold at a fair by a kindly woodcutter. After being reconciled with his former master, Emmi's dedication to his work is rewarded in typical fairy-tale fashion by an unexpected inheritance from the old beggar, marriage to his master's daughter, and the position of warden of the forest.

In several of the *Contes* Sand presents aspects of that most momentous of issues in the nineteenth century, the question of evolution. Charles Darwin's theories in *The Origin of Species* (1859), with their emphasis on change, development, and transformation, had fuelled renewed interest in folk and fairy tales and stimulated the nineteenth-century imagination to contemplate the infinite possibilities of creation.[68] Darwin's theory of evolution, a 'new myth of creation' that replaced the idea of the Fall with an image of the ascent of humankind from the primeval swamp, offered many varied possibilities for narratives of cycle and renewal, of individual and social growth, degeneration, survival, and progress.[69] Evolutionary theories also fitted well with the fairy-tale world of proliferation, metamorphoses, strange hybrid creatures, and the powerlessness of humans in the grip of unseen and uncontrollable forces. Although Darwin claimed that his work had little effect in France, there had been ongoing debate about evolution for some time, notably in the work of Jean-Baptiste de Lamarck in the early nineteenth century. Religious factions were inevitably hostile to Darwin, and although various evolutionary models were proposed there were few supporters for the key theory of natural selection, which rejected the idea of a 'plan' in the development of higher forms of life.[70] Nevertheless, as has been seen, there was widespread interest in natural history, the investigation of different species, and the interaction of humans with the environment. In the second half of the century, of course, scientific theories on cause and effect had invaded fiction in the work of writers like Zola, whose Naturalist novels were informed by theories of social and biological determinism and sought to explain human personality and behaviour in terms of certain fixed laws. Sand sought a different approach in order to mediate to young readers information about evolution and her enthusiasm for the workings of what she called 'cette fée qui ne laisse rien perdre, qui répare tout et qui recommence tout ce qui est défait. Cette reine des fées, vous la connaissez fort bien: c'est la nature.'[71]

In 'Ce que disent les fleurs', also addressed to Aurore, Sand embeds a partial myth of creation in an account of her own alleged childhood experience of trying to listen to the flowers in her garden talking amongst themselves. The child in the tale overhears a conversation between the flowers and the breeze, who tells the flowers its life story, representing its former self as the eldest son of the king of storms, a fearsome creature with great black wings whose task was to sweep over the earth destroying the creative work of the spirit of life. He is cast out by his father and doomed to live on earth when he is seduced by the beauty and heady scent of a rose and seeks to save her from destruction, but, in a reversal of the Lucifer story, he is rewarded by the spirit of life and is changed into a gentle feminised breeze who becomes the sister and friend of all the flowers. The child's account of her experience is dismissed by her tutor as a sign of illness but supported by her grandmother as evidence of a special faculty of childhood that she once shared.[72] The natural world itself is the protagonist in 'Le Marteau rouge', in which Sand's interest in minerology informs the life history of a piece of pink cornelian through the ages. The fairy—who splits into smaller fragments the large chunk of rock, eroded from a mountain and undisturbed for centuries, in order to dam the mountain stream and prevent it from flooding the water meadows—plays only a brief and mediating role, creating an atmosphere of magic that contrasts with the real 'magic' in the text, which is that of the constant renewal of matter. Thereafter the rock's various transformations throughout the centuries (as a Stone Age weapon, a Bronze Age vegetable knife, a scraper in medieval times, a specimen on a velvet cushion in the collection of an eighteenth-century aristocrat, a child's plaything, and finally a tiny fragment set in a pretty ring) underline the permanence of nature and invite the reader to contemplate the relative insignificance of human beings in the great scheme of things.

In 'Le Gnome des huîtres' an oyster gourmet learns more than he ever wanted to know about the genealogy of oysters when he dines with a strange, gnomelike little man who reveals to the narrator his treasure trove of ancient fossilised molluscs. The hallucinatory quality of the gnome's recitation of the Latin names of the fossils and their different properties induces a dreamlike nausea in the narrator, exacerbated by overindulgence in wine, which results, according to the narrator's confused memory, in a violent struggle. In this tale both the gourmet, whose only interest in the oysters is a gustatory one, and the man of science, who is obsessed with classification, are implicitly satirised. The fecundity of nature is also the theme of 'La Fée aux gros yeux', a tale more likely to appeal to younger readers not least because it focusses on the experience of a child. The merveilleux here resides in the infinitesimal variety and complex exquisiteness of the miroscopic insects who are attracted to the lamp of the protagonist's eccentric governess Miss Barbara ('la fée aux gros yeux'), whose myopic vision enables her to see her minute visitors. The child, Elsie, intrigued by her governess's nocturnal activities, is initiated into the magical world of nature in miniature, unsuspected although coexisting with her own, by means of a magnifying glass. The lasting impression created by this tale is of the ephemeral nature of life and the inexhaustible wonders of creation that often go undetected by humans.

The tale that is most clearly related to contemporary scientific debates is 'La Fée Poussière', in which the fantastic is most fully employed to take the young protagonist and narrator, together with the reader, on a journey through the development of the universe. The protagonist here is, once again, the grandmother herself who, in presenting the tale as her own experience as a child, reinforces the idea of continuity in life. The journey undertaken to the bowels of the earth recalls Verne's *Voyage au centre de la terre* (by which it may have been influenced) except that the narrative strategy employed is that of a voyage in a dream. Unlike the fastidious adults in the household, the young protagonist is fascinated by household dust, personified as a tiresome little old woman in grey cobwebby clothes who transports the child, after she has fallen asleep, to her fairy palace. Transformed into her real self, the beautiful and magnificently attired Fée Poussière reveals how all the precious stones, trees, plants, swans, and fish in her lakes are her own creation: 'Tout cela est fait de poussière; c'est en secouant ma robe dans les nuages que j'ai fourni tous les matériaux de ce paradis.'[73] The universe is seen to be the product of the fairy's laboratory, as she leads the child down into the bowels of the earth to witness 'le commencement des choses'.[74]

As they pass through different levels and geological periods, the child sees evolutionary processes firsthand in fast-forward mode as vegetation springs up and reptiles, insects, and strange animals appear and disappear as the centuries scroll by. Destruction and death are a necessary part of the renewal of life, and therefore human life is both relatively insignificant and will continue to evolve and progress. Sand's religious belief merges with both fairy tale and evolutionary theory as the whole of creation is also seen, rather confusingly, as the work of 'le roi des génies', who is also described as 'l'activité incessante et suprême' and 'le grand esprit de la vie'.[75] The development of life on earth, the processes of adaptation, and the survival of the fittest appear to the child to be like magic as the Fée Poussière demonstrates that all that is created from dust will return to dust but will be transformed into new forms of life. In a linking of dream and reality characteristic of the *conte fantastique*, the child finds, on awakening, that she has a little pile of dust in her hand and is still sufficiently under the spell of her dream to be able to perceive the myriad life forms present within it. The fairy's gift is thus knowledge of the history of the universe and an awareness of the relativity of one's own existence.

In the *Contes d'une grand-mère*, Sand recuperates the role of the female storyteller of old, and, speaking with the voice of a grandmother, passes on the secrets of nature, like the Fée Poussière, to a new generation. The female principal is, moreover, elevated to a central and dynamic role in the process of creation of both the narrative and the universe itself. For Sand, the forms and motifs of fairy tales were entirely consistent with the merveilleux of nature and science and hence an appropriate vehicle not just for models of maturation and socialisation but for the dissemination of ideas that revised the way human beings perceived themselves and their place in the universe.

ADVENTURE STORIES: THE SUCCESSORS TO VERNE

The expansion of colonial enterprise in the second half of the nineteenth century opened up the way, in France as in England, for a wave of young readers' adventure stories exploiting the fascination of the unknown, many of which were more overtly politicised than Verne's works. Like their real-life counterparts, the intrepid literary travellers of the second half of the century visited exotic regions that, in some cases, had only comparatively recently been opened up to the West. Aimed at an essentially white, male, middle-class, adolescent audience, adventure stories both promoted an individualistic ethos of courage, initiative, and manliness and supported the French colonial enterprise, reinforcing the sense of national pride and cultural superiority.[76] This patriotic agenda was particularly urgent after the defeat of France in the Franco-Prussian War in 1870, and invaded books and magazines for both adult and child readers. The embracing of the colonial ideal by the rulers of the Third Republic and the aim of enlarging the French empire in Africa has been seen as 'baumes appliquées à une nation blessée' and the creation of a myth of imperial glory.[77] In the heyday of French colonial expansion after 1880, school textbooks and adventure stories alike shared an emphasis on conquest and the heroism of French explorers and soldiers against rebels and fearsome natives in Algeria, Tunisia, and many other more remote parts of the African continent. The colonising ideal was shared by both lay and church groups who were otherwise at war over the issue of education, although the school books and magazines they produced between 1880 and 1914 emphasised different aspects: the lay books for the *écoles publiques* praised the achievements of soldiers, explorers, and doctors, while the Catholic publications highlighted the work of missionaries.[78] Both agreed, however, that France was engaged in a necessary civilising mission against the barbarism of inferior races, a vision that continued to be presented to young readers in the new century in both educational and leisure reading, and in toys, games, illustrated papers, and the newly emerging bande dessinée.

Although the adventure story genre was dominated by English-speaking writers like Cooper, Haggard, and Robert Louis Stevenson, a large number of French writers set out to cater to the demand for such works. A specialist website currently lists forty-five authors of adventure novels of different sorts, including those from the first half of the century, like Gustave Aimard, Alexandre Dumas, and Gabriel Ferry.[79] Not all of these, by any means, were writing specifically for the young, although many, especially those whose works were first published in feuilleton form, certainly reached a dual audience. The Dreyfous and Hetzel publishing houses initiated series titled, respectively, Bibliothèque des voyages et aventures (c. 1878) and Les romans d'aventures (1880) that were aimed at a young readership, while a magazine, the *Journal des voyages et des aventures de terre et de mer*, founded in 1877 and specialising in exciting tales of travel and adventure, offered fiction by a wide range of authors. It has been argued that because of its assimilation to low, rather than high, culture, the adventure novel genre did not take itself seriously and writers developed a tendency to humorous extravagance and an ironic, even parodic, distancing from the events recounted.[80] In respect of those books specifically directed at the young, it has also been asserted that this approach was a strategy adopted by writers with republican sympathies to emphasise an ideological or pedagogical agenda rather than the adventure aspect.[81] Indeed, in less able hands than those of Verne, the didactic element of the texts is frequently ostensibly burdensome and damaging to both the coherence of the plot and the development of the psychology of the characters. Unfortunately, many of these novels have long been out of print, and even secondhand copies are difficult to obtain. The following discussion considers briefly some examples of writers whose works were either overtly directed at a young audience or are known to have been enjoyed by a dual readership.

A blend of fantasy and realistic adventure with a topic of contemporary relevance and a strong ideological subtext is found in Alfred Assollant's entertaining novel *Les Aventures merveilleuses mais authentiques du Capitaine Corcoran* (1867). Assollant (1827–1886), a fervent and politically active republican and opponent of Napoleon III, spent some of his early life in America and contributed articles titled 'Scènes de la vie américaine' to the *Revue des deux mondes* before turning his hand to writing novels. In the 1850s he exploited the contemporary taste for stories set in North America in thrillers like *Walter et les émigrants américains* (1856), and in historical novels like *La Mort de Roland, fantaisie épique* (1860), now largely forgotten. The fantastical exploits, humour, and sheer exuberance of *Les Aventures merveilleuses mais authentiques du Capitaine Corcoran*, which appeared in Hachette's Bibliothèque rose illustrée list for children ages eight to fourteen, with illustrations by A. de Neuville, have ensured its survival, however. Despite its contemporariness, the narrative draws on devices of fairy tale to maintain a tongue-in-cheek attitude towards the events depicted.

The novel begins with the sensational arrival of Corcoran, a mysterious and fearless young Breton of great strength and initiative, at a meeting of the Académie des Sciences in Lyon in 1857 to offer his services in the search for an ancient, sacred Hindu book. The tone of humour and hyberbole is established from the start in his account of his past exploits (as a ship's captain in the China seas he has killed some thirty pirates), his self-presentation (he bends the iron bars on the window), and the appearance of his companion, the young lioness Louison, who leaps over the heads of the astonished *académiciens* and obeys Corcoran's every word. Once in India, Corcoran, who appears to be a cross between Indiana Jones and El Cid, soon becomes the heir to an Indian prince whose daughter he marries, and then a maharaja himself, a charismatic and wise ruler venerated by his subjects as a descendent of the god Vishnu. Assollant apparently has little interest in the depiction of other races and their customs, as only an artificial and anecdotic exoticism is apparent in his descriptions of the settings of the action. There are no lengthy digressions to instruct the reader, as the action is paramount. The characters are familiar stereotypes: Corcoran's Indian friends are courteous and noble while his enemies are vicious and cowardly. The real villians, however, are the English, and Assollant's Anglophobia is rampant in his presentation of the 'goddams' who are arrogant, ruthless, and cruel, determined to destroy the Indian princedoms and consume their wealth. In repeated bloody encounters with the English troops,

Corcoran easily triumphs, outwitting them with his ingenious military tactics. The battles are described in lurid and bloodthirsty detail, and Corcoran's victories against tremendous odds and his repeated escapes from danger leave the reader teetering on the brink of delighted incredulity. The fantastical aspect of his heroic exploits is increased by the presence of his two animal helpers, the lioness Louison and Scindiah, an elephant. Louison, who understands instinctively when and how to save her master, obeying his commands and terrorising his enemies, is a source of much excitement and humour as her very appearance by his side causes the pusillanimous English to flee. Like Louison, Scindiah responds instinctively to Corcoran's needs, shielding him against bullets with her bulk and flattening his attackers, and eventually gives her life for him in battle. Her death may be a matter of narrative necessity, however, as Corcoran's family make a dramatic escape from India in an air balloon sent opportunely by his friend Quaterquem. The appearance of the balloon at the very moment that the wounded and exhausted Corcoran, abandoned by his troops, seeks help from God, certainly taxes the reader's willing suspension of disbelief but delights with its ironic deployment of the deus ex machina. Equally incredible but quirkily satisfying is the dénouement in which the English are finally routed and Corcoran, sickened by the treachery and cowardice he has seen and disgusted with power, abdicates and also leaves by balloon to live happily ever after with his family in an island paradise. The narrative hints tantalisingly at the possibility that he may return one day, like a saviour, to rid the Indian subcontinent of its English oppressors forever but leaves the reader on tenterhooks. Assollant, like Verne, is severely critical of English colonialism but, with no apparent awareness that this represents a paradoxical position, sees France's colonial exploits as the justified spread of civilising ideals. The ending in effect implies that only the intervention of a French hero can save India from enslavement and generate the republican ideals of liberty, justice, and brotherhood. The text is resolutely male-centred, with a love interest that merely serves to provide Corcoran with a family to save and a happy ending in tune with the family-orientated ethos of the time. The suggestion that Corcoran, his wife, and his children are to visit the 1867 Exposition in Paris, in the very year of publication of the novel, adds a touch of credibility to their existence as an ideal French family.

The novels of the prolific Louis Boussenard (1847–1910), one of the writers most closely associated with the *Journal des voyages*, which serialised his works from 1877, followed the same agenda as Jules Verne in seeking to both instruct and entertain the reader. Boussenard, too, was prone to interrupting the narrative at critical moments to launch into didactic digressions on the geography, climate, people, and fauna and flora of the countries visited by his protagonists, but they amount to little more than enumerative lists and are less well integrated than in Verne's novels.[82] His works also reveal the characteristics of narratives that are written for serialisation, for the plethora of colourful events succeed each other at breakneck speed with repeated cliff-hangers and reversals of fortune in order to preserve the reader's interest over weeks or months. As with many adventure novels, Boussenard's titles are enticing and the geography wide ranging: *Les Robinsons de la Guyane* and *Le Sultan de Bornéo* (1883); *Les Français au Pôle Nord* (1892); *L'Enfer de glace* (1900), set in the Klondike; *Le Capitaine Casse-cou* (1901), set in South Africa; and *Le Zouave de Malakoff* (1903), describing the campaign in Italy. His most widely read novels were those that featured his adventurer hero, Friquet, the *gamin de Paris*, a French answer to the English heroes. Embodying what was deemed to be the *esprit parisien*, Friquet is courageous, optimistic, and good-hearted, hates authority, and loves practical jokes and scams. Boussenard's admiration of Verne is explicitly signalled in the first novel, *Le Tour du monde d'un gamin de Paris* (1879–80), for the protagonist's decision to embark on his journey is inspired by his reading of Verne's novel. The indefatigable Friquet features in a whole series of stories that take him all over the world, and which appeared in book form a year or so after serialisation: *Aventures d'un gamin de Paris à travers l'Océanie* (1883); *Aventures d'un héritier à travers le monde* (1885); and *Aventures d'un gamin de Paris au pays des lions, Aventures d'un gamin de Paris au pays des tigres*, and *Aventures d'un gamin de Paris au pays des bisons* (all in 1886). In 1897, Boussenard exploited his popular creation further with *Voyages et aventures de Mademoiselle Friquette* and in 1909 with *Le fils du gamin de Paris* (serialised four years earlier). Boussenard's vision of the world, like that of Assollant, is a colonialist and essentially racist one, condemning colonial exploitation as practised by other European nations while advocating the superiority of the French and glorifying attempts to save indigenous populations from the hands of the British or the Germans. The latter in particular, in the spirit of revenge for 1870, are constantly ridiculed and tricked by the triumphant and energetic protagonist. Despite the humour inherent in the narration of the often extravagant adventures, Boussenard's novels, like many others in the genre, also display a delight in bloodthirstiness and violence that demonstrates the way in which approaches to reading matter deemed suitable for the young were undergoing rapid changes.

Another important contributor to the *Journal des voyages* and a prolific novel writer, Paul d'Ivoi (pseudonym of Paul Deleutre, 1856–1915) also acknowledged his admiration of and debt to Verne in his series of eighteen adventure novels published by Boivin under the title Voyages excentriques. Boivin's eyecatching editions, aimed at a young readership, were clearly imitations of Hetzel's editions of Verne's Voyages extraordinaires in their format, with a large number of illustrations and bright, gilded illustrated covers.[83] Like Boussenard and Verne, Ivoi knew the value of attracting the reader with tantalising titles like Le Docteur Mystère (1899) and Les Voleurs de foudre (1910) and glamorous characters with exotic names like the Corsaire Triplex, Jean Fanfare, Docteur Mystère, and Miss Mousqueterr. His novels also reveal close similarites to those of Verne in the nature of their plots, which invariably involve momentous journeys, stupendous deeds, and a fascination with machines and inventions (fast cars, telephones, and the cinema now play their role in the later novels). Ivoi's best-known work, Les Cinq sous de Lavarède (1894), which was staged in 1903 and made into a film in 1927 and again in 1939, gestures overtly towards Verne's Le Tour du monde en quatre-vingts jours in a number of ways. The protagonist is an impoverished journalist who stands to inherit a fortune if he can complete a round-the-world trip in a year with only five sous in his pocket, and the motif of a race against time and the struggle against the many difficulties encountered are replicated here. But Lavarède is a very different character from the upright, honourable Phileas Fogg, resorting frequently to unscrupulous methods, including fare dodging, scrounging, and blackmail, to achieve his goal. Two secondary characters, the villainous Bouvreuil and Lavarède's travelling companion Sir Murlyton, strongly recall Verne's detective Fix and Phileas Fogg himself. Lavarède, who reappears in further novels, notably Le Cousin de Lavarède (1895), represents, like Boussenard's gamin de Paris, the attempt to create a specifically French adventure hero, an attractive and energetic rogue, brave and determined with a strong sense of justice. Other links with Verne are clearly discernible in both the titles and plots of Ivoi's Voyages excentriques: L'Aéroplane fantôme (1910) is reminiscent of both Robur le conquérant and Le Maître du monde, for example, and the eponymous protagonist of Le Corsaire Triplex (1898) who captains an electrically powered fortress that can travel over land and sea recalls Verne's Nemo. Docteur Mystère in the novel of the same name (1900) is really a Hindu prince who seeks revenge, like Nemo, for the slaughter of his family. Ivoi also shares Verne's ambivalent attitude towards technical progress, for many plots have frightening global implications, like the attempts to control the climate in Les Semeurs de glace (1903). His machines, too, are both wonderful and highly dangerous: like the Nautilus and Robur's versatile flying machine in Le Maître *du monde*, the plane in *L'Aéroplane fantôme*, which is in danger of falling into the hands of the Germans, is capable of large-scale destruction. As in the novels of his contemporaries, there is a clear element of jingoism and racism in his treatment of the peoples and culture of other nations. Despite his interest in communicating geographical and scientific information to the reader, Ivoi is judged to be less serious in his didacticism than Verne, privileging amusing anecdotes over a pedagogical agenda, but his fertile imagination and lively style ensured that his works remained in print well into the twentieth century.[84]

In addition to his books on school life, André Laurie's contribution to the adventure novel genre should be noted. He is perhaps best known for having written the first drafts of three novels subsequently rewritten by Jules Verne and published by Hetzel: *Les Cinq cents millions de la Bégum* (1879), *L'Etoile du Sud* (1884), and *L'Epave du Cynthia* (1885). He was also, however, the author of a number of novels for young readers published in Hetzel's 'Romans d'aventures' series, which displayed the same enthusiasm for bizarre adventures in exotic settings, like *Les Chercheurs d'or de l'Afrique australe* (1897) and *Atlantis* (1895), and the same exploitation of scientific and technological advances (*De New York à Brest en sept heures* [1888] describes a tunnel beneath the Atlantic). Like Verne, he has a claim to being one of the first science fiction writers: *Les Exilés de la terre: Séléné Company Limited* (1887) is based on an attempt to draw the moon down to earth in the Sahara desert with a giant magnet in order to explore it firsthand. Just as Laurie was more actively involved in politics than Verne, so the didactic element of his novels reveals a greater political engagement and, characteristic of much post-1870 writing, an extremely militant patriotism.

Any discussion of the adventure story should include at least a mention of Alphonse Daudet's entertaining spoof on the genre, *Tartarin de Tarascon*, published in 1872. Best known for his portrayal of Provençal life and scenery in such texts as *Lettres de mon moulin* (1869), Daudet (1840–1897) here offers a satirical perception of the flamboyance and romance-loving aspects of the southern character. This text, quickly appropriated by a young readership and still available today in Gallimard's Folio Junior series, draws on all the conventions of the adventure story in its depiction of the vain, formidable middle-aged Tartarin, whose longing for heroic adventures is constrained within the walls of his village home, packed with exotic weapons, where he sits and devours novels by Aimard and Fenimore Cooper. Daudet evokes the model of Miguel de Cervantes's Don Quixote in his protagonist's boredom with his everyday life ('en vain se bourrait-il de lectures romanesques, cherchant, comme l'immortel Don Quichotte, à s'arracher par la vigueur de son rêve aux griffes de l'impitoyable réalité'), but Tartarin also has a Sancho Panza side to his character that prefers caution and comfort and keeps him in his armchair.[85] The prestige he enjoys in his village because of his prowess in the local pastime of shooting hats (there being no other prey available) leads eventually to a new reputation as a hunter of lions through his own boastfulness and bravado in the face of a caged lion at a visiting menagerie. A victim of his own self-mythologising, Tartarin is eventually forced to set out for Africa in search of big game. There is much humorous description of the travels of this innocent abroad that mimic and satirise the journeys into the unknown of his literary predecessors and recall the self-deluding exploits of Cervantes's hero. In fact, he gets no farther than Algeria, is easily duped by a con man who steals all his money, and is sidetracked by the attractions of a life of sybaritic ease in Algiers with a voluptuous Arab woman who, unsuspected by him, is well known to male visitors to the city for her charms. Eventually he succeeds in his mission to kill a lion, but nothing is ever as it seems for Tartarin (as for Don Quixote), and his victim is only a poor tame blind creature used to raise funds for a monastery, an exploit that lands him in trouble with the law. Nevertheless, he is able to send the promised skin back to his cronies in Tarascon, thus confirming his reputation as a great hunter. The text ends with his triumphant return, accompanied by his adoring and loyal camel, which the embarrassed Tartarin has desperately tried to shake off but which only adds to his kudos in the village, and the beginning of his own version of the narrative, which transforms his journey into the great adventure his avid listeners expect. Despite the racist depiction of the Arab and Jewish inhabitants of Algiers and the exploitation of animals, Daudet's novel is still a very readable and humorous corrective to an addiction to adventure stories in its depiction of the way that heroes are made and the collision between literary adventures and real life. Lists of local flora and fauna are deployed in a comic fashion and the constant humorous reversals of fortune successfully deflate the hyperbole of contemporary works (as when Tartarin awakes believing that he has shot a lion during a night in the desert to find himself in a cabbage patch on the outskirts of the city under attack from a peasant woman whose donkey he has killed).[86]

While it seems that the implied reader of adventure stories was mainly an adolescent male, it is likely that in reality they were also read and enjoyed by young females, especially in the family context of the *Magasin d'éducation et de récréation*. It would be unwise, therefore, to see the development of books for young readers in the second half of the century as simply evolving along strictly gendered lines. With this in mind, the next chapter explores a different application of the adventure story and considers how it was pressed into the service of education in the specific context of the nationally traumatic events of 1870–71 and their aftermath during the Third Republic.

4

SIGNS OF THE TIMES

There was an increased interest in the second half of the nineteenth century in the portrayal in literature for all ages of the plight of orphaned, abandoned, exploited, or abused children. This can be explained in part by demographic and social factors. Despite society's huge investment in children and the promotion of family values, the decline in the birth rate in midcentury, and a still high infant mortality rate, the problem of abandoned children (*enfants trouvés*) was particularly acute in France. Largely because of the scandal and shame attached to illegitimate births, the number of abandoned children had increased from 67,000 in 1809 to 121,000 in 1835.[1] Hospices run by nuns took in abandoned babies left at their door, and children were often placed by the authorities with rural families and, in the second half of the century, in orphanages. The state, which in the nineteenth century began increasingly to direct its attention to the family, used foundlings as labourers, soldiers, and colonists.[2] Because the stigma of illegitimacy was commonly associated with potential delinquency, the illegitimate child was, however, often subjected to humiliation and was vulnerable to exploitation.

A consequence of the Industrial Revolution was the employment of children from an early age in sweatshops, factories, mills, and mines and the physical, mental, and moral toll of the conditions under which they worked was incalculable. As in Britain, child labour had been a political and social issue from the early part of the century, culminating in a formal attempt to improve conditions in the 1840s.[3] A law of March 1841 banned children under the age of eight from working for large enterprises or in factories that used machinery or kept a fire burning. Working hours were to be limited (to eight hours a day for ages eight to twelve, and twelve hours for ages twelve to sixteen). Children under thirteen were not to be employed for night work, and employers were required to ensure that their young employees had some schooling. Because these requirements were not consistently enforced, however, in many areas they had little impact. The impetus for reform was lost under the Second Empire, a situation exacerbated by indifference and resistance from parents and industrialists, and it was considerably later that further measures to protect children in the workplace and ensure them their rights to education were put in place.[4] The 1874 *Loi sur le travail des enfants et des filles mineures dans l'industrie* raised the minimum working age to twelve, although it remained at ten for some industries, with a maximum twelve-hour working day, no night work, and, for those under twelve, two hours of schooling a day. Penalties for breaking the law were stiffened with the creation of a centralised factory inspectorate, but, as in Britain, the effect of such legislation was often to drive child labour underground.[5]

THE CHILD AS VICTIM

The appearance in literature of the theme of child as victim is generally attributed to the influence of Victor Hugo's portrayal of the abuses suffered by Cosette at the hands of the Thénardiers in *Les Misérables* in 1862 and to that of Charles Dickens, many of whose novels were published by Hachette and who had been in Paris in 1856 to oversee the translation of his works.[6] But George Sand had also explored the plight of the foundling in *François le champi* (1848) and made a heroine of the abused child, marginalised by society because of the reputation of her grandmother as a witch, in *La Petite Fadette* (1849). Although these were not specifically books for children, the latter incorporating a covert post-1848 political agenda, they have been considered suitable for the young because they are brief, pastoral tales foregrounding young protagonists; they still find a place amongst books for children in bookshops today. Marie-Thérèse Latzarus describes two non-fiction works of the 1860s that aimed to bring home to the children of the privileged classes the reality of life for those less fortunate. Edouard-Thomas Charton's *Histoires de trois pauvres enfants qui sont devenus riches, racontées par eux-mêmes* (1864) drew on the memoirs of three boys who overcame poverty, hardship, and physical abuse to achieve highly successful careers and respected positions in society in the eighteenth century by dint of persistence, determination, and hard work.[7] These biographical narratives were intended to inspire pity and admiration in readers and to encourage a positive and proactive attitude to their own potential, but it is, of course, doubtful that many children in analogous positions would have had access to the book to benefit from it. Edouard Siebecker's approach was different; his work, *Les Enfants malheureux* (1868), was based on his observation of, and interviews with, working children of the day and was intended as a corrective to the idealised views of childhood current at the time. He talked to children of both sexes engaged in various activities, all of which involved hard labour, physical exhaustion, deprivation, and dangers to health and moral welfare: a little girl whose job was to pull a cart along a mine shaft, a chimney sweep, a flowergirl, ship's boys, and apprentices in laundries, glassblowing, and printing workshops. His accounts of children initiated into thieving by their parents or getting drunk in the street must have made startling and distressing reading for a middle-class child more used to the fiction of the Bibliothèque rose series.

Children of all social classes were also abused in the home. Parents— or rather, fathers—had complete authority where their children were concerned, and children had few legal rights until late in the century. Three widely read works aimed at adult readers appeared in the second half of the century that portrayed childhood and family life, as exalted in the Third Republic as it was in the Second Empire, in a very negative light. In Alphonse Daudet's *Le Petit chose* (1868), Jules Vallès's *L'Enfant* (1879), and Jules Renard's *Poil de carotte* (1894), children are brutalised, tormented, or neglected by their parents and oppressed at school. Daudet's Jack is humiliated at school because of his poverty and subjected to brutal treatment and, after running away, is sent by his surrogate father to work in hellish conditions at a forge. In the case of Vallès's novel, the portrayal of Mme Vingtras, the wife of an impoverished teacher of peasant origins, with her obsession with appearances, and the tormenting of her son Jacques through her control of his clothes, food, and daily activities is an attack on social pretensions and how they affect children. Her son's humiliation and suffering as the result of her attentions is an indictment of the consequences of investing in the child as the vehicle of the family's fortunes. The fate of Jacques's friend, the little girl beaten to death by her father, is a potent condemnation of a society in which there were no organisations to protect children, and thus an attack on the forces of patriarchy at the level of the family and the state.[8] In *Poil de carotte*, the torment the child undergoes is ascribed to the mother's cold, inexplicable, and seemingly gratuitously sadistic attitude to her youngest child (notably removing his chamber pot and then punishing him for soiling his bed). His unhappiness and frustration result, inevitably, in confused feelings of hatred and a desire to please, and in outbursts of viciousness towards animals. These texts were not initially aimed at child readers, although *Poil de carotte*, which evokes the little incidents of childhood in short, impressionistic, and often humorous chapters, was subsequently appropriated by children and Hetzel published a revised and expurgated version of *Le Petit Chose* for young readers in 1878. But such overt condemnation of parents and a bleak view of the exploitation of the vulnerable by those with power over them was more or less taboo in children's books, which continued to promote, by and large, an idealised view of the family. Similarly, the portrayal of delinquency and transgressive behaviour resulting from a deficient upbringing was modified in children's books, and often shown to be easily corrected by loving care.

The child as victim in the workplace was already a widely exploited theme in literature in English, particularly amongst writers published by the Religious Tract Society who catered for both juvenile readers and the newly literate. In France, the condition of the offspring of the industrial or urban proletariat was a less common theme generally than in Britain because of the predominantly rural nature of the country and the relatively late introduction of industrialisation. It has been claimed that French books for children virtually ignored the crucial social issues of exploitation, child abuse, and infant mortality. It is true that most fictional works that touch on the subject of exploitation depict what Ganna Ottevaere–van Praag calls a 'faux réalisme' in that the protagonists are frequently well-born children who find themselves dispossessed or who have been abducted and are able to emerge from dreadful experiences and vile environments apparently without having been affected physically or morally to be restored to their family and rightful inheritance. Such texts also display a kind of biological determinism based on class assumptions in that, despite the experience of immersion in a sordid milieu, in some cases from babyhood, the bourgeois child's inherited characteristics of noble sentiments and linguistic refinement are shown to be uncontaminated.[9] In the popular deployment of the theme of abduction, children's books were both playing on the bourgeois child reader's fear of dispossession and manipulating events to create a reassuring ending rather than offering a portrayal of what real-life children, especially those born into a life of poverty and hardship, experienced. There are, however, portraits of children who play minor roles in the texts (like Panouille in Louis Desnoyers's *Les Mésaventures de Jean-Paul Choppart*) who are more representative of a true picture of the nineteenth century's cruelty to children.

Rather than depicting an industrial environment, preference in books for young readers is for the portrayal of the plight of beggars, street performers, or circus children, of which Desnoyers's novel was a precedent. The child protagonists of the later novels are, however, usually the victims of criminal acts rather than scamps or runaways, and the picture of life on the road has lost the humorous edge. The portrayal of their situation is sometimes accompanied by a description of the ways in which a stolen child is disguised, even disfigured, by his or her abductors to avoid detection (like the little girl Diélette in Hector Malot's *Romain Kalbris*) or their limbs dislocated so that they could perform contortions and acrobatics in circuses and travelling shows, as in Mme Marie Delorme's *Les Filles du Clown* (1893). The beatings, starvation, and humiliation of such an existence are contrasted with the tawdry sparkle of the costumes they are forced to wear, destroying the romantic notion of liberty and spontaneity often associated with a life in the open air, free from social constraints. As noted above, most such novels for young readers end happily, however, with the lost or stolen child recognised and rescued, or running away and eventually being reunited with family or adopted into a new home. Typical of this approach was Julie Colomb's very successful *La Fille de Carilès* (1874), published in the Bibliothèque rose illustrée and still in their catalogue around 1912, in which an old man who sells paper windmills in the streets adopts a little girl who has escaped from gypsies. The plot quickly turns into a sentimental tale of the relationship between the child and the old man (a theme much beloved by the Religious Tract Society writers in Britain) and of mutual self-sacrifice.[10] The girl Miette, who is torn by remorse at becoming ashamed of the shabbiness of their existence, resolves to devote her life to her surrogate father Carilès, refusing an offer of marriage, while he, now blind and feeling himself to be an impediment to her happiness, decides to remove himself from the scene. Coincidences and contrivances effect a happy ending: saved from falling into a river by a passerby who, fortuitously, is a doctor, Carilès is cured of his blindness and Miette is able to marry, but continues to care for Carilès as he had cared for her. A number of novels of this type are listed by Latzarus, including the Bibliothèque rose's widely read *La Maison roulante* (1869) by Mme Stolz, who also authored *Les Enfants volés* (1882).[11]

HECTOR MALOT'S BEST-SELLERS

One of the most widely read and loved children's books of the second half of the century was Hector Malot's *Sans famille* (1878), the story of a foundling's search for his real family, although it is little known and studied outside France today.[12] Malot (1830–1907), a liberal humanist and moderate anticlerical, was also a prolific and successful writer of well-documented realist novels for adults set in different social environments, including the world of horse racing (*Un Beau-frère*, 1868), the linen industry (*Baccara*, 1886), and army life (*Le Lieutenant Bonnet*, 1885), in which he explored the social problems of bourgeois family life and presented a critical view of bureaucrats, the clergy, and members of the medical and legal professions. Although not so radical as his friend Jules Vallès, whom he supported both financially and as his literary agent when Vallès was in exile in England after the period of the Paris Commune, Malot's work manifests a deep concern about social conditions and, in particular, in his novels for young readers, the plight of children in the labour market. Whereas the suffering children in the Comtesse de Ségur's novels are generally oppressed by individuals or seen as the victims of specific circumstances or, indeed, of aspects of their own personality, Malot's novels offer a wider picture of social conditions affecting the poor or dispossessed.

In the autobiographical account of his literary career, *Le Roman de mes romans* (1895), Malot explains that he had been moved to write for the young by the memory of his own boredom with children's literature.[13] In all his children's books Malot employs thematic and narrative strategies specifically designed to appeal to a young reader: the familiar plot structure of initiation and maturation, a sympathetic and energetic protagonist who leads an active, outdoor existence full of tests of endurance, the introduction of a faithful friend and confidante, a number of attractive animals, and a wise elderly adult who acts as mentor. The novels feature a wide range of different environments and dramatic events, a fast-moving plot full of surprises and reversals of fortune, comedy and tragedy, a large amount of dialogue, a straightforward but colourful style, and a satisfyingly happy ending. A travel enthusiast himself, Malot uses the travel motif as a central structuring device in his novels, a strategy that links his work with the first prose narrative written specifically for the instruction and amusement of a young reader, *Les Aventures de Télémaque* (1699), François Fénelon's spin-off from Homer's *Odyssey*. This adventure story of a young man's quest for his father, originally written for Fénelon's pupil the Duc de Bourgogne, was still in print and widely used as a pedagogical text in the second half of the nineteenth century.

Malot's first book to find favour with young readers was *Romain Kalbris*, initially serialised in *Le Courrier français* in 1867 and published in book form two years later. It is both a Bildungsroman and an 'on the road' novel that recounts the experiences of the boy Romain, a child from a long line of Normandy fishermen who, after the death of his father in an attempt to save the victims of a shipwreck, determines to earn his living and support his mother as a *mousse*, or ship's boy.[14] As in Malot's other novels, Romain's formative experiences reflect the author's dislike of the conventional school system and his preference for a Rousseauistic upbringing that favours the development of the individual's mental and physical faculties free from social constraints and close to the natural world. This is inscribed overtly in the text in the person of M. Bihorel, an eccentric old man living on an island nearby, who takes Romain under his wing and educates him in the ways of birds, animals, and sea creatures, telling him that 'il y a plus d'une façon de s'instruire, on peut s'instruire en jouant et se promenant'.[15] M. Bihorel's bible is Daniel Defoe's *Robinson Crusoe*, a book on which he has based his own life (his servant has been named Samedi), and from which he believes, like Jean-Jacques Rousseau, his protégé will learn 'ce que peut chez un homme la force morale'.[16] Romain's exposure to this text serves more to encourage dreams of adventure, however, which after the old man's disappearance at sea and an acutely unhappy period for the boy with his uncle (a miserly bailiff), renew his determination to go to sea. His travels, which form the bulk of the text, have a definite goal, to reach Le Havre and seek work on a ship, but the circumstances to which he falls victim en route not only deflect him from this but represent a harsh initiation into adulthood. Malot portrays in great detail the physical and psychological effects of a hand-to-mouth existence in the open air, of hunger, inadequate clothing, exposure to the elements, and fear of strangers and the authorities. Like Jean-Paul Choppart, Romain is taken up by a troupe of travelling circus people, but Malot's emphasis is on the real physical and psychological hardships of this way of life, his concern about the exploitation of children mediated through the story of the young girl Diélette. Initially stolen at a fair in Paris and sold into virtual slavery, she has spent her short life as a beggar and child entertainer, starved, mutilated, and passed from master to master, her only solace being her affection for an old lion.

The flight of the two children and their journey to Paris to find Diélette's mother allow for highly affective scenes of a bitterly cold night spent under a hedge (an unflinchingly realistic babes-in-the-woods scenario), and of trudging through a snowstorm in the countryside and the muddy, slushy streets of the capital in their fruitless search. Unlike the authors of the Bibliothèque rose, Malot produces no kindly benefactor to watch over them or solve their difficulties at a stroke. Although they are given food and a few coins by people who pity their plight, they find no permanent respite in the city, which is clearly associated with solitude, misery, and a largely uncaring society. The children are turned out of a church where they have sought shelter, and wander through dark streets of houses with closed doors, until, in a bleak scene on the banks of the Seine, Diélette falls so ill that she is taken to a hospital. Malot frequently confronts his protagonists with a choice of survival between a life of crime on the margins of society and an opportunity to make their way through honest work, and Romain, rejecting the offer of a former companion to join his company of adolescent thieves, chooses to wait for Diélette to recover by working for a kindly market trader. Although Diélette's troubles end when she goes to live with Romain's mother, he has more tribulations to endure in his determination to be independent and earn his own living at sea. A self-conscious gesture towards the fictionalising of lived experience is incorporated by Malot when Romain later becomes a celebrated shipwreck survivor like his fictional hero (after stowing away aboard a ship bound for South America) and is invited to perform his experience repeatedly in a stage play. Ultimately happiness for Malot lies in a rural setting, and a series of contrivances are deployed to bring the narrative to a comforting close with all the characters united and Romain, having conveniently inherited a large sum from a distant uncle, becoming the owner of six fishing boats. Thus determination, honesty, and perseverance are rewarded, as they are in fairy tales, with material success and personal happiness.

Of Malot's novels for young readers, *Romain Kalbris* (1869), *Sans famille* (1878), and *En famille* (1893), *Sans famille* was by far the most successful. A blockbuster tearjerker, it was widely translated (even into Japanese, Russian, and Vietnamese), made into film and television versions and is still in print today. It features in many writers' memoirs as the book by which they were most moved and, to Malot's delight, excerpts were regularly published in French readers for English schoolchildren.[17] The genesis of *Sans famille* is an interesting one. Shortly after the publication of *Romain Kalbris*, Malot was approached by Pierre-Jules Hetzel, who asked him to write a book for serialisation in the *Magasin d'Education et de Récréation*. Hetzel envisaged an educational novel and the contract of 1869 stipulated that it should incorporate descriptions of different parts of France and of local industries. The provisional title was to be *Les Enfants du tour de France*.[18] Already ill at ease with Hetzel's directions, Malot was displeased when the publisher wanted a number of significant changes to the manuscript he submitted in 1870—notably, the removal of passages on social and religious questions. Matters were put on hold during the period of the Franco-Prussian War and the Paris Commune, when a large part of the manuscript seems to have been lost; when Malot eventually returned to the book, what he produced was radically different and only on the insistence that Hetzel release him from his serialisation rights. *Sans famille* was eventually serialised in the newspaper *Le Siècle* between December 1877 and April 1778 and was published in book form in 1878 both by Dentu, Malot's usual publisher, and by Hetzel, the latter with illustrations by Emile Bayard.

Malot was clearly at pains to make the subject matter, although often disturbing, accessible to the child reader. The dedication to Malot's daughter Lucie (then age ten) reveals that she was a pilot reader for the work and that he kept her probable reactions in mind throughout the composition of the text. The first-person narrative of an *enfant trouvé*, or foundling, named Rémi, *Sans famille* represents one of the fullest expressions of the 'on the road' novel, but also owes something to the quest narrative, the family romance, the picaresque novel, and fairy tales in Malot's treatment of the themes of exile, separation, a peripatetic existence, lessons in self-reliance and survival, and the search for identity and social integration.[19] Rémi's journey is both literal and metaphorical, an initiation into both the geography of France and into adulthood through his experiences and encounters in different social environments. In all, he makes several journeys across France, and to England and Switzerland and back, in search of his real identity, a family, and love. The narrative viewpoint is that of the adult Rémi recounting his childhood from a position of bourgeois security and wealth (although this is only revealed at the end of the novel), but from the first words ('Je suis un enfant trouvé') the reader is immersed in the child's experience, which the narrative relives vividly as if in the present. The reader only learns the truth of his situation as Rémi himself discovers it, and the novel is structured on a pattern of expectations, false hopes, and frustrations, although there are clues throughout to a happy outcome that both intrigue and reassure.

Paradoxically, the plot of *Sans famille* offers a multiplicity of potential family scenarios to confuse Rémi and tantalise the reader. As in the traditional fairy-tale plot, Rémi's hardships begin with an exile from home and the woman he thought was his mother when he discovers that he is really a foundling and is sold by his brutal foster father to a travelling musician, Vitalis. With this kindly surrogate father figure Rémi experiences many physical privations as a street performer, but also undergoes an apprenticeship to life in terms of character-building lessons and survival strategies as they travel 'au hasard' through France. Vitalis teaches him to read print, maps, and music and to play the harp, which opens up new worlds of possibility, but Rémi learns from the firsthand experience of his travels rather than from books. Vitalis is not a cruel exploiter of children but a kind teacher, guardian, and philosopher of life whose identity, like Rémi's, is a mystery. It is later revealed that his life has also been blighted by harsh reversals of fortune, for he was an international opera star reduced by the loss of his voice to performing in village squares with his small troupe of dogs and a monkey. The animals play an important part in reconciling Rémi to his new life, especially his bond with the performing poodle, Capi, which helps to ease his misery and solitude and creates a new sense of 'family'. The animals are also the catalyst for one of his hardest lessons, that of personal responsibility. When left in charge of the little troupe in a makeshift shelter in the forest on a snowy night, Rémi falls asleep and is indirectly responsible for the deaths of two of the dogs, who are eaten by wolves, and for the death of the monkey from the cold. The pathos of this scene, with no reassuring reversal or happy conclusion, does not spare the child reader's sensibilities in underlining the harsh reality of Rémi's plight.

His meeting with the English Mme Milligan and her invalid son Arthur aboard their canal boat Le Cygne, with its veranda garden; the instant and instinctive attraction he feels towards them (which is reciprocated by the doting mother and the pale, weak child); and the few idyllic days he spends with them, briefly enjoying a new status as 'brother', companion, and teacher to Arthur are obvious narrative contrivances that offer a major clue to the truth of Rémi's past and identity. The boat itself can be seen as a symbolic locus of maternal love and family affection, desired but elusive, but it also, unknown to all concerned, links his past and his present, as at the end of the second part of the novel Mme Milligan turns out to be his real mother from whom he was stolen as a baby. However, before this revelation, Rémi must experience other family structures and dynamics. It is his winter sojourn in Paris as a street musician and beggar in the charge of Garofoli, a figure surely influenced by Dickens's Fagin, that most fully testifies to the foundling's vulnerability in contemporary society. Malot's view of cities as the locus of misery, perversion, and cynicism informs the portrayal of this cruel and capricious monster whose brutality to the little chimney sweeps and street entertainers in his charge is revealed in a grim account by one of his victims, the sick and abused boy Mattia, who becomes Rémi's friend and fellow traveller. The home that he finds with the Acquins, the family of a wallflower grower, after Vitalis's death from hunger and cold in a dismal Paris suburb allows Rémi to become, temporarily, part of a family with siblings and a shared occupation, but this potentially satisfying form of closure is disrupted when the father is imprisoned for debt after his flowers are ruined in a hailstorm and the Acquin family is dispersed. His new loss provides Rémi with a goal in his resumed travels: to be reunited with his surrogate siblings, especially the dumb child Lise, and this provides the link between the first and second parts of the novel.

The second part of the novel depicts Rémi's travels with Mattia (now restored to health) and Capi, and his reinvention of himself in his new career as a musician. The themes of friendship and solidarity come to the fore in what becomes the joint enterprise of visiting his foster mother and finding the Acquin children. The episode in which Rémi becomes, briefly, a coal miner, reveals, like the depiction of Garofoli's hostel, Malot's concern about child labour. The atmospheric description of the miners' lives, work, and homes and the accident in the mine (written ten years before Émile Zola's *Germinal*, which *Sans famille* may well have influenced) lays bare the hardships and danger of the desperate working conditions of adults and children alike. Yet Malot is no radical social reformer in that there is no overt condemnation of social conditions and the politics that have produced them, nor suggestions for positive change. The episode nevertheless would have succeeded in exposing the bourgeois child reader to unfamilar and possibly unsuspected ways of life. Significantly, help comes to Rémi not from any intervention of the authorities but from other poor or marginalised members of society: the old miner, an example of the popular literary figure of the working-class autodidact, who encourages the sharing of knowledge; the barber who teaches Rémi and Mattia more sophisticated musical techniques; and, later, Bob the black busker, who helps Rémi escape from prison in England.

Malot's depiction of the dirty, foggy London slums of Bethnal Green, where Rémi goes with Mattia and Capi to find the Driscolls, whom he is led to believe are his real family, is Dickensian in its grimness, and the episode presents Rémi with another dilemma that problematises the conventional form of closure of the family romance.[20] While he feels only disillusionment and disgust at the Driscolls and resists being drawn into the criminal underworld of which they are a part, Rémi is torn by the compulsion to be loyal to them until Mattia's commonsense observations persuade him that he cannot be a product of the Driscolls' thieves' kitchen. Upon their return to France after a suspenseful account of Rémi's wrongful arrest, the various threads are pulled together into a highly satisfying if blatantly contrived manner. Miracles start to happen: Lise regains her voice and Arthur his health, the evil uncle who was responsible for Rémi's loss as a baby is routed, and Rémi and Mme Milligan are reunited. Ironically, his real family is still not what he expected, for the child brought up by a French peasant woman is, in fact, both rich and English. In the final chapter the reader is brought into the present with the adult Rémi a propertied English gentlemen with a stately home and gardens with real swans on the lake. The former foundling, married to Lise and sharing his home with Arthur and Mme Milligan, has created his own cosmopolitan extended family from his surviving friends, including Mattia, now a famous musician, and Lise's siblings. This, plus the prevalence of real or surrogate families in the text that are dysfunctional, fragile, or lacking in one respect or another, may suggest a covert undermining by Malot of the traditional notion of the ideal nuclear family.[21] The genesis of Rémi's narrative is revealed: it is a gift of gratitude to his friends and a tribute to the part they have played in his life, and copies are distributed when he brings them together to celebrate the birth of his first child. The two halves of the book are brought together, and closure given to all of their struggles as a scene from his childhood is reenacted with Rémi and Mattia performing a Neapolitan song and Capi (whom the reader is enchanted to see still alive and sharing in the good fortune) playing his old role of passing a cap around for a collection. In a final gesture to stimulate the reader's social conscience, Malot has Rémi and Mattia donate the proceeds to a refuge for child street performers.

The success of *Sans famille* was undoubtedly due to its depiction of a variety of environments, colourful characters, and the deployment in rapid succession of melodrama, sentimentality, horror, and humour. Despite seemingly insuperable odds, virtue, goodness, courage, and truthfulness are seen ultimately to prevail. A large part of its success must have been the opportunity to indulge vicariously in the wandering life, free from constraints of parental, school, or church authority. The first-person narrative allows for intimacy with the protagonist's thoughts and dreams as well as his moments of despair, and his capacity for self-criticism acknowledges his weaknesses, like the temptation of fantasies of wealth that threaten at one point to distort his personality and the preoccupation with his own goals that makes him insensitive to Mattia's needs. The plot privileges male agency, for apart from the two mothers Mère Barberin and Mme Milligan, who are absent for large stretches of the novel, it is surrogate father figures who move the plot on and are responsible for both exploiting Rémi (Barberin, Garofoli, Driscoll, James Milligan) and supporting and helping him (Vitalis, Père Acquin, the old miner, the barber). There is a degree of conventional stereotyping in many of the characters: Arthur, for example, represents a favourite nineteenth-century literary type, the ethereal sick child whose patience and courage confer blessings all around, his immobility contrasting with the robust Rémi's way of life. The female characters are the most consistently stereotyped, however, as passive and self-sacrificing: Etiennette, the little surrogate mother of the

Acquin family, is a melancholy, resigned creature who has never had time to be a child; and the mute Lise, regarded by Rémi as an ideal being and a kind of guardian angel, is patient and stoical. Significantly, it is the singing of Rémi when he finds her again that gives her back her voice. This imaging of women nevertheless reflects the feminine ideal promoted by many writers of the Bibliothèque rose.

En Famille, published fifteen years later, offers girl readers a more dynamic female protagonist, another dispossessed child who shares her name with Malot's granddaughter, Perrine, who was born the same year. This novel, the title of which is taken from the last chapter of Sans famille, is a study of willpower and survival set against the background of the jute industry. Malot's original intentions were to portray the modern improvements in the working and living conditions of the workers, but during his research in the factories of the valley of the River Somme he was horrified at the lack of a concerted view on the implementation of, and even the need for, such improvements and was struck especially by the contrast between the luxurious homes of the factory owners and the dwellings in the workers' village, full of squalor, misery, drunkenness, and debauchery. He reports in Le Roman de mes romans that, in raising at the end of En famille the question of the duty of the manufacturers to improve the material and moral situation of their workers, he incurred the criticism that such notions perverted the purely economic relationship of capital and labour, but reaffirms his belief that enlightened employers could not fail to be moved to action by such a disparity in conditions. By implication, he also endorses the duty of the writer to arouse their sense of natural justice. To personalise this theme, he added the portrayal of the achievements of willpower in one child's struggle for survival, 'sa formation dans un caractère, son fonctionnement, les miracles qu'elle peut accomplir'.[22]

As with Sans famille, the initial situation of the protagonist in En famille seems to belie the book's title, for Perrine finds herself an orphan when her mother dies shortly after they have arrived at the outskirts of Paris in a dilapidated gypsy caravan pulled by a donkey. As with Rémi, her family origins are obscure, but her goal is to continue to make her way to the village of Maraucourt, where, it is hinted, their fortunes will be revived.[23] Other clues to her real identity are embedded in the description of her unusual, exotic features (she has blond hair and dark eyes) and her gentle but proud bearing despite her rags and the near destitution of their wandering, hand-to-mouth existence as travelling photographers. Malot thus conforms to the literary convention, common in nineteenth-century children's novels (as in fairy tales), that good breeding can be detected in physical appearance. The first part of the novel is an 'on the road' narrative, recounting Perrine's encounters as she walks to the village in the north and her arrival and employment in the jute factory. Malot presents a graphic and thoroughly researched depiction of the factory with its constant deafening clatter of machinery, the scurrying child workers, and the shouts of the overseers, and of the overcrowded, noisy, stinking conditions of the workers' dormitory where Perrine is initially lodged. The social-problem plot is juxtaposed to an interlude that is a *Robinsonnade* in miniature, when, alienated by the squalor of her surroundings, Perrine seeks peace in self-imposed isolation in an abandoned hunters' hut on a tiny island in the river and develops her ingenuity and skills in making her own clothes, sandals, and cooking utensils from the natural resources of her surroundings. The description of her rural idyll (for which Jules Verne supplied information about fish, birds, and hunting) stands in stark opposition to that of the village, with its dirty streets and seedy bars beneath a pall of black smoke from the factory chimneys.[24] Apart from furnishing the opportunity for Perrine to demonstrate her willpower and initiative, the function of this episode is, of course, to remove the protagonist from the degrading life of the other workers, thus providing comfortable reassurance for the reader, but such a strategy also inevitably avoids confronting fully the issue of the influence of such an environment on the individual. This is displaced from the protagonist to Rosalie, the factory girl who befriends Perrine and introduces her (and the reader) to the factory, and is injured in her work. The contrast between the portrayal of Perrine and, say, the child Nana in Zola's *L'Assommoir* (1877), may suggest, apart from the evident differences between the two writers in their literary techniques, the constraints which writers for the young felt compelled to observe.

The second half of the novel conflates social concern with a fairly predictable family romance plot. Her intelligence, diligence, cleanliness and quiet dignity quickly winning admiration and approval at the factory, Perrine's fortunes improve when she is employed as a translator (she speaks English) and then as a guide to the blind factory owner, M. Vulfran Painavoine, himself. The relationship between the girl and the old man presents an emotive depiction of two emotionally deprived people, in this case the loneliness of the orphan and of old age blighted by a longstanding rift with an only son over an unsuitable marriage. After several incidents, including a disastrous fire that kills a number of small children in the village, Perrine helps convert the embittered and grieving M. Painavoine, whose physical infirmity symbolises his moral blindness to his responsibilities, to a recognition of what might be achieved for the betterment of the factory and the lives of its workers.

Together they establish a crèche, better family housing, and every kind of amenity in the surrounding villages, with even the gardens of M. Painavoine's château becoming a public park and playground. The revelation, soon suspected by the reader, that M. Painavoine is in fact Perrine's grandfather is not presented as an arbitrary melodramatic contrivance but is a fact known to Perrine who, because of her innate nobility of spirit, wished to make herself loved before she revealed her identity. Perrine's fortunes thus depend less on coincidences that tax the reader's belief than on her own deliberate efforts, a modulation of the orphan story that invests the protagonist with a greater degree of autonomy and control over her circumstances. Malot does, however, produce a characteristic manipulation of events to effect a finale strong in the 'feel-good' factor with M. Painavoine regaining his sight, Perrine reunited with her donkey friend Palikare, and the new family surveying the fruits of their collaboration from a hilltop. The transformation of hard-hearted factory owner to model employer is a familiar theme in nineteenth-century novels of social concern, but the blending of the theme here with the narrative of Perrine's self-development is an affecting introduction for the young reader to a major issue of the time. Malot's own recognition that individual endeavour is only a starting point in the elimination of social injustice, however, is made explicit in M. Painavoine's assertion that his improvements are only 'l'ABC de la question sociale et ce n'est pas avec cela qu'on la résout; j'espère que nous pourrions aller plus loin, plus à fond; nous ne sommes qu'à notre point de départ'.[25] The obvious corollary of this is that, if social justice comes from personal conviction, then a novel that can move and inspire its readership from an early age has an important part to play.

JULES VERNE AND THE RAGS-TO-RICHES NARRATIVE

It was perhaps the success of Sans famille that prompted Jules Verne to write P'tit Bonhomme (1893), one of his lesser-known novels, which also details the life of a dispossessed orphan and his travels around Ireland. This is an unusual novel in Verne's oeuvre, for there is no scientific element, and it has more in common with the Bildungsroman, or novel of self-development, than the adventure story genre. However, it is more politicised than Malot's novel, depicting the widespread poverty and hardship in town and countryside alike. Verne highlights in particular the parlous situation of the small peasant farmers and touches on the growth of nationalist activism in a starving and desperate nation where absentee British landlords have the power to evict a family from their farm on a whim. P'tit Bonhomme also deals more extensively than

Malot with the plight of the foundling and the theme of child abuse in grim vignettes of the protagonist's progress from the squalid hovel of a drunken baby minder, to the hands of a travelling puppeteer where he lives, at age four, like an animal in a cramped cart, to a ragged school, and eventually to life on the road. Nothing is known of the child's background and he has no identity other than his nickname of P'tit Bonhomme. Verne ironically deconstructs a convention of the family romance in insisting that, despite his sensibility, honesty, and love of order the child is *not* of high birth, a coincidence only fit for a novel. Indeed, after the ragged school burns down, P'tit Bonhomme is briefly taken in by an actress who sees his plight and their relationship precisely in terms of the melodramatic scenario of the foundling whose air of distinction reveals his noble birth and the lady bountiful who rescues him. The difference between literary convention and real life is startlingly apparent when she requires P'tit Bonhomme to perform this role on stage, confusing the child and revealing her egotism when it ends in comic disaster.

Like Rémi, P'tit Bonhomme finds successive surrogate families and helpers who will feature in his later life, notably Grip, an older boy who protects him at the ragged school and becomes a lifelong friend, and the MacCarthy family, on whose farm he spends the happiest years of his childhood until, after their sudden eviction, he finds himself dispossessed once more with only a dog for company and his own resources to call upon. Verne's depiction of the destitution of the poor during a cruel winter, the harsh measures of the landlords and their middle men, and the cynicism of the aristocracy is as powerful an indictment of this aspect of British rule as his portrayal of more farflung colonised territories. As with Rémi, P'tit Bonhomme's meeting with a younger boy—also an orphan to whom he becomes a protector, in turn—provides the opportunity not just for companionship, but for a shared project. In Cork they start a small business selling matches, papers, and stationery from a cart before walking to Dublin to try their luck there. P'tit Bonhomme's career diverges radically from Rémi's at this point, for he makes his own fortune and thrives through his own initiative, willpower, capacity for hard work, and sound business sense, opening a small shop that flourishes under the name of 'Little Boy and Co.'. However improbable the prospect of a business run by two young boys (with a little help from a kindly adult advisor) may seem, the venture succeeds precisely because of its novelty, with P'tit Bonhomme's youth and personality attracting admiration and patronage. A concession is made to the family romance genre in the bringing together at the end of the novel all the people dear to P'tit Bonhomme and the establishment of a happy extended family, as in *Sans famille*, but not before the introduction of a typically Vernian surprise episode that strongly recalls that in *Romain Kalbris*. P'tit Bonhomme, returning from Londonderry on a ship of goods he has purchased, remains on board alone when the ship founders and becomes something of a hero. The plot of *P'tit Bonhomme* is thus both a manipulation and an implicit critique of the orphan story in order to present an image of the destitution and despair of rural Ireland in the 1880s.

G. BRUNO: LEARNING PATRIOTISM

The wave of patriotism that engulfed France after the shock of military defeat in the Franco-Prussian War, the period of the Paris Commune (1870–71), and, in particular, the loss of Alsace and Lorraine had a seminal impact on children's books. With national cohesion under threat from recent social upheavals and ongoing ideological divisions between church and Republic, the provision of a uniform education for all that would consolidate republican ideals became an urgent issue in the 1870s and patriotic sentiment was deemed to be an identifiable shared ethos and unifying force.[26] The involvement of the young in the project of working together to regenerate France, including, if necessary, readiness to fight for the *patrie*, infiltrated school textbooks, fictional works, and journals alike. Hetzel, in July 1871, left the readers of the *Magasin d'éducation et de récréation* in no doubt about his own views of the disaster of 1870, urging his readers to recognise their future role and responsibility:

> C'est à nos fils et à nos filles elles-mêmes qu'il appartient de prouver au monde que si la France, mal élevée, mal instruite et mal dirigée, a pu faiblir et être vaincue, que si, peut-être, elle a mérité ses revers, elle n'a pas cessé cependant d'être la nation forte et généreuse qui, avec l'aide de Dieu, peut, toujours, se relever plus grande et meilleure de ses chutes les plus profondes.[27]

The comparison of France to a badly brought-up child lays the blame for defeat, by implication, squarely at the door of Napoleon III and his domestic and foreign policies and suggests that for the nation, as for the individual, calamities can be good for the soul. An article in *L'Ami de l'enfance*, in condemning war, also suggested that France had an important lesson to learn: 'Prions-le [Dieu] enfin, chers enfants, qu'il éloigne de notre chère patrie ces quatre fléaux de l'humanité: l'égoïsme, la violence, l'esprit de ruse et l'amour des conquêtes'.[28] Nevertheless, the spirit of revenge and anti-German sentiment continued to manifest itself in both the teaching of history in schools and in leisure reading for the young alongside the broader agenda of instilling a love of the *patrie* and the moral and psychological preparation of its future soldiers. Ernest Lavisse, author of the *Histoire de France* widely used in schools, also produced a work geared precisely to this end titled *Tu seras soldat* (1887). Children were thus exposed to the propaganda of 'le culte du drapeau' repeatedly in their reading, in the images of Epinal and on postcards, in songs, and in games, very much as they had been during the revolutionary period.

This patriotic agenda produced the text that became by far the best-selling work for young readers in the second half of the century, *Le Tour de la France par deux enfants* by G. Bruno (1883–1923) the pseudonym of Mme Augustine Fouillée. First published in 1877 by Eugène Belin, *Le Tour de la France* was a book for use in elementary schools and sold three million copies in its first decade, reaching six million by 1901.[29] For decades this text and, to a lesser but still significant extent Bruno's other works *Francinet* (1869) and *Les Enfants de Marcel* (1887), were known in the majority of French homes. Although detailed discussion of textbooks in this period are beyond the scope of this study, Bruno's work merits consideration because of its approach, which links it with developments in fiction for young readers, and its clever integration of text and image. Described on the title-page as a 'livre de lecture courante avec 212 gravures instructives pour les leçons de choses et 19 cartes géographiques', the book employs a slim fictional narrative set in 1871 as a framing device for the mediation of a vast amount of information about the geography, history, industry, agriculture, monuments, people, and ways of life of the different regions of France. The title itself suggests a gesture towards Jules Verne's *Le Tour du monde en quatre-vingts jours*, which had achieved enormous popularity when it was published four years earlier and evokes the tradition of the journey made by apprentice craftsmen to learn different working methods.

The plot features two brothers—André, age fourteen and Julien, age seven—who leave their home town of Phalsbourg in Lorraine in secret after the death of their father to seek their only surviving relative, an uncle in Marseilles, in order to have a guardian in France to allow them to continue to claim French citizenship.[30] In obedience to their father's final wish (he dies with the word 'France' on his lips), the journey of André and Julien is thus a quest narrative of a fundamental kind with a strong contemporary relevance, a search not just for family or self-discovery but for identity and nationality. The subtitle *Devoir et Patrie* indicates the text's urgent patriotic agenda, and the two notions are intimately linked throughout. In her preface, Bruno asserts that 'la connaissance de la patrie est le fondement de toute véritable *instruction civique*' and explains her appropriation of the popular travel narrative to stimulate the interest of a child reader: 'Pour frapper son esprit, il faut lui rendre la patrie visible et vivante.'[31] Her use of two fictional child protagonists sets her book firmly in the tradition of the exemplary narrative and the 'leçon de choses', for their experiences and active engagement with the landscape in town and country offer the child reader the vicarious opportunity to 'voir et toucher', to be initiated along with André and Julien into 'la vie pratique et à l'instruction civique en mème temps qu'à la morale'.[32] The book about the great men of France (inventors, scientists, painters, philanthropists, and the like) that Julien is given mirrors the aim of the text itself in showing the pleasure that the brothers derive from learning about the achievements of their fellow countrymen as they visit the places where they lived and worked. In a kind of *mise en abîme*, the words of the woman who gives the book (one of the many kindly people who offer assistance to the boys) reflect the pedagogical agenda at the heart of Bruno's text: 'Lisez-le: il est à votre portée; il y a des histoires et des images qui vous instruiront et vous donneront, à vous aussi, l'envie d'être un jour utile à votre patrie.'[33] It is not just a question of presenting facts, therefore, but, through a sense of identification with both the boys and the great men, of inculcating patriotic pride and the desire to imitate their qualities and contribute to the greatness of France. This strategy links Bruno's work with the exemplary lives genre popular during and after the Revolution, while her description of her work as 'une sorte de morale en action d'un nouveau genre' is an overt gesture of insertion in the tradition of pedagogical texts in its reference to Bérenger's successful *La Morale en action* of 1783.

At first sight, Bruno's text seems to be a straightforward celebration of republican patriotic and lay ideologies, of the promise of scientific progress and capitalistic enterprise, a view apparently confirmed by Bruno's acceptance of the removal of all religious references in Belin's 1906 version in order to conform to the spirit of laicisation after the formal separation of church and state in 1905. However, it has been convincingly argued that it can be seen to reflect a compromise not uncommon at the time between republican homogenising ideology and an acknowledgement of diversity in its portrayal of rural France and local artisan trades and its celebration of the traditional humanistic values of compassion, kindness, generosity, and charitableness.[34] In this respect there are close similarities to the Romantic view of rustic life and to the traditional linking of nature and virtue in children's literature. Similarly, while elements from all the different regions come together in Paris where the boys see regional produce in the market and the sum of French achievement in monuments, shops, museums, libraries and the Grandes Ecoles, this is less an endorsement of centralisation and the supremacy of the capital than a vision of the nation as the culmination of the best of all its different parts.[35] This interpretation is consistent with the narrative strategy employed by Bruno, in which the discrete vignettes of the different regions are like pieces of a jigsaw puzzle, the complete picture of which is made available to André and Julien when they reach Paris.[36]

The role of the illustrations in the text is one of diverse complementarity that recalls earlier didactic works for the young. There are images of single objects with a brief description beneath (an animal, a tree, a shell), reminiscent of the approach taken by Noël-Antoine Pluche in *Le Spectacle de la nature* (1732–50), the Comte de Buffon in *Histoire naturelle* (1749–89), and Antoine-Nicolas Duchesne and Auguste-Savinien Le Blond in *Portefeuille des enfants* (1784–98), and of scenery and natural wonders as in the Chevalier Girard de Propriac's *Merveilles du monde* (1821) or of scenes incorporating a number of features (the workshops of a tanner, potter, carpenter, sculptor, winemaker, and papermaker; a railway station; a farm; a port) like those in Jan Amos Comenius's *Orbis sensualium pictus* (1658) or, indeed, Jean d'Alembert's and Denis Diderot's *Encyclopédie*. Unlike other illustrated fictional narratives, the illustrations do not depict the events of the story itself but represent what the boys see and learn, or reproduce the portraits of the great from Julien's book. In some of the images, nevertheless, two tiny figures carrying bundles on sticks can be discerned to encourage the reader's sense of sharing the travellers' experiences. Even here there is always a double discourse apparent on a didactic level, for just as the factual title of each chapter is accompanied by a moral reflection ('Enfants, la vie entière pourrait être comparée à un voyage où l'on rencontre sans cesse des difficultés nouvelles'), an accompanying illustration—in this instance, an image of four people huddled in a boat on a storm-tossed sea that might be taken to represent the boys, their uncle, and a ship's captain narrowly escaping shipwreck—has a caption beneath it explaining the nature of storms off the northwest coast of France. By offering visual evidence, the images help the young reader make the transition from their own lived experience to the acceptance of knowledge acquired from books.[37] The maps of each region visited allow the reader to follow the brothers' itinerary but also form another step in the transition from knowledge of local detail to a wider picture, from the familiar to the new. This pedagogical process continues for André and Julien, too, for in Paris the horizons of their knowledge are broadened further when they marvel at the exotic animals in the Jardin des Plantes and, later, listen entranced to tales of the colonies.

Although the didactic agenda is uppermost throughout and the characters neither evolve nor share their innermost thoughts with the reader, there is a certain amount of action, and melodramatic or emotional situations are deployed to sustain the reader's interest. The vicissitudes of the boys' journey include being lost in the forest in a fog, nearly trapped in a fire, endangered by a drunken wagon driver, and shipwrecked. However, in a convenient reversal of fortune, their uncle, who has been ruined in a speculation, has his fortune returned, and at the end all the central characters are reunited and resolve to spend their lives together in a manner reminiscent of a novel by Malot or Ségur. This conventional ending is placed in a contemporary context, however, for the sea captain's farm has been destroyed in the war, and the efforts of the new family are invested in restoring it. The role of the text in encouraging participation in the regeneration and reconstruction of postwar France is presented in the words of the boys' uncle: 'Si la guerre a rempli le pays de ruines, c'est à nous, enfants de la France, d'effacer ce deuil par notre travail, et de féconder cette vieille terre française qui n'est jamais ingrate à la main qui la soigne.'[38] To endorse this resolution, the family group is shown six years later in their flourishing farm and the reader is assured that they have all remained faithful to the three watchwords of their lives: 'Devoir, Patrie, Humanité'. The absence of any reference to God or religion in this context is very striking in the context of traditional moral tales for the young. The message that emerges through the boys' experiences is that everything in life, from food and shelter to recreational facilities and public libraries, is provided by the land, the state, or the goodness of the French people. Bruno's original text did contain references to prayers, descriptions of churches, and an awareness of the cultural significance of religion (although references to God were vague), but these were expunged completely in the 1906 version when overtly religious books were banned from schools. There remains, arguably, a quasi-religious aura to the fervent patriotism, as when even the echoes of the hills repeat Julien's shouted 'J'aime la France!' and at the end of the book when the courage and determination of the characters are rewarded with a home and family contentment.[39] An epilogue added in 1906 is set on New Year's Eve 1904, on the occasion of a visit from one of the boys' former benefactors and his son, and brings the scientific information up to date with descriptions of submarines, trams, vaccinations, telephones, the cinema, and the Paris Metro. Perhaps with an eye on the 'Etrennes' market, the text closes with a New Year's wish recited by Julien's little son Jean, in which the qualities of filial piety, family feeling, obedience, diligence, and honesty are lauded and the engagement of even the youngest reader is solicited once more in the communal project of reviving France's fortunes in the assertion that 'ce qui fait la gloire de la patrie, son honneur, sa richesse et sa force, c'est la valeur morale de ses enfants'.[40]

A CONTINUING PATRIOTIC AGENDA

The patriotic agenda in books for the young at this period has been seen as revealing the influence of the historical novels of two writers from Alsace, Emile Erckmann (1822–1890) and Alexandre Chatrian (1826–1890) that were coauthored largely in the 1850s and 1860s under the Second Empire and retained their popularity well into the twentieth century. Indeed, Bruno's choice of Phalsbourg as the home of André and Julien was, allegedly, because 'grâce à Erckmann-Chatrian, la petite forteresse lorraine était devenue, après 1870, familière à tous les français, et le symbole des provinces perdues'.[41] Having begun their literary career with a collection of *Contes fantastiques* (1860) in the manner of E.T.A. Hoffmann, which combined the fantastic and supernatural with local realism, Erckmann and Chatrian embarked upon a series of *Romans nationaux*, the aim of which was to educate readers in the history of their country through a vivid evocation of past events often narrated by ordinary characters who had been firsthand participants and witnesses. Amongst the best known are *Madame Thérèse ou les volontaires de '92* (1863); *Histoire d'un conscrit de 1813* (1864) and its sequel *Waterloo* (1865); *L'Invasion* (1866), which deals with events of 1814; *Le Blocus* (1867); and the four-part *Histoire de la Revolution française racontée par un paysan* (often simply called *Histoire d'un paysan*; 1868–70). Although not written specifically for children, these works nevertheless achieved a wide readership amongst adolescents when they were taken up by Hetzel in 1865 for publication first in *feuilleton* form and subsequently in the Bibliothèque d'éducation et de récréation. These editions featured in school libraries (which had been in place in every public school since 1862) and as school prizes, and were bought or recommended by parents and teachers who had themselves enjoyed the writers' skill in evoking the spirit of the France of the past.[42]

Despite the events of revolution and conflict covered in the *Romans nationaux*, the message preached by Erckmann and Chatrian is not a glorification of war but one that promotes a desire for universal peace and the revolutionary ideals of liberty, equality, and justice. The novels in effect deplore the aggressive conflicts of the Napoleonic era, depicting the horrors of war and its consequences for the poor, although action in defence of the patrie or for justice against social abuses is celebrated. In *Histoire de la Révolution française racontée par un paysan*, for example, a novel that condemns the dictatorship of Napoleon, the differences made to the lives of the peasants by the Revolution after the abuses of the ancien régime are highlighted to present an image of a just conflict in liberating the oppressed. Their evocations of history are not without implications for the present time of the reader. Thus, the criticism of the first Empire suggests, by inference, the authors' views on the state of the nation under the Second. After 1870, the popularity of the novels as educative tools for young readers rested not just upon their historical interest but upon the support they offered to the promotion of the ideals of the Third Republic, which shared Erckmann and Chatrian's faith in progress and the importance of educating the masses. They also helped to keep the memory of Alsace and Lorraine alive with their evocation of the scenery, people, and way of life, evoking not just nostalgia in the portrayal of nature and rural sights and pursuits but also the hope of regaining the lost territory, as extracts chosen for textbooks prior to the First World War exemplify.[43] The inclusion of a poem titled 'Dis-moi! Quel est ton pays?' (from *Histoire d'un sous-maître*, an autobiographical novel of 1871), preceded by a brief history of Alsace in *Le Livre de la patrie* (1883), a reading manual by Gabriel Vicaire, for example, and in other collections of passages intended for memorisation in the classroom, was clearly intended to reinforce in the minds of the novice readers that Alsace-Lorraine was still, if only in a moral sense, French.[44]

The strategy of portraying history 'from below', through the eyes of fictional characters of humble origins, offers the reader an insight into the implications of historical events for ordinary people. The narrative voice in, for example, *Histoire de la Révolution française racontée par un paysan* or *Histoire d'un conscrit de 1813* is thus not that of an historian, but of a participant in history. The detailed narration of their experiences—by a soldier, a peasant, an artisan, or a teacher in a rural school—that replicates the oral tradition of one generation transmitting knowledge to another in straightforward language inserts the reader directly into the period and fleshes out the bare bones of fact derived from history books. This approach implies a subjective viewpoint, of course, but all the protagonists and narrators are shown to be sympathetic and trustworthy, motivated by love for their family, humankind, and country and showing a strong regard for truth and the principles of liberty and justice. Their role inevitably presupposes a greater degree of education and political awareness than that of many of their comrades, although in order to maintain a sense of realism they are not omniscient, and information often has to be supplied from other witnesses.[45]

There are strong female characters too who play an active role in civic life, like the energetic and informed Marguerite in *Histoire de la Révolution française racontée par un paysan*, who sells radical pamphlets and encourages the narrator, Michel, to read and to improve himself. Although the majority of the *Romans nationaux* depict events earlier in the century, more recent history is featured in *Histoire du plébiscite, racontée par un des 7,500,500 Oui* (1872), the story of the consolidation of Louis Napoleon's position as Prince President (shortly to become Emperor) after the coup d'état of December 1851. Erckmann, in particular, was traumatised by the outcome of the Franco-Prussian War, as a result of which he had to leave his birthplace, and the later novels, including *Histoire du plébiscite*, are more bitter in their approach.[46] When approached, however, by English publishers for a book about the events of 1870, his refusal, communicated to Hetzel, demonstrates his sensitivity to the issue: 'Vous pensez bien que j'aurais été honteux de spéculer sur nos malheurs et de repaître les étrangers de nos misères.'[47]

Apart from enjoying a popular following, Erckman and Chatrian were admired by their fellow writers, including George Sand and Jules Verne, and it is clear that they were regarded as highly suitable for young readers. The moral aspect of the novels was evidently deemed to be beyond reproach, for the reissued novels were classified under 'Littérature et morale' in the 1880s by the body responsible for controlling school libraries.[48] Extracts were regularly chosen for inclusion in books used to teach reading in the public elementary schools, which meant that these ideas reached a wide audience of working-class children from an early age. Particularly popular choices were passages depicting school life (as in *Histoire d'un sous-maître*) and the importance of education, which offered young readers an intriguing picture of the life of children in the past and responded to one of the prime preoccupations of the period. The words of Michel Bastien in *Histoire de la Révolution française racontée par un paysan* ('Celui qui ne sait rien, et qui n'a pas le moyen de s'instruire, passe sur la terre comme un pauvre cheval de labour') had as much political and social resonance under the Third Republic as in the period to which they referred.[49] When Hachette took over Hetzel's business in 1914, a number of expurgated versions of their major works were published in the Bibliothèque verte illustrated series for young readers with the result that they became closely associated with juvenile literature. Notably, after the First World War, when Alsace and Lorraine had been returned to France, Erckmann and Chatrian's works were still deemed by educators to exhibit contemporary preoccupations with education, work, temperance, and civic and patriotic duties and it has recently been demonstrated that extracts from their novels are still to be found in school textbooks in the 1990s.[50]

The pacifism of Erckmann and Chatrian was by no means a universal sentiment in reading matter for the young. We have already seen that even in the novels of domestic realism of this period, an element of militarism was apparent as the child characters play at soldiers and chant patriotic sentiments. Hetzel, whose father was from Alsace, contributed to the promotion of active patriotism not just with his editorial comments but with what became most popular fictional work, *Maroussia*, a rewriting of a Ukrainian story by Mme Markowski. This had already been translated into French by Ivan Turgenev, who as an associate of Hetzel, was charged with looking out for books that might interest French readers, but Hetzel in fact rewrote the text to serve his own purpose. First serialised in *Le Temps* in 1875, and then specifically for young readers in the *Magasin d'éducation et de récréation*, it tells the story of a ten-year-old, sweet-faced Ukrainian girl who acts as guide to a Cossack, a champion of Ukrainian independence, in his mission across enemy lines. She accompanies him through battles in deep snow and storms, displaying courage and a dogged determination in protecting him, and eventually is herself shot as she seeks to warn a group of soldiers hidden in a wood of an imminent ambush, her tragic death saving the lives of many others. Hetzel claimed that it was his favourite work and that the story of his 'Maroussia alsacienne', 'une petite Jeanne d'Arc enfantine' would be 'compris par tous les coeurs dans lesquels vit l'amour de la Patrie'. In response to a reader who wrote to him asking that Maroussia should not be allowed to die, Hetzel offered in print his view of the beauty of dying for one's country, an honour open even to the young: 'Est-ce que ce n'est pas l'honneur de l'humanité que les petits et les petites puissent être des grands par les belles actions qu'ils peuvent faire et par les grands exemples qu'ils peuvent donner?'[51] It is striking that much of the language used and the sentiments promoted at this time are very similar to those employed in books for the young during the Revolutionary period.[52] The success of this text can be judged by Latzarus's description in 1924 of the effect on her of reading *Maroussia* as a child: 'Petite Maroussia! les larmes que nous avons versées sur toi, nous, les enfants des bannis, sont de celles qui laissent au coeur, avec la haine de l'envahisseur, le désir fou des justes revanches.'[53]

The values of *travail, famille, patrie* that underpinned the ideology of the Third Republic were manifested in a rather different way in the works of Edmond About (1828–85), a dramatist, satirical novelist, polemical journalist, and founder of *Le Dix-neuvième siècle*. Several of his novels were published by Hachette in the Bibliothèque des écoles et des familles series, and his *Le Roman d'un brave homme* (1880) featured amongst the *livres de prix* of the Republic for decades. The critical view of modern Greece of his 1854 essay, *La Grèce contemporaine*, also informed *Le Roi des montagnes* (1857), a satirical portrait of the country with much picturesque detail, in which a young German herbalist sent to study the local flora in Greece finds himself kidnapped, together with the two Englishwomen he is accompanying, by the infamous bandit chief Hadgi-Stavros. The novel satirises the power and prestige enjoyed by this outlaw, a former hero of the War of Independence, and during their prolonged stay the hostages are surprised by his courtesy and hospitality and by the scale of his highly organised enterprise, which he runs as a limited company. There are many humorous scenes: Hadgi-Stavros is first seen dictating a letter to his daughter encouraging her to apply herself in her studies and discussing the arrangements he has made to supply her with books and a piano, and one to his bank in London about his investments. There is some drama in the protagonists' attempts to escape, but the main thrust of the book is an amusing, if cynical, satire on tourism, the political situation in Greece, the different nationalities involved, and human nature as a whole. The plot of *L'Homme à l'oreille cassée* (1862), perhaps About's best-known work, is a bizarre mixture of the *fantastique*, scientific improbabilities, historical reflection, and melodrama. Léon Renault, a young civil engineer, returns from working in the Russian mines with, amongst his souvenirs, the desiccated body of a French soldier, mummified after nearly freezing to death in an experiment by a famous scientist in 1813. After much debate about the ethics of resurrecting him, the soldier Fougas is brought back to life in a complicated procedure of rehydration and proceeds to tell his life story as a war hero and spy for Napoleon. Understandably loath to believe that he is now in 1859 and that Napoleon is dead (his first words are 'Vive l'Empereur!'), he is dismayed and distressed to hear the résumé of French history in the intervening years. He believes that his failure to deliver a message to a French general before he was captured led to the defeat of the French army and that history would have been different if he had survived. The mystery of the fascination that his mummified body had exerted over Léon's fiancée Clémentine, who is moved to inexplicable and hysterical sobs when she first sees him, is gradually unravelled when Fougas talks of a child conceived by his lover—also named Clémentine—just before his capture, and it transpires that he is this younger Clémentine's grandfather. The juxtaposition of scientific discourse, suspense, horror (Clémentine is distraught when Léon accidentally breaks off a bit of the mummy's ear), prophetic dreams, and emotional revelations make this novel an intriguing blend of genres. Perhaps surprisingly, it is listed on the current Ricochet children's literature website as suitable for readers ages twelve and upwards.

Around the turn of the century, the patriotic sentiments in works for young readers took a different direction in the adventure novels of Capitaine Danrit (pseudonym of Colonel Emile-Cyprien Driant, 1855–1916).[54] Although, as in Verne's novels, Danrit's settings depict different parts of the globe and are concerned with questions of colonisation and empire, the main thrust of his plots is a militaristic one, glorifying the French army and depicting battles against enemies both old and new. For Danrit, the interest in technological marvels is subordinate to the role they might play in support of patriotic idealism. His portrayal of army manoeuvres, military strategies, and the potential of weapons (including those of mass destruction like poisoned gas) bring together both detailed technical information and descriptions of brave and patriotic deeds by his protagonists. In novels like *Les Robinsons sous-marins* (1908), *L'Aviateur du Pacifique* (1909), and *Les Robinsons souterrains* (reissued as *La guerre souterraine*, 1913) he presents a specific military problem, describing in the first of these, for example, the situation faced by two sailors trapped in a submersible craft that is sunk by enemy action and their struggle to save themselves and their vessel. Writing at a time when much of the world had already been colonised and tensions between the great powers were simmering, Danrit presents a vision of a world where an inevitable cataclysm is on the horizon. His attempts to alert readers to this situation resulted in descriptions of dangers of which he believed much of society was unaware and in predictions of conflict in all directions: with Britain in *La Guerre fatale. France-Angleterre* (1902–3), with Germany in *La Guerre de demain* (1889–93, in six volumes), and with new menaces from the colonised world that represented a threat to French culture and way of life in *La Guerre au XXe siècle. L'Invasion noire* (1894) and *L'Invasion jaune* (1909). The fear of invasion and of the threat of the 'other' was a common obsession of the period and a consequence of colonial expansion that generated awareness of the size, and hence potential military might, of other continents and was exacerbated by the continuing preoccupation with the relative decline of France after 1870 when contrasted with other countries in Europe.[55] The need to be ready to defend France against potential enemy action and a fundamental distrust, even of France's allies, underpin all the narratives. In *L'Invasion jaune*, the *entente cordiale* with Britain is blamed for, amongst other moral disasters, the weakening of the power of the army by the controversy surrounding the court martial of Alfred Dreyfus and the blatant miscarriage of justice.

In the three texts of the series *Une famille de soldats* (1898–1901), Danrit offers a history of nineteenth-century French military action through the different generations of 1792–1830, 1830–70, and 1870–86, highlighting the Battle of Valmy, the campaign in Algeria, and post-1870 colonial conquests. His admiration for the great figures of French history, especially Napoleon, is apparent in the second of the series, *Filleuls de Napoléon* (1900), while *Evasion d'empereur* (1904) depicts a plot to save Napoleon from Saint Helena by submarine. Danrit's conviction that the French republic was failing to support its army is evident in his attempts through his works to encourage the young to see a military career as a glorious one and the manifestation of true patriotism. The pedagogical aspect of his works is, therefore, predicated upon a far narrower and more specifically political agenda than that of many of his contemporaries. Having predicted the First World War in *La Guerre de demain*, it is tragically ironic that Danrit himself was to be killed at Verdun in 1916.

Finally, a less inflammatory but nevertheless still energetically patriotic approach appears at the turn of the century in the works of Pierre Maël, many of which were published by Flammarion, Hachette, and Mame with the market of *livres d'étrennes* or *livres de prix* in mind. The name Maël was in fact a pen name used by Charles Vincent (1851–1920) and Charles Causse (1862–1905), under which they specialised in books for the young of both sexes, producing a series of works ranging from domestic realism to adventure stories. The former, with titles like *Fleur de France* (1890), *Seulette* (1899), *Mademoiselle Pompon* (1902), and *Poucette* (1910), exhibited strongly traditional family values based on a markedly Catholic morality. Maël also catered for the taste for stories about abandoned children (*La Lande aux loups*, 1912) and the hardships of working children (*La Marmotte*, 1925, which describes the life of a young chimney sweep). Their versatility extended to travel adventure (*Une Française au Pôle Nord*, 1893), seafaring tales (*L'Alcyone*, 1889; *Les Pilleurs d'épaves. Moeurs maritimes*, 1891; *Le Sous-marin 'Le Vengeur'*, 1902) and a Robinsonnade designed to appeal to both boys and girls, *Robinson et Robinsonne* (1895). The popularity of the adventure novels with both educators and parents as well as the young recipients of the books themselves rested upon the blend of lively, dramatic, imaginative plots and—unlike many of the contemporary novels of adventure—an irreproachable moral tone. Maël's novels are not concerned with scientific or military information but with promoting a clear-cut patriotic agenda. While Maël's novels do not glorify war as Danrit does, conflicts between nations often form the background and are the catalyst for the heroes' adventures. The action of *Un Mousse de Surcouf*

(1901), for example, is set against a struggle with the English; *Blanche contre jaunes* (1904) is set in the war between Russia and Japan; and *Terre des fauves* (1894) features conflict in a colonial setting. The plots encapsulate a heroism based on courage, initiative, and self-sacrifice in the service of one's country, but are distinguished from the majority of adventure stories by their comparative lack of bloody scenes of brutality and slaughter, elsewhere described with so much relish. There is a marked sobriety to the descriptions of conflict and a moral seriousness in Maël's narratives rather than the exaggerated, tongue-in-check excess characteristic of much of the genre, and the characters are inspirational models of decency, bravery, and a devotion to family and country rather than performers of superhuman feats simply to amaze and entertain. The protagonists are thus not flamboyant adventurers or mercenaries seeking adventure or fulfilling bets but, for the most part, brave, intelligent, and upright young army officers. These qualities must have contributed to a large extent to their acceptability and popularity in lists of books suitable for gifts or prizes. It seems that Maël was regarded as one of the 'auteurs phares' of the Hachette list at the turn of the century and, although adaptations were still in print in the 1950s, their close association with the editorial policies concerning a pedagogical dimension that governed the production of *livres de prix* may account for the failure of Maël's works to gain lasting success, unlike those of Jules Verne.[56]

The popularity at the beginning of the twentieth century of both Maël's novels of domestic realism and the adventure stories exemplifies the survival of both these genres after 1900. Indeed, many of the texts by the writers discussed in these first three chapters continued to enjoy new editions, albeit often in abridged or expurgated form, for many decades. The next two chapters look at the development of literature for young readers in the first half of the twentieth century, which, after the explosion of books for the young in what is often seen as the 'golden age' of children's literature, is often judged to be a period of comparative stagnation exacerbated by the two world wars and an invasion of reading material from abroad that threatened to stifle homegrown creativity. The new century also, conversely, saw developments that changed the face of children's literature.

5

THE EARLY TWENTIETH CENTURY

The output of juvenile literature in the first decades of the twentieth century is often seen as repetitive, insipid, and mediocre. Several factors have been adduced as responsible for the decline in quality in children's books after 1890.[1] The developments in printing techniques meant that larger print runs were capable of being produced more cheaply, and the publication of children's books had become a significant profit-making enterprise. Such commercial developments did not, however, contribute to the quality of the product; Marc Soriano writes that 'l'édition est submergée par une littérature de pure consommation, fade, larmoyante ou invraisemblable et qui, par surcroît, semble toujours coulée sur le même moule'.[2] Isabelle Jan goes further, noting, 'La littérature des années 1930 à 1960, prise dans son ensemble, est assez médiocre, et si elle se trouve dévalorisée, c'est à juste titre.'[3] The shortage of good-quality materials, resources, and indeed a labour force during the First World War inevitably impacted upon the material quality of books, which with the publishers Hachette and Hetzel had reached extremely high standards in the nineteenth century. Moreover, the increase in literacy consequent upon the Ferry laws on education had produced a much enlarged reading public, many of whom had had little or no access to or experience of the culture of the past and were perceived by publishers as being relatively undemanding (and consequently easier to please). There was also, of course, a greater demand for reading material that was cheap to buy. Although a number of collections with titles like Bibliothèque du Petit Français (A. Colin) or Bibliothèque des Ecoles et des Familles (Hachette) appeared around the turn of the century to cater for these new generations of readers, few of the writers who contributed to them achieved anything like the stature of their predecessors.[4]

Numerous magazines also appeared during this period, although their lives were often short. The most significant developments in reading material for the young were, however, the shift in emphasis from text to image and the rise of the illustrated paper and comic book, which soon came to dominate the market. With this innovation the artistic and educational formulas that had become entrenched in the expectations of the middle-class purchasers of children's books were set to change dramatically.[5] The 1920s and 1930s saw the beginnings of changes that heralded a more fertile and innovative period in the production of reading material for the young. However, production was once more interrupted by the Second World War, in which the material problems and difficulties in distribution were exacerbated by the presence of the German occupying forces in half of the country, including Paris, and the consequent requisitioning or displacement of some publishing firms.[6] This chapter looks first at some examples of the narrative genres surviving into the twentieth century, the measures taken to revive children's literature with the development of new publishing strategies and new forms of narrative, and the impact of the two world wars on the development of children's books. Chapter 6 will consider the role taken by the image in books for the young, including the rise of the picture book, the illustrated paper, and the *bande dessinée* in the twentieth century.

FIRST-HAND TESTIMONIES

We have interesting evidence from two avid young readers of the time, Jean-Paul Sartre (born in 1905) and Simone de Beauvoir (born in 1908) of the range of works to which they had access and found pleasure in reading. Sartre, in *Les Mots* (1964), recalls how he learnt to read through Hector Malot's *Sans famille* and graduated from 'les petits livres roses' to fairy tales and then *Les Enfants du capitaine Grant, Le Dernier des Mohicans, Nicholas Nickleby*, and *Les Cinq sous de Lavarède*. He describes his love of Hetzel's volumes of the *Bibliothèque d'éducation et de récréation* ('Je dois à ces boîtes magiques … . mes premières rencontres avec la Beauté'), how he preferred the extravagant tales of Paul d'Ivoi to Jules Verne, and was entranced by the illustrated papers *Cri-Cri* and *L'Epatant*, both of which carried serialised adventure stories.[7] Beauvoir also testifies to a very catholic appetite for reading:

A plat ventre sur la moquette rouge, je lisais Mme de Ségur, Zénaïde Fleuriot, les contes de Perrault, de Grimm, de Mme d'Aulnoy,
du chanoine Schmidt, les albums de Töpffer, Bécassine, les aventures de la famille Fenouillard, celles du sapeur Camember, *Sans
famille*, Jules Verne, Paul d'Ivoi, André Laurie, et la série Livres
roses, édités par Larousse, qui racontaient les légendes de tous les
pays du monde et pendant la guerre des histoires héroïques.[8]

In Beauvoir's case, it is interesting to note that her choice of reading
matter embraced a wide range of genres and was not restricted to material explicitly targeting girls.

SURVIVORS AND IMITATORS

Editions of many of the works of the writers discussed in the previous
chapters (particularly Zénaïde Fleuriot, Hector Malot, the comtesse de
Ségur, and Jules Verne) were still in print in the first decades of the new
century, and children's books continued to be dominated by the two
main genres of adventure and family stories. The writers still publishing
new works in the first decades, like Capitaine Danrit and Pierre Maël,
were not, however, in the same league as their predecessors, despite
their adherence to established formulas, and their works have not stood
the test of time; they are no longer in print, and therefore are unlikely
to be read widely by young readers today. Similarly, Hachette continued to publish new edifying novels in the Bibliothèque rose illustrée
collection, but they are generally judged to be monotonous and unin-
teresting compared with the colourful works of the comtesse de Ségur
and other early exponents of the family novel.[9] These, too, are rarely
reissued in modern editions and tend to be known only to researchers
into the period. A catalogue for 1912, for example, lists works by Mlle
Chabrier-Rieder (*Une enfant terrible* and *Les Epreuves de Charlotte*);
Mme de Witt (*Enfants et parents* and *Un nid*), Mme Chéron de Bruyère
(*Petite nièce* and *Les Idées de Jacqueline*), and Mme Cazin (*Histoire d'un
pauvre petit* and *Les orphelins bernois*) that suggest a social and moral
ethos and a literary approach not very different from those of some
thirty or forty years earlier. The sentimentalised image of the child and
the family persisted alongside narratives portraying a transgressive
child whom the reader is encouraged not to emulate. Although plots
were translated into a more contemporary world and the scope of the
fictional children's experiences was enlarged to an extent, this realism
still served a familiar edifying agenda. Despite the increased awareness
of, and interest in, developments in child psychology at the turn of the

century, publishers and writers were caught between, on the one hand, appealing to the tastes and inclinations of young readers and portraying realistic and admirable characters, and, on the other, maintaining a responsible stance that would satisfy parents by not violating acceptable social and moral values.[10]

APPROPRIATIONS

Two books published before the outbreak of the First World War that are now often associated with classics of juvenile literature, although neither were initially specifically addressed to children, are Louis Pergaud's *La Guerre des boutons* (1912) and *Le Grand Meaulnes* (1913) by Alain-Fournier (Henri Alban Fournier). In the preface to *La Guerre des boutons*, subtitled *Roman de ma douzième année*, Pergaud asserts that the book 'ne s'adresse ni aux petits enfants, ni aux jeunes pucelles' and that in portraying a period of 'notre vie enthousiaste et brutale de vigoureux sauvageons dans ce qu'elle eut de franc et d'héroïque, c'est-à-dire libérée des hypocrisies de la famille et de l'école', he sought to create 'un livre sain, qui fût à la fois gaulois, épique et rabelaisien'.[11] The novel depicts the epic gang warfare between children in neighbouring villages in a rural area. Their activities mimic the realities of war except that they only cut buttons from their opponents' clothes as booty. Although regarded as shocking because of its consistent employment of vivid, colloquial language, Pergaud's novel was widely translated and made into a film in 1962. *Le Grand Meaulnes*, the only completed novel of Alain-Fournier, who like Pergaud died fighting in the First World War, portrays the pains and pleasures of growing up, hero worship, and first love in a first-person retrospective narrative that tantalises the reader with withheld information, flashbacks, and a view of events coloured by the narrator's emotional and vicarious involvement with his friend's adventures. The calm existence of the timid and overprotected François Seurel, the son of a provincial schoolmaster, is transformed by the arrival of the more mature and dynamic August in Meaulnes, whose chance encounter with Yvonne, a beautiful young girl at a *fête étrange* in a château, during an unplanned escapade triggers a quest that comes to dominate their thoughts and days. After a number of intricate misunderstandings and misadventures, complicated by the melodramatic actions of Yvonne's brother Frantz, François is left to pick up the pieces when Meaulnes rejects a happy ending to embark on a new quest to find Frantz leaving his new wife after their wedding night. This poignant story of complex adolescent emotions, longing, doomed love, and bereavement—inspired by Alain-Fournier's own torment over a brief meeting with a young woman with whom he fell instantly in love—did not specifically target young readers, but it, too, has been appropriated by them (and has featured as a set text for A-level examinations in Britain, to this author's certain knowledge).

THE IMPACT OF THE FIRST WORLD WAR

It has been estimated that there was a dramatic fall in the production of children's books during the First World War. Whereas in 1912 some 331 titles were published, this had more than halved by 1914 (to 144); in 1915 only sixty-nine titles, including reissues of older texts, appeared, and the number was reduced to thirty-nine by 1918. Fifteen publishing houses specialising in books for the young had disappeared in 1914 alone. The war loomed large in children's books and magazines, however. Although patriotic exhortations were most noticeable in the illustrated papers, the *Catalogue des livres d'étrennes* for December 1916 revealed that the war was either the subject of, or the background to, nearly all the new titles on offer.[12] Just as during and after the French Revolution the different genres of children's books were manipulated to promote Republican values, so once again alphabet books, *contes*, songs, exemplary biographies, and moral tales were appropriated to serve the war effort. Thus, the *Alphabet de la grande guerre 1914-1916. Pour les enfants de nos soldats* (1916) encouraged even the very young to feel involved in the struggle, and in Emile Moselly's intensely patriotic *Contes de guerre pour Jean-Pierre* (1918), the revised tale of 'L'Ogre et le Petit Poucet' represents the war in images that would already be familiar to most child readers, recounting that 'il y avait dans un pays du Nord un ogre très méchant. Il commandait à des légions de sujets dociles, travailleurs, têtus et soumis.'[13] The traditional image of Germany as the enemy of France easily translated into such stereotyped figures of aggression and brutality. Stories of exemplary lives, which were popular during and after the Revolution, came back into fashion, featuring child soldiers and martyrs in the uniform of the characteristic First World War soldier, the *poilu*, in such texts as *Petits héros de la grande guerre* (1918) by J. Jacquin and A. Fabre and Joachim Renez's *Le Petit poilu* (1918). The express aim of Larousse's *Livres roses* series was to 'mettre à la portée des petits les actes de bravoure et les glorieux exploits de nos vaillants soldats et de nos héroïques alliés'.[14] The immense national rejoicing at the return of Alsace and Lorraine after the war inevitably found its way into children's publications, as had their loss nearly a half century earlier. Jean-Jacques Waltz's *Histoire d'Alsace racontée aux petits enfants d'Alsace et de France par l'Oncle Hansi* (1913), which depicted the author reading his book to a group of children in the national costume of Alsace while being watched by some disapproving German tourists dressed in green, was followed in 1919 by his *L'Alsace heureuse, la grande pitié du pays d'Alsace et son grand bonheur racontés aux petits enfants par l'Oncle Hansi avec quelques images tristes et beaucoup d'images gaies.*[15] In the latter, Alsace was depicted as 'la belle au bois dormant' awakened by the forces of liberation.[16] Animals, too, were recruited to play their part in the struggle against evil in order to help make events accessible to a young reader, as in Benjamin Rabier's *Flambeau, chien de guerre* (1916), which will be discussed in chapter 6, and *Les Mémoires d'un rat racontés aux enfants* (1924) by Pierre Chaine, which included the tantalising section 'Comment j'ai défendu la ville de Verdun'.[17]

THE REVIVAL OF THE BOOK TRADE

After the war, children were seen as crucial instruments of future reconstruction, and there was an unprecedented international interest in child development on the part of psychologists, paediatricians, sociologists, and teachers.[18] The training of children to fulfil their role as builders of the new Europe had to begin at a very early stage. The exponents of L'Education Nouvelle, a system proposed by a group of like-minded individuals including Maria Montessori, advocated in the wake of psychological and sociological studies of the child a new, enlightened method of teaching that differed radically from traditional methods. The pedagogical premises of this system were to respect the child's individuality and autonomy and encourage spontaneity in learning rather than to subject the child to constant constraints and repressive authority. The role of educators was to furnish the materials for children's physical, intellectual, and moral development and allow them to grow through personal experience while encouraging a sense of personal responsibility, self-government, and a social conscience. Children's literature had, of course, an important part to play in reflecting these new ideas, and at this time also became recognised as a legitimate subject for study.[19] The most important exponent of L'Education nouvelle in France was Paul Faucher, whose Père Castor albums are discussed in chapter 6, but the efforts made to revive children's books and habits of reading in the interwar years all responded to the desire for regeneration and for a radical departure from previous approaches to writing for the young. Access to children's books was no longer seen as the prerogative of a privileged minority but as the right of every child.

Change was not immediate, however, and traditional forms of narrative and established texts continued to be produced to ensure sales. In the 1930s, Hachette's Bibliothèque rose illustrée, for example, now under the direction of Magdeleine du Genestoux, herself an author (see below), produced editions of the novels of the Comtesse de Ségur with new illustrations and jacket covers by the contemporary artist André Pécoud and, for the Nouvelle collection illustrée, illustrations by Félix Lorieux; these placed the settings firmly in contemporary times. In both the 1920s and 1930s, strenuous efforts were made to generate new inspiration and initiatives. New collections were launched by various publishers to feed the high demand for *livres d'étrennes*, and contes and historical tales appeared in luxury editions in response to the cheap, mechanised exploitation of colour in the illustrated magazines. Hachette, for example, having acquired Hetzel's business in 1914, relaunched the Nouvelle Bibliothèque d'éducation et de récréation which later became the Bibliothèque verte in 1924, as well as the Bibliothèque blanche. Such collections, which often included the same texts in different formats and bindings, also answered the marketing needs of publishers, of course, because they stimulated the desire for ownership, and sales and standardisation led to cheaper production.[20] In 1924, as part of the campaign for the reconstruction of countries devastated in the First World War, a significant step was taken in the shape of a gift to the city of Paris from the American Book Committee on Children's Libraries, which funded the establishment of the Bibliothèque de l'Heure Joyeuse.[21] This first specialist children's library was to be run according to a new American model of open access, user-centred public libraries, and encouraged participation by organising reading sessions and exhibitions. Its furniture and environment were child-friendly and offered a space for leisure reading and study that was free and open to all. Inspired by the principles of L'Education nouvelle, the collaboration of readers in the organisation and work of the library was actively sought to encourage children to develop a lifelong interest in books.

In the 1930s established writers were recruited to produce books for young readers. Short stories by Marcel Aymé, Sidonie-Gabrielle Colette, Georges Duhamel, Maurice Genevoix, and François Mauriac appeared in Hartmann's series Les Grands auteurs pour les petits enfants. Although they dealt with themes relating to childhood, they do not always seem to have been written with a child reader in mind. Mauriac's *Le Drôle* (1933), for example, is a conventional moral tale of the taming by a new young governess of a problem child indulged by a weak and besotted father and grandmother. The viewpoints are resolutely adult ones, however; the suspicions of the villagers that she is brutalising the boy and starving him to death are juxtaposed to the truth presented from the standpoint of the governess. She reconciles the impossibly egoistic child to her presence by tending his wounded dog and exploits his liking for music to impose order and discipline and a balance between work and play in his life. The satirical portrait of the adult characters reveals the writer more used to dissecting human nature and social manners for adult readers, and, of course, the theme of the difficult relationship between child and parents appears elsewhere in Mauriac's work.[22] Children and family life also feature regularly in Duhamel's work, but in *Les Plaisirs et les Jeux* (1922), although portraying the small child's daily life, the focus is on the father's delight in watching and analysing his son's movements, gestures, and changing facial expressions. To encourage authors to participate in the project of renewal, prestigious literary prizes, including the Prix Jeunesse and Hachette's Prix Jules Verne were set up in the 1930s and new formats and new topics, as well as new authors, were actively sought. Major players in initiatives at this time were Hachette, Larousse, Mame, and Nathan.[23] The greatest expansion and experimentation in this period were achieved in picture books, illustrated magazines, and comics (discussed in chapter 6), but prose fiction also began to explore new images of children, departing from the traditional middle-class settings to portray children of different social classes and nations in order to appeal to and reflect the concerns of the new wider audience. On the eve of the Second World War children's literature was again flourishing, with some forty publishers producing around five hundred titles, and was trying, as Mathilde Leriche, librarian of the Bibliothèque de l'Heure Joyeuse remarked in an essay of 1939, to free itself from the stranglehold of the past.[24] The next section considers some of the products of this interwar period.

MAGDELEINE DU GENESTOUX: BREATHING NEW LIFE INTO OLD FORMULAS

The novels by one of the better-known names from the second quarter of the century, Magdeleine du Genestoux (d. 1942) demonstrate both the continuation of narrative elements characteristic of the Bibliothèque rose tradition and the introduction of nuances and references that transplant these elements into a more modern context. The titles of Genestoux's works published by Hachette in the late 1920s and 1930s are conventional enough: *Les Vacances de la famille Plumet* (1928),

Mademoiselle Trouble-fête (1930), *Une Petite vaniteuse* (1931), and *La Famille Hurluberlu* (1932). The focus is on a child or children and relationships within a family context, with carefully reproduced details of daily life and perceptive insights into child psychology and questions of upbringing. Parents are not always shown in a positive light, however, signifying the retreat of unquestioned parental authority, and in some of the novels the child characters are liberated from adult constaints and given an unusual degree of autonomy and agency. There is also often an element of rackety mayhem that, while not condoned, imparts an air of energy and life to the narrative. In *Pompon et Pomponettte* (1934), for example, we find a 'home alone' scenario in which a ten-year-old boy and his younger sister are left with an elderly, incompetent female cousin, nicknamed Ficelle, by their work-obsessed father, a scientist at the Institut Pasteur, while he goes on a trip to India. The children are remarkably self-sufficient, enjoying a freedom to come and go as they please that was rare in children's books hitherto. (The sense of them being older than they are said to be is increased by the rather terse black-and-white sketches by Pécoud that accompany the text.) Pomponette, unlike her more responsible brother Pompon, is uninhibited, undisciplined, emotional, malicious, and demanding, and spends her days tending stray cats and dogs in the garden of their apartment. There is criticism, both implicit and explicit through the views of other characters, of their father's neglect, and Pomponette's lies and outbursts are seen as attention-seeking and a need for love and care. Her attempts to make friends with a neighbouring family of four well-brought-up boys are greeted initially with reservation by their mother, although the boys delight in her company and the comparative liberty of her chaotic household. The scene (more reminiscent of the freedom and fun in Richmal Crompton's *Just William* books than of a traditional French family story) in which the elaborate tea laid on by Pomponette ends in gleeful havoc with her pet dog and monkey running riot must have proved provocative and exhilarating reading. The slender plot hinges upon a missing document containing an important scientific formula, and the children's attempts to discover whether this has been stolen or is simply a victim of their father's absentmindedness. It is Pomponette's noble gesture in drawing the blame upon herself in order to protect Ficelle when she is accused of theft by their father's colleague that persuades her neighbouring family of her good heart, and, after the 'thief' (Pomponette's pet monkey Zozo) is unmasked, the children are taken into their household, thus providing them with a surrogate family in which they can find the care, stability, and order that they secretly crave.

Les Exploits d'Hispano, chien terre-neuve (1933, illustrated by Félix Lorioux), which exploits the contemporary popularity of animal stories, is a mixture of the domestic and the adventure genres. Although the novel draws on familiar themes and narrative contrivances, references to telegrams, telephones, planes, guns, tennis, and cigarettes place it firmly in the interwar context. The plot is relatively complex and features a large cast of characters of different nationalities. The child characters Benoît (age ten) and Anne (age eight) Lenoir are more foregrounded than in the generality of late-nineteenth-century adventure stories and are transported into a strange and dangerous outside world when the liner in which they are travelling to join their father in Saigon catches fire and sinks in the Red Sea. The children, the slightly comic but devoted old soldier and family retainer Séraphin Pédoncule, and the equally loyal dog Hispano are washed ashore, but their mother is believed to have drowned. The central episodes in which the shipwrecked group find themselves in a Somali camp are in the tradition of the *Robinsonnade* and are reminiscent of a similar sequence in the Comtesse de Ségur's *Les Vacances*, but their link with the outside world is soon reestablished as they are conducted to a railway station three days' trek across the desert, where they catch a train to Djibouti. The plot is driven by the search for news of their mother, and the second half of the novel brings to the fore the friendship between Benoît and Pierre, a boy his own age whose wealthy shipowning father neglects him emotionally but allows him apparently limitless funds and freedom. Indeed, Pierre's self-confidence in dealing with people in different situations and his stock of cash and cigarettes makes the reader wonder at times whether the author has forgotten his supposed age. Like Vernian heroes, Benoît and Pierre embark together, accompanied by Hispano, for the shores of Arabia on a ship rather improbably under Pierre's command, and after many mysterious and dangerous encounters, eventually rescue Mme Lenoir from unscrupulous men who hope to gain a substantial reward for saving her. The racism inherent in most examples of the adventure story genre is slightly modified here: the Somalis are depicted warmly as handsome, brave, and kind although they are also patronised occasionally (they are thrilled to be addressed by a French naval commander), but the black assistant station master is ridiculed for his pomposity and violent rages while the Arabs are seen as sinister and conniving. Neither Pierre—nor it seems, the author—see anything wrong in teasing the little Arab girl Aïcha, who has cared for Mme Lenoir in her captivity, as Pierre promises to buy her as his slave in order to free her from her brutal existence. Despite the foregrounding of Hispano in the novel's title, the dog's active involvement in affairs other than as companion and guard is sporadic: he saves Anne from the overturned lifeboat and is instrumental in discovering where Mme Lenoir is hidden. Occasionally the reader is given Hispano's viewpoint, as when, for example, he chooses to join the boys in their search, swimming out to the departing ship, but this is not consistently exploited. The conclusion is a conventional one, with all the family reunited and rewards distributed, while the theme of informal adoption found repeatedly in Ségur's novels is reiterated here as Pierre and Aïcha are offered a home in France with their friends and a more modern ordering of relationships is established as Séraphin is promoted from servant to family friend and Aïcha from slave to lady's companion.

These novels give some idea of Genestoux's attempts to breathe new life into an old formula and signal the emergence of a new kind of child character with greater mobility and independence and a more active role in energetic plots. At the same time, other writers were exploring different approaches to a child-centred literature that would both entertain a child readership and offer food for reflection.

ADVENTURES UNDERGROUND

Although patriotic triumphalism continued to appear for some time in works such as *La Grande guerre racontée aux enfants par un poilu* (1920) by N. Sevestre, a different form of discourse promoted tolerance and understanding. *Patapoufs et Filifers*, by André Maurois (1885–1967) published in 1930, uses fantasy to satirise chauvinism and jingoistic rhetoric in order to encourage young readers to think about the futility of war. The text suggests comparisons with Lewis Carroll's *Alice's Adventures in Wonderland* (1865) but here there is a clear political edge. When two brothers, Edmond and Thierry (one fat and the other thin), explore a deep crevice between the rocks in the forest of Fontainebleau, they enter a strange underground world that mirrors their own physical difference, divided as it is between the two races of the Patapoufs and the Filifers. After their descent on an escalator from a brightly lit hall reminiscent of the Paris Metro, they find themselves before an underground sea under a sky lit by balloons filled with blue fluorescent gas (an intertextual gesture, perhaps, to Jules Verne's *Voyage au centre de la terre*). They are then, like Alice, swept along by circumstances, scrutinised by officials, and sent to different countries according to their shape and size. In the description of the Patapoufs and the Filifers and their environments and habits, which are revealed in parallel chapters and a bewildering array of puns, Maurois's imagination and comic linguistic inventiveness run riot. Everything in the Patapouf kingdom reflects the inhabitants' roundness: the buildings are short and squat with curved walls and domes, the trains and ships are broad and bulging, and the air is filled with balloons. Food and drink are everywhere and meals are taken every hour on the hour, followed by a quarter of an hour's rest. The people, ruled by Obésapouf XXXII, are peaceable, easygoing, and cheerful. In the Republic of the Filifers, under Président Rugifer, the buildings are tall, thin towers, their vehicles are long and narrow, and the people are abstemious and energetic, obsessed with time and accuracy and, unlike the Patapoufs, envious, ambitious, and power hungry. The line drawings by Jean Bruller, founder of the Editions de Minuit and author, under the name of Vercors, of the famous novel of the Occupation, *Le Silence de la mer* (1942), establish the 'reality' of the underground world with maps and complement and extend the central conceit of the novel in their parallel and contrasting comic representations of Patapouf and Filifer cities, homes, families, games, food, and armies.[25] The two races have a long-standing history of conflict crystallised in their current dispute over whether an island in the gulf between the two countries should be called Patafer or Filipouf, a covert reference perhaps to Alsace and Lorraine.[26] Nevertheless, like the brothers, who are always fighting but are mutually dependent, the Patapoufs and the Filifers depend on trade with each other to satisfy their needs. Edmond and Thierry, appointed through their status of *Surfaciens* as secretaries to the respective rulers of their adoptive nations, soon find themselves reluctant enemies, are exposed to diametrically opposed, chauvinistic rhetoric, and participate in the great peace conference that ends, predictably, in disaster. After the catastrophe of war in which the Patafoufs are defeated and their country annexed, the boys witness the gradual and unexpected influence of the vanquished over the victor as Patapouf habits are assimilated and the Filifers start to relax and indulge themselves. Through mediation and promptings, the boys participate actively in the process of reconciliation and the construction of the Royaumes Unis du Sous-Sol, and acquire something like heroic status (the final illustration shows a monument erected in their honour). The story ends with a return to the surface, where the boys discover that they have only been away for an hour. Although exuberantly humorous, the narrative conforms both to the narrative of initiation and to the katabatic tradition (which involves a visit to the underworld in the quest for knowledge, derived from Homer and Virgil) as reworked in François Fenélon's *Les Aventures de Télémaque* and Carroll's *Alice's Adventures in Wonderland*. Here, the boys' journey beneath the ground leads to the acquisition of knowledge—in this case, of trench warfare, summit meetings, the sensitivities of relationships between nations, and the atrocities of war. Maurois's portrayal of the absurdity of xenophobia and inherited hatred, of belligerent national pride and the obsession with pure blood mirrored recent events in Europe in a very different way from earlier children's books, and, indeed, was a chilling fore-shadowing of events to come. The final image, of two peoples united in a peaceful coexistence and of the role of children in reconciliation and reconstruction, nevertheless offered a message of tolerance and hope to young readers of the day.

ANOTHER WAR

The impact of the Second World War on children's literature was different from that of the Great War in many crucial respects, not least because of the tangible consequences of the Occupation.[27] After the invasion of 14 June 1940, and during the Occupation, the press, including children's books and papers, was closely monitored and censored by the German authorities. Many publishing houses were forced to relocate outside of Paris, and of those that remained, Gallimard operated with a much reduced list, Hachette was requisitioned, Mame was bombed, and others, like Calmann-Lévy, Nathan, and Offenstadt (the publisher of a large number of illustrated magazines) were 'Aryanised'. As in the First World War, material resources were scarce and paper rationed, and distribution problems were exacerbated by the division of the country into two zones. Libraries in Paris closed upon the declaration of war, and although the Bibliothèque de l'Heure Joyeuse reopened in October 1940, its purchases of books plummeted.[28] Because of these restrictions, the destruction of the records of many publishing houses, and the incompleteness of official bibliographies from the period it is difficult to assess the state of children's publishing with any accuracy.[29] It seems, however, that the war and the portrayal of conflict were rarely evoked in books and magazines at this time, as it had been so consistently during the First World War, and that publishers played it safe with a mixture of escapist works like fairy tales, animal stories, and traditional Robinsonnades.[30] A major reason for this, apart from the factors outlined above and an understandable desire not to evoke miseries that were being experienced all too vividly, was that in 1914 there was a clear enemy, the traditionally hated Boche (as the French were wont to call the Germans), against whom patriotic sentiment could be mobilised, but after the armistice signed between the Germans and Maréchal Pétain on 22 June 1940 brought into force a policy of collaboration, political and moral issues were less clear. France's perception of its position in the war, its relationship with former allies, and, indeed, of a sense of national identity were further complicated by the activities of the Resistance movement and the broadcasts of General De Gaulle from London.[31] As will be seen in the next chapter, children's reading also came under attack from the Vichy regime, which blamed unhealthy literature, in particular American comics, for undermining the morals of contemporary youth.[32]

ROBERT DESNOS (1900–1945): WORDS AS FREEDOM

The escapist spirit of books for children published during the Second World War is evident in the poet Robert Desnos's collection of verses titled *Trente chantefables à chanter sur n'importe quel air*, published in 1944. Shortly before their publication, Desnos, a member of the Resistance, was arrested by the Gestapo in Paris. He had already written and illustrated some poems for the children of friends and these were, in fact, to be his last, as he died in 1945 after a period spent in concentration camps. A second edition of the *Chantefables*, to which were added thirty unpublished poems titled *Chantefleurs*, was published in 1952 and a complete edition with another twenty *Chantefleurs* appeared in 1955. In a preface to this edition, his wife, Youki Desnos, wrote that 'il me plaît que ce qui reste de cette sinistre époque soit ces belles fleurs et ces paisibles animaux, dédiés avec amour aux enfants, donc à l'avenir'.[33] The poems are for the most part brief snatches of verse for speaking or singing or to serve as an accompaniment to chanting, skipping, clapping, or dancing games. Each poem is based on a flower or animal, evoking in many cases a pastoral idyll that is, as the explicit use of names of rivers and places indicates, the French countryside. Others feature exotic animals like the whale, the alligator, the gnu, or the kangeroo. Surprising juxtapositions create lyrical associations: in one poem, for example, a weathervane and a giraffe are linked by a swallow that visits each in turn as the seasons change. Fables without morals and frequently without much apparent meaning, the poems evoke, variously, moods of melancholy, nostalgia, cheerfulness, and joy through the variety of rhyme schemes and rhythms and the exuberance and musicality of the words. The beauty of the names of flowers is savoured and enhanced by repetition and emphasis, which are brought alive when spoken aloud. Many are pure nonsense verses, the surreal humour deriving as much from the symmetry or the repetition of sounds as from the juxtaposition of elements. 'La fourmi' is an assertion of the delight in fantasy:

Une fourmi de dix-huit mètres
Avec un chapeau sur la tête,
ça n'existe pas, ça n'existe pas.
Une fourmi traînant un char
Plein de pingouins et de canards,
ça n'existe pas, ça n'existe pas.
Une fourmi parlant français,
Parlant latin et javonais,
ça n'existe pas, ça n'existe pas.
Eh! Pourquoi pas?

The poems often end on an exclamation, a question or a punchline to be shouted gleefully or revel in an unsuspected surprise note: in 'Le Pélican', the never ending cycle of nature is evoked as a pelican belonging to the eighteen-year-old capitaine Jonathan lays an egg that hatches a pelican that lays an egg, and so on, until the pattern is disrupted by the matter-of-fact cruelty of 'Cela peut durer pendant très longtemps / Si l'on ne fait pas d'omelette avant'. Occasionally, something of the mood of the time surfaces—for example, in 'Le Myosotis', in which the forget-me-not has lost its memory and with it, its future and its past, and in 'L'Edelweiss', in which the tiny white flower on the slopes of Mont Blanc 'fleurit, beau mystère / Pour la France et Paris'. However, for the most part, the poems are celebrations of the beauty of nature and words and as such have survived and are still known to French children today.

SERGE DALENS (1910–1998) AND THE SCOUT NOVEL

The first French scouting organisations, the Eclaireuses et Eclaireurs de France and the Eclaireuses et Eclaireurs Unionistes de France, for Protestant children, were founded in 1911; the Catholic 'Scouts de France' and 'Guides de France' emerged in 1920 and 1923, respectively. Forbidden in theory under the Occupation and regarded with suspicion by the Germans because their activities could be construed as a kind of military training, the scouting movement was nevertheless approved by the Secrétariat général à la jeunesse in 1942, and the movements united in a federation called le scoutisme français, by which time there were some 115,000 boys involved.[34] The movement generated not only a magazine, Le Boy Scout, which ran from 1913 to 1914, but also inspired a collection aptly named the Signe de Piste, published by Alsatia Colmar in Paris, which produced some two hundred works inspired by the values and activities of scouting between 1936 and 1971, many of which were reissued when the list was subsequently taken over by Hachette. The novels, published in different series for different ages, promoted ethical character development and scouting skills within exciting adventure narratives. Amongst its publications was one of the best-selling novels of the prewar period, Serge Dalens's *Le Bracelet de vermeil* (1937), the first in the Prince Eric series, which encompassed six novels in all. *Le Bracelet de vermeil* was followed by *Le Prince Eric* (1939), *La Mort d'Eric* (1943), and *La Tache de vin* (1947).[35] Two further volumes have appeared subsequently: *Eric le magnifique* (1984) and *Ainsi règna le Prince Eric* (1992), which depict the dramatic events in Eric's life before and after the adventures depicted in the earlier texts and resolve many of the remaining puzzles in the novels. The Prince Eric novels have been reprinted many times in all the Signe de Piste collections, most recently in the new collection Signe de Piste Fleurus, and the first two novels have sold well over a million copies.[36] Dalens described his hero as 'la cristallisation d'un ensemble d'aspirations qui sont le fait de la plupart des adolescents', embodying the values of honour, loyalty, friendship, courage and love of family and country.[37] They were illustrated by Pierre Joubert, and the images depict slim, fair-skinned, clear-eyed, and strong-limbed adolescents in either dramatic situations (galloping on a horse, striking heroic poses in the face of danger) or moments of comradeship and solidarity.

Le Bracelet de vermeil and *La Mort d'Eric*, the first and, in terms of narrative logic, the last of the series, are radically different novels in terms of both content and narrative techniques. *Le Bracelet de vermeil* is a mystery and adventure story with a touch of the gothic that depends to a large extent on elements of scoutisme. Not only are the central characters members of a scout troop, but the adventure plot takes place during a scout camp in the grounds of a mysterious château at Birkenwald in Alsace and exploits and mimics the conventions of the *jeu d'aventure*, a central scouting activity. The *jeu d'aventure* is a group test set up and monitored by the troop leaders and usually involving tracking, hiking, following directions and clues, and outdoor survival. As the name suggests, it provides the participants with the stimulus of an adventure within carefully controlled, and hence relatively safe, parameters and promotes initiative, teamwork, and other life skills. The plot of *Le Bracelet de vermeil* involves both a conventional *jeu d'aventure* and an exciting and sinister real-life adventure that threatens the lives of the central characters and has no such reassuring constraints. The setting of the camping holiday allows for the exemplification of the ethos of the scout troop (loyalty to the leader and fellow scouts, discipline, honesty, a sense of fair play), and the characters are all decent, brave, and clean-cut

boys. The relationship between the two central characters, Christian d'
Ancourt, the son of a Paris surgeon, and the Nordic prince Eric Jan-
sen, a newcomer to the troop, is marked from the start by a strange
sense of foreboding despite their friendly attraction to one another, and
the admittedly improbable plot is based on an assumption that their
meeting is somehow predestined, their fates linked through a family
feud going back to the fifteenth century. A prologue to the story points
towards this by whetting the reader's appetite with a list of deaths and
disappearances of members of the Ancourt family on the same date
every hundred years, and Christian's father's initial reluctance to let
him go away to camp indicates a mystery of which the parents, but not
the adolescents (those most at risk), are aware.

The plot involves secret underground passages and chambers in the
château complete with instruments of torture and old manuscripts and
a race against time to rescue Christian when he falls into a deep dungeon. The central dilemma belongs to Eric, who, having discovered in
the labyrinth beneath the château a manuscript containing details of
the revenge regularly exacted by a member of his family against a member of Christian's, is faced with a decision whether to carry out what he
now understands to be the mission entrusted to him by his father or to
follow his instincts and save his friend. The narrative refuses the anticipated form of closure and increases the suspense, for Eric's unexpected
decision is to keep his promise to his father and abandon Christian,
resolving to die himself if Christian is not rescued. The agony of the
choice leads him to smash the bracelet, the symbol of his servitude to
an ancient vow of revenge that causes him to break his own scout's vows
by not helping someone in need and, for the first time in his life, telling
a lie. However, honour is restored when, after an attempt to kill himself,
he reveals the whereabouts of Christian, and the scouts engage in a real
life-and-death adventure to save him.

La Mort d'Eric, written between 1940 and 1942, is set in the first
half of 1940 and, in this explicit depiction of the horrors of warfare
informed by his own experiences, Dalens takes the extraordinary step
of allowing his young hero to be killed in grim circumstances. In his
'Avertissement' to the first edition in 1943, Dalens explains that while
the first books in the series were written for fourteen-year-olds, this
work is aimed at the seventeen-year-old reader, the age at which Eric
and Christian are engaged as officer cadets in the French army, and
defends the decision not to hide the realities of the situation: 'Je pense
qu'il peut tout comprendre, aussi bien, mieux peut-être, qu'une "grande
personne"—précisement, parce qu'il allie pour un temps très court la
générosité de l'enfant à la vigueur de l'homme. Parce qu'il sait tout ce

qu'on lui cache et n'en dit rien.'[38] Dalens describes this work as a *récit* rather than a novel, since the fictional plot is grafted onto real events and is presented through passages of narration, fragments of Christian's diary, and passages resembling a military logbook.

In following the fortunes of Eric and Christian, who are serving in the same regiment (and both receive citations for bravery), the novel shows how the activities and qualities of the scout troop are readily transposed into the arena of war. The illustrations depict the same beautiful young boys as in the earlier novels, looking far too young for the military uniforms they now wear. Dalens provides a brutally realistic representation of the sights, sounds, and smells of combat in woods and muddy fields, the field hospitals and constant movements on the roads of troops and evacuees, and the frustration and demoralisation of the French soldiers at the decisions of their superiors and the prospect of imminent defeat. Several of Christian's old scouting companions featured in the earlier novels are reported to have been killed and, in the last pages, Eric finds himself lying severely wounded in a ditch, and eventually dies alone waiting for attention in the corridor of a makeshift hospital in Vittel on his eighteenth birthday. The handsome boy prince is buried without a coffin and with just a brief prayer as the armoured troops of the enemy roll into the town, eight days before the armistice accepting the defeat of France is signed. Christian is taken prisoner and the saga comes full circle as, during a forced march, he finds himself spending the night in the château at Birkenwald where he first met Eric.

The intense and impeccably chaste relationship between the two young men is warmly depicted, as is the homosocial camaraderie amongst the soldiers, and the theme of the power of friendship that underpins all Dalens's novels is expanded here in the context of global strife. *La Mort d'Eric*, functioning as an 'eyewitness' account of events leading up to the collapse of France, is a striking and thought-provoking work that deserves to be more widely known. In his 'Avertissement' Dalens underlines the didactic agenda of his text: 'Pour que, songeant à la mort d'Eric, mort obscure, inutile, mais non pas inféconde—au destin de Christian, symbole des prisonniers, ils [les lecteurs] sachent qu'ils doivent rebâtir la France d'aujourd'hui et non la France de demain.' He urges his readers 'crois au travail, à l'intelligence, à la force' and to build their character and their friendships to prepare themselves for the task ahead. They are encouraged to ask questions of their parents and other adults and to demand answers.[39] When *La Mort d'Eric* was published in Germany in 1950, Dalens wrote a special 'Avertissement' that amounts to a plea to a new generation to work together for peace and 'le triomphe final de l'Amour sur la Haine'.[40] In two passages in *La Mort d'Eric*,

Dalens shows young French and German soldiers lying wounded side by side and he alludes to his own friendship with Germans, which have withstood the test of war. Outside of his writing, Dalens worked tirelessly for young people. In his position at the Secrétariat général à la jeunesse, he founded centres for the rehabilitation of young delinquents and, under the Vichy régime, succeeded in saving many young boys from being sent to work on the *Service de Travail Obligatoire* scheme agreed with Germany. His later novels in the trilogy *Les Voleurs—Les Enfants de l'espérance* (1954), *Le Juge avait un fils* (1967), and *Jimmy* (1977)—depict the plight of adolescents in trouble with the law and the lasting effects of delinquency. These novels, which feature a young boy, Jacques, who becomes involved with thieves and finds that he cannot escape from his past even when he is given a second chance, are an early attempt to address this subject in children's literature.

COLETTE VIVIER: SAGAS OF EVERYDAY LIFE

The novels of Colette Vivier (1889–1979) represent a significant move away from the nineteenth-century model of the novel of domestic realism towards the child-centred novels of family life that developed in the latter half of the century. Although her works are like the Comtesse de Ségur's in offering a vivid portrayal of the child protagonist's environment and relationships with parents, siblings, friends, and neighbours, Vivier focuses on working-class settings in the urban environment of Paris. The narrative style is simple and direct, privileging the child protagonist's viewpoint, and characters are revealed through their words and actions. The description of the material world is concrete and minimal. Vivier's novels do not concentrate reality into larger-than-life eccentric characters or melodramatic circumstances, nor indulge in bizarre boisterous farce or corrosive sentimentality like her nineteenth-century predecessors, but present to the reader of the middle of the twentieth century a highly realistic image of the daily concerns of their own lives and the difficulties, both public and private, by which they were beset. Vivier was a member of a Resistance network during the Second World War and *La Maison des quatre vents*, published in 1946, depicts the lives of the occupants of a tenement building in Paris under the German Occupation. The dangers and misery of the situation invade every aspect of the life of the inhabitants: in one family the father of three children is a prisoner of war in Germany; another family is Jewish while their neighbours are pro-Nazi. The implications for everyday existence of constant uncertainty, fear and deprivation, rationing, the presence of soldiers in the streets, and antagonism between neighbours, some of whom seek to exploit the situation for their own gain, are portrayed with an immediacy and freshness of perception. Children are shown to be intimately involved in the moral dilemmas of the time and the dangers to themselves and others of their actions are energetically rehearsed: the child of a collaborator denounces a Jewish family while another takes messages for members of the Resistance.

In *La Porte ouverte* (1954), the continuing vicissitudes of postwar daily life are depicted in the lives of the protagonist Lise, her parents, and her two brothers who all live in a one-room apartment. Food and comforts are sparse, but the novel celebrates the altruism and neighbourliness born of shared circumstances as Lise's mother regularly feeds her daughter's friends, Etiennette, neglected by her older sister who is preoccupied with clothes and romance, and Thérèse, an orphan lodging with an elderly concierge. Although there is a third-person narrator, the narrative positions the reader within the child's viewpoint so that the adults and their actions are seen only from the outside. The children's fluctuating friendships and the minutiae of their lives are perceptively delineated, the plot focussing initially on the rivalry over tickets for the raffle of a gorgeous doll. The self-seeking befriending of Thérèse, the lucky winner, contrasts with her own unselfish gift of the doll to her little sister, from whom she is separated. The children's shared fantasy of living in a tumbledown house glimpsed in the countryside makes their troubles bearable, and Lise's parents are soon equally seduced by the dream of a rural idyll. Having negotiated an exchange with the elderly owner, Lise's father sets about renovating the house with the willing help of local people, and Lise's mother agrees to take in Etiennette, Thérèse, and her sister Alice on a permanent basis. The final image of the extended family and their home in a field of flowers makes this a 'feel good' novel to lighten postwar austerity, but also illustrates the power of kindness, persistence, determination, and hard work in effecting change and building a better future through shared projects. Moreover, the responsibilities that the girls take on in looking after the smaller children, dragging them with them through the dirty streets and on the Metro, and their detailed planning of their ideal house reveal them to be in training to be mothers in a brighter world.

However, it is Vivier's first novel, *La Maison des petits bonheurs* (1939), and for which she won the Prix Jeunesse, that has become her most famous—perhaps because of its very innovative approach and difference from other contemporary fiction. It is written in the form of a diary by the eleven-year-old girl Aline Dupin and documents the events, both trivial and momentous, that constitute daily life over a period of two months in her family's tenement apartment in Paris.

Aline, who has been described as 'l'héroïne la mieux individualisée du roman français conçu pour l'enfance depuis la fin du dix-neuvième siècle', is an energetic and occasionally malicious observer and honest and perceptive in describing her own emotions.[41] The narrative reproduces the thought processes and language of the protagonist without authorial asides or interpretation and adopts an engaging and, for the most part, convincingly childlike register and vocabulary. The language is lively, direct, and conversational, full of digressions, associations of ideas, lists, exclamations, and rhetorical questions. The mood swings constantly from contentment to euphoria to annoyance and short-lived misery and back again in response to situations that acquire an intensity of meaning far beyond their actual significance and loom large to a tender ego. Although Aline appears, like so many fictional diarists, to have the gift of almost total recall of conversations, her interpretation is restricted by her youth and inexperience and the reader is therefore encouraged to look beneath the surface to grasp the dynamics of the relationships within the family and with the extended family of the other occupants of the house. Of course, it is impossible to assert the extent to which a child reader would in fact have identified with Vivier's portrayal of Aline, or indeed would do so today, but the similarity of her style to that of recent, highly successful writers for children is a measure of her innovativeness.

Aline's life is bounded by home and school and a relatively small network of parents, siblings, friends, and neighbours. As in the two novels discussed above, Vivier creates a strong sense of community. In the first diary entry, Aline self-consciously introduces herself and her family with brief factual information of the kind important to a child: the names and ages of herself and her siblings (Estelle, twelve, and Riquet, six and a half); their address; her favourite toys, books (*Sans famille, La Roulotte, David Copperfield*), foods, and dresses; her prowess at school; and the childhood illnesses they have had. Interspersed with these facts are entertaining asides that evoke her personal view of her circumstances and evoke the energy of the child's mind in pursuing a kaleidoscope of ideas. The dynamics within the family soon become clear. Estelle, who is pretty and clever, is also vain, sulky and manipulative, using her studies as an excuse to get out of sharing the housework or to avoid situations she is unwilling to face, and is often spiteful towards her siblings. Riquet, a determined but sensitive little boy, is adored by all and is a constant source of anxiety to Aline, to whose care he is often entrusted. Aline herself, despite her age, is sensible, practical, and mature, and takes on many of the burdens of the household, which is a happy if slapdash one. Both parents, although affectionate and caring, are impractical and tend to depend upon Aline's common sense, keeping her home from school to help out in minor family emergencies. Aline records, but clearly does not understand, an obliquely perjorative comment about their upbringing made by a neighbour, but her home is depicted as warm and safe. In her relationships with her friends she is kind, generous, and sensitive to the needs of others, organising a lottery to provide a new pinafore for a friend neglected by her stepmother; but she is also capable of malice, mocking a fat child and neglecting her longtime best friend for a new one. The *petits bonheurs*—both private and public—of life in the apartment building constitute the subject of the first part of Aline's diary. The birthday party of one of the neighbours, to whom all are invited, is a high spot, while other events (the scandal caused by a new occupant, an eccentric violinist, who disturbs the house at midnight with his playing, and the concierge's horror at the drawings on the newly painted wall by the trouble-prone Armand) bring all the neighbours out onto the staircase and delight the younger members.

Aline's character is tested in the main section of the novel when, during her mother's protracted absence caring for a widowed friend, an aunt is brought in to look after the family. Tante Mimi is everything that the mother is not: efficient, authoritarian, and house-proud. The 'improvements' that she makes to the home (replacing chipped china and mending a broken clock and the window of the girls' bedroom) unnerve and destabilise the children because they seem to efface their mother's presence, and their father, conscious of their indebtedness to Tante Mimi, is too weak and afraid of upsetting her to object. Tante Mimi soon emerges as a 'control freak', and her constant battles with the children over trifling matters, and the favouritism she shows towards the flattered and sycophantic Estelle, are a great source of tension and resentment in the family. She ruins Aline's excitement at being invited to tea with her beloved teacher, insisting on curling Aline's hair against her protests (with unhappy results), and punishing Aline for lending the necklace she gave her to an underprivileged schoolfriend. This episode encapsulates the lack of understanding between child and adult and Aline's keen sense of injustice, her hurt exacerbated by her father's failure to intervene on her behalf, although he later comes to console the devastated child as she lies sleepless in bed. The diary evokes effectively her pain and sense of helplessless as she continues to be victimised by Tante Mimi while doing her best to survive at school and shouldering responsibilities beyond her years at home, protecting Riquet, resenting Estelle's refusal to become involved, and longing for her mother's return.

The plot culminates in a crisis when the inoffensive and increasingly nervous Riquet runs away from home with his friend Armand after being beaten by Tante Mimi for a supposed misdemeanour. It is suggested that the older Armand has masterminded their flight to fulfil his love of adventure stories, and indeed their setting off to find Riquet's mother in the south of France with only a page torn from an atlas, a rough itinerary, and minimum provisions has echoes of a grand expedition, although they only get as far as the forest of Fontainebleau. They attempt to model themselves on the characters in *Sans famille* by deploying their meagre performing talents to earn a crust of bread after two nights lost in the forest, but their families' distress and anxiety and the boys' subsequent illness and exhaustion underline the crucial difference between fiction and reality. This episode provides insights into other people's true characters: it triggers a reconciliation between the sisters, and on the eve of the mother's return, Aline glimpses the neediness and jealousy underlying Tante Mimi's harshness and lack of sensitivity when the latter comes to gaze at the sleeping Estelle and goes home early rather than witness the joy of the family reunion. Although thankful for the familiar situation of her childhood reestablishing itself, Aline can recognise that it has been a formative experience for her: 'ça vous change, d'avoir à faire face aux choses et, quand il arrive qu'on soit triste, de ne pouvoir compter que sur soi'.[42] Although the theme of the 'little mother' is a familiar one in nineteenth-century children's fiction, the sentimentality and idealism with which that theme was generally treated are a far remove from Vivier's down-to-earth portrayal of Aline's endeavours to save her family from collapse, not least because Aline never casts herself in the role of a heroine or *petite fille modèle*.

POSTWAR NOSTALGIA: CHILDHOOD AND THE NATURAL WORLD

In the years following the Second World War, fictional works for adults and children alike were frequently marked by a nostalgia for childhood and a rural past and a longing for a safe, calm existence lived close to nature. It is important in this respect to distinguish books that overtly addressed and sought to appeal to young readers from those portrayals of childhood intended to satisfy adult longings for escape from a dreary and uncertain world. The portrayal of childhood days in such works as Marcel Pagnol's *La Gloire de mon père* (1957) and *Le Château de ma mère* (1958), for example, has led to these texts being considered as suitable for young readers, although it is doubtful whether they can really be considered as *littérature de jeunesse*. The gently ironic and nostalgic tone and the romantic depiction of the innocence and freedom of a childhood in the Provençal countryside, characteristic of much writing in the 1950s, suggest a targeted adult audience, although the attempt to capture a child's view of adult relationships (like the disputes between the narrator's republican father and his Catholic Oncle Jules) and the self-conscious portrayal of the trajectory of growing away from dependency on home and family could be seen as having appeal for both an adult and older adolescent readership. The texts considered below have similarly been recommended for or appropriated by young readers although arguably they reveal a highly subjective concept of childhood founded on both the authors' personal preoccupations and the adult desires and regrets characteristic of the period.

Henri Bosco (1888–1976): Escapism and Obsession

Although the themes of childhood and adolescence are central to Henri Bosco's work, it is debatable whether many of his novels would be regarded today as suitable for or likely to attract young readers. Nevertheless, a few were included in Gallimard's Bibliothèque blanche, which published works by established authors of a high literary quality that were either designed for or deemed suitable for the young, and in 1959, Bosco was the recipient of the Grand Prix de la Littérature pour les Jeunes.[43] His novels are set mostly in the Provençal countryside, which Bosco knew from his own childhood, and are imbued with nostalgia and an intense sensitivity to the moods of the seasons, sights, sounds, and smells of the natural world and the power of ancient superstitions. He reworks, almost obsessively, different aspects of the themes of lost paradises and enchanted souls in interconnected stories in which the borders between dream and reality and the visible and invisible worlds are blurred and the same characters repeatedly appear and disappear. His fictional world is an isolated and intense one of strange beauty with primitive religious undercurrents inhabited by sinister gypsies, poachers, fanatical hermits, and enigmatic, tormented adolescents. Like Alain-Fournier in *Le Grand Meaulnes*, Bosco effects almost imperceptibly the transition from a realistic rustic scene described in lingering detail, to a domain of mystery where violence and danger lurk beneath the surface, achieving a poetic balance between the everyday and the supernatural.[44] The plots are slow to unfold and focus on the psychological struggles of the characters and their communion with nature, which promises to reveal the secrets of the unseen world. Despite Bosco's evident perceptive understanding of the longings and fears of childhood, the combination of bizarre events, the pagan spirituality and superstitiousness by which the characters are driven, the psychological cruelty inherent in the plots, and the lengthy descriptions of the natural world make his works seem rather unusual additions to the field of juvenile literature and certainly different from other contemporary works. Unlike the works discussed above, Bosco's novels are free of contemporary echoes or political overtones, although the recurrent theme of the quest for an earthly paradise or a childhood past was very much in tune with the escapist trend in adult literature in the middle decades of the century.[45]

Of the novels selected by the Bibliothèque blanche, *L'Enfant et la rivière*, first published in 1945, seems the most accessible to young readers and has seen frequent new editions. In this novel of initiation, which recounts a young boy's escape from the confines of home and adult supervision and his discovery of friendship and adventure on and around the forbidden river, the child is placed at the centre of the text and the focus is on his longings, pleasures, and uncertainties. The first-person narrative is retrospective, however, so that the child's thoughts and emotions are still subjected to adult interpretation as the now elderly narrator seeks to reconstruct and give voice to the feelings that he claims he felt as a child. One wonders to what extent the poetic quality and occasionally slow-moving pace of the novel would have appealed to a postwar adolescent readership that enjoyed a diet of Ivoi and Verne or the abundant comic papers of the time. Yet this story of escape to a different and exciting world set within a realistic environment has clearly continued to be read with pleasure by many young readers: in Gallimard's best-seller list of 1993, *L'Enfant et la rivière* featured in fourth place.[46] Bosco's novel is reminiscent of Alain-Fournier's *Le Grand Meaulnes* in its portrayal of the transformation effected in a protected only child through an unsought adventure in the company of another boy. For Pascalet, whose life with his parents and great-aunt Tante Martine in an isolated house in the countryside is peaceful and safe, the river represents a fascination that both frightens and irresistibly attracts him. The poacher Bargabot, with his tales of fishing and exploration of the hidden inlets and islands, is a glamorous outsider figure for Pascalet, offering a temptation to which the child eventually succumbs, emboldened by his parents' absence and stimulated by the arrival of spring to follow the lure of the forbidden. He is, however, a timid wanderer, in that his first flight from home takes him only to a secluded part of the river bank where he sleeps in the shelter of the bushes and hastily returns home at nightfall alarmed by the sight of footprints in the sand and a thread of smoke from the island opposite. The second time he intends only to sit in a boat moored on the river but is carried off into the current, thus embarking on a journey that immerses him in a sinister and exotic situation on the island. The river thus represents a transition, a crossing from the safety and familiarity of childhood to another, more dangerous world. The gypsy camp, seen through Pascalet's eyes, with a young girl sitting by a cauldron over a fire with a crow on her shoulder and a performing bear wandering loose is an almost caricatural adventure story scene.[47] Pascalet's involvement in this world begins when, braving discovery, he rescues a young boy who has been tied to a tree and flogged by the gypsies, and they escape together by boat.

There follows a magical time, 'hors du temps et de l'espace', hiding in secluded backwaters amongst the reedbeds ('les eaux dormantes') rife with fish and waterfowl, during which Pascalet's experiences of learning to row, fish, make fires, and sleep under the stars are seminal in stimulating his imagination and opening up the wonders of the natural world.[48] Life is concentrated in the present, where the intimate contact with nature and the elements assaults his senses and invades him with a deep happiness free from any sense of guilt or remorse at his flight. Bosco excels in the description of such an environment and its effect on the psyche, and this long central chapter is poetic and evocative, imitating the languorous pace of their days. Like François Seurel in *Le Grand Meaulnes*, Pascalet is intrigued by his new companion, Gatzo, who is strong, practical, and fearless but also silent and enigmatic. Although he is clearly experienced in the ways of life on the river, Gatzo's identity and past remain a mystery, and, like the figure of Meaulnes, he seems the ideal friend of his inexperienced companion's imaginings, or his alter ego, the child that the timid dreamer wishes he could be. With his instinctive, primitive qualities, Gatzo represents the freedom of the savage and reveals to Pascalet the unimagined depths of his own aspirations.[49]

The second half of the novel increases the atmosphere of enchantment when, on a moonlit night near a ruined chapel, they meet a strange girl, Hyacinthe, who is endowed with an otherworldly, mysterious quality, and is at first mistaken by the boys as a ghost. We know only that she comes to the chapel at night to pray for the return of her absent surrogate family, and her history in fact relates to another Bosco book, *L'Ane Culotte* (1937). After the disappearance of the increasingly preoccupied Gatzo, Pascalet goes in search of him, following a pathway that draws him onwards towards the village and succumbing, like Meaulnes himself at the *fête étrange*, to a feeling of unreality in a dreamlike world, 'un lieu de féeries innocentes créé pour le plaisir des enfants rêveurs et fantasques, juste sur les confins du paradis'.[50] The events at a puppet show that holds the villagers entranced beneath a huge elm tree hung with lanterns blur the boundaries between reality and fantasy. After the show, which portrays the theft of a child from his parents and his return after a period of corruption amongst gypsies, Pascalet is witness to the reunion of a weeping Gatzo with the puppeteer, his grandfather, and learns the secret of his past as a child stolen from home. The narrative seems to gesture at this point towards the contrived reunions of novels like Sans famille, but the emphasis again is on the psychological effect on Pascalet, who is left alone to suffer the agonies of sorrow and loss until he is tracked down by the poacher Bargabot and taken home—a tame return far from the usually triumphant homecoming of the adventure-story hero. The transition back to the familiar world is marked, once again, by a period of sleep, a recurring motif in the novel. The secret of Pascalet's flight is kept safe by Tante Martine, who, despite her bustling domesticity, herself seeks escape from the humdrum everyday world in rummaging through old trunks in the attic, reliving her memories of the past and, in a later novel, communing with the spirits of the dead. Like Le Grand Meaulnes, this novel has a provisionally happy ending, for Gatzo returns one night a year later and is taken in to live with Pascalet's family, the brotherhood of the river thus becoming a reality, if only temporarily.

The characters in this novel had already appeared, and subsequently reappear, in other texts in which events overlap and are of uncertain chronology. The girl Hyacinthe had featured in a trilogy of which the first novel, L'Ane Culotte, also appeared in the Bibliothèque blanche. In this novel the attempts of a fanatical old man, Cyprien, to create an Eden in the Provençal hills with the aid of his donkey, Culotte, and charm the beasts and birds with his music are seen through the eyes of a young boy, Constantin, who is drawn to the hills as Pascalet is to the river. Cyprien is a threat to children, however, stealing Hyacinthe, an orphan waif over whom he has cast a spell, and joining a band of gypsies. The other novel by Bosco that has seen most editions in collections for adolescent readers is Le Renard dans l'île (1956). Although it is the sequel to Gatzo's story that is promised at the end of L'Enfant et la rivière, this novel is arguably less accessible to young readers, with its central theme of the transmigration of souls. Moreover, the pace is slow, the stifling summer days punctuated with small events like a disagreement between the boys or a visit from the poacher, which are presented as of great significance in their isolated existence. The attempts of Tante Martine to tame Gatzo and encourage him to leave his wild life for domesticity are reminiscent of Miss Watson's efforts to 'sivilise' Huckleberry Finn in Mark Twain's eponymous novel, although here the tone is poignant rather than humorous. As in Le Grand Meaulnes, again, the theme of adolescent obsession motivates the plot. Gatzo, tormented by the superstitious obsession that a quasi-supernatural white fox is searching for the body of a child who has gone mad in order to reincarnate its soul, fears for the girl they have seen with the gypsies. Pascalet is a less willing companion in this quest, hovering between sharing and disbelieving the superstition, although he, too, is drawn by his friend's intensity to the island once more. Hyacinthe herself is seen only once, as an unearthly, vacant-eyed, and vulnerable figure standing in the moonlight in the gypsy camp, and the reader is given no intimation of her feelings or thoughts on her situation. She remains a distant and enigmatic figure, the object of the fascinated male gaze on the part of characters and author alike. At the end of this strange novel, after a burst of dramatic action in which Gatzo strangles the fox and is shot by the gypsies, he takes off again, abandoning Pascalet and resuming his life as a wanderer in search of the soul of the girl, the centre of his fears and yearnings. Pascalet appears again in the two short pieces *Bargabot* and *Pascalet*, both published in 1958, which further the theme of Gatzo's quest to rescue Hyacinthe. The latter depicts Pascalet's escape from his bleak, cheerless boarding school in search of his imaginative inheritance, and his reunion with a secretive Gatzo, who has rescued Hyacinthe and is hiding her in an old farmhouse. There is no fairy-tale ending here, however, for when the old man Cyprien comes to claim her, Hyacinthe is passive and unresisting, having lost her will because of the gypsy spell that enslaves her spirit. This curious and deeply pessimistic portrayal of the female character must have been as uncomfortable for female readers as that of Alain-Fournier's Yvonne, for both young women are, in their different ways, the tragic victims of male arrogance and obsession. The ending of *Pascalet* also recalls *Le Grand Meaulnes* as Gatzo once more resumes the mission that consumes him: a quest, perhaps, for a love that remains forever elusive.

Jean Giono (1895–1970): Fables for a New World

The same ideal of the reconstruction of postwar life in the countryside through hard work and solidarity found in Vivier's *La Porte ouverte* informs Jean Giono's short tale 'L'Homme qui plantait des arbres', written in 1953, initially for an adult readership and published by Gallimard in a children's collection in 1983. This trajectory is an interesting one: originally commissioned by *Reader's Digest* for a series titled 'The Most Unforgettable Character I've Met' but rejected because it was a fictional piece, the tale was published by *Vogue* in 1954 under the title 'The Man who Planted Hope and Grew Happiness'.[51] Although not originally targeting young readers, it would seem that the return to an interest in ecological concerns in the 1980s after the technomania of the 1960s and 1970s caused this text to appear a suitable addition to Gallimard's catalogue of children's books.[52] 'L'Homme qui plantait des arbres' is a parable denouncing modern civilisation which is at risk of destroying nature, and hence the planet, through rural exodus, wars, incompetent management of the countryside at local and national government levels, and the incessant depletion of natural resources to satisfy the needs of mechanisation in a technological age, and thus reflects issues that are still highly relevant and topical today. It tells the story of the young adult narrator's encounter with a shepherd, Elzéard, a patient, solitary, and altruistic man with an almost messianic mission who has taken it upon himself to plant a hundred acorns a day and eventually creates a new forest in formerly desert lands in Haute Provence. The narrator's first visit takes place in 1913 on the eve of the First World War and his subsequent regular visits after the war allow him to observe the progress of Elzéard's trees and realise that 'les hommes pourraient être aussi efficaces que Dieu dans d'autres domaines que la destruction'.[53] Elzéard diversifies his planting until, in 1935, a substantial forest has grown and is visited by forestry officals who regard it as having sprung up spontaneously and want to give it government protection from the local charcoal burners. By 1945, after yet another war that appears to leave Elzéard and his work untouched, the whole region has been transformed. The trees have worked ecological and social miracles: there is water in the springs and wells once more, and the dead or dying villages have been rejuvenated and repopulated by healthy, happy people. More than ten thousand people, the reader is told, owe their happiness to one man, a humble apostle of peace who dies quietly in a hospice in 1947, contemplating his handiwork. This story, motivated by Giono's own love of planting trees, promotes a message, for the end of the twentieth century as it did for the 1950s, of endorsing the value of individual effort in transforming both the environment and human lives, and the rejection of a world consumed by the pursuit of profit in favour of a return to the calm, equilibrium, and wisdom of a life lived in harmony with the natural world.[54]

Giono's "Le Petit garçon qui avait envie d'espace" was written especially for children in response to a request in 1949 from four Swiss chocolate firms who were sponsoring a volume of contes. This tale of a little boy who is frustrated on his Sunday walks with his father by the high hedges and tall trees that impede their view of the wider countryside and who, in a dream, climbs a spiral staircase in a tree and succeeds in following the birds and flying freely through the air, can be read as a simple fantasy of escape into nature or as a metaphor for the desire to grow up and transcend the confines of childhood. Comparisons have been made with Carroll's *Alice's Adventures in Wonderland* but the unnamed boy here converses with no strange creatures nor, as in fairy tales, encounters hazards to be overcome.[55] As he flies over the countryside he sees only a bird's-eye view of villages, lakes, windmills, fields, and mountains, thus keeping contact with the known world to which he returns, reassured, when he awakes with a cry to see his mother bending anxiously over him. The dream reveals to the boy that he now knows how to break through the constraints of everyday life and achieve freedom through an imaginative recreation of reality, an adjustment in the way of seeing the world that can be interpreted as the underlying principle of literary creation.[56]

The employment of the narrative device of a dream that allows for excursions into fantasy without actually leaving the safe confines of the familiar world was a popular strategy in children's books in the first half of the twentieth century before the explosion of full-blown fantasy writing that came to dominate the market in the latter half. This phenomenon and the renaissance of the *merveilleux* are discussed in chapter 7.

6
THE ROLE OF IMAGES

We have seen how the importance of images in children's books was recognised by publishers in the nineteenth century, with Hachette and Hetzel employing established and highly regarded artists to illustrate their publications. The images served to complement and visualise the text, but, despite the excellence of the results, in many cases few concessions were made to the age and ability of the young reader to read these images fully. Few artists produced specifically child-oriented images like those of Kate Greenaway and John Tenniel in Britain. Towards the end of the century, however, the status of the image began to change, moving from a position of addition to the text or educational aid to become the main focus of the reader's attention and pleasure. As has been seen in chapter 5, the general increase in literacy resulting from the Ferry laws on education had produced a new mass public who had little or no experience of reading as a leisure activity.[1] To cater for this new enlarged readership, publishers in the early years of the twentieth century were producing increasing numbers of illustrated papers and *histoires en images* in large print runs. In magazines and *albums*, or picture books, aimed at young children, the image was served by the text rather than the other way round, creating a new genre in which 'le visible supplante le lisible'.[2]

Images had played an important role in popular culture in France from the eighteenth century on, with the crudely coloured wood engravings of the Images d'Epinal. These separate sheets of images, originally disseminated by pedlars and depicting, for example, saints, heroes, military uniforms, and animals or reproducing in a series of images tales from the Bibliothèque bleue, developed in the nineteenth century under the direction of Nicolas Pellerin and with more sophisticated printing technology to include images of contemporary events or other matters of interest to the illiterate.[3] Children's versions portrayed brief, brightly coloured versions of fairy tales, fables, moral tales, and pictures of dolls, animals, or soldiers and offered a stimulating if simplified view of the world to young and inexperienced eyes. Although the *Images d'Epinal* flourished in the first half of the nineteenth century, their popularity declined after 1850 as the availability of cheap illustrated papers and books with more subtle and well-produced images increased. Images had also been employed to appeal to children learning to read in *abécédaires*, or alphabet books, since the seventeenth century. In the nineteenth century, the *Croix Depardieu*, a cheap chapbook so named because of the cross on the title page, which traditionally contained letters of the alphabet, syllables, prayers, and a short catechism, was eventually eclipsed by more sophisticated and secular products, the thematic abécédaires, in which letters and images were combined and followed by brief reading passages on different themes, the most popular of which were natural history and artisan crafts. Ségolène Le Men claims that the abécédaire, the market for which was linked with the successive education laws in the nineteenth century, represented 'le premier genre de large diffusion de la littérature illustrée pour l'enfance' and has demonstrated the great variety and ingenuity of the complicity between text and image in such texts.[4]

It is impossible to do more here than give an overview of the development of the *bande dessinée* and the significance of the influx of material from America in particular in the first half of the century. Attention will therefore be focussed on Francophone products, in particular the histoires en images and comic strips that were reproduced in albums and thus assimilated into the category of children's books.

PREDECESSORS: THE PICTURE ALBUM
Maurice Boutet de Monvel (1850–1913)

By 1900, long before the comic strip entered the arena, the picture book was a best-selling product in France. Heinrich Hoffmann's *Struwwelpeter* (1845), a collection of comic verses and images depicting the gruesome consequences of various examples of children's bad habits or misbehaviour (thumb sucking, playing with matches, refusing to eat) had been successful in translation in France as it had in Britain. The success of Hetzel's *Mlle Lili* series has already been noted. The albums of Maurice Boutet de Monvel (1851–1913) are stunning examples of the high standards of children's book production at the end of the nine-teenth century. His work was inspired by a variety of wide-ranging influences, from medieval illuminated manuscripts to contemporary French lithographic art and, like that of his contemporary, Walter Crane, the aesthetics of Japanese prints. After the Exposition univer-selle of 1889, oriental art was highly fashionable, the influence of its stylised portrayals of nature, and its flat, unshaded use of colour dis-cernible everywhere—in painting, posters, domestic decoration, and dress design.[5] Boutet de Monvel's illustrations were also influenced by the stylised realism of Kate Greenaway's child figures. This is most clearly seen in his illustrated edition of Anatole France's *Nos enfants: Scènes de la ville et des champs* (1887), in which pretty, static infants are posed with birds and animals, and his illustrated songbooks *Vie-illes chansons pour les petits enfants* (1883) and *Chansons de France pour les petits français* (1883). On the cover of the *Vieilles chansons*, the four formally posed child figures standing in a line on the bottom edge of the rectangular frame between two stylised plant containers, three facing the reader (two of them identical little girls) and one with her back towards the reader as she conducts the others, recall Green-away's elegantly attired little children in *Under the Window* (1879) and *Marigold Garden* (1885). The title page of *Chansons de France* depicts a line of boys and girls of different ages marching in a line from left to right and bearing French flags. The flag carried by the leader is a huge scrolling banner containing the title of the book. Although portraying movement, the scene is curiously immobile. The gait of the children is repeated with slight variations; all appear to be singing loudly, with two of them looking out towards the reader, and the flags are all stretched with identical rigidity except for the last one, which is carried by a tod-dler at a rakish angle, thus disrupting the pattern. These techniques of repetition and stylised movement are used repeatedly throughout the two books, in which Boutet de Monvel uses a palette of predomi-nantly pastel colours: blue, pink, green, and brown with splashes of red and black for emphasis. Each page or pair of pages contains the music and words of a song within a box or white space that is surrounded by vignettes of children, animals, and plants in stylised arrangements, or used dynamically as part of the action. In *Vieilles chansons*, for exam-ple, to accompany the follow-my-leader tune of 'La Queue Leu Leu', a continuous line of children step out across the top of the text box holding on to each other's skirts or jackets, tumble down the right-hand side, continue along the bottom of the page with just their feet showing beneath the box, and are pulled up by one another on the left-hand side, the circular, continuous motion echoing the nature of the song and the game. For 'La Pêche aux moules' in *Chansons de la France*, a similar line of children, this time dressed in peasant clothes and carrying baskets, walk in identical motion along the top of the song box as though it were one of the breakwaters on the beach that forms the background in order to avoid the crabs, their pincers menacingly raised, below. For 'Chanson de la mariée', also in *Chansons de la France*, a throng of revellers in blue, black, pink, and white Breton peasant dress crowd the vertical and horizontal space beside and above the music, drawing the eye up and around. On the left side of the page, one dancing couple look over their shoulders as though to invite the reader to join in, while on the right we see only the backs of the heads of a group who wait to pay their respects to the bride and groom. The happy couple are flanked along the top of the page by pairs of dancers and musicians. The mise-en-page here creates a sense of involvement and celebration (somewhat at odds with the rather gloomy prognostications about marriage in the song itself). The text box is used as an integral part of the action in the two facing pages of 'Margoton va-t-à l'eau' in *Chansons de France*. On the left-hand side of the first image a girl is seen falling into a stream, witnessed by three boys in the distance, their arms identically outstretched. On the facing page, the boys stand on the text box, their hats neatly arranged in a line behind them, hanging comically on to each other and pulling the girl, her bloomers showing, up from the water. The humour and repetition of gestures and shapes mirror the repeated refrains of the verse.

Boutet de Monvel also produced an album of La Fontaine's fables, in which the vignettes accompanying the text employ the same techniques of repetition and variation and are arranged in a sequence following the key stages of the fable so that they can be read almost like a comic strip. His most famous work, however, is *La Vie de Jeanne d'Arc* (1896), his first narrative work, for which he provided both the text and the images.[6] The depiction of Jeanne's transformation from peasant girl to heroine and her mission to rid France of an invader had considerable contemporary significance, for her birthplace was Lorraine and for many writers she had become the symbol of France itself. She has, in fact, been appropriated at various times as a symbol by monarchists and Republicans, by religious and secular groups, and by adherents of both the political Right and the Left. Statues were commissioned all over France, including that by Emmanuel Frémiet in the Place des Pyramides in Paris in 1875.[7] A large number of biographies appeared in the last third of the century and in many school textbooks, Epinal prints and stories for children, her courage, faith, and patriotism were represented as qualities towards which all should aspire, especially at times of national distress. In G. Bruno's *Le Tour de la France par deux enfants*, for example, she is seen as the perfect role model for the young citizen of the future.[8] In his 'Avant-propos' to his *Jeanne d'Arc*, Boutet de Monvel emphasises the power of patriotic fervour and urges his readers: 'Souvenez-vous-en, le jour où le pays aura besoin de tout votre courage.'[9] The title page conflates three levels of historical reference, depicting Jeanne in armour on horseback leading a troop of French foot soldiers with the uniforms and rifles of the 1890s, their banners inscribed with the names of some of France's more glorious conquests under Napoleon Bonaparte (Jena, Lützen, Valmy). After this, however, his version of Jeanne's life transcends any particular contemporary or ideological interpretation.[10] The elegant stylised realism of the full-page illustrations and the unmodulated flatness of the colours in which muted blues, browns, greys, and yellows dominate with splashes of dark red evoke both Japanese prints and the work of Henri de Toulouse-Lautrec. The historical detail is accurate, but the evocation of medieval life and culture in the pictures is undeniably idealised: the costumes are clean and bright and the battles, although energetic, appear blood-less. Boutet de Monvel adheres to nineteenth-century literary conventions associating purity and goodness with blondness, and portrays Jeanne initially as a demure young girl, a *petite fille modèle* in every way. Once embarked on her quest to save France, she is consistently pale and handsome and, in some of the pictures the scalloped sleeves of her tunic flow like angel's wings from her shoulders. The rejection of contemporary conventions of passive femininity implied in her militant role is justified by an assertion of divine inspiration in pictures showing visitations from the archangel Michael and Saints Catherine and Margaret. The pictures often spread across two pages forming crowded, panoramic scenes at court or in battle, of which Jeanne is always the focus. The development of the narrative is mediated through a combination of static, theatrically posed tableaux (Jeanne appearing before the council or addressing her judges) and scenes full of figures and movement. The chaos of battle scenes is structured by the use of mirroring effects in double-page spreads, by the arrangement of spears, the position of horses, and the figure of Jeanne herself. In a siege scene, for example, the crowded diagonal lines of ladders, swords, and arrows draw the reader's eye upwards to the bold figure of Jeanne ascending a ladder, sword pointing heavenwards and banner flying. These two symbols of her inspiration (the banner linking her with the temporal power of the king and her gesture with God) are foregrounded throughout the book. In a number of pictures she is portrayed as a solitary figure with her arm outstretched either towards the heavens or pointing towards the dauphin, the soldiers or the clerics at her trial, underlining her defiance and determination. Boutet de Monvel's experimentation with space in the juxtaposition of text and image is an innovative aspect of this work. The text appears within white boxes set into the illustrations, usually a horizontal rectangle at the bottom of the page, thus privileging the image above the word, but different positionings of the insets often form a comment upon the action depicted. Vertical inserts placed beside the figure of Jeanne in scenes where she addresses the dauphin or his council support her dominance and the power of her words. In the scene with the archangel Michael, the text box containing his instructions to her seems to emanate from the point of his sword. Elsewhere, the text box forms a staircase mimicking that which she must climb to reach the dauphin, or is an obstacle over which her horse leaps to lead her men in an attack on an English stronghold. In the scene where the English Lord Stafford threatens Jeanne with a dagger as she lies chained to a prison bed, the inset text above her seems to oppress her and emphasises her vulnerability. This gorgeous picture book represents the best in children's book illustration at the end of the nineteenth century.

Benjamin Rabier (1864–1939)

The works of Benjamin Rabier, a former designer of Epinal images who produced elegant illustrated editions of La Fontaine's fables (1906), the *Roman de Renart* (1909), and *Le Buffon de Benjamin Rabier* (c. 1917) and created the trademark image of 'La Vache qui rit', is regarded as precursors of the bande dessinée for his privileging of image above text in his albums for children.[11] The first, *Tintin le lutin* (1897), written in collaboration with Fred Isly, featuring the misadventures of a mischievous little boy, has obviously sparked suggestions that herein lie the origins of Hergé's famous character. However, Rabier's Tintin is a small boy, often dressed in knee breeches and a tam-o'-shanter, whose exploits, like those of nineteenth-century books for the very young, are resticted to the environment of his home and the surrounding fields and woods.[12] Perhaps the most interesting of these albums is *Flambeau, chien de guerre*, published during the course of the First World War in 1916, which capitalises on the popularity of animal stories of the period to present a patriotic view of the terrible realities of the conflict, an agenda not obscured by the humour with which events are depicted throughout.[13] Flambeau is an ugly puppy, rejected by his owners and ill-treated by the other farm animals, who decides to sign up as a *chien de guerre* when war breaks out. Dreaming of glory but rejected and humiliated by the recruitment officers, too, he decides to go solo and embarks upon a campaign of guerilla warfare, displaying initiative and heroism, and, of course, an intense patriotic hatred of the *Boches*. He witnesses the horrors of war in bombing raids and experiences them himself when he is nearly blown to bits, is shot in the thigh, gets tangled in a stretch of barbed wire, and almost drowns on two occasions. Assisted by an equally patriotic rabbit and other wild animals, and, eventually, by the other farmyard animals who have come to admire his heroism, he succeeds in passing provisions to a patrol of imprisoned French soldiers through a tunnel, drags a mine into a trench, blows up a German command post, commandeers a barge carrying supplies by blocking the chimney and asphyxiating the Germans on board, and deflects a torpedo from its path with his bare paws.

The images in this rectangular album, in both colour and black and white and varying constantly in size and shape, fill their pages, accompanied by a few lines of text beneath. Full double-page spreads depict crowded scenes in which the terrified woodland creatures flee from a missile, a dozen different fish endure the turbulence caused by a torpedo exploding underwater, and farm animals react with horror to the appearance of a German soldier from a hole in their yard. Flambeau's activities are depicted in a succession of long rectangular strips or squares—sometimes three to a page—or in full-page illustrations that carry the action along energetically. The comic perspective of Flambeau's ruses and the witty tone of the accompanying narrative are superbly reflected in the action-packed scenes and the postures and facial expressions of both animals and humans. The collaboration of the other animals, who each contribute according to their natural talents, can be seen as symbolic of a largely rural France united in solidarity to defend the nation's ideals of peace, liberty, and labour, and indicate the need for all, even the young, to become mobilised in whatever way in the war effort.[14] The German soldiers are depicted as easily duped, cowardly, and incompetent. The album finishes in an optimistic vision of the end of the war (still not in sight at the time of publication), with Flambeau's return to the farm and the farmer's joyful proclamation, 'Après la guerre par les armes, la guerre par le travail. Nos troupes sont triomphantes. L'ère de la liberté est enfin venue.'[15] The range of emotions depicted in this tale of suffering and triumph and the resilience and determination of the animal heroes make Rabier's album far more authentic and compelling than the bare jingoistic exhortations of many other contemporary works of propaganda.[16]

Although Rabier's drawings do feature humans, he is known above all for his drawings, both realistic and comic, of animals. The ambitious edition of over two hundred fables by La Fontaine exemplifies an innovative concept of the mise-en-page in which, as in Boutet de Monvel's edition, text and image work harmoniously together. The text appears in a box or white space in different positions on the page and is surrounded by multiple images of varying shapes and sizes that encapsulate the stages of the fable and can be read like a comic strip, a concept employed in a similar way in Hoffmann's *Struwwelpeter*. The images are free-floating vignettes in elegant pastel colours set within a large frame or contained in a combination of rectangles, lozenges, and medallions, with occasional decorative Art Deco panels reminiscent of the work of Alphonse Mucha, making each page unique. The animals are naturalistically portrayed, although their faces display the relevant emotions of cunning, greed, malice, or surprise. In contrast, Rabier initiated for Tallandier in 1923 a series of sixteen humorous albums featuring Gédéon the duck, in which the image once again takes precedence over the text.[17] The style here is more cartoonlike, with bright, flat colours (Gédéon is yellow and has a preternaturally long neck for a duck) and the animals are anthropomorphised in their facial expressions, behaviour, and relationships, although they do not wear human dress. These tales were initially set in a farmyard where the animals live in a recognisably human social hierarchy and, as in La Fontaine's fables, Rabier's animals represent human foibles. Amongst Gédéon's companions and sometime antagonists are Aglaé, a pretentious goat; Serpolet, a mendacious rabbit; and the two dogs, Placide and Grognard. Gédéon is an ugly duckling who becomes a hero, fêted initially by his companions for ridding the farmyard of the predatory fox and wolf, and then becoming a passionate righter of wrongs and protector of the weak in different scenarios. As the series progresses he moves beyond his farmyard and, like the heroes of adventure stories, becomes involved in a number of adventures and activities (*Gédéon en Afrique*, (1925), *Gédéon traverse l'Atlantique*, (1933), *Gédéon fait du ski*, (1938), *Gédéon, chef de brigands*, (1931)). The exploits are often topical: in *Gédéon, sportsman* (1924) he and his companions attend the Olympic Games (held that year in Paris and Chamonix), and in *Gédéon mécano* (1927) he and Placide terrorise the countryside in a bright red sports car driven by Bout-de-Zan the monkey. After returning to his farmyard, marrying, and starting a large family, Gédéon is a kind of elder statesman, dispensing advice and generally keeping the peace, and eventually, in *Gédéon, grand manitou* (1938), after organising and winning elections, becomes a much respected leader of a happy country.[18] Although Rabier's vision is essentially optimistic and the images are in bright and cheerful pastel colours, there is also an undercurrent of cruelty and horror in some of his tales, like the furious battles between the dogs and the fox family.

The struggles against oppressive forces and Gédéon's efforts to bring harmony to all communities of animals and keep aggression at bay carried profound contemporary resonances in the 1930s. In *Gédéon fait du ski* (1938), his refuge for animals, a kind of Noah's Ark, is unexpectedly invaded by zoo animals, a situation that he has to act quickly to rectify (a clear reference to contemporary dangers) and in the last album, *Les Dernières aventures de Gédéon* (1939), Rabier portrays a very pessimistic image of the state of his hero's country, for discord and oppression have returned and Gédéon is forced to try to overcome the apathy of the other animals before it is too late and the country slides into moral chaos and outright conflict. Like *Flambeau, chien de guerre*, some of the Gédéon albums have been revived and are once again in print.

ILLUSTRATED PAPERS, HISTOIRES EN IMAGES, AND BANDES DESSINÉES

If the novel in the first two decades of the century failed to furnish many fresh approaches, original plots, or memorable characters or to provide new and exciting models of childhood free from the constaints of the adult world and the authors' didactic agenda, these were, on the other hand, beginning to be found in abundance in the new histoires en images and comic strips, many of them in colour, that featured colourful characters that captured the imagination of young readers. Unlike the admirable virtuous characters of the traditional novel, the new stars were often mischievous, disruptive, and incompetent or scatterbrained and always in trouble. While their fictional predecessors were representatives of social and moral values or overcame their faults in order to find happiness in conformity, the exploits of the characters of the histoires en images and comic strips often result from their inability to adjust or conform to a changing world, or a downright refusal to do so.[19] In the years following the First World War it was abundantly apparent that the didactic and artistic formulae in children's books that had found approval with bourgeois readers prior to 1914 were undergoing rapid and fundamental changes.[20] The comic strip, usually humorous and often anarchic in nature, implied a different kind of reading experience, requiring less imaginative and intellectual effort on the part of the reader, perhaps, but offering a strong visual involvement with the action and the characters and access to a world where the usual rules and constraints were overturned. Characters like Bécassine, Tintin, and Mickey Mouse who appeared regularly in magazines and albums in different adventures over a long period of time while rarely ageing or changing in personality, offered the pleasure of both anticipation and satisfaction, familiarity, and surprise. The most successful comic strip characters acquired a huge following that spanned a generation and more and, in some cases, spawned an industry in merchandising in the shape of dolls, jewellery, china, postcards, and soft furnishings just as many children's book and television characters do today. Soft toys and other souvenirs of Bécassine, whose last adventures were published in 1950, for example, can still be found for sale on the Internet, and the worldwide Disney industry speaks for itself.

Christophe (1856–1945): A Forerunner of the Bande Dessinée

The father of the bande dessinée in France is generally accepted to be Georges Colomb, teacher at the Sorbonne and populariser of science who under the pen name Christophe produced the earliest home-grown forerunners of the genre at the end of the nineteenth century. He has been credited with both revitalising school textbooks with a greater amount of illustration and with the innovation of introducing histoires en images suitable for different ages to encourage children to enjoy reading.[21] Christophe, in turn, was influenced by the French-speaking Swiss artist and schoolmaster Rodolphe Töpffer, whose histoires en images produced in the first half of the nineteenth century are regarded as the first in the comic-strip genre. In his satirical portraits of society Le Docteur Festus (1829), Histoire de Monsieur Jabot (1833), Les Amours de M. Vieuxbois (1837), and Monsieur Crépin (1837), Töpffer took the first step towards exploiting the potential of the interaction between text and image, his black-and-white line drawings dominating the page in a sequence that presented a narrative with just a line or two of complementary handwritten text beneath.[22] Christophe followed this format and even borrowed some episodes from Töpffer's work.[23] His speciality is the pompous, naïve, or incompetent adult whose comic misadventures ensured a following amongst young readers more used to the portrayal of adults as admirable role models. A prototype for his most famous creation, La Famille Fenouillard, appeared in 1889 in the form of the misadventures of the Famille Cornouillet in a visit to the country (Une Partie de campagne) in Hachette's Journal de la Jeunesse. He was asked to produce a similar piece for Le Petit Français illustré: journal des écoliers et des écolières, with the family visiting the Exposition Universelle in Paris that same year, and strips featuring the Famille Fenouillard ran in this journal from 1889 to 1893.[24] The family consists of the vain, pompous, and authoritarian father Agénor, bored with his existence as a shopkeeper; his bossy wife Léocadie; and two raucous daughters with comically illustrious names, Artémise and Cunégonde, and the strips feature the hazards of their daily life and the journeys they undertake to brighten their existence. The strips were histoires en images rather than bande dessinées, in that the black and white images, arranged in the traditional format of the Images d'Epinal of three rows of two images (six images per page), were confined within frames, with an explanatory text beneath.

In 1893, the adventures of the family were reproduced in album form in colour. The satire of petit bourgeois life and the narrative style suggests that the strip was aimed more at an educated middle-class audience than a popular one. While much of the action is slapstick, the text is written in a parodic formal style containing cultural references, scientific information, and linguistic jokes like the names of the daughters and the Fenouillard emporium's speciality (since prehistoric times!) of waterproof hats and antineuralgia stockings for the unmarried of both sexes. The scholarly language of school textbooks is employed humorously to entertain the readers of secondary school age who would be more than familiar with such discourse.[25] There are allusions to the cautionary tale tradition of children's literature, moreover: in the first episode, for example, one daughter falls from the window, landing in a dungheap, while the other falls down a well, the former's accident described in mock serious scientific terms.[26] To ridicule the conventions of bourgeois life, Christophe often employs a comic disparity between text and image (the girls' music recital before their proud parents is illustrated by two ducks with a sheet of music singing their hearts out). The family's trip to Brussels is abandoned after they are beset by a series of minor irritations at the station that culminate in a farcical scene in which M. Fenouillard hurls a large squishy Camembert cheese at a porter and hits his own wife instead. This episode finishes with her resolution never to leave home again, but it is one that is soon forgotten, for in later episodes they succumb once more to tourism fever and venture further abroad, including, in Jules Verne fashion, a trip around the world. The subtitle to an episode of 1893 described the piece as an 'ouvrage destiné à donner à la jeunesse le goût des voyages', a further tongue-in-cheek reference to the didactic tradition in children's books.

In subsequent strips, Christophe created other entertaining types: the sapeur Camember, a none-too-bright soldier whose naïveté gets him into all sorts of trouble as the victim of circumstances; Cosinus, an absent-minded and obsessive savant who longs for adventure; and Plick and Plock, too mischievous gnomes who wreak havoc in a household.[27] The misadventures of the soldier Camember generally result from his disingenuousness and misguided good intentions, and the series' popularity with a dual audience of young and adult readers stemmed to a large extent from the comic colloquial language of the characters—notably, the peasant register of speech of Camember and the elaborate military insults of Camember's superiors. The *Cosinus* series also demonstrates a satirical approach to the traditions of children's literature, encouraging the reader to view them with a more critical eye. The lengthy subtitle of *L'Idée fixe du savant Cosinus* (1899) introduces the story as offering both intellectual and moral instruction, with Cosinus's misfortunes evidence that 'il est sage d'avoir la plus grande déférence pour les règlements, surtout s'ils sont contradictoires'.[28] Inspired by the reading of the travels of his cousin M. Fenouillard, Cosinus engages in elaborate preparations for a journey of his own, including the invention of an extraordinary travelling machine (the name of which contains fifty-one letters) but, unlike the self-confident scientist explorers in the novel of adventure, never succeeds in leaving Paris. *Les Malices de Plick et Plock*, fairy-tale stories of two household gnomes in search of a magic formula that will control their urge to do stupid and naughty things, is an album for younger children. The language is simpler, presupposing no prior knowledge of the discourse of school textbooks, but the tone of the stories is anarchic, the gnomes indulging freely in all the disruptive and antisocial behaviour denied to well-raised children in the real world. The magic formula in effect turns out to be 'Réfléchissez avant d'agir', a fairly conventional form of self-policing, if less draconian and prescriptive than the recommendations for good behaviour generally found in moral tales for the young.

Early Illustrated Magazines

It has been estimated that some sixty-two illustrated magazines appeared between 1904 and 1939.[29] These were of different sorts, serving different social, political, and religious agenda, and not all were aimed exclusively at children. Indeed, many addressed the whole family and the content varied correspondingly in its appropriateness for a young audience. In the first decade, papers such as *Le Petit Illustré* (1906), *L'Epatant* (1908), *Fillette* (1909), *L'Intrépide* (1910), and *Le Cri-Cri* (1911), all published by Offenstadt, were aimed largely at a working-class readership. *L'Epatant*, in particular, was criticised by Catholic groups for its portrayal of violence and immorality, for it was often in questionable taste and focussed on comic characters who operated on the margins of society and the law. These groups, in response to *laïcité* in education and the separation of church and state in 1905, produced their own magazines for boys and girls with titles like *L'Echo du Noël* (1906) and *Bernadette* (1914) that continued to promote Christian and family values and offered supplements to assist in home education. Established publishers like Gautier-Languereau, Geffroy, Albin Michel, and Tallandier also sought to woo young readers and create future customers for their books by entering the illustrated paper market. In brief, a choice existed between magazines that were unexceptionable in terms of their moral and edifying approach, and those less so, like some of Offenstadt's products, in which the comic, sensational, and cynical took precedence.

Many magazines, including Hachette's *Journal de la Jeunesse*, which started in 1872, and the *Magasin d'éducation et de récréation*, did not survive the First World War although many were revived after a hiatus. Two short-lived papers appeared during the war, however: *Trois Couleurs* (1914–19) and *La Croix d'honneur* (1915–18) specialised in topical and patriotic histoires en images, tales from the Front celebrating French bravery in the face of enemy perfidy and brutality. Many of these short narratives featured the deeds of boy soldiers who, like their counterparts in children's books published during the French Revolution, were prepared to sacrifice their lives for France. After the decades of preoccupation with the loss of Alsace and Lorraine in 1870, it is not surprising that, after the armistice of November 1918, the return of these regions to France was widely celebrated. *L'Echo du Noël* carried a picture of two children with the French flag with the legend, 'Alsacien et Lorraine saluent la France avec enthousiasme, remerciant Dieu d'avoir fait cesser enfin la captivité de leur province sous le joug des allemands.'[30]

The interwar years saw a new burgeoning of publishing projects that evolved under the widespread influence of the influx of comic books from America.[31] Hachette published *Tarzan*, *Félix le chat*, and *Silly Symphonies*. The most influential arrival, the *Journal de Mickey* in 1934, which featured Mickey Mouse and his friends, was widely disseminated and triggered a veritable Disney invasion, including albums of Mickey's adventures like *Hop-là*, published by Hachette. Homegrown magazines gradually altered their comic style and adapted techniques in order to compete. Perhaps the most significant influence from American comics was the introduction of speech balloons, which reduced the importance of supporting text and altered the perspective of the narrative. Legends in text boxes were employed only for brief contextualising remarks, and the story was carried forward almost entirely through the highly colloquial dialogue or musings of the characters in balloons containing speech or exclamation or question marks, and special effects 'noises' like 'Boum!' or 'Paf!' This strategy was first used consistently in France by Alain Saint-Ogan in *Zig et Puce* (see later discussion).

In response to the evolving international situation, many French children's magazines in the 1930s attempted once more to politicise their young readers, debating contemporary issues like Communism, the class struggle, and the rise of Nazism, and events like the Spanish Civil War, some even creating unions for readers to join or supporting religious and political groups. *Mon camarade*, begun in 1933 and aimed at children of the proletariat, declared that it put itself at the service 'de toutes les organisations qui veulent faire des enfants non des matraqueurs fascistes ou de la chair à canon, mais des travailleurs libres et fiers, des hommes dans le sens le plus beau de ce mot'.[32] *Benjamin*, on the other hand, deplored in 1936 the sight of children in red berets singing the *Internationale* and urged its readers in 1933 to devote themselves to their studies and obey their parents, for 'La France en aura tant besoin quand vous aurez dix-huit ans'.[33] Condemnation of Nazism was unanimous: a defiant letter to Hitler declared that 'c'est avec tout notre enthousiasme et tout notre patriotisme que nous vous crions, M. le chancelier Hitler, si vous avez espéré nous impressioner, c'est complètement raté. Vive la France!'[34]

During the Second World War, children's magazines were subject to the same conditions affecting book production discussed in chapter 5. Many disappeared altogether, while others, like *La Semaine de Suzette*, stopped publication for the duration. American comics were banned after the Americans entered the war in December 1941 and ten comics in the occupied zone closed between January and March 1942. During this period, children's magazines were manipulated for both positive and negative propaganda purposes. Propaganda publications were largely the products of a small number of publishers in Paris and shared the preoccupations and prejudices of the occupying forces. The targets of the Vichy regime were essentially the same as those of the Nazis (Americans, Bolsheviks, the English, Freemasons, and the Jews) and publications for young readers were used to disseminate distrust and hatred. The image became a powerful tool in this campaign, as the alleged evil of the enemies was externalised in the grotesque and frightening physical appearance of villains—particularly Jews—who were seen as the new bogeymen. As has been seen in the case of the Comtesse de Ségur and other nineteenth-century writers, anti-Semitism was not a new element in French children's literature, and the existing current of antagonism led to the identification of the Jews as scapegoats in a campaign that sought to attribute responsibility for the defeat of 1940.[35] Children's literature was involved more broadly in anti-enemy propaganda in the allegations made by Henri Croston in his pamphlet *Les Corrupteurs de la jeunesse. Mainmise Judéo-maçonnique sur la presse enfantine* (1941–42) that children were the targets of Jewish and Freemason attempts to demoralise French youth through their reading.

Croston attacked the threat represented not just by schools and youth movements but by comics like the Communist *Mon camarade* and the *Journal de Mickey*.[36]

Le Téméraire, which ran for thirty-eight issues and three special issues from January 1943, was the organ of fascist propaganda run by collaborationists and extreme anti-Semites who were close to the German *Propaganda Abteilung*.[37] It was quite a luxurious product, with a large cover image, and sought to continue the traditional balance between education and amusement with a mixture of didactic articles, stories, and a bande dessinée in the centre pages. There were, however, insidious political overtones in all its material and it exploited all the existing conventions of the genre to preach the values of the New Order.[38] The heroes exemplify the Nazi agenda: Marc le Téméraire is a dynamic, virile, athletic, blond young French policeman whose mission is to save France from destruction, and he shoots down a Soviet plane in the process; Docteur Fulminante, an inventor, is pitted repeatedly against Vorax, a villain with exaggerated Jewish features who embodies rapacity and evil. Other corrupt, decadent, fanatical, and sadistic villains are English, Jewish, or Russian, while the evil king of the swamp men in the science fiction story *Vers les mondes inconnus* is a grotesque creature with dark skin, huge bulbous eyes, a hooked nose, and a red star on his crown. The educational articles duplicate the propaganda: an essay titled 'Du singe à l'homme' purported to be a scientific demonstration of the position of white Nordic types at the top of the evolutionary chain while a story about Atlantis showed how the civilisation degenerated through interbreeding with undesirable types, thus promoting to young readers an analogous image of their own world under threat. The magazine initiated Cercles des Téméraires, with associated clubs, camps, and competitions to involve children more actively. Alain Jeff's *Le Fantôme de minuit* in the 1943 special summer issue borrowed from scout literature the plot of a group of Téméraires on a camping trip who foil villains in a mysterious château, and appropriated scout songs and games to serve the paper's agenda.

In the southern zone, to which some publishing companies had relocated, some fifteen titles were produced between 1940 and 1944, although all adopted a reduced format because of material restrictions.[39] These magazines, which already promoted the nationalist ethos as a reaction to the influx of American comics, supported the Vichy regime and, like *Siroco* (December 1942–July 1944), celebrated 'France, Empire, Héroïsme, Fierté, Labeur, Espérance, Enthousiasme'.[40] As during the French Revolution, children were perceived as a symbol of the future and thus were central to the ideology of the *Révolution nationale* and prime targets for Vichy propaganda. (Some examples of children's books produced by Vichy will be considered in chapter 7.) In complete contrast, *Le Jeune Patriote, organe des jeunes du Front National,* was an underground publication that emerged in October 1944 and carried stories and bandes dessinées of real and fictional heroes of the Resistance.[41] *Fifi, gars du maquis,* for example, which ran between 1945 and 1947, featured a young worker who was a member of the *Francs-Tireurs-Partisans de France,* a mostly communist organisation.

Against this background, discussion will now focus on some of the most successful histoires en images and comic-strips that appeared in albums of the twentieth century.

BÉCASSINE (HISTOIRE EN IMAGES)

An early but long-lasting creation lacking the vulgarity and amorality of some of the comic strips in illustrated papers and a best-seller in album form was Bécassine, the moon-faced Breton maid who is good-hearted, energetic, and enthusiastic but naïve and repeatedly prone to mishaps. Her adventures were the fruit of collaboration between, initially, Jacqueline Rivière and J.-P. Pinchon and first appeared in the illustrated paper *La Semaine de Suzette* in January 1905. In 1913, Maurice Languereau (who adopted the pseudonym of Caumery), the editor of the magazine, took over responsibility for writing the text. Each episode of her adventures was depicted in a series of images of varying sizes and shapes with a passage of text, in straightforward and accessible language, beneath. Despite the fact that she is an adult figure, or perhaps *because* she is a comic, scatterbrained, and disaster-prone one, Bécassine was an extremely popular character with young readers, her adventures continuing—with only a six-year interruption during the Second World War—until 1950. *La Semaine de Suzette* was initially designed for girls of the Catholic bourgeoisie between the ages of eight and eighteen although it sought a wider audience after the Second World War up to its last issue in 1960.[42] It was committed to acting as a complement to a religious and intellectual education, promoting Christian values in stories, poems, articles of contemporary interest, and homemaking advice in accordance with an editorial ethos of good taste and moderation. The paper's endorsement of traditional morals, respect for the social and domestic hierachy, and gender-specific roles and activities ensured its success with parents as well as young girls.[43] The exploits of the paper's star Bécassine also appeared in twenty-six albums published between 1913 and 1950, incorporating various episodes into an overarching lengthy narrative, many of which are still available in modern reprints.

Bécassine (her real name is Annaïk Labornez) began her career as a servant in the Parisian home of the Marquise de Grand-Air and acts in a variety of capacities in later stories including teacher, war worker, and nursemaid to Loulotte, the Marquise's adopted goddaughter, who first appeared in 1922. Bécassine is an instantly recognisable figure, dominating the images in her unchanging traditional Breton costume of a wide-sleeved, full-skirted green dress with black velvet trimmmings, a red bodice, and a white apron, her hair completely hidden by a white-winged cap. The rustic simplicity of her character is underlined by contrast with the elegant period clothes of the other characters that contextualise the images immediately in the well-to-do milieu of the early twentieth century. Although the images, printed in primary colours, contain accurate period detail, many of the characters are essentially caricatures, their faces represented very impressionistically. Bécassine herself has dots for eyes, high-arched eyebrows, and a little stubby nose, but appears to have no mouth.[44] The stories are informed by a very conservative ideology, depicting a social milieu long disappeared, although after 1913 Caumery introduced a more ironic view of a social class whose way of life was under threat from the modern world.[45] In later albums Bécassine's kind and endlessly patient employer becomes simply Mme de Grand-Air and wears the smart fashions of the interwar years. The characters are shown moving into the modern world: Bécassine learns to drive, and travels in trains, on an ocean liner, and on a plane. Although often bewildered, she is nevertheless endlessly resourceful and prepared to have a go at anything. The stories feature a vast array of representatives of different social classes, professions, and occupations, and frequently the introduction of a new character, even in a minor role, is accompanied by anecdotes of their past history, which interrupt the main plot and contribute to the overall humorous and satirical scheme. The third-person narrative of the early albums had maintained a mocking distance from Bécassine, too, but the strategies employed in later titles have significant implications for the narrator-character-reader relationship. In many, Bécassine narrates events herself and, although she is a keen observer of human nature, her views are kinder and more indulgent. The reader is also given an insight into her own thoughts and motivation, and this adds considerably to the interest and humour of the story. In some albums, both first- and third-person narratives are employed, creating the illusion of a collaboration between the fictional character and her creator. This illusion is extended in *Bécassine fait du scoutisme* (1931), for example, which opens with Bécassine shown in the process of writing, struggling with a pile of papers and books, and harassed by M. Caumery and M. Pinchon to provide her manuscript ('Ah! Tout n'est pas rose dans la vie d'écrivaine!').[46] The introduction into the story of the editor and illustrator themselves and Bécassine's occasional references to her status as a writer for *La Semaine de Suzette* suggest that she enjoys a real existence in the same world as her readers.

As with the Comtesse de Ségur's Sophie, Bécassine's bright ideas go awry, and her well-intentioned efforts to obey her mistress's orders or please Loulotte usually result in further complications from which she must try to extricate herself. Frequently she is the victim of circumstances, misunderstandings, or her own childlike silliness that lead to confusion and farcical situations and at times stretch the reader's credulity. In the very first episode, 'L'Erreur de Bécassine', she thinks that her mistress's instruction to ensure that the *homards* expected for dinner are red and fresh refers to the military men in their scarlet uniforms who arrive as guests. There is humour at the expense of the Marquise here, too, portrayed with her hair in curlers and a little dog who mirrors her reactions. Although most of Bécassine's exploits take place in France, she occasionally ventures further afield, most notably in *Bécassine voyage* (1921) in which, like so many contemporary comic-strip characters, she goes to America, meets up with some *Peaux rouges* and, after some conflict with their medicine man, earns respect by curing the chief. Not to be outdone, she even participates in current events during the First World War, in *Bécassine pendant la Grande Guerre* (1915), *Bécassine chez les alliés* (1917), and *Bécassine mobilisée* (1918).[47] In *Bécassine pendant la Grande Guerre* she is depicted on the cover between two children in the national dress of Alsace and the *patriotisme revanchard* of the times is apparent in her implacable hatred of the Boches and the final image of all the characters saluting a tattered flag, 'image de la France meurtrie mais héroïque, sûre de son droit, forte de sa bravoure, confiante en la victoire'.[48] Through her comic misadventures, tending the wounded, helping to fortify her home village, and her encounters with pistols and bombs, the real horror of the war is reduced to a farce, a strategy presumably intended to protect the sensibilities of the readers of *La Semaine de Suzette*. In *Bécassine mobilisée,* evidence of the more general implications of the war for the civilian population is incorporated, but again manipulated for comic effect. After Mme de Grand-Air's household move to a small apartment in Versailles because of her straitened circumstances, Bécassine resolves to earn her keep by responding to an advertisement for the mobilisation of women to take on the jobs vacated by men serving in the war. After negotiating the bizarre bureaucracy involved, she awaits the call by taking a job as a ticket collector on a tram, where she is teased by schoolchildren and cheated by the old men collecting firewood who hide behind huge branches to avoid paying their fares. Although she becomes something of a celebrity with the passengers, she loses her job when she reroutes the tram to drop her mistress at her door in the rain. Much humour is directed at the pointlessness of the department in charge of the renovation of old, damaged motor vehicles to which she is eventually assigned, her own incompetence as a mechanic matching the bureaucrats' lack of success despite their grandiose titles. The draconian regulations relating to national security are also lampooned when Bécassine visits a factory and, terrified by a poster announcing that any theft is regarded as treason, is subsequently tormented by having involuntarily 'stolen' a speck of coal dust in her eye.

After the introduction of Loulotte in *Bécassine nourrice* (1922), the stories became more child oriented, following Loulotte's activities and interests, and the focus on their relationship imparts coherence to the subsequent albums as she grows up under Bécassine's care.[49] Much humour is derived from Bécassine's anxieties about the child's health and welfare and her attempts to keep up with Loulotte's changing moods. Loulotte is often difficult, rude, and naughty, thus presenting the young reader with a portrait of the problems of child rearing. Together they go to school (*Bécassine au pensionnat*, 1929), visit the seaside (*Bécassine aux bains de mer*, 1932), take up mountain climbing (*Bécassine alpiniste*, 1923) and travel in a plane (*Bécassine en aéroplane*, 1930). In *Bécassine fait du scoutisme* (1931), Bécassine makes acquaintance with the Jeannettes, the junior branch of the Guides, preparing Loulotte for her induction and joining in their games and camping activities. The events in this album would have been a closer reflection of the lives of her readers and is a clear promotion of the ethos of the Jeannettes and the suitability of such an occupation for well-raised young girls. Loulotte is seen to improve dramatically, becoming less wayward and more sensible and considerate.

Although she continues to have many fans and the albums are still in print, the portrayal of Bécassine seems old-fashioned and problematic to modern readers, not least because she seems to be demeaned by continuing to be depicted in the same national costume while other characters have moved with the times. Physically she remains more of an unchanging caricature than do the other characters. Moreover, the association of her simplicity and naïveté with her regional origins is a more sensitive issue today than it was when she began her career over a century ago. The strip has frequently come under attack for ridiculing

Brittany and its inhabitants as staid and backward, thus diminishing the status of regional values and enhancing a sense of cultural superiority in the eyes of Parisian readers.[50] Bécassine's goodheartedness is attractive, but even the celebrity status that she acquires amongst people she encounters often seems (with the exception of the Jeanettes) based as much on a patronising amusement at a curiosity as on genuine respect or affection.

NEW HEROES

In contrast, the entry into histoires en images of a popular young character endowed with the liberty to be independent and transgressive without sacrificing likeability was *L'Espiègle Lili*, created by Jo Valle (storyline) and André Vallet (illustrator) in 1909 for Offenstadt's *Fillette*, and subsequently taken over by other writers. The episodes were presented like a comic strip, with a section of text beneath each picture, and *Lili* albums appeared from 1915 on. As the title indicates, Lili, a dynamic little blonde, is mischievous rather than wicked and continually gets into scrapes, each episode displaying her fondness for playing practical jokes on her unsuspecting family and friends as well as her capacity for kindness. Lili is far from a 'petite fille modèle', and like the Comtesse de Ségur's Sophie is attractive for her energy and ingenuity and her very subversiveness. In the early episodes, which ultimately conform to a more traditionally moralising tone, she is seen as a schoolgirl with no respect for authority and in conflict with hostile adults—particularly her unscrupulous rich cousins, who seek to cheat and exploit her at every turn. Lili's parents are absent on their travels for the most part and Lili is left in the care of a diligent and long-suffering guardian, Monsieur Minet, a professor of philosophy at the Sorbonne. She is thus released from the constraints of a conventional family life and is able to enjoy a certain amount of autonomy without being totally cut off from adult influence and protection. Unlike many comic-strip characters, Lili is seen to grow older (although with no correlation with real time, and sometimes going backwards in years between series) and her adventures consequently broaden in scope. After the Second World War, Lili appears in a series of albums in which she is a dynamic and headstrong teenager and, after 1974, a young adult (she even acquires an American fiancé, although their relationship is suitably chaste). In the early albums, she is seen at home and at school, appears in a circus with her friends (and learns that it is not all glamour and glitter), and visits England. Later she travels widely and, when her family falls on hard times, takes on a variety of jobs in a pâtisserie, on a farm, in a hotel, and as a salesgirl, an actress, an air hostess, a reporter, and an apprentice in a fashion house. In the latter capacity, she is engaged to carry a wedding dress to India, the plot involving an encounter with her cousins on board ship, while as a reporter and photographer she is sent to the South Seas to cover an eclipse. In 1962, she joins bandits in Corsica and in 1996 mingles with top models.[51] The changing nature of Lili's experiences as she grows from childhood to young adulthood, thus continuing to appeal to new audiences as well as an established fan base, may well account for her durability, with albums still in print until the late 1990s.

An example of characters who demonstrate their ingenuity and nonconformism outside the traditional moral framework and in less conservative environments appeared in Louis Forton's widely read, satirical *Les Aventures des Pieds Nickelés,* which appeared in *L'Epatant* from 1908 on. These stories in pictures with supporting text featured morally dubious adult characters and were clearly intended for a wider age range. Indeed, in their comic celebration of misdoings and scams, they would not have been first choice reading material for the young in homes aspiring to respectability. The three amoral, cynical, idle but cheerful characters Ribouldingue, Filochard, and Croquignol are drunks, cheats, liars, and rebels against all authority. They are unshaven, snaggle-toothed and scruffy, and speak invariably in slang. They engage in numerous anarchic and unscrupulous exploits and experience wild fluctuations of fortune, rubbing shoulders with presidents, politicians, and gangsters, enjoying brief periods of prosperity amongst the rich and powerful or, conversely, being hunted by the police. The series continued during the First World War when, in 1915, even the Pieds Nickelés became patriotic, their adventures taking them to the Front, where they were able to use their wiles to good effect against the enemy. The episodes in the album series became more elaborate and implausible and their resilience and daring increased. To some extent, their exploits can be viewed as a crude parody of the adventures of Jules Verne's protagonists, taking them to Britain, America in the heyday of gangsters, and the North Pole and down into the ocean (*Les Pieds Nickelés sous les eaux,* 1938). This exploitation of the world as a resource for humour and the picturesque rather than for educational purposes is characteristic of histoires en images and comic strips of this period. The characters engage in every activity under the sun in the most unlikely occupations, endlessly reinventing themselves as trappers, sailors, volcanologists, journalists, vets, pharmacists, radio reporters, bankers, hippies, footballers, spies, firemen, ghost-hunters and travel agents (where they organise holidays in the Stone Age). They operate both outside the law as burglars and, occasionally, as representatives of it (in *Les Pieds Nickelés, policiers de la route*, 1960). The plots often involve topical issues, as in *Les Pieds Nickelés, rois du caoutchouc* (1938), *Les Pieds Nickelés, as du Contre-Espionnage* (1950), *Les Pieds Nickelés aux Jeux Olympiques* (1957), and *Les Pieds Nickelés et leur fusée atomique* (1958) in which they appear as rocket scientists. Like Lili, the Pieds Nickelés had a long life, passing to other artists and other magazines including their own paper (1971–72) and a series of albums with brightly coloured caricatured images on the covers that were still in print in the late 1980s and inspired three films, the last of which came out in 1964.[52]

A nonconformist character that was more obviously aimed at young readers was *Bibi Fricotin*, created by Louis Forton in 1924 for *Le Petit Illustré*. Initially Bibi was a cheeky and wily stable lad whose main aim in life was to get away with playing tricks on adults. A resourceful and none-too-scrupulous urchin teetering on the verge of delinquency—although he too is sometimes the victim of other people's wickedness—he can be seen as a caricatured version of the *gamin de Paris* type found in Louis Boussenard's novels. With other writers and artists, a period in *L'Epatant* after the Second World War, a magazine of his own (*Le Journal de Bibi Fricotin*, 1965–76) and a series of albums, Bibi branched out into ever more extraordinary and comic adventures that can also be seen as parodies of the adventure story genre. His travels—accompanied by an African boy, Razibus Zouzou, and the eccentric Professor Radar—and his encounters with his enemy Professor Trublion resemble the quest narratives of Verne, to which some of the titles clearly allude (*Bibi Fricotin fait le tour du monde*, 1930; *Bibi Fricotin et le Nautilus*, 1962) and bring him into contact with ancient civilisations (*Bibi Fricotin découvre l'Atlantide*, 1963). In the 1950s and 1960s, Bibi joined in the contemporary craze for science fiction with a series of fantastic space adventures (*Bibi Fricotin et les soucoupes volantes*, 1955; *Bibi Fricotin et les Martiens*, 1955), the latter featuring little green Martians who look like elephants walking on their hind legs and wearing yellow motorcycle helmets, and an excursion into the distant future (*Bibi Fricotin en l'an 3000*, 1963). The albums use a range of bright colours, with Bibi himself in his red pullover with his shock of reddish hair always remaining the same. The other characters are conventional cartoon caricatures—especially Razibus, whose shiny black face, huge white eyes, and red rubbery lips betray the racism still inherent in comic stereotyping in the middle of the century.[53]

The adventures of Zig and Puce by Alain de Saint-Ogan, which first appeared in the *Dimanche illustré* in 1925 and in a variety of different papers after 1940, are regarded as the first *bande dessinée* proper because of the consistent use of speech balloons rather than accompanying narrative.[54] With their mixture of humour and fantasy and bright, clear semicaricatural images, they were an immediate success with young readers and quickly made the transition into album form: Hachette published a series of eleven between 1927 and 1941, with five more after the war. In 1963 the strip was given over to Greg (pen name of Michel Régnier), who produced new stories for *Tintin* magazine and six albums between 1965 and 1969.[55] This comic strip features the escapist tales of two adolescent boys of comically contrasting appearance. Zig is tall and thin while Puce is short and sturdy, with spiky hair like that of Dennis the Menace (created in 1951). Like Bibi Fricotin, they undertake extraordinary journeys to all the different continents and travel in space and time, including trips to New York, India, and Venus, and, many years before Bibi, a visit to the future (*Les Aventures de Zig et Puce au XXIe siècle*, 1935) and to Atlantis (*Zig et Puce en Atlantide*, 1948). Saint-Ogan eventually introduced an animal companion for the boys in the shape of a penguin, Alfred, who is adopted during a visit to the North Pole and became an even more popular character than Zig and Puce themselves and the chosen emblem of a major French comics award. In later episodes they also acquire other travelling companions—Marcel, a horse, and a little girl, Dolly—in order to expand the possibilities of interaction and adventure. Like Jules Verne's universe, Saint-Ogan's fantasy world featured strange and wonderful machines, including one unthought of even by Verne, for delivering kicks up the backside. The adventures of Zig and Puce gave rise to radio shows, cartoon films, and, as in the case of Bécassine, toys, posters, and artefacts of all kinds. Saint-Ogan created other comic-strip characters including *Mitou et Toti* (1932) and *Prosper l'Ours* (1933), but none achieved the lasting popularity of *Zig et Puce*.[56]

POSTWAR REACTION

These energetic and endlessly inventive, self-determining characters—especially the young ones, enjoying autonomy unfettered by adult or social restrictions and roaming the world like the adult heroes of adventure stories—undoubtedly owed their popularity to the fact that they represented an ethos totally contrary to that traditionally preached in children's books. Indeed, their colourful and dynamic exploits were a celebration of the mocking rejection of the moral and literary conventions of children's literature. Although hardly suitable role models for young readers, such picaresque characters as Bibi Fricotin and Les Pieds Nickelés testify to the challenge to aesthetic and moral values instigated by the illustrated papers early in the century. They have been seen by commentators who deplore their influence on children's literature as the beginnings of a cultural transformation in which humour, aggression, and amorality replaced the inculcation of traditional moral values and in which language, like content, was reduced to its lowest common denominator—one of slang and vulgarities. The conformism of earlier children's books was thus in danger of being replaced by a different and more insidious kind of conformity to an ethos of egotism and disregard for all social, moral, literary, and linguistic standards.[57] Serious reservations were expressed after the Second World War about the corruptive influence of imported comics on the nation's youth by educationalists and literary critics specialising in children's books. Marie-Thérèse Latzarus had already in 1924 contrasted nineteenth-century histoires en images with children's magazines of her day, finding them 'grotesques par leurs couleurs, et de mauvais goût par leur inspiration'.[58] Georges Sadoul, editor of the communist Mon camarade, saw a political danger, considering the Mickey Mouse comics as fascist ('C'est ainsi qu'une innocente souris peut cacher, dans son ombre, un grand fauve hitlérien').[59] Jean de Trigon, in his 1950 survey, describes the influx of weekly comics in which text was reduced to a few syllables in speech balloons as 'le sabotage de tout art et de toute littérature'.[60] These anxieties became of such concern after the war that they resulted in the law of 16 July 1949 'sur les publications destinées à la jeunesse', which imposed a rigorous censorship on children's publications. This law required above all that a publication aimed at a young readership should contain no text or image that presents in a favourable light 'le banditisme, le mensonge, le vol, la paresse, la lâcheté, la haine, la débauche ou tous les actes qualifiés crimes ou délits ou de nature à démoraliser l'enfance et la jeunesse, ou à inspirer ou entretenir des préjugés ethniques'.[61] This law is still invoked in the publisher's declarations in children's books today.

Despite such concerns, it was the potential of the marriage of word and image that led to a revival of high standards in both the content and the material aspects of children's books in the second half of the century.

ALBUMS AND THE RENAISSANCE OF CHILDREN'S LITERATURE

The Albums of Père Castor

An innovative project that has lasted to the present day and is generally accepted as having had an immense influence on the development of children's books was begun in 1931 by Paul Faucher (1898–1967), a keen supporter of the theories of L'Education Nouvelle.[62] In response to the relative poverty of children's book production, Faucher initiated a new project of publishing good quality, low-priced albums with interesting and easily assimilable content for young children that would both assist in and encourage the reading process and, in line with the pedagogical ideas of L'Education Nouvelle, serve as support for other activities. The Albums du Père Castor, published by Flammarion and involving a team of writers and artists under Faucher's direction at his atelier, were designed to appeal to different levels of reading competence, addressing the child readers directly and stimulating their imagination, powers of observation, memory, creativity, dexterity, and sense of logic and order. They included abécédaires, picture books with a small amount of text for the very young, colouring and cut-out books, and books of games, folktales, and stories about animals and children from different lands. The series began with two *livres-jeux* illustrated by Nathalie Parain titled *Je Fais mes masques* and *Je découpe* and grew rapidly, with five titles in 1932, including an illustrated version of the Russian folktale *Baba Yaga*; twelve in 1933; and eighty by 1939.[63]

The year 1934 saw the appearance of the first of the *Roman des bêtes*, the most popular collection of the Albums du Père Castor, which employed lively, informative, and interesting narratives and attractive images to introduce readers to the wild life around them and other representatives of the animal kingdom. These albums were immensely successful, with the first, *Panache l'écureuil*, written by Lida Durdikova and illustrated by Rojan (Féodor Rojankovsky), selling more than 600,000 copies.[64] Other titles include *Froux, le lièvre* (1935), *Scaf, le phoque* (1936), *Bourrou, l'ours brun* (1936), and *Quipic, le hérisson* (1937). Each album is dedicated to one creature, but introduces other aspects of nature in painting a detailed picture of the animal's habits and environment, often seen from the animal's viewpoint and therefore in close-up detail. *Plouf, canard sauvage* (1935) for example, charts the stages in the life of eight ducklings from birth to adulthood, immersing the reader in their experiences. Their development follows the seasons of the year; thus, when the cow parsley is out in summer, the ducklings can expect to be ready to learn to fly. To enable the child reader to identify with the ducklings, their lives are conceived in human terms: their first introduction to water is a christening celebrated by the other waterfowl, their activities are games and adventures, learning to fly is a longed-for skill, and their first moult, through which they obtain their new winter plumage, is a rite of passage to full adulthood. The ducks converse amongst themselves, and exhibit human emotions: when they are born, their mother dreams uneasily of threats to her brood, such as enormous frogs and giant weeds, and advises them constantly of dangers in the world. Their existence is not idealised or sentimentalised, however, for predators are everywhere and the ducklings themselves prey on frogs and worms. They have to learn to negotiate aggression and rivalry in the reed beds and the unknown hazards of the open lake and surrounding marshes and fields. Ploof, who is more adventurous than his siblings, escapes from encounters with a hawk and a dog, and is deemed mature enough, at the end, to go with the migrating wild ducks and discover the world. The brightly coloured, naturalistic lithographs and black-and-white drawings on every page replicate the ducklings' view of their environment: when they learn to fly, an aerial view of the countryside fills an entire page in order to allow the reader to share the experience. The instructive aspect of the text is broadened by the inclusion of labelled images of other waterfowl and the creatures that inhabit the margins of the lake.

The aim of the Père Castor series was to encourage child readers to see themselves as part of both nature and the wider world. After the Second World War, an important part of the Père Castor agenda was to encourage children's understanding of other cultures. In the series on children from other lands, *Les Enfants de la terre*, a single-named child figure was introduced as a representative of nationality, thus assisting the reader's identification and stimulating interest in unfamiliar ways of life. The first, *Apoutsiak le petit flocon* (1946) which featured a little Inuit child, was followed by *Mangazou le pygmée* (1952), a pygmy boy; *Amo le peau-rouge* (1951), an American Indian; *Jan de Hollande* (1954); *Antonio un petit italien* (1961); and *Féfé des Antilles* (1962), amongst others. The Albums du Père Castor were quickly adopted by primary schools and for leisure reading, and Faucher won the Prix Européen du Livre pour Enfants in 1962. The Editions du Père Castor have diversified over the decades into numerous collections on different topics, including history, travel, and science, and new formats, notably the Montreur d'images series, which employed photographs to show the stages of a bud bursting into flower or a chick hatching from an egg; the paperback series Castor Poche (from 1980), which published fiction for different age groups including adventure and detective stories, science fiction, and folktales from around the world; and books with an accompanying audiocassette from 1989 on. By 1967, Faucher's atelier had sold some twenty million books at home and abroad.[65] The current Flammarion website lists some nine hundred titles, and a special, collected edition of four of the 'Roman des bêtes' (*Quipic le hérisson, Coucou, Panache l'écureuil*, and *Plouf, canard sauvage*) was published by Ecole des Loisirs in 2004.[66]

The Babar Albums

The adventures of Babar the elephant began life as a story told by Jean de Brunhoff's wife Cécile to their two boys, which was subsequently recast as a histoire en images by Brunhoff, and published in 1931 as *Histoire de Babar, le petit éléphant.* Brunhoff produced five more albums and a Babar alphabet book (1934) and after his premature death in 1937, the stories were continued by his son Laurent from 1946. Unlike portrayals in the Père Castor realistic nature studies, Babar is anthropomorphised as a stylised elephant figure who adopts human dress and has human faculties, emotions, and ambitions. In the first album—which, like fairy tales, brings together the world of humans and that of animals—we read of Babar's birth, his happy childhood in the jungle, and his journey to the city after his mother is shot and killed by a hunter. There, with the help of a kindly, rich old lady, he emulates the humans he envies by buying himself a smart green suit, shirt, tie, shoes and spats, and a bowler hat. He shares the old lady's home, drives a car, and learns to read and write, all without any apparent surprise on the part of shop assistants, teachers, or the old lady's friends, whom he regales with tales of his life in the jungle. Still prone to bouts of nostalgia for his early life, he eventually revisits the jungle where his experience and savoir faire lead to his being invited by the venerable old elephant Cornélius to become their new king. The story ends with an animated scene of the marriage and coronation of Babar and his cousin Céleste. Brunhoff's illustrations use clear cheerful colours (largely green, brown, and yellow) with the occasional splash of red; these colours form a contrasting background to the grey of the elephants and are simply and elegantly drawn. The mise en page varies, with large images of Babar alone, Babar with one other character, or crowded panoramic scenes. In the first album, thirty-one young elephants are shown playing ball, digging in the sand, playing follow-the-leader, or amusing themselves in a pool of water. There are many humorous details that delight the eye and flesh out the accompanying lines of narrative: one elephant floats on his back, his trunk in the air, while four of different sizes stroll along, the last three of which link their trunks into the tails of those in front of them. In the wedding scene, animals of different species enjoy music provided by a monkey band and a chorus of parrots, an ostrich dancing with a snake, a rhinocerous with a hippopotamus, a giraffe with a lion, and, of course, a host of prancing elephants. Apart from Cornélius, who wears a bowler hat and spectacles (and whose outline is drawn with wavy lines to depict his great age), only Babar, Céleste, and their other cousins wear clothes at this stage, although all the elephants dance on two legs.

The covering of their nakedness is seen as a significant civilising factor, for in *Le Roi Babar* (1933), after the building of an ideal city, Célesteville, Babar presents clothes to all the elephants and they are depicted thereafter in smart outfits dating from the first decades of the century or, on fete days, in costumes and uniforms of every nationality and from every period of history. Babar's closest friendships cross the boundaries of species, notably with the old lady and Zéphir the monkey, and life in Célesteville promotes an ethos of harmony and happiness. With their exotic settings and delightful animal protagonists, the Babar books endorse traditional moral and social values and mirror an idealised version of human existence, celebrating family and community spirit. The reader is encouraged to see the development of this ideal with fresh eyes through the elephants' unspoilt and sincere enthusiasm for the achievements of human civilisation.[67] Célesteville is seen as the distillation of the best in human cities, with every civic amenity, and the elephants have homes to themselves overlooking a huge lake where they can indulge in water sports. Life is divided between hard work and fun (a *palais de travail* and a *palais des fêtes* stand side by side), including fairs, musical evenings, tennis, and the theatre. Every citizen has a particular profession and all work together for the common good. The panoramic illustrations again provide a wealth of details to be noticed on successive readings: in the double-page spread depicting the parade to mark the first anniversary of the founding of the city, the marchers include elephants dressed as Roman soldiers, *mousquetaires*, and groups of workers decked with the emblems of their professions; a guard of young elephant scouts lines the road. However, in what is perhaps an echo of the clouds gathering in the real world, a note of disquiet is introduced in this book when, after a day of triumphant celebration, disaster strikes two of the inhabitants (the old lady is bitten by a snake and Cornélius is injured when his house burns down) and Babar's confidence in his perfect happy world is shaken. His dream, in which the hideous *Malheur* and her monster acolytes (*mollesse, peur, ignorance, paresse, lâcheté, colère, bêtise, maladie, découragement,* and *désespoir*) are routed by a flight of angel elephants (*bonté, intelligence, espoir, travail, amour, santé, patience, joie, savoir, persévérance, courage,* and *bonheur*), offers an encouraging message for the times and reassures Babar of the validity of the social prescription that if all continue to work joyfully they will continue to find happiness.

One of the most attractive elements of the original editions is the elegant cursive handwriting used for the text, which imparts an informal tone and forms a pleasing decorative contrast to the vigorous, animated images. This unusual aspect is, regrettably, not replicated in many English editions. Jean de Brunhoff's albums, which also include *Le Voyage de Babar* (1932), in which the newly wed Babar and Céleste depart for their honeymoon in a balloon and are stranded on an island amongst cannibals; *Les Vacances de Zéphir* (1936), in which Zéphir, on holiday in his monkey town, teams up with a mermaid to rescue a princess from monsters; *Babar en famille* (1938), which depicts his growing family of three children, Pom, Flora, and Alexandre; and *Babar et le Père Noël* (1941) sold some four million copies.[68] In Laurent de Brunhoff's later albums, like *Babar et le coquin d'Arthur* (1946) and *Pique-nique chez Babar* (1949), Babar travels farther afield, even visiting New York, thus inscribing the series in the literary tradition of Jules Verne and the adventure story, despite still privileging the themes of home and family. In a special English-language album published in 2003 (*Babar's Gallery*), Babar turns a deserted station in Célesteville into an art gallery that bears a striking resemblance to the Musée d'Orsay. The reader joins a tour of the gallery and, together with Babar's children and friends, is invited to admire all the most famous paintings in the world, recast to feature elephants. The attempts of Cornélius to explain the paintings are juxtaposed with the spontaneous reactions of the others (Sandro Botticelli's *Birth of Venus* is greeted by the children as a picture telling us how to dry off when we come out of the water), imparting the message that art does not have to be subjected to scholarly analysis to be enjoyed. The Babar stories have been widely translated and imitated, and, because of the clarity and originality of the style and the gentle and reassuring humour of the content are seen as a landmark in the history of children's picture books.[69]

FAVOURITES FROM THE SECOND HALF OF THE CENTURY

It would be impossible to do justice in this chapter to the range of illustrated magazines, comic books, and picture albums published in the second half of the twentieth century, so brief consideration is given to two publications that have enjoyed a wide circulation, one read largely by girls and the other largely by boys, before introducing what are undoubtedly two of the best-known Francophone bande dessinée characters, Tintin and Astérix. In the early 1950s, Hachette initiated a series of albums written and illustrated by Pierre Probst about a little girl, Caroline, and her group of animal friends. The *Collection Caroline*, for younger readers, remained a favourite for more than a decade amongst the Albums roses series, and many of the albums have been reissued in recent years. The Caroline books are not comic strips but stories in which the illustrations take precedence, with the narrative, which contains a large amount of dialogue, generally occupying part of one page in each double-page spread. Caroline, who appears from the illustrations to be under ten, is recognisable by her blond hair tied in bunches and her trademark red dungerees worn over a neat white shirt. Despite her youth and gender, her adventures take her to all the places visited by the comic-book heroes (a ranch, a circus, a mysterious island, the North Pole, America, Canada, Egypt, Russia, and into space), and she engages in an implausibly wide range of activities including winter sports, detective work, and animal liberation, and encounters not only people of different nationalities, but Liliputians, robots, extraterrestrials, and the Loch Ness monster. She is accompanied by a retinue of small, feisty animals who are realistically drawn but wear articles of clothing and have the power of human speech. These attractive characters (a white and a black kitten, named Pouf and Noiraud, respectively; three small dogs, Bobi, Pipo, and Youpi; a little bear cub, Boum; a leopard cub, Pitou; and the lion cub, Kid) had appeared in albums by Probst from 1946 on and have their own distinctive personalities. They participate actively in the adventures—even, for example, building an igloo and flying a plane in *Caroline au Pôle Nord* (1962). The Collection Caroline thus ingeniously brought together two of the genres most popular with young readers in the twentieth century, the adventure narrative and the animal story. Probst's large and colourful illustrations not only accompany the narrative but add innumerable touches of humour that repay careful scrutiny. The activities and facial expressions of the animals in both the foreground and background of the illustrations expand the significance of each episode by contributing multiple responses to, and engagement with, the action. The reader is, of course, expected to accept unquestioningly the independence and autonomy of Caroline (which are seemingly also accepted by the adults with whom she and her friends come into contact) and the ease with which she is able to commandeer cars, planes, ships, or whatever mode of transport and equipment she needs for her exploits. With this demand upon the reader's willing suspension of disbelief and the conceit of the anthropomorphised animal companions, the Caroline albums present a blend of realism and fantasy characteristic of much twentieth-century children's literature. Like many of the characters featured in this chapter, Caroline has evidently retained her fan base for expressions of enjoyment and requests for information about the availability of the books can be found on the Internet.[70]

The character Spirou was first created in the Belgian *Le Journal de Spirou* in 1938 and, with various changes of writer and artist, has survived in albums to the present day. The strip is most commonly associated with André Franquin, who took over in 1946, and by the 1950s *Spirou* was one of the best-selling bande dessinée magazines in Europe. The character of Spirou began life as a lift operator in an hotel, dressed in a red jacket with gold buttons reminiscent of Mickey Mouse, and, like other bande dessinée characters, with an unruly shock of red hair. Later the illusion was created that he was, like Tintin, an investigative journalist on his own magazine, and he was taken on longer adventures fighting injustice and defeating villains. His companions include his friend and fellow reporter Fantasio and two animal helpers; Spip, his pet squirrel, whose grumpy reactions to their adventures are mediated to the reader in thought balloons; and one of Franquin's most successful creations, the Marsupilami, a fantastic creature with a long prehensile tale. Franquin retained the rights to the Marsupilami character when the strip changed hands again in 1969 and the creature's popularity earned its own series in the 1990s. The Spirou strips reveal the influence of Disney comics in their highly coloured, rounded, elastic, caricatural graphic style.[71] In terms of content and scope, they essentially conform to the conventions established by their predecessors. Spirou has an eccentric scientist friend, the Comte de Champignac whose 'double' is Zorglub, a madman bent on world domination, and his adventures take him and his companions far and wide, to colonial Africa (*Spirou chez les Pygmées*, 1950), and, in later albums, to Australia (*Aventure en Australie*, 1985), New York (*Spirou à New York*, 1987) and Moscow (*Spirou à Moscou*, 1990). Extraordinary machines regularly feature, in, for example, *Spirou et les plans du robot* (1948), *La Boîte noire* (1983), and *La Machine qui rêve* (1998). From the mid-1950s on, topical and polemical issues began to be introduced, like *Le Dictateur et le champignon* (1956), involving Third World Fascism, and in the 1970s Jean-Claude Fournier introduced issues like nuclear energy (*L'Ankou*, 1978).[72] A new series of special albums with guest writers and artists was launched in 2006 to appear alongside the regular series.

Franquin's other bande dessinée, *Gaston Lagaffe*, is a more anarchic creation that depends more on short visual gags and verbal humour. An office boy at *Spirou* magazine, Gaston is lazy and gaffe-prone but energetic and imaginative and, rather like Bécassine, his original and well-intentioned ideas usually end in disaster. His inventions and ideas for improvement around the office (enabling him to spend less time working and more time snoozing), which backfire and enrage his superiors, are a major source of humour (he invents an ultrasonic kettle, keeps several animals in the office, and trains a lobster to sort the mail). Running gags are his hindrance of his bosses' business activities (notably, signing contracts with a wealthy businessman), his passion for creating bizarre gastronomic delights, and his efforts to outwit the parking meters outside the office. The series of albums published between 1963 and 1996 have titles—*Gala des gaffes* (1963), *Les Gaffes d'un gars gonflé* (1967), *Le Gang des gaffeurs* (1974), *Gaffe à Lagaffe!* (1996) that suggest the anarchic nature of the content just as, visually, the strip is chaotic with distorted shapes and frantic movement.[73] To celebrate his fortieth anniversary in 1997, Editions Dupuis republished the whole series of nineteen albums. Gaston, an antihero for readers of any age, has become an icon of popular culture in France and Belgium but has not been translated into English.

TINTIN: A UNIVERSAL HERO

Although Hergé (Georges Rémi, 1907–1983), the creator of Tintin, was Belgian, the character Tintin has been thoroughly appropriated by French readers and has become (along with Babar and Astérix) one of the most widely acclaimed exports of children's literature in French; as such, the Tintin albums merit inclusion here.[74] Tintin first appeared in January 1929 in *Le Petit Vingtième*, the children's supplement of the right-wing Catholic newspaper *Le Vingtième siècle*, and his appearance and personality have changed little since. Although his neat sweater, white open-necked shirt and plus fours were eventually replaced by jeans and a polo shirt, his round, closely barbered head with the distinctive tuft of ginger hair and his snub nose have remained relatively unchanged by age. Accompanied always by his white fox terrier Milou, Tintin is both youthful and mature, ordinary and exceptional, but his talents are in no way superhuman, and he has no need to affect fantastical disguises or persona, a major respect in which he differed from the American superheroes of the mid-twentieth century. Hergé, a keen scouting enthusiast, also produced a series for *Le Boy Scout Belge* in 1926, involving a character called Totor, and indeed, his later creation does exhibit many qualities of the scouting ethos: a sense of fair play, courage, resourcefulness, determination, and a dedication to helping the weak or exploited. Tintin is highly intelligent, virtuous, chaste, and clean living (he disapproves of drinking and smoking after the early albums), devoting his life to the righting of wrongs and the defeat of villains worldwide and is an attractive and empowering role model for young readers. His family background and circumstances are never revealed, and he is known only by the one name; he never lacks the financial means to travel nor appears to have constraints like parental or educational pressures or responsibilites to inhibit his activities. Initially he was conceived as a roving reporter for the very newspaper in which he appeared, thus integrating the character firmly with the real world, although later this formal career became less foregrounded as he was called upon repeatedly to travel, track down criminals, or help to solve some difficult international situation. When the first episode, *Tintin au Pays des Soviets*, ended, the newspaper nurtured the allusion that Tintin worked for them by staging his 'return' with a youth dressed like Tintin arriving at the Gare du Nord in Brussels, to the delight of fans.[75] Tintin's adventures, aimed at an audience of ages seven to seventy-seven, according to Hergé, appeared in *Le Petit Vingtième* from 1929 to 1940, and then in *Le Soir jeunesse* (1940–45) and subsequently in his own magazine, *Le Journal de Tintin* (1945–76), and after serialisation, each story was published by the Belgian publisher Casterman in hardback albums.[76] Initially the images were in black and white, but were redrawn in colour by Hergé after 1946. The albums have been translated into some fifty languages, and have sold millions of copies worldwide.

Hergé's graphic style, which was influential on a number of other graphic artists, is distinctive and immediately attractive. Known as *ligne claire*, or 'clear line', it employs well-defined lines, precisely proportioned shapes, and fresh, bright, unmodulated colours that give a strong sense of realism yet create a world too clean and lacking in shading and clutter to exist outside the bande dessinée.[77] Each page of the albums contains four rows of panels that are generally square or rectangular with variations in size and shape for effect. The speech balloons are also uniformly rectangular, with neat, regular lettering, varied only by the occasional balloon containing a large exclamation or question mark to indicate puzzlement, confusion, surprise, or outrage. There is the absolute minimum of external, contextualising narrative, with events set in motion by newspaper reports read by Tintin or by explanations or requests from other characters and carried forward by the action itself. Each page in the albums ends on a suspenseful note that draws the reader onwards, a reminder of Tintin's serialised origins, and interest is maintained by a clever alternation of tense and humorous moments.

The first two Tintin albums, *Tintin au Pays des Soviets* (1929) and *Tintin au Congo* (1930), exemplify the social and racial prejudices of the day. The first reveals the influence of *Le Vingtième siècle*'s editorial policy, which, twelve years after the Russian Revolution, presented the totalitaran regime of Bolshevik Russia as corrupt and terrifying, and was the only one of the stories not to be reprinted in the album series.[78] The satire on the mendacity of the Russian propaganda machine, the country's disastrous economy (a factory visited by Tintin is a mere cardboard frontage, its belching chimneys merely piles of burning straw), the activities of the secret police, and the poverty and starvation of the people in the food queues was intended by the newspaper's director, Abbé Norbert Wallez, to show young Belgians what was happening under the Communist regime. This album, like the second, *Tintin au Congo* (1930), is structured around a series of episodes with visual jokes rather than the more complex plots found in the later albums. Tintin is sent to report on the state of the Soviet economy, and various attempts are made to kill or imprison him to prevent him from telling the truth—all of which fail. Tintin is drawn as a more burly and aggressive figure than he later became, and his expertise and love of speed are seen in frenetic chase sequences involving a car, a motorcycle, a plane, a motorboat, and an adapted railway trolley. He and Milou adopt a variety of disguises, and at one point they both get drunk on champagne. The second album, *Tintin au Congo*, first published in black and white in 1931 and redesigned, like all prewar albums, in colour at a later date (in this case, 1946), also reveals the prejudices of Hergé's background, and has been out of favour for many decades. Tintin, visiting the Belgian colony of the Congo on safari, encounters a number of near-fatal situations involving wild animals and the henchmen of an archvillain (eventually revealed to be Al Capone) out to control the diamond trade. There is much here to disconcert the modern reader: the impression that Africa and its resources are simply a kind of theme park for the amusement of white tourists is implicit in Tintin's unashamed killing of a number of animals (he blows up a rhinocerous with dynamite and kills a monkey in order to dress in its skin), and the portrayal of the Africans is characteristically racist and paternalistic. They are comically stereotyped with huge red lips and wearing a motley collection of Western outfits, from dress uniform jackets with shorts to fur-trimmed coats or battered top hats. (One man wears only a collar and tie and white cuffs on his bare torso, a long yellow skirt and a jaunty boater.) They are depicted as lazy, childlike, and easily dominated by Tintin, whose ingenuity and modern European equipment quickly lead to his being acclaimed leader of a tribe after routing the evil witchdoctor. They speak in pidgin French, as fictional black characters invariably did at this period. Hergé later regretted the easy assumption of contemporary prejudices in these early albums, describing them as his 'péchés de jeunesse'.[79] After the Second World War, he was also a controversial figure for having continued to work for the collaborationist newspaper *Le Soir* after 1940 and for his connections with Belgian fascist writers.[80] However, it has been argued recently that the evidence of papers in the Hergé archives seems to suggest that despite his undoubted right-wing tendencies, Hergé was more absorbed in the production and progress of his work than in active political engagement and propaganda.[81] The war years were, in fact, amongst his most successful, with huge sales despite the paper shortage, and the creation of some of the most popular titles, which avoided political topics and took Tintin on exotic and mysterious adventures. Furthermore, two albums, *Le Lotus bleu* (1936), in which Tintin meets Tchang, a Chinese boy who becomes a close friend, and *Le Sceptre d'Ottokar* (1939), set in a fictional troubled Baltic state, Syldavia, can be seen as strong antifascist statements. Tintin himself, as he evolved, remained politically unaligned, fighting evil and corruption whether it be in communist countries, the Middle East, Europe, or the United States. Arguably, he owes his longevity to his embrace of the universal values of courage, compassion for the underdog, and a strong sense of justice without subscribing to any particular ideology.

From the mid-1930s on, the episodic structure of the earlier volumes, which relied on the repeated build-up to comic situations, was replaced by a more complex and unified linear narrative with the situational and visual jokes integrated into the plot. In effect, the albums become more like a mixture of the full-length adventure narrative best exemplified by Jules Verne, of whom Hergé was an admirer, and the mystery and detective story, like those of Gaston Leroux.[82] The structure of the stories has been seen as basically conforming to the traditional pattern of the folktale and fairy story, with the hero leaving home on a journey, encountering and overcoming difficulties caused by villainy or misfortune and, with his exceptional talents, returning triumphant.[83] An important ingredient of this model is not applicable to Tintin's adventures, however, in that they are not narratives of initiation or self-development. Although Tintin certainly gains knowledge in his travel, it is never formative in the sense of leading to maturation, for his qualities remain essentially the same. Nor is Tintin's return home ever rewarded with marriage and riches, as in the traditional folktale model. After *Le Lotus bleu*, the stories also exhibit a greater attention to realistic detail based on research into the history and culture of the countries depicted rather than dependence on clichés.[84] The depiction of streets, buildings, vehicles, clothes, and objects are strongly anchored in contemporary reality. This documented realism, which includes not just physical landscapes but local colour and customs, encourages the conviction that Tintin inhabits the same world as his readers.[85] Moreover, the story lines introduced young readers to issues that were (and continue to be) of strong social and political concern.

Each album involves Tintin in different parts of the world, investigating dangerous situations that have clear topical resonances. He goes, by invitation or chance, to America (*Tintin en Amérique*, 1932) where he is pitted against gangsters in Chicago and witnesses the exploitation of the native Americans; Egypt, in *Les Cigares du Pharaon* (1934), where he tackles heroin smugglers; China, in *Le Lotus bleu* (1936), which again deals with drugs, political intrigue, and the Japanese invasion; Scotland, in *L'Île noire* (1938), where he outwits forgers; the Middle East, in *Coke en stock* (1958), which deals with illegal arms dealing, a rebel coup d'état, and the slave trade; and Tibet, in *Tintin au Tibet* (1960), in which he meets the Yeti. The latter album is unusual in that there are no villains to be pursued (even the Yeti turns out to have friendly qualities) and the plot involves a personal quest motivated solely by Tintin's determination to find his friend Tchang after a plane crash in the mountains of Tibet. Here the boy scout in Tintin comes to the fore, as most of the story concerns the tracking of his friend through the snow covered mountains.[86] In two albums in the 1950s, *Objectif Lune* (1953) which appeared four years before the launch of the first Sputnik, and *On a marché sur la Lune* (1954), fifteen years before the Apollo XI moon landing, he and his companions undertake a rocket trip to the moon and Hergé provides an impressively accurate depiction of scientific equipment and conditions in space, unlike the stereotyped fantasy of other contemporary comic strips. On the moon there are no aliens, although there is a glacier and a cave with stalactites.[87] Hergé also invented fictitious countries for some of the more politically sensitive plots. Thus, in *Le Sceptre d'Ottokar* (1939), Tintin saves Syldavia, a fictitious country in the Balkans, from invasion by its fascist neighbour and the villain Müsstler, an extraordinarily topical and risky subject at a time when Adolf Hitler had just invaded Austria.[88] He visits the equally fictitious South American republic of San Theodorus in *L'Oreille cassée* (1937) and *Tintin et les Picaros* (1976), a country torn apart by the commercial interests of warring Anglo-American oil barons, the activities of arms dealers, guerilla warfare, and rival would-be dictators. The latter, Hergé's last album, manifests a troublingly pessimistic view of Tintin's moral campaigns and the consequences of his efforts to defeat evil and restore harmony. Travelling to San Theodorus reluctantly to rescue a friend who has unaccountably been imprisoned on suspicion of plotting to overthrow the regime, he assists the rebel General Alcazar (who appeared earlier in *Coke en Stock)* against the corrupt and unscrupulous General Tapioca, but at the end, San Theodorus still remains in the grip of an oppressive dictatorship. Alcazar, moreover, is supported by the International Banana Company, a clear suggestion that American concerns were supporting rebellion in unstable South American countries.[89] It is no wonder that Tintin is initially reticent about becoming involved. In the penultimate panel, Alcazar's soldiers are seen patrolling a street of a squalid shanty town, swinging their batons while two shrinking inhabitants look on and the plane carrying Tintin and his companions back to the haven of Moulinsart flies off in the distance. This mirrors closely the earlier panel in which another plane flies over a similar scene, except that the soldiers' uniforms are different and a wayside notice reads 'Viva Alcazar' instead of 'Viva Tapioca'.[90]

Tintin's most frequent companions have become memorable characters in their own right. The wonderful Milou is his inseparable companion and loyal partner in troubles from the start, and the source of much of the humour in the stories. Although a realistic dog, he has a hugely expressive face that often mirrors Tintin's reactions, and is also subject to human reflections and reactions portrayed through thought balloons, even engaging occasionally in a conversation with Tintin. He is cocky, boastful, and brave but on other occasions can be nervous and superstitious. The first few pages of *Tintin au Congo* portray the series of comic mishaps that plague Milou on board a ship after he has been frightened by a spider and broken a mirror, including having his tail bitten by an aggressive parrot and falling overboard. (Milou recuperates his dignity later in the story when he attacks a lion that has hurt Tintin and bites off its tail.) His doggy attributes are used to good effect, sniffing out dangers and following scents, but his penchant for bones sometimes leads to trouble: in *Tintin au Tibet*, he is torn between desire (a large bone) and duty (delivering an urgent message), his quandary represented by an angelic dog and a demon dog, both replicas of himself, who appear in thought balloons and lecture him. Humour is derived on several occasions from Milou's greed and his liking for alcohol, and in *L'Ile noire* he incurs Tintin's displeasure when he develops a fondness for Loch Lomond whisky and becomes incapably drunk. Not only subject to murderous attempts by various villains, Milou also comes under attack from other animals, both domesticated and wild— notably, in *Tintin au Congo*. In *L'Ile noire*, however, his initial terror of a giant gorilla, kept chained in a tower as the villains' secret weapon, turns to smug self-confidence when the fearsome creature proves to be scared of his bark, an event that causes him to reflect mockingly on the gorilla's sensibilities until he himself flees ignominiously from a spider.

The earliest of Tintin's extravagantly comic human companions to appear were the identical twin detectives Dupond and Dupont, in *Les Cigares du Pharaon* (1934). Their appearance and mannerisms and their role in the adventures are the source of multifunctional humour. Dressed alike in black suits with bowler hats and walking sticks, they mirror each other's movements, gestures, and speech, repeating each other's words with comically clumsy distortions. Their involvement in the adventures invariably aggravate a situation through misunderstandings or their incompetent notion of discreet detection work. In *Le Lotus bleu*, they dress as Chinese mandarins in order to go undercover and become immediately the centre of bemused attention in the streets. Their pompous language, in which absurdities abound, and their dogged insistence on observing the rules ridicule the conventional forces of law and order. Tintin's most notable human companion, however, is the irascible, stubborn, but loyal and courageous Capitaine Haddock, who first appears in 1941 in *Le Crabe aux pinces d'or*, in which he is portrayed as an incompetent sailor and a violent drunk whose ship is being used to smuggle opium without his knowledge—a situation from which he is saved by Tintin. He is an unusual character in a book for young readers, even more so as an heroic figure. His drinking becomes less threatening and, together with his pipe smoking, more the occasion for humour in later albums, but he remains subject to violent but short-lived outbursts of enthusiasm, rage, or frustration expressed in extravagantly comic and inventive curses and insults ('mille milliards de mille sabords!', 'tonnerre de Brest!', 'coloquinte à la graisse de hérisson!') which by both their resemblance to and difference from conventional expletives are designed to appeal to a juvenile audience. Depicted throughout the series in a sailor's dark blue jersey and peaked cap with a black beard, he is of indeterminate age and driven by protective feelings towards Tintin, accompanying the youngster, often against his better judgement, in dangerous situations in which he is routinely the victim of attacks from humans, animals, and natural forces. A less frequent companion is the eccentric Professeur Tournesol, a type frequently found in comic strips where marvellous inventions are often called upon to save the day. Once again, Hergé modulates the stereotype, for his deafness, which causes him to mishear and repeat erroneously what others say is the source of much of the verbal, as opposed to visual, humour in the stories. Tournesol is the motivating force for the adventures in *Les Sept boules de cristal* (1948) and *Le Temple du soleil* (1949), when he has to be rescued from the curse of an Incan mummy. He constructs the rocket that takes them to the moon in *On a marché sur la Lune*, and plays an important role in the hunt for the treasure of Haddock's ancestor, François Hadoque, a captain under Louis XIV, in *Le Secret de la licorne* (1943) and *Le Trésor de Rackham le Rouge* (1944), in which his shark-shaped submarine enables them to explore a sunken galleon. As a result of this adventure, the three friends acquire the château of Moulinsart, where they live peacefully together between adventures in later albums, a ménage which has inevitably given rise in more recent years to speculation about the sexual orientation of Tintin, fuelled by the absence of any romantic attachments to young women or, indeed, of any significant young female characters in the stories.[91] The only female of any consequence is the grotesque opera singer Bianca Castafiore, who surfaces sporadically and unexpectedly in several volumes, her arrival always heralded by a burst of the 'Jewel Song' from Charles-François Gounod's *Faust*; despite her alleged worldwide fame, her talents are derided by Tintin and Haddock as shrill caterwauling. Tintin's world, in short, is a very homosocial one, and in this respect his exploits are characteristic of the adventure story genre.

The Tintin albums are still both topical and entertaining, and continue to sell in the thousands. His adventures have been transferred to animated films and are currently available, in English, on DVD. Several websites are dedicated to the albums and list numerous events, including those celebrating the seventieth and seventy-fifth anniversaries of his first appearance.[92] One can only wonder what use Tintin himself could have made of the Internet.

ASTÉRIX

The Astérix series has arguably achieved even greater success than that of Tintin. Created by René Goscinny and Albert Uderzo in 1959 for the first issue of *Pilote*, a new magazine aimed at adolescent readers, the Astérix strips then appeared in hardcover albums published by Dargaud in Paris. The thirty-third Astérix story, *Le Ciel lui tombe sur la tête*, was published in 2005. After Goscinny, who wrote the text, died in 1977, Uderzo continued to produce new volumes, and by the 1980s Astérix was outselling Tintin. The popularity of the comic adventures of the little Gaulish hero and his companions in the year 50 B.C.E. have been attributed to the welcome positive self-image they promoted for French readers at a period of loss of empire and of American dominance in cultural and political terms, and hence to a boost to national pride.[93] Astérix lives in a fictional village in Armorique (Brittany), the only place in Gaul to hold out against the Roman invaders thanks to the superhuman strength of the inhabitants gained from a magic potion concocted by their local Druid Panoramix. Each album contains a wealth of comic episodes, visual and verbal jokes within an overarching, loosely constructed plot that takes Astérix and his sidekick Obélix all over Europe and beyond, engaging in battles or helping the locals to resist Julius Caesar and the Roman legions. The stories are less straightforward in moral terms than the Tintin albums, relishing constant fast and furious violence and excess of feasting and fighting, with Astérix and Obélix and their companions engaging in ruse after ruse to defeat their enemies. Uderzo's images, unlike Hergé's, are brightly coloured, crowded, and full of comic detail, and the figures are caricatured, with extreme body shapes, huge noses, and big feet. The breathless pace of the plot demands a multitude of 'movement' lines, giant exclamation and question marks and 'sound' words ('Paff!' 'Boum!' 'Schplokk!').

Astérix is a hero of immense intelligence and resourcefulness as well as superhuman strength, despite his small stature, and is immediately recognisable by his sleeveless black tunic, red trousers, and helmet with wings that point jauntily upwards or droop disconsolately according to his mood. He is the ringleader and decision maker and, like all super-heroes, is the first to be called upon in a crisis. He fights mainly with his fists, even against a whole legion of sword- and shield-bearing Romans. His companion Obélix, a carver of stone monoliths, is correspondingly large and always ready for action but slow on the uptake, prone to fits of giggles, and constantly preoccupied with where his next meal of roast boar is coming from. Obélix is permanently strong because he fell into a vat of the magic potion as a baby, and his resentment at being excluded from the drinking ritual is a running gag throughout the albums. The comic effect of his bulky shape, which contrasts with the tiny, lithe fig-ure of Astérix, is enhanced by his blue-and-white-striped tight-fitting trousers and the neat black bows that secure the ends of his plaits. The Roman leaders are portrayed as aggressive, unscrupulous, and deca-dent but are easily outwitted and defeated in battle, and the Roman soldiers are often reluctant and fed up. There are regular jokes about the well-honed efficiency and discipline of their military manoeuvres, which nevertheless cannot withstand an encounter with the two Gauls. Obélix's favourite remark, 'Ils sont fous, ces Romains', has become a popular catchphrase. Although Astérix shows no scruples in his deal-ings with the Romans, he and his fellow villagers do not, like their enemies, seek to invade or impose themselves on others. At the start of each album, the inhabitants of the Gaulish village are seen peaceably going about their business before an emissary or news from outside prompts a new adventure. In *Astérix gladiateur* (1964), the tiny warrior is shown sweeping the doorstep of his neat little stone cottage, complete with a vase of flowers on the windowsill. Many of their exploits are undertaken to help others in trouble. In *Astérix aux jeux olympiques* (1968), he even helps the Roman competitors avoid the wrath of Cae-sar. After allowing them access to the magic potion and then having them disqualified for employing a forbidden substance, he gives them the prize he has won in the race. Each album ends with a scene of feast-ing and good fellowship after Astérix's return home from his adven-tures. It is possible to see the Gauls' existence as simple, enjoying the basic pleasures of life as opposed to the corrupt, power-hungry politics and consumer culture of Rome, and hence the Gauls as representative of resistance to any dominant, aggressive force, but the humour is too wide-ranging and the morality too relative for Astérix to be adopted as the representative of any one modern political stance.[94]

The unrelenting humour takes many different forms to appeal to a wide readership, from situational farce and visual jokes to sophisticated linguistic humour. As well as the humour resulting from the many short episodes that make up the overall plot, there are running gags: in several stories, when Astérix and his companions find themselves imprisoned, they sit and talk for a while before calling to the perplexed guard that they are coming out and breaking the door down. This joke is taken to the extreme in *Astérix et les Goths* (1963), in which several cell doors are broken and are eventually replaced with a curtain. A minor character, the Gaulish bard Assurancetourix, is always denied the opportunity to sing by his fellow villagers and is depicted at each feast scene tied up and gagged in his tree house in a corner of the picture. This situation is exploited to the full in *Astérix, gladiateur* when Astérix and Obélix become gladiators to rescue the kidnapped Assurancetourix who is about to be thrown to the lions in Rome. His appalling singing causes the lions to flee, and Astérix and Obélix teach the gladiators party games (such as answering questions without saying yes or no) that enrage Caesar but delight the audience at the Circus Maximus. On his travels by sea, Astérix repeatedly encounters a group of pirates and sinks their ship so that they dread the sight of him on the horizon. The characters and places all have comic, punning names: the Gauls' names end in -ix (Obélix's tiny dog is Idéfix and the leader of the village is Abraracourcix), the Egyptians in -s (Courdeténis), the Goths in -ic (Téléféric, Electric) and, of course, the Romans in -us (the four encampments surrounding Astérix's village are Babaorum, Aquarium, Laudanum, and Petitbonum).[95] The cultural specificity and stereotypes of the different countries to which Astérix's adventures take him are the source of much of the varied humour. In *Astérix chez les Bretons* (1966), where he goes to Britain to help a village like his own to fight the Romans, there are repeated jokes about the bad food, the weather, and the warm beer. The Britons, whose leader is Zebigbos, wear handlebar moustaches, are formal and polite, drive their chariots on the wrong side of the road, and stop whatever they are doing at five in the afternoon to drink hot water with milk. At the end of this album, Astérix makes a magic potion with some mysterious (tea) leaves he has acquired from the Druid and creates their national drink. In *Astérix et les Goths* (1963), the brutal and belligerent Goths eat cabbage and wear spiked helmets, and their soldiers goosestep into battle. Spain in *Astérix en*

Hispanie (1969) is renowned for its cheap holidays for tourists, and the people are colourful and fiesta-loving. The different French regions are satirised, as well: in *Astérix en Corse* (1973), for example, the heroic duo encounter pride, blood feuds, and stinking cheeses. The humour of stereotyping not only alludes to modern prejudices and perceptions but draws on modern perceptions of the past based on cultural legacies: in *Astérix aux jeux Olympiques* the Greek athletes are seen in poses like those on vases, and in *Astérix gladiateur* a group of Egyptian tourists in Rome are depicted walking in line in profile as though in a frieze on a wall painting. The strip contains relatively little narrative exposition, and speech is a major source of humour in both linguistic terms and in its visual representation. The Goths speak in Gothic script and the Egyptians in hieroglyphs, while the stiff-upper-lipped Britons speak in French constructed with English syntax (the placing of adjectives before the noun annoys Obélix) and react to events with 'Bonté gracieuse' and 'Oh, je dis!' Plenty of comic use is made of Latin, not only in names: Julius Caesar's disgust at the hijacking of the gladiatorial games by the Gauls is expressed as 'Veni, vidi, et je n'en crois pas mes yeux!' while the traditional 'Ave César, morituri te salutant' of the gladiators is echoed by Astérix's 'Salut, vieux Jules!'[96]

Although firmly set in 50 B.C.E., a number of anachronistic elements and contemporary cultural, historical, and political references are introduced to comic effect. In *Astérix et Cléopâtre* (1965), Cléopâtre's arrival in a chariot like a great gilded Sphinx irresistibly recalls that of Elizabeth Taylor (to whom she bears some resemblance) in the 1962 film *Anthony and Cleopatra*. Astérix and Obélix enjoy a violent game of rugby complete with teams in striped jerseys and a large gourd for a ball in *Astérix chez les Bretons* and glimpse four famous bards, easily recognisable as the Beatles, amidst a crowd of screaming groupies. In *Obélix et compagnie* (1976), a Roman official is a caricature of the young Jacques Chirac, while figures resembling Superman and Mickey Mouse appear in *Le Ciel lui tombe sur la tête* and two Belgian soldiers in *Astérix chez les Belges* (1979) look and talk like Hergé's comic policemen Dupont and Dupond. The panoply of modern advertising at sporting events is paraded at the gladiatorial games in *Astérix gladiateur*. History is rewritten to attribute events and discoveries to Astérix and Obélix: Astérix has the idea of building a tunnel to connect Britain with Gaul (*Astérix chez les Bretons*) and for a canal linking the Red Sea with the Mediterranean in *Astérix et Cléopâtre*; and in *Astérix en Hispanie*, he invents the bullfight when a woman drops a red cape into the arena where he confronts a bull. The stalls in the desert in *Astérix et Cléopatre* that sell models of the Sphinx have to adapt their wares with a chisel after Obélix breaks the original's nose by climbing up it (a reference to the belief that Napoleon's troops were responsible for destroying the nose of the Sphinx by using it for target practice).[97]

The Astérix albums have been widely translated and turned into films (one featuring Gérard Depardieu as Obélix in 1999) and computer games. Astérix's world itself became accessible to fans when a theme park opened near Paris in 1989. The popularity of the series surely derives not just from the boisterous humour and witty use of language but from the universally cherished motif of the little man who gives two fingers to a powerful empire and has the muscle to redress his grievances. For young readers, the colourful, energetic exploits provide the same kind of stimulus as cartoon films. The characters undergo extreme physical punishment but readily bounce back, and even amongst the enemies of the Gauls nobody is killed. The busy pictures provide a wealth of comic detail to look at and there is verbal humour to appeal to all ages. Although it could be argued that there is a didactic dimension to the albums in portraying aspects of life in the distant past, the historical material is so overlaid with fiction, anachronism, and distortions that its documentary value is minimal. Rather, the comic effects depend upon the reader's recognition of that distortion. The albums therefore do not aim to teach although the level of intellectual engagement required to appreciate fully the multilayered humour and the intertextual and cultural references raises the Astérix series above the level of most comic books.

The next chapter returns to the earlier years of the twentieth century to explore the re-entry of the merveilleux in forms old and new into children's literature and a renaissance of fantasy that is continuing to intensify in the twenty-first.

7

THE RENAISSANCE OF THE IMAGINATION

We have seen how, after the debate about the pernicious nature of fairy tales in the eighteenth century and their harnessing by writers like Mme Le Prince de Beaumont and Mme de Genlis to a didactic purpose, the traditional *merveilleux* almost disappeared from new children's books in the nineteenth century.[1] In the twentieth century, however, writers turned once more to fairy tales, myths, and fantasy to express a variety of ideas, rewriting familiar tales or creating new ones in response to perceived contemporary needs or tastes or as a personal statement. In literature for adults, especially that written in English, fairy-tale themes and constructs have been reworked in order to explore and throw new light on political, social, racial, and gender issues and to encourage readers to look at their society's beliefs in a different way. In children's literature, too, a significant shift in emphasis can be seen in the agenda informing the use of the merveilleux. Whereas the underlying aim is often still moralistic and concerned with social or existential questions fairy tales have also become humorous and anarchic. Occasionally such tales are merely escapist, but many writers have employed fantasy not to shield children from reality, but, as Ganna Ottevaere–van Praag puts it, to 'l'aider à découvrir sa vie intime ainsi que son entourage par le biais de la fantaisie et de l'humour, il veut lui faciliter l'accès au monde que chemin faisant il lui enseigne à critiquer sinon à contester'.[2] The agenda is thus frequently not one of socialisation and the promotion of contemporary social and moral values but one of stimulating the young reader's critical spirit to interrogate the assumptions and prejudices of the adult world and of the genre of the merveilleux itself. Such an innovative approach introduces a hitherto extremely rare note of subversion into children's books, one that goes hand-in-hand with a move towards a more child-centred literature. At the same time, traditional fairy stories, particularly the tales of Charles Perrault, have continued to appear in new editions and have successfully made the transition to comic strip, television, and film (notably, those of Disney, which are known worldwide).

Many attempts have been made by critics to define exactly the differences between the *merveilleux,* the *fantastique,* and *la fantaisie.* In *Le Conte fantastique en France* (1951), Pierre-Georges Castex claims that the *fantastique* is characterised by 'une intrusion brutale du mystère dans le cadre de la vie réelle', and, according to Tzvetan Todorov, involves a hesitation on the part of character and reader as to whether the strange events are supernatural or have a rational explanation.[3] The merveilleux, most familiar to readers in fairy tales, involves the depiction of a world in which strange events, like talking animals, provoke surprise in neither characters nor the reader.[4] However, there are many different modified applications of both the merveilleux and the fantastique evident in children's books in the twentieth century, and the last ten years has seen a huge craze for what is generally termed 'High Fantasy', in which the action takes place entirely in a complete fantasy world. This chapter considers some of the most innovative appropriations of the fairy tale and the renaissance of fantasy in books for children in the course of the last century. It is concerned with five different types: fairy tales; works in which the fantastique intrudes in the real world; works in which the merveilleux coexists with a realistic portrayal of everyday life creating a kind of magical realism; stories that feature a child with special powers in a spiritual, mystical, existential sense; and high fantasy located in a fictional world in which a child protagonist has magical powers.

PREWAR MANIFESTATIONS OF THE MERVEILLEUX
Fantasy Islands and Wish Fulfilment

The theme of a journey to a delectable and utopian island where all desires are satisfied has a long history in books for the young. It was deployed in the late seventeenth century by François Fénelon in his fables for his pupil the Duc de Bourgogne, in imitation of Lucian's fantastic travel narrative *True History* and by writers of fairy tales like Mme d'Aulnoy, whose stories for adults were also published in children's versions. In the interwar years it was reworked by Charles Vildrac (1882–1971) in *L'Ile rose* (1924) and by André Maurois in *Le Pays des 36,000 volontés* (1928). The former, described by Annie Renonciat as 'ce premier texte moderne écrit pour les enfants au XXe siècle', also has something in common with the *Robinsonnade* in its story of a boy removed from his drab existence in a poor, working-class suburb to a children's colony on an idyllic island. Illustrated by Edouard-Léon-Louis Edy-Legrand, *L'Ile rose* does indeed have many of the characteristics of modern children's literature. The novel is child-centred and the protagonist, Tifernand (short for Petit Fernand) is a psychologically complex character, sensitive and a dreamer as well as energetic and active, relishing the opportunities offered by the island but also manifesting fears and sensitivities, missing his home, and feeling guilty at being so happy. Children's activities are foregrounded both in the streets of Paris and on the island where everything is provided for their pleasure and stimulation. There is no overt religious or moral agenda and some of the adult characters, like the bullying schoolmaster who blights Tifernand's days at school, challenge the convention of the adult authority figure.

The transportation of Tifernand (the middle of three children of a working-class family) to a new life on the island (somewhere off the coast near Marseilles), with its pink rocks and palatial white mansion, involves a slippage in the narrative between reality and fantasy, not least because it appears to be the fulfilment of a wish. While playing in the street with his little sister and friends, Tifernand is overheard by a passing stranger expressing a longing to be transported by an enchanter to the 'Pays du soleil', a glamorous world he has seen at the cinema. Moreover, after a particularly tiresome series of accidents and punishments at school, he takes one of his mother's aspirins and, as he falls asleep, is engulfed in a confused dream of the events of the day and of an enchanter who, after talking to his parents, carries him from his bed to a waiting car. In the manner of Todorov's 'hesitation', the reader is left uncertain at this point whether such a conversation has really taken place, so that the journey to the island—which is undertaken, in the care of the strange man M. Vincent, in an amazing plane that can hover and descend by folding its wings like a butterfly—retains an air of dreamlike mystery. M. Vincent explains that he is really a wealthy benefactor who has established a colony for deserving boys in order to bring some happiness into their lives and his island is a child's paradise: apart from the exotic location, food and toys are plentiful and there are a gymnasium, and canoes in the lagoon. The boys enjoy almost unrestricted freedom, with only a few hours of lessons every day in which the innovative teaching methods delight and encourage them to learn. Although M. Vincent acts with the permission of the boys' parents, the background and motives of this modern Pied Piper make him an uncomfortably ambiguous figure. He reveals that he has assumed the role of a self-styled 'enchanteur des enfants' after his own two boys were taken away by their mother because he was always too preoccupied with his business affairs.[5] He selects boys the same age as his own children to take to his island and, assisted by a team of teachers and domestic workers, dedicates himself to their welfare. However, his motives are not entirely altruistic, for he is irritated at Tifernand's homesickness and does not tell Tifernand of the letter informing him of his mother's serious illness. The reader is informed explicitly that M. Vincent tries to make the boys (many of them orphans or neglected) forget about their past lives, dreaming of making them 'peu à peu ses fils adoptifs'.[6] Although this reason for his reluctance to let Tifernand return home is presented as one that he perhaps did not even admit to himself, it is difficult to see M. Vincent as other than a flawed philanthropist. Vildrac clearly did not envisage this situation as potentially exploitative and alarming to a child reader in the way that it strikes the adult reader today, but this aspect of the text may well account for the fact that it is not available in modern editions.

Only after Tifernand's courageous attempt to reach the mainland in a canoe when he overhears the news of his mother's illness, and the dramatic rescue scene when his craft is overturned in a storm, does M. Vincent revise his selfish agenda. An artificially contrived ending brings all Tifernand's friends and his favourite teacher as well as his parents and siblings together on the island. Vildrac's promise of a sequel telling of the transformation of the colony is reminiscent of the ending of many a Robinsonnade in which new ideal communities develop in a remote location. This novel clearly reflects the postwar awareness of changing times after the destruction of traditionally held values, and, despite its ambiguities, a desire for a new humanitarianism and a better world of peace, enjoyment, and personal fulfilment that also characterise Vildrac's poetry.

Maurois' Le Pays des 36,000 volontés incorporates a more traditional fairy tale for younger readers that depends more overtly upon the wish-fulfilment motif but employs various devices to intimate that the journey to a fantastic locality takes place in a dream and therefore has a rational explanation. At the beginning of the short work, Michelle (age seven), frustrated in her attempts to learn La Fontaine's fable of the fox and the crow by her brothers' loud repetition of their own homework which ruins her concentration and disgruntled by a day in which her desires have all been thwarted, goes to bed wishing that there existed a place 'où l'on peut faire ses trente-six mille volontés'.[7] Once again, there is a hesitation as to whether Michelle is awake or asleep as the light beneath her bedroom door expands and she finds herself in a desert, but her adventure is distinctly oneiric, incorporating the last things to intrude upon her consciousness before she goes to bed: elements from the homework tasks (the desert itself; a Pharaoh, seen only in profile as in Egyptian paintings; his own strange dream, which Michelle is asked to interpret; and the talking crow who acts as gatekeeper to the magic kingdom). In order to enter the *pays des 36,000 volontés,* Michelle must become a fairy, and her transformation is conceived in familiar scholastic and domestic, rather than magical, terms: she must pass a brief examination, for which it does not seem to matter if the answers are wrong, and the essential wings for a fairy outfit come in different sizes according to body weight. When she flies to the magic kingdom where the inhabitants do exactly what they want all day, she finds, as in dreams, her brothers and her friends as well as two eccentric characters, M. Knockbottom, a crazed Scottish golfer, and a fairy queen with a mania for transforming things simply because she can. From this point, the narrative adopts the stance of a traditional moral tale, for Michelle and her friends soon discover that having free rein to do whatever one wants inevitably clashes with other people's desires and leads to frustration, irritation, and enmity rather than fun (chaos ensues at the queen's party when the musicians all play different tunes and the children are perpetually fighting each other). The desired return home is represented as an awakening, and after finding herself back in her bed on a sunny morning, Michelle soon begins to forget the adventure. However, the simple explanation of a dream is complicated when, after a disappointing ninth birthday, she wishes to visit the *pays des 36,000 volontés* again but is denied entry by the crow gatekeeper because her entry permit has expired. She further disqualifies herself by providing the right answers to his examination questions. Michelle has finally crossed the threshold into the age of reason: her subconscious refuses a regression to childhood and the fantasy world of flying and self-indulgence is no longer open to her. This charming little tale, with the fantasy sections framed by events of Michelle's daily life, is reminiscent of Lewis Carroll's *Alice's Adventures in Wonderland* in its structure, the surreal nature of the inhabitants of the magic kingdom, and the bizarre conversations they hold. Still available and marketed by Hachette for readers age eight or over, it is clearly perceived not just as a simple fairy tale but as one with a psychological as well as a moral dimension masked by the humour of the jaunty narrative.

Blaise Cendrars: New Myths for Old

The *Petits contes nègres pour les enfants des blancs* (1928) by the Swiss poet and novelist Blaise Cendrars (1887–1961), can be seen as an example of the attempts made, after the First World War, to introduce children to other cultures in order to generate understanding, tolerance, and friendship. This brief volume of tales exemplify the author's own fascination with the exotic and the traditional culture of other lands that led him to travel constantly. But Cendrars, who had published in 1821 an *Anthologie nègre*, from which the short prose tales here are reproduced for young readers, was also exploiting the contemporary fascination with 'la mode nègre' in art, sculpture, and music that was at its height between 1925 and 1930. The interest in ethnology and folklore had developed since the beginning of the century; black soldiers from the African colonies had fought in the war, and black workers were visible in factories and ports. Jazz was all the rage and the black artist Josephine Baker was a sensation in Paris in the 1920s.[8] The dedication of the *Petits contes nègres pour les enfants des blancs* presents the tales to two named children (Danie and Claude) as traditional folk tales 'que se racontent les grands enfants d'Afrique pour s'amuser la nuit autour du feu et ne pas s'endormir à cause des bêtes qui rôdent'.[9] Arguably, in thus infantalising the original tale tellers, Cendrars was, in effect, endorsing a widely held colonialist view of Africans as childlike and primitive, held in thrall by fetishes and superstitions, a view used to underpin contemporary theories of the racial superiority of white people. The tales can also be seen as catering for a public attracted, at a turbulent period in their own history, to the seductive image of a naïve people living picturesque lives dominated by an intense and magical spirituality.[10]

The tales in the collection do indeed portray an unfamilar and exotic world of rural simplicity, a universe peopled by spirits in which humans and animals live in close contact with the soil, rivers, and trees of an exacting and sometimes pitiless landscape. The wild animals and the elements are anthropomorphised and engage dynamically with human beings in fantastic narratives that seek to explain the origins of natural phenomena and human and animal behaviour. Cendrars's poetry has close affinities with surrealism, of which he is seen as a precursor, and in these short prose tales the juxtaposition of images for poetic effect without logical or rational explanation is exploited to the full to create an atmosphere of the *merveilleux*. Throughout, the effect of orality is re-created by colloquial interjections and direct address to the listening or reading audience. As in European folk tales, the structure of these stories often involves repetition of both events and refrains, sudden surprise changes in direction, and abrupt, dramatic denouements. In some of the stories, no human characters appear. 'Le vent', for example, extols the power of the wind, perceived successively as a playful, greedy, and sometimes destructive monster who lives in a mountain grotto, a magician, and the offspring of the moon and sun. Although he can never be seen nor grasped, his omnipresence and hyperactivity are the cause of the movement not just of clouds and swirls of dust but of flocks of birds and fish in the sea and everything the listener sees. The story ends with a lyrical evocation of the dependence of life in these climes on the wind:

> Voici la pluie! Voici la pluie!
> La saison sèche est bien finie!
> Et c'est encore le vent.
> Merci, vent.[11]

In 'Pourquoi personne ne porte plus le caïman pour le mettre à l'eau', the narrator offers a fable structured largely on dialogue and based on the traditional folkloric device of the deceiver deceived to explain the origin of the relationship between human and beast. A naïve hunter, persuaded by a stranded caiman and its young to carry them back to the water, is saved from the ungrateful and treacherous creature's clutches by a passing hare who outwits the caiman. Pretending not to believe that the hunter has been able to carry the reptile on his head, the hare persuades them to repeat the exercise. The hunter, who is as slow on the uptake as the caiman, is then urged to kill the creature quickly. The moral of the story is set out overtly at the end: 'Depuis, personne ne porte plus le caïman pour le mettre à l'eau. C'est un ingrat.'[12] The tale 'C'est bon, c'est bon' is a circular narrative built on the motif of the echo, which explores the dichotomy of good and bad luck through the actions of the myriad spirit helpers summoned by a mysterious, unseen voice to assist a peasant who dares to clear and plant a piece of scrub land that belongs to their king. Since their actions merely repeat his, his good fortune in maximising his efforts soon turns to disaster when his disobedient son eats a stalk of the millet, for the crop is instantly devoured by the spirit helpers. Things go from bad to worse, for the son, whom the peasant hits, is beaten to death by a thousand unseen hands, his wife is drowned in a flood of tears, and the peasant himself is scratched to death when he is stung by an insect. The purpose of this story seems to be to suggest the supernatural power of echoes, which may presage misfortune, and, on a more practical level, to emphasise the need to police and take responsibility for one's own actions. It also serves to explain the existence of uncultivated terrain shunned by superstitious human beings.

The irrationality and injustice of the law is humorously depicted in 'Le mauvais juge', in which a tailor whose garments have been eaten by a mouse takes his case to a judge, a sleepy baboon. The mouse, who denies the deed, blames the cat, and there follows a sequence of denials and accusations involving a sequence of animals and inanimate objects (a dog, a stick, the fire, water, an elephant, and an ant). The baboon's judgement is to make each punish the next in line, thus explaining the relationship between water and fire, cat and mouse, and so on. Although the organisation of relationships in nature is thus explained, the tailor, whose family is also tormented by an old woman personifying hunger, remains unsatisfied ('l'homme attend toujours la justice. Il a toujours faim').[13] Hardship and suffering are thus humorously and fatalistically presented as an inevitable part of the natural scheme of things.

In their own way, Cendrars's tales are as fantastic as those of Mme d'Aulnoy and Perrault, but introduce the young reader to a different type of magical universe peopled by exotic, unfamiliar animals and ruled by powerful, capricious, and awe-inspiring spirit forces.

Marcel Aymé: *The Merveilleux in the Farmyard*

Marcel Aymé (1902–1967) was a writer of humorous and satirical novels for adults and presented his *Les Contes du chat perché*, now a classic of French children's literature, as 'pour les enfants âgés de quatre à soixante-quinze ans'.[14] Indeed, Aymé suggests that he initially envisaged an adult readership:

> je ne savais pas encore, sauf pour le dernier, qu'ils seraient des contes d'enfant. Je les écrivais pour reposer mes lecteurs éventuels de leurs tristes aventures où l'amour et l'argent sont si bien entremêlés qu'on les prend à chaque instant l'un pour l'autre, ce qui est forcément fatigant. Mes histoires sont donc des histoires simples, sans amour et sans argent.[15]

The first four tales—'Le Loup', 'Les Boeufs', 'Le Chien', 'Le Petit coq noir'—appeared in 1934, followed by others published separately in soft card covers with illustrations by, amongst others, Nathalie Parain, up to 1946. Several collections with varying contents followed, including the *Autres contes du chat perché* (1950), the *Derniers contes du chat perché* (1958), and the *Contes bleus du chat perché* and the *Contes rouges du chat perché* (both in 1963). A modern Gallimard edition contains seventeen tales. In his prefatory remarks Aymé declares that he wishes to preempt criticisms 'touchant les règles de la vraisemblance' from 'certaines personnes raisonnables et bilieuses', notably on the question of animals talking. Turning the tables neatly on such critics, he affirms that he is quite prepared to accept that, if animals talked, they would in fact talk about politics and science, even 'qu'elles feraient de la critique littéraire avec distinction', and therefore his tales should be regarded as 'pures fables, ne visant pas sérieusement à donner l'illusion de la réalité'.[16] In fact, the most attractive aspect of the tales is precisely the mixture of reality and the merveilleux, which, as in the tales of Perrault, inserts the magical in the form of talking animals and strange happenings into a vividly depicted, recognisable world without explanation or justification. In Aymé's tales, however, the merveilleux is used to create a gently humorous effect and never to inspire horror or fear.

The tales depict events in the lives of two little girls, Delphine and Marinette, who live with their parents on a typical farm in an unspecified rural area. The children are placed firmly at the centre of the text, and the narrator privileges their thoughts, experiences, and fantasies. The theme of play is foregrounded in each tale and the ludic dimension of the text is signalled in the title itself, which alludes to one of their favourite games. This, however, is an imaginative and unpredictable world where the boundaries between reality and fantasy are constantly blurred, events are governed by the logic of childhood (which rarely coincides with that of the adults), and the merveilleux is frequently brought into play by the narrator to contradict or demolish adult authority and wisdom.[17] The slippage between reality and the merveilleux manifests itself immediately in the relationship between the humans and the animals of the farmyard and the surrounding woods. The animals (cows, oxen, chickens, ducks, a pig, a dog, a cat, a fox, a deer, and a boar) converse freely and naturally with the children and interact closely with them in their daily lives. This is not a question of the special intuitive relationship between child and animal that is sometimes found in children's books, however, because the animals also converse with each other and with the parents without evoking any surprise. Although they fulfil their respective roles on the farm, they also participate in the children's games and identify with the dilemmas that beset them, frequently acting as advisors and helpers. In 'Le Problème', for example, when the girls are unable to solve a mathematical problem involving the calculation of the number of trees on a certain piece of land, the animals conceive and execute the idea of counting all the trees and bushes in their own area, and triumphantly confront the schoolmistress with the result, to her consternation. Their personalities demonstrate a further slippage between the stereotypical and the unexpected. Thus, the cows are passive, the fox cunning, and the cat haughty, but the pig is both grumpy and vain, a little grey cow is an incorrigible tattletale, and the duck demonstrates initiative and leadership.

The portrayal of the parents is a provocative one, refusing and caricaturing the convention of the unassailability of parental authority. Although they clearly love their daughters, they are bad-tempered and oppressive with the girls and the animals alike. They fail to grasp the value of play and are inconsistent, shortsighted, and inadequate, obsessed with utility and hard work, grumbling incessantly about time-wasting, abusing the children verbally, and inflicting draconian punishments. The narrative approach here is humorous rather than condemnatory, however, for they are constantly subjected to ridicule, the description of their 'voix d'ogre' running like a refrain through the tales. They are bemused by happenings at the farm, and their rages at the children's misdemeanours are presented from an external viewpoint that renders them comic rather than threatening ('les parents furent si en colère qu'ils se mirent à sauter comme des puces au travers la cuisine').[18] The animals regularly complain about the injustices to which they, too, are subjected by the parents and are always ready to assist in thwarting or deceiving them, helping the children to rebel against the constraints of the adult world. In 'La Patte du chat' the parents are manipulated and outwitted by the animals when they attempt to drown the cat because he is presumed to conjure up rain by washing behind his ears with his paw. The animals conspire to replace him with a piece of wood in the sack, and a period of drought makes the parents regret their action such that when the cat is discovered alive and well in the children's bedroom they welcome his return and beg him to bring some more rain.

Like their predecessors, the *contes* of Perrault and the fables of La Fontaine, Aymé's stories do contain morals, although they are often implicit and sometimes ambiguous. The traditional targets of disobedience, vanity, and arrogance are discernible but treated in a more subtle and less obviously didactic way than in much children's literature. Vanity is punished in 'Le Paon', for example, when the children, seduced by the prettiness of their cousin, become obsessed with their looks and are only persuaded of their folly when they witness the foolishness of the vain pig who tries to become a peacock. The moral here is ambiguous however, for the story ends with the colours of a rainbow reflected on the pig's back, briefly giving the illusion of a magical transformation. The majority of the transgressions on the part of the children are a result of their games. The theme of transformation is a crucial one in this respect, as in traditional fairy tales, but it is not seen as a positive or life-enhancing experience, confusing relationships and issues of identity and invariably leading to problems. The children's deceitfulness leads to trouble in 'Les Boîtes de peinture', when, instead of working, they play with their magic paintboxes that transform the animals they paint: the donkey has only two legs as in his portrait; the horse is smaller than the cockerel; and the white oxen, whom the children have refused to paint because they will disappear on the white paper, do in fact disappear, leaving only their horns visible. As usual, the imminent arrival of the parents creates suspense, and it is the magic power of tears, shed by the despairing children and animals, that restores them to their rightful size and shape in the nick of time. In 'L'Eléphant' the children bring all the animals indoors on a rainy day to play at Noah's Ark and persuade a white hen to change itself, through an effort of will, into an elephant. The children's enchantment at her transformation turns to despair when the parents return and they have to resort to lies and prevarication to prevent discovery of the elephant trampling around in the bedroom. The situation is resolved only by the intervention of magic wielded by the narrator, for after much suspense, when the parents finally open the door, the transformation has been reversed and out flutters the hen.

The parents' return from their frequent absences, a dreaded event threatening discovery in a number of stories, does not merely effect closure, signalling a return to normality that might suggest that the strange happenings are to be construed as manifestations of the children's imaginations, for magical occurrences, like the noises made by the elephant here, often persist in their presence. A troubling tale is 'L'Ane et le cheval', in which the children's wish that they were animals comes true overnight and the parents soon overcome their initial grief and, avoiding confronting the question of their daughters' disappearance, begin to treat them as beasts of burden. The children, too, begin to forget who they once were until they turn back into their proper forms as unexpectedly and inexplicably as before. With its oneiric quality this tale could be read as an externalisation of a childhood fantasy or simply a dream, but the transformation is depicted as no less real than other events, mundane and marvellous, that happen on the farm.

Questions of identity, desire, and individual liberty underlie many of the tales. In 'Les Boeufs' the children persuade one of the oxen to allow them to teach him to read, and he conceives a passion for learning that leads him to astound his master by quoting a poem of Victor Hugo, but the same passion also proves detrimental to his daily work. His companion at the yoke, on the contrary, becomes obsessed with play such that the work in the fields becomes impossible, and the beasts only escape the butcher by being sold to a travelling circus where they become a star attraction. The reflection that teaching an ox to read is counterproductive might suggest that Aymé intends a comment on the value of mass education, but the lighthearted tone of the tale militates against such a draconian, and indeed at this time outmoded, prejudice. Rather, the inference is that neither all work nor all play are desirable and that, for animals as for humans, it is folly to go against one's natural talents and instincts to wish to be other than what one is (a theme explored elsewhere in Aymé's novels for adults).[19] In 'Le Petit coq noir', a story reminiscent of the fables of La Fontaine, the naïve girls are influenced by an apparently amiable fox's denunciation of the cynicism of adults and aid and abet the little cockerel in liberating all the fowl in the village to spite their parents. The consequence of their action and of the cockerel's naïve desire to be a hero, is, inevitably, that a number of the birds are eaten by the fox and his companions. The remainder resolve that the prospect of being eaten by their masters is the lesser evil and return to their homes.

'Le Loup' has a strong intertextual dimension that adds to the humour. It depicts the encounter between Delphine and Marinette and a wolf who is cold and wounded and, he alleges, feels himself converted to goodness by the sight of the little girls through their window. The children, who have been forbidden to open the door in their parents' absence, pity him, but like the reader, they hesitate before the wolf's attempts to revise his traditional reputation. Mindful of his past in fairy tales, they tax him with having eaten *le Petit Chaperon rouge*, a charge he accepts as a 'péché de jeunesse', but eventually accept his reassurances and encourage his weekly visits. He becomes, it seems, truly reformed, throwing himself into the games they teach him and enjoying the warmth and fun of friendship. The dangers of distorting one's nature surface again, however, and their confidence and good intentions are the girls' undoing, for in a game where he is encouraged to pretend to be a wolf who jumps out on the girls, he gets carried away in his role playing and swallows them up. In a gesture towards other, later versions of Perrault's tale, the children are saved easily enough when the returning parents cut open the wolf's stomach, but, in an original twist to the plot, the wolf's resolution never to have anything to do with little girls again revises, ironically, the motif of victimhood.

Although the outcome of many of the stories seems to confirm the warnings of the parents and hence the values of the adult world, the narrator nonetheless appears to condone, even celebrate, disobedience and the refusal to be bound by those values. The affectionate bond and collusion between Delphine and Marinette and the animals allow their fantasies to come alive and provide both them and the reader with an escape from the boredom and frequent harshness of daily life. In effect, the parents' recognition of and participation in the merveilleux amounts to a kind of complicity, albeit often uncomprehending and reluctant, in the world of the imagination and its effects, just as the adult readers are invited to suspend their disbelief and enjoy the humour and magic of the stories. Moreover, the stories contain provocative reflections on existential questions of identity, individual freedom, friendship, responsibility, good and evil, and death represented in terms that appeal to both young and adult readers. *Les Contes du chat perché* have remained in print, and in 2002, Gallimard issued new illustrated editions of the *Contes Bleus* and the *Contes rouges* to mark the anniversary of Aymé's birth.

FAIRY TALES INTO TOADS: PROPAGANDA IN THE SECOND WORLD WAR

Traditional fairy tales continued to be published during the Second World War and, since they remained popular with children, were a sure source of income for publishing houses. Indeed, between the wars, editions of fairy tales and of the novels of such writers as the Comtesse de Ségur and Jules Verne had continued to help publishers to fill their catalogues.[20] However, fairy tales underwent a brief metamorphosis themselves when they were manipulated for political and propaganda purposes during the Occupation. Fairy tales had already proved themselves conducive to political exploitation in Germany. In the first decades of the twentieth century they were cultivated by both the social democrats and the communists in order to shape the attitudes and perspectives of a young readership, and in the Nazi period, the traditional tales of, for example, Hans Christian Andersen, the Brothers Grimm, and Wilhelm Hauff were appropriated to serve national socialist ideology, glorifying Adolf Hitler and the Third Reich.[21] In France, too, as has been seen, fairy tales with their fundamentally socialising imperative had been harnessed to a political agenda after the First World War. With their straightforward and dramatic plots, stereotyping of characters, clear identification of good and bad, and their tendency to violence, exaggeration, and predictability, fairy tales were eminently suitable for revising for propaganda purposes.

The French tradition of the merveilleux was mobilised by the Vichy regime to attack the enemies of the Nazis and to promote the ideology of the *Révolution nationale*. The blatant perversion of the fairy tale is seen clearly in the following two examples, which were specifically intended to stimulate hatred and prejudice in their young readers.[22] In the illustrated rewriting of the most famous of all cautionary tales, *Le Petit Chaperon rouge*, published by the Nouvelles Etudes françaises and titled *Doulce France et Grojuif* (1942), the wolf is a grotesque, cynical, and exploitative monster with curly dark hair, grasping claws, and an immense hooked nose and his speech is marked by a Jewish accent. Having killed the grandmother, who is named Vérité, the wolf puts on her clothes, thus masquerading as Truth in order to deceive the child, as Jewish publishers and writers were alleged to have done. The author of this tale, identified only as 'N', follows Perrault's text very closely but deviates from it with the ending, preferring that of the Grimms' version in which the child is saved from the wolf's clutches by a passing woodcutter. Here, Doulce France, horrified by having trusted the wolf, screams for help and is rescued by 'un des fils de la nouvelle France', represented in the uniform of a *légionnaire* in the illustration. The last line lifts the allegory to a specifically contemporary political level: 'Et dans l'azur, la "Vérité" de ses chauds rayons, put emplir le ciel de France pour se mêler à la clarté de la nouvelle Europe.'[23]

The Bolsheviks are the targets of the anonymous and undated *L'Homme aux mains rouges*, which reworks Perrault's *Barbe-bleue* in an unsubtle and overtly allegorical manner to portray the perceived communist threat to Europe.[24] The role of the murderous husband is incarnated here in a tyrant, eventually revealed to be Joseph Stalin, who wishes to marry the princess Europa and has lured her to his domain, the illustrations of which feature red stars, and hammers and sickles, in abundance. True to Perrault's version, the princess transgresses by seeking to discover the forbidden secret of the tyrant's castle and finds the murdered bodies of his previous consorts Polonia and Lithuania, amongst others.[25] The tyrant swears by the damned soul of his master Vladimir Lenin to kill her, but she is saved by the arrival of the valiant prince Germain, accompanied by soldiers wearing 1940s German helmets, under whose protection she places herself and her oppressed people after Germain has killed her suitor. The last line of the story again confirms the significance of the allegory: 'De longues années de Paix et de Prospérité furent alors assurées au Monde entier.'[26] Perhaps not surprisingly, these tales disappeared from view after the end of the war, and extant copies are now rare.

The merveilleux was also employed to promote a positive vision of Philippe Pétain's *Révolution nationale*, with the Maréchal himself playing a central role as a kind of fairy godfather in some texts. The cult of Pétain between 1939 and 1943 emphasised his status as First World War hero and his glorious military past, and presented him, despite his great age, as the figurehead who would lead the nation to a glorious future in the new Europe.[27] Judith Proud has shown that propaganda texts endorsing the Vichy regime also drew on the school textbooks of the Third Republic, like G. Bruno's *Le Tour de la France par deux enfants*, which were predicated on the same ideals of family and individual effort. In effect, the fundamental tenets of the Révolution nationale—*Travail, Famille, Patrie*—reflected the same values as had underpinned the socialisation agenda of much children's literature for many decades.[28] Texts like Bruno's were, of course, also propaganda in the sense that they sought to illustrate and promote the qualities, values, and achievements that had made France great and in which the child protagonists and readers were intimately implicated. The approach taken in the Vichy texts was to show that these values had declined, with catastrophic consequences, and that it was up to a new generation to assist in the reconstruction of the nation. Whereas Bruno had employed a basically realistic approach in her narrative, the Vichy message was presented in fairy-tale form, evoking an image of an idyllic rural past to be revived by the Révolution nationale. In A. Paluel-Marmont's *Six petits enfants et treize étoiles* (1942), for example, a group of six children from different social backgrounds befriend a whitehaired old man in a wood who promises them help if the need should arise. The wood here is not a locus of evil but an idyllic, enchanted place in which the anthropomorphised animals and flowers are friendly and unafraid of the children. As in other texts of this kind, a great storm threatens to destroy the country, and the children seek him out to beg for help.[29] He carries a baton marked with thirteen stars (the baton of a French *Maréchal*, which regularly featured as a symbol of Pétain's authority) with which he not only calms the storm but, throwing each star to the ground, conjures up farming and domestic equipment with which the children begin to rebuild a more harmonious and prosperous village. Although the wise old man is cast in the role of a magician, he makes it clear to the children that the real magic is to be wrought by them. At the end, when the children join hands, they understand that their names (François, Rose, Anne, Noël, Clément, and Estelle) spell out the name of the *patrie* of which they are the representatives. The role of the patriarchal figure in such tales represents an important part of the Vichy propaganda machine's transformation of Pétain from man into myth, although the fairy tales do not explicitly identify him. Already presented in children's magazines as a grandfatherly figure with a close affinity with children and an object of affection and veneration, Pétain is here metamorphosised by implication into a saviour of the nation with quasi-supernatural powers, an image that complemented the hagiographic techniques employed in allegedly factual biographies like *Il était une fois ... un Maréchal de France* (1941), also by Paluel-Marmont.[30]

The fairy tale, with its universality and easily grasped and persuasive implications, was thus perceived as a powerful weapon to motivate and enlist the energies of the youth in whose hands the country's future would lie. It is, of course, difficult to know how young readers actually did react to these stories and the extent to which they understood the underlying propaganda. It is rare, understandably, to find testimonies to the enjoyment of such works, particularly the flagrantly anti-Semitic texts, but this does not obscure the significance in literary and historical terms of the insidious manipulation of a central genre in children's literature to entertain, instruct, and corrupt a generation.

THE SPECIAL CHILD

Saint-Exupéry's Le Petit Prince

The Romantic image of the child as a being endowed with special powers of intuition and empathy with nature clearly continued to be attractive to writers and found a new impetus after the middle of the century in the wake of the horrors of the first half. In two of the texts discussed below, the special child becomes a vehicle for the mediation of reflections on crucial issues of social, existential, and personal concern. However, this image can be seen as essentially promoting an adult idealised construct redolent with nostalgia and regret that objectifies the child and moulds him in the image of the adult's desires. The construction of the *enfant merveilleux* has been described as the product of 'un consensus culturel fondé non pas sur la raison, mais sur la logique des relations affectives'.[31] It is not insignificant that these texts have been regarded as addressing a dual audience, and have found favour with both an adult and a child readership.

The best-known children's book emanating from the Second World War is Antoine de Saint-Exupéry's *Le Petit Prince*, which was written and published in the United States in 1943, although it was not available to French readers until after the Liberation. The works written by Saint-Exupéry (1900–1944) while he was living in New York between 1940 and 1943 are intimately connected with the war: his novel for adults, *Pilote de guerre* (1942), was inspired by his own experience as a reconnaissance pilot in 1940, and the *Lettre à un otage* (1943) was addressed to his Jewish friend Léon Werth, a journalist and novelist, and his other compatriots in occupied France. Saint-Exupéry himself was to become a victim of the war, for having returned to flying under the auspices of the Americans in 1943, he never returned from a reconnaissance flight on 31 July 1944. The status of *Le Petit Prince* as a book for children has been much debated, and it is possible to see Saint-Exupéry's appropriation of the format and style of a children's book as a challenge to adult readers as much as an attempt to appeal to the young. It can certainly be interpreted on a number of levels as the apparently simple fairy-tale plot incorporates both metaphysical implications and social and political satire.[32]

The address to a dual readership is evident in the dedication, once more to Léon Werth. Saint-Exupéry begins by apologising to child readers for dedicating the book to a 'grande personne', and offering as his excuse the facts that Werth is his best friend and that he is capable of understanding everything, 'même les livres pour enfants'.[33] This suggestion that a children's book is too difficult for adults signals the approach developed throughout the book, privileging the child and the child's vision of the world above that of grown-ups, who have lost the ability to see with the eyes of the imagination. The introduction of the motif of friendship also supports the main theme of the novel, one that is lent added significance by the third excuse offered, an oblique reference to contemporary times: 'cette grande personne habite la France où elle a faim et froid. Elle a bien besoin d'être consolée.' Finally, Saint-Exupéry revises his wording to dedicate his book to the child that the adult once was ('A Léon Werth, quand il était petit garçon'), reminding the reader that all adults have once been children, even if they fail to remember it. The dedication thus points to the dual purpose of the book: to delight children and introduce thought-provoking issues but also to act as a reminder to adults at a time of conflict and despair of the capacity within them to recall what the author sees as the child's instinctive and intuitive view of life and the fundamental significance of factors important to children, friendship, trust, and love.

Le Petit Prince employs the short chapters and clear, simple vocabulary and uncomplicated syntax of a book for very young readers, with an emphasis on conversation and a host of childlike illustrations drawn by the author himself in bright primary colours. The first-person retrospective narrative recounts the meeting of a pilot who crashes his plane in the desert (as Saint-Exupéry himself had once done when competing to beat the flying record from Paris to Saigon in 1935), with a vulnerable and enigmatic little prince who claims to have come from another planet.[34] The use of an adult narrator who experiences a new way of looking at life and feels compelled to communicate this to others thus invites identification on the part of an adult reader. The framing narrative establishes the link between the pilot's childhood self and the qualities that made him receptive to his present role as recorder of the prince's message. The illustrations are crucial in this respect, for his awareness of the difference between a child's view of life and that of adults derives from his own early attempt to represent reality as he saw it with a drawing of a boa constrictor that has swallowed an elephant and the inability of adults to see it as anything other than a hat.[35] The ridiculing of adults' lack of comprehension and their need for explicit explanations acts as a challenge to the adult reader, for whom the drawing does indeed look like a hat. The pilot tells us that as adults continued to fail his test of their imaginative powers, he felt isolated and alienated from his peers until he capitulated and resolved to reduce his conversation to their level. The use of the expression 'à sa portée', employed so frequently in children's books in the past to imply talking down to children, establishes the idea that it is the subjects dear to adults (bridge, golf, politics, ties) that are trivial and inferior. This introductory first chapter thus establishes the reversal of roles pursued throughout the book, with the adult's pretensions and obsession with facts and figures constantly ridiculed and diminished in contrast with the child's intuitive grasp of essentials. Adults are patronised and pitied by a narrator who places himself firmly on the side of the child reader ('Mais, bien sûr, nous qui comprenons la vie, nous nous moquons bien des numéros').[36] The centrality of a drawn image also reinscribes the important function of illustrations as communicators of ideas, a function increasingly relegated to children's books.

The narrator's meeting with the prince takes place when he is in a life-or-death situation stranded in the desert, therefore suggesting a hesitation between reality and hallucination. The development of their relationship is, in effect, built upon the motif of the ability to engage imaginatively with reality, as the first words of the little prince, who appears out of nowhere, are to ask for a drawing of a sheep, and the pilot's initial failed attempts to satisfy him remind him of his status as a 'grande personne' in the face of the child's demands. Their rapport is established, however, by the prince's instant understanding of the pilot's boa constrictor drawing, and approval of his new offering of a drawing of a box, which leaves the prince's imagination free to imagine the sheep inside. Although the little prince is more inclined to ask questions than to answer them, the story of his solitary life on his minuscule planet and his journey to earth gradually emerges. The description of his visits to a series of tiny planets occupied by a solitary human type represents a level of satire of human foibles unusual in a children's book and might be deemed to be aimed more at an adult readership.[37] However, the little prince's puzzled reactions to his encounters with a series of self-obsessed and deluded adults (a king possessed by a lust for power, but with no subjects; a vain man with no admirers; a drunkard caught in a vicious circle of drinking to forget that he is a drunkard; a businessman greedy for possessions, who spends his life counting the stars; and a geographer whose life's work is based on secondhand information) reveal a childlike intuitive apprehension and rejection of absurdity. These chapters thus work on two levels and encourage the adult reader to share Saint-Exupéry's frustration with bureaucracy and hatred of materialism and to see the pointlessness of much adult activity through the eyes of the child, an exercise facilitated further by the cartoonlike drawings of the individuals.

The little prince's preoccupation, on the other hand, is with relationships. Driven to leave his planet by the capricious demands of a beautiful rose, of which he finds many on earth, he comes to understand that the uniqueness of his rose lies in their mutual emotional dependency. This can be interpreted as a jaundiced depiction of sexual jealousy and the lack of understanding between men and women, but the issue of the rose is only part of the overall theme of relationships in which affection is predicated upon mutual reponsibility and need. Drawing upon the fairy-tale convention of talking animals, Saint-Exupéry invests this central message of the book in the person of a fox, traditionally seen as a marginalised and hunted predator, who begs to be tamed in order to create a special connection that will give meaning to life. He teaches the little prince that life is transformed by friendship even in separation and communicates his secret: 'on ne voit bien qu'avec le coeur. L'essentiel est invisible pour les yeux.'[38] The importance of 'connecting' and creating links with others and of ignoring externals and seeing with the eyes of the imagination stands in sharp contrast to the egocentric and materialistic priorities of 'les grandes personnes'. Kindness, empathy, responsibility, and usefulness are thus key attributes in personal and social relationships.

Le Petit Prince is also unusual in that it tackles the subject of death, presenting the disappearance of the little prince in a melancholy but ultimately consolatory and empowering manner. The sacrifice of his own life, which could be interpreted as a suicide since in order to return to his planet he chooses to be bitten by a mysterious golden snake that claims to have the power of resolving all enigmas, is seen as an act of courage in embracing the inevitable. The pilot's assertion that he could not find his body the next morning further mystifies the interpretation of both his death and, indeed, of his existence and the pilot's testimony. Finally, the truth of the little prince's view of the transformative power of friendship is exemplified in the return to the framing narrative in which the pilot's happiness or sorrow is bound up with his concern for the little prince and his flower. The two final illustrations depicting a sweep of sand dune beneath a star—identical except that in one the little prince is present while in the other he is not—offer, apart from the humour in Saint-Exupéry's injunction to the reader to remember and recognise the spot, a poignant depiction of loss and a sense of the transcendental.

Le Petit Prince is rare in its presentation of themes that strike a chord with both adults and children and in its blending of narrative strategies and simple, vivid illustrations designed to appeal to both a child and an adult readership. The book lends itself to both a universal and a specific contemporary meaning and allusions to France's particular position can be discerned in, for example, the little prince's description of the need to root out the bad seeds on his planet before they turn into monstrous, all-consuming trees. The reference to the different meanings attributed to stars calls to mind the stars associated with Pétain (see above) and the yellow stars that Jewish people were forced to wear during the Holocaust. In the fragile figure of the little prince, so different from the dynamic or transgressive characters of the bande dessinée, Saint-Exupéry encapsulated a message of hope and encouragement to his readers at a time of extreme pessimism and personal and national anguish. Le Petit Prince has transcended its specific context, however, and although critical opinion on its success as a children's book varies—as, indeed, do the views of young readers themselves—the figure of the little prince, like that of Tintin, Astérix, and Babar, has become widely recognised and associated with French children's literature.[39]

Maurice Druon (1918–): A Fantasy of Miracles

Tistou les pouces verts (1957), which shares a similar Romantic view of the child as Le Petit Prince, was the only book for children written by Maurice Druon, author of the seven-volume historical novel Les Rois maudits (1955–77), member of the Académie Française, and French Ministre des Affaires Culturelles (1972–74). In his 'Avant-propos', Druon states that he refuses to adopt a false childish voice to address a young readership and elects to narrate a partly realistic, partly fantastic tale in a simple, conversational register. Tistou is a special child who constantly questions the explanations that his parents and teachers give him and has the chance to improve the world about him when he discovers that he has a green thumb and can make flowers grow by causing seeds everywhere to burst magically into life. He uses his gift to transform a prison, a zoo, a hospital, and a shantytown in order to bring pleasure and hope into the lives of the inmates whose dreary, hopeless existence he pities. Druon argues in the 'Avant-propos' that the child's characteristic desire to work miracles and change the world is usually endstopped by their lack of power to effect any change, and when the child attains adulthood, this desire is forgotten or renounced ('il y a seulement une grande personne de plus, sans miracle').[40] The merveilleux aspect of the story, Druon informs us, is that Tistou has the opportunity to act on his altruistic instincts while he is still a child. Like Saint-Exupéry, Druon contrasts the child's fresh and unprejudiced view of the world with that of adults whose judgement is skewed by habit and who can only explain the world by means of ready-made ideas. The narrative opposes good and bad, justice and injustice, freedom and constraints, and war and peace, and the choices and explanations made by the adult world, seen through the eyes of Tistou, seem incomprehensible. As in Maurois's *Patapoufs et Filifers*, the depiction of the futility of war is comic but still extremely topical, for the two nations fight over a piece of desert, beneath which lies oil. The explanation that they go to war over the oil because oil is indispensable to going to war is merely an absurdity to the child, as is the fact that both armies are supplied by the factory belonging to his father, an arms manufacturer. When Tistou single-handedly stops the war by causing the canons, rifles, machine guns, tanks, and supply wagons to be immobilised by climbing plants simply by touching them, Druon turns the horror of warfare into a humorous situation, as the only injuries are to the behinds and dignity of the wagon drivers from the stinging nettles which infest their seats. Tistou's father undergoes a conversion, refusing to have his son incarcerated as a subversive and turning his factory to the production of flowers instead. Their new motto, heralding the flower power movement of the 1960s, is 'Dites non à la guerre, mais dites-le avec des fleurs.'[41]

The specialness of Tistou is not unlike the transformative power of the child so often reworked in nineteenth-century novels, but his power is performed through magic rather than pious sentiments. Ultimately, like the Petit Prince, he cannot continue to survive in the real world. After the death of his friend and first mentor the gardener Moustache, Tistou learns that death is 'le seul mal que les fleurs n'empêchent pas de passer' and it is his desire to find Moustache in heaven that leads to his creating and ascending a ladder into the clouds. His companion, a wise pony, who understands that Tistou will never return from this journey, reveals the secret of Tistou's existence, causing golden flowers to appear in the meadow where he grazes that spell the words 'Tistou était un ange!'[42] Such an ending is contrived and disappointing, since it puts an end to the hope of Tistou retaining his values into adulthood and, arguably, undermines his potential value as a role model for the youth of the day. However, Druon's highly moralistic and poetic book deals with issues of contemporary and ongoing concern, like society's treatment of prisoners, the plight of zoo animals, the demoralising environment of hospitals, the evils of poverty and aggression, and the virtues of pacifism. The message is a positive and inspiring one, seeking to instil a questioning attitude to received ideas and to germinate the seeds of kindness and love—which, like the seeds in the story, are deemed to be lying dormant everywhere, waiting to be fertilised and brought to life by anyone who can retain a vision of hope and fulfil the promise of childhood.

J. M. G. Le Clézio (1940–): The Child's Empathy with the Natural World

J. M. G. Le Clézio's *Voyage au pays des arbres* (1978) continues the Romantic theme of the child's empathy with nature in the brief tale, reminiscent of George Sand's 'Ce que disent les fleurs', of the little boy who learns to listen to the conversation of the trees of the forest. The figure of the child plays a central role in the works of Le Clézio, where the purity and intuitiveness of childhood is seen to be capable of communicating directly with nature and understanding the world without the prejudices and preoccupations of adulthood ('Il n'y a rien entre les enfants et la vie').[43] His child protagonists, like Mondo in *Mondo et autres histoires* (1978), are often apparently solitary and rootless and mediate to the reader a fresh and imaginative perception of the world. This ability, as described in *L'Inconnu de la terre*, also published in 1978, is construed as akin to magic ('leur pouvoir est magique, surnaturel, il ne ressemble pas à celui des adultes') and allows the reader to rediscover, or in the case of a young reader, to discover perhaps for the first time, 'le pur, le sacré, le merveilleux'.[44] This theme is reworked in several of Le Clézio's short, highly poetic novels that, despite featuring a young protagonist, are not specifically addressed to a young readership, although some have been published by Gallimard in the Folio Junior editions. All his enigmatic fictional children crave freedom from social and domestic restraints and prefer to wander at will or sit and surrender themselves to the sensations of the natural environment. They all have heightened senses and are particularly susceptible to light, the wind, and the sounds and smells of the sea. Mondo lives a life of complete independence, sleeping in the open air, eating when and where he can, and evading the authorities who pick up vagrant children. His transitory relationships are with outsiders (street entertainers, beggars, recluses) like himself. The boy Daniel in *Celui qui n'avait jamais vu la mer* (1997) disappears after leaving his school early one morning to find the sea and his whereabouts are never discovered. Daniel is not an orphan like Mondo, but his impoverished parents seem to resign themselves to his departure. Lullaby (1978) the protagonist of the novel of the same name, is a young girl who plays truant from school in order to spend the day on the rocks by the sea and think of her absent father. Her reverie is alarmingly interrupted when she finds herself followed by a strange man, the perverse and uncomprehending nature of adults further exemplified upon her return by the schoolteacher's assumption that she has probably been spending the day with a boy. The most extreme example is the blind child Petite Croix in *Le Peuple du ciel* who has an almost supernatural capacity for sitting still, waiting, and experiencing the light and warmth of the sun, the shadow of the clouds, and the wind on her skin, the touch of bees who feed from her hands but do not sting her, and the feel of snakes that slither caressingly over her legs. Again, we know nothing of her circumstances or background and the static narrative lures the reader into sharing the silent stillness and intensity of her sensations.

In *Voyage au pays des arbres*, Le Clézio offers young readers a manifestation of these ideas in an accessible and highly imaginative form. The tale is cast as a fairy tale, with the traditional opening ('Il y avait une fois') in which the forest is a place not of fear but of knowledge and communion with its benign inhabitants. The only human character in the story is an unnamed boy, of whom we are told nothing but that he, too, longs to escape from the boredom of his life, and that, having no means to fulfil his dreams of flight to the unknown realms beyond the horizon, resolves to embark upon a voyage of discovery to 'le pays des arbres'. His potential for empathy is clear from the start, as he senses that the trees want to talk to him, and, by sitting and waiting quietly in their midst and whistling to them softly, he encourages them to be at ease in his presence and to reveal their voices, eyes, and movements to him. Like many other child characters of Le Clézio, the boy exhibits the qualities of passivity and patience that, in their implicit refusal of activity, would seem to be the antithesis of the spirit of adventure. Yet their very immobility allows them to open all their senses to the exterior world, and their escape from everyday life and society is effected through contemplation rather than movement and action.[45] Unlike the novels of Jules Verne and his imitators, in which the plausibility of the travellers' adventures is stretched to the limit, Le Clézio immerses the reader in the natural world that exists around them and that they too can experience.[46] In this sense, his stories can be seen as a different model of an initiation narrative for character and reader alike.

The assertion that 'il faut apprivoiser les arbres' in this text reflects Saint-Exupéry's concept of creating a sympathetic bond with another creature, and the view of trees as immobile, blind, deaf, and dumb is overturned as they are revealed to have a social hierachy and a life of their own when human beings are not around, talking amongst themselves endlessly and recounting stories 'sans queue ni tête qui ne sont pas pour les hommes'.[47] The superior powers of observation, participation, and sensitivity to sounds characteristic of Le Clézio's child characters allow the boy to become a trusted confidant, discovering the different voices and personalities of the many species of trees in the forest, and to take part in their night-time dance. The description of the stately movements and sounds of the swaying branches clashing together transforms the effects of a windy night into a magical experience, after which the child, like the trees, falls asleep in the forest until dawn. The lack of realistic exterior contextualisation and the intense focus on the boy's experience create a text that is both poetic and oneiric.[48] The illustrations by Henri Galeron for the Folio Cadet edition (recommended for ages eight and up) reproduce these qualities in the images of trees in which human features or profiles can be discerned that dwarf the figure of the child. These images, both full-page and vignettes predominantly in green, brown, and grey, are, in effect, rather more frightening than the text—especially the vignettes depicting leaves with eyes and a shouting mouth. The last illustration, reproduced on the cover, of the boy sitting on the moon apparently simultaneously high above the tree-tops and beneath the spreading roots of a great tree, does not relate to a particular episode in the text, but captures the dreamlike quality of the narrative and reflects the association of children with magical powers and the merveilleux in Le Clézio's works.

Claude Roy (1915–1997): Magic and the Child's Imagination

Claude Roy, a poet and novelist who also wrote for adults, attempts in his books for young readers to present a context and an image of childhood that are closer to their experience while still privileging the role of the imagination in both childhood and his narrative. *La Maison qui s'envole* (1977) is, in essence, a cautionary tale since the four children's magical adventure comes about as a punishment for their disobedience and passion for dismantling objects about the house in their parents' absence. The parents' warning that they should neither tamper with the clocks nor play with matches is the catalyst for the ensuing disorder, and the grandfather and two servants in whose care the children are left are incapable of controlling the situation. But it is also a fantasy tale built upon a constant hesitation between what is real and what is not and exemplifying the same love of life, nature, and the world of the imagination that inform Roy's poetry. A number of fairy-tale motifs are introduced (the motif of the good deed returned, a flying Persian carpet, and the intervention of animals and objects endowed with speech and autonomy of action) and the fictional status of the whole is established in the reference to other children's books: the parents have been invited to stay with Général Dourakine along with other fictional characters such as Alfred Assollant's Capitaine Corcoran, Verne's Capitaine Grant, and, by contrast, Christophe's le sapeur Camember. Eventually the household objects rebel and collude to teach the children a lesson, terrorising them by behaving in unexpected and painful or frustrating ways, and when the children respond by dismantling more and more objects, outright war is declared and the four siblings are spirited away on a bedside rug on a journey to the North Pole. The reader's disbelief is manipulated by the narrator: the chapter that narrates the kidnapping advises the reader that the children's adventures 'qui sont pourtant strictement vraies, commencent à prendre un tour absolument invraisemblable', although the description of the surprise of aeroplane passengers at seeing the carpet fly past is followed by the tongue-in-cheek assertion that 'aujourd'hui, il ne faut s'étonner de rien'.[49] The adventure mirrors aspects of the first half of the book: the journey on the rug echoes the imaginary voyages at which the children play in a pine tree in their park, and the mysterious young angel violinist who appears from nowhere and is instrumental in saving them is the same young man helped earlier by the children when he comes to seek work and is dismissed by the parents as a vagrant.

Only when the cold and frightened children have repented of their misbehaviour can they return home, and the violinist repays their earlier good deed in a neat reversal of the traditional fairy-tale motif of homecoming by summoning their house to come to fetch them. The house, finding itself empty, silent, and safe from childish interference, has become bored, and rather than fulfilling the traditional function of home as a safe haven to which the wanderer returns, opts for adventure as well. Its stately progress through the skies, like that of a great galleon, is a delight to all the occupants and the children are even allowed a little touristic detour, flying over New York where the Americans are perturbed to see the little French house sailing over their skyscrapers. The motif of the flying house has itself been set up at the start of the story when two sorts of houses are identified: the solemn and sad houses firmly rooted on the ground and those carefree houses that fly away at the slightest provocation, their doors and windows open to the sun, moon, and stars. The children's house thus represents both safe family life and a love of life and the capacity for imaginative adventure. Since neither the grandfather nor the servants offer any comment on their journey, the return to normality opens the way for the interpretation of the adventure as one of Eric's tales or a fantastic game. The narrative can therefore be read as a parable of play as a means of escape, via the imagination, into the unknown. The reader's response is best summed up, however, in Hermine's reply to her little brother when he objects that the stories she tells him are not true: 'Bien sûr. Seulement c'est joli'.[50]

The enhancement of life by fantasy and Roy's whimsical humour is also apparent in the titles of two books of poems and fables, *Enfantasques, fables pour enfants* (1974) and *Nouvelles enfantasques, poèmes et collages* (1978), and in stories that derive from his love of cats. In *Le Chat qui parlait malgré lui* (1982), for example, the tale of Gaspard, a cat who suddenly acquires the power of speech, Roy extends the fairy-tale conceit of the talking animal by admitting that his cat Myrna suggested the topic to him although he denies that the tale was actually dictated by her, as she claims.

Jacques Prévert (1900–1977): Tales of Transgression

The poet and screenplay writer Jacques Prévert was another established writer who turned his hand to writing children's books in the postwar period. Childhood and the family are repeated themes in his poetry, and to some extent he, too, shares the Romantic vision of the child as a symbol of purity and vitality with a special relationship with the natural world. The influence of the family and social forces on the child are seen as oppressive and corruptive, as in the prose poem 'L'Enfant abandonné', in *Spectacle* (1951), in which the group of friends encountered in a public park by a well-raised and deeply frustrated little boy horrify his family but help him to embrace transgression and refuse socialisation ('ils apprennent mal leurs leçons, ils ne font pas bien leurs devoirs, ils changent la morale des fables, il se battent, ils pleurent, voyant à travers les grilles un cheval blessé. Et le Vendredi Saint, ils pensent à Robinson Crusoe'). In contrast, the polite little girls, the boy scouts, the obese babies, and the infant prodigies are seen as monstrous or profoundly sad creatures irremediably spoilt by society, 'déchirantes petites figures du musée de cire familial'.[51] A joyous rejection of traditional education based on memorising facts, figures, dates, and names is articulated in 'Le Cancre' (in *Paroles*, 1946), in which a nameless child, interrogated in class, responds by a sudden burst of laughter and 'avec des craies de toutes les couleurs / sur le tableau noir du malheur / il dessine le visage du bonheur'.[52] It is not surprising, therefore, that Prévert's writing for children, informed by these same ideas and accompanied by imaginative new illustrative techniques, is innovative and subversive.

The title itself of his *Contes pour enfants pas sages* (1947), published in album form with illustrations by Elsa Henriquez, is a challenge to the conventional assumptions of children's literature.[53] In the *livres de prix* tradition, the gift of a book was perceived as a reward for good behaviour and the satisfactory fulfilment of adult expectations. (Robert Desnos's *Chantefables* was first published in the Librairie Gründ's Pour les enfants sages collection.) While children's books traditionally condemned transgression against social and cultural conventions and were intended to encourage less-well-behaved readers to mend their ways, Prévert's fantastic tales feature a variety of animals and celebrate and encourage revolt against the more cynical, inhumane, and stultifying aspects of contemporary society. The subversive nature of such an approach, rare in a book for children, is only lightly obscured by the use of fairy-tale motifs and humorous surreal images akin to those of nonsense verse.

The first tale, 'L'Autruche', the only one actually to feature a child, is introduced as the true story behind Perrault's *Le Petit Poucet*. It tells how an ostrich swallows the white pebbles dropped by Le Petit Poucet in order to find his way home, and persuades the child to embrace freedom by travelling with him on his back to distant lands. The ostrich's joyous dancing and his pride in his ability to consume all manner of things, including bells and trumpets, represents a limitless and unconstrained ability to sample all that life has to offer. He overcomes the child's reluctance to abandon his parents by criticising their social pretensions (symbolised by the ostrich feathers the mother wears in her hat) and their cruelty, articulating what the child recognises as his own feelings. The ostrich's words 'tu ne verras plus tes parents, mais tu verras du pays' exemplify a triumph of liberty and self-determination over parental guidance and authority that responds to a common childhood dream, and is supported here by the reader's knowledge of Le Petit Poucet's plight as an abandoned child.[54] This tale thus portrays, through the rebellion of two individuals, the revenge of animals and children against their adult oppressors. Personal liberty is also the central issue in 'Cheval dans une île', an allegory of class conflict, in which a horse, alone on an island, dreams of mobilising all the other horses in the world in a revolt against the cruelty of man. He is alert to the irony of the much-advertised 'Be kind to animals' campaign by humans, while horses are constantly subject to the whip, the spur, and the branding iron, and envisages horses confronting their masters with their demands. Prévert's sympathy for the proletariat is evident here as the mockery of the horses pulling the carriages of the wealthy and the fearful reluctance of the wagon horses to speak out in support are evoked. Despite the condemnation of war apparent in his poetry, Prévert appears to concede here the legitimacy of bloodshed to achieve freedom from oppression. The horse's cry of 'Vive la liberté!' is echoed by the horses on other islands but is rashly ignored by the humans who have no conception of what is lying in wait for them.

The inhumanity of man to animals also informs 'Les Premiers ânes', in which the wild donkeys welcome the arrival of men but are soon harnessed and used by the conquerors as beasts of burden because they are stupid and inedible. This scenario is depicted through the eyes of the donkeys, whose generosity and hospitality towards the odd-looking, pale, two-legged creatures is in marked contrast to the men's cynical appropriation and exploitation of them. The white men's assumption of superiority and ownership can be interpreted as reflecting Prévert's dislike of colonialism, which is even more overt in 'Scène de la vie des antilopes', in which black Africans are treated like animals by the white colonisers, lassooed and forced to build roads and railways, and shot if they try to escape. This is recounted in a matter-of-fact manner but the issue is complicated by the delight engendered in both black and white by the killing of an antelope, the blacks celebrating the prospect of food with music and dancing while the whites enjoy the spectacle. The death of the antelope is also seen from the perspective of the animals, however, who await in vain for the return of one of their number and, eventually recognising the significance of the fires and shouting in the valley, and thus accepting the inevitable, sit down without appetite to their own silent and sad meal. The structure of 'L'Opéra des girafes' is a masterpiece of economical theatricality, with its scene of exposition by a chorus of giraffes singing, paradoxically, of their muteness, the complication of the plot in the hypocrisy of the two old men, one with a giraffe-skin coat, observed by the silent animals who pass by, and the dramatic denouement in which the old man's son, a giraffe hunter, meets his nemesis when he is bitten by a tsetse fly and falls on the body of the giraffe he has just shot. Prévert is clearly rehearsing one of his favourite themes, condemning the insensitivity and indifferent cruelty of the bourgeoisie, but the protest of the peaceable and silent victims who are nevertheless avenged is a theme of tragic intensity worthy of grand opera and skillfully condensed into a few vivid images, focussing, as Prévert does in his poetry, on the drama of individual experience.

Prévert's fondness for exotic animals is apparent throughout the *Contes pour enfants pas sages*, and wild animals, like those described above, often represent the freedom and spontaneity of human beings that are constrained or perverted by social forces. In 'Jeune lion en cage', the animal watches his own transformation into a circus animal with amusement, welcoming the spectators, but leaps upon the lion tamer when he brandishes a chair and shoots a pistol in the air. From the animal's viewpoint, which creates a different perspective on human affairs, the lion tamer is perceived as a madman and the animal seeks to restore order. The disruption that ensues in the circus tent when an English spectator declares that he had predicted what would happen seems to confirm a view of humans as eccentric, erratic, and aggressive. It is tempting to interpret this tale as a warning against awakening the aggressive nature of other nations, but the lion is the more civilised creature and watches the humans' actions with an ironic eye. The elephant seal in 'L'Eléphant de mer' lives happily enough in captivity as long as he is treated well and and fed regularly, but Prévert invites the reader to imagine 'si tous les animaux se fâchaient, ce serait une drôle d'histoire'.[55] One of Prévert's other favourite targets, the intellectual, appears in the humorous 'Le Dromadaire mécontent', in which a young dromedary is disappointed and bored at a much anticipated lecture in which an academic drones on repetitively about the difference between dromedaries and camels but does not know the difference when his young listener gets up and bites him.

That the *Contes pour enfants pas sages* were incorporated in an edition of *Histoires et d'Autres histoires* in 1963 suggests that Prévert did not envisage children as the sole audience for the tales. In proposing disobedience and insurrection, these tales were perhaps intended also to appeal to those adult readers who did not share their society's values.[56] Elsa Henriquez's original drawings of 1947, reproduced in full colour in modern editions, capture the fantastic nature of the tales by ignoring conventional rules of scale and perspective and creating a childlike and imaginative perspective on reality. Prévert introduced the same theme of freedom from familial and social restraints in the innovative *Le Petit lion*, also published in 1947 and the fruit of collaboration with Ylla (Kamilla Koffler), a photographer specialising in pictures of animals. Prévert's story of the lion cub who is inspired by his mother's tales of the wild to escape from the zoo and finds himself in an apartment with a little boy's family is tailored perfectly to the photographs in which the animals' faces and postures appear to express a variety of emotions. The sentimentality of a conventional story of friendship between child and animal is rejected here, for the cub is soon left like an abandoned toy at the mercy of the other members of the household, who all want to exploit or change him. Instead of roaming with wild animals he finds himself lying on a zebra-skin rug. The artificiality and abnormality of his existence is encapsulated in a photograph of the cub in a small knitted coat, and his rage at thinking that his own reflection in a mirror is his brother mocking him exacerbates his unease at this restricted and oppressive environment. He dreams of virgin forests full of exotic creatures where he runs free with his own family, but when he is returned to the zoo he feels forced to rewrite his story for the benefit of his younger brother, transforming his experiences into an extravagant tale of adventure and fantasy, of which he is the triumphant hero. The text thus portrays the gap between dreams and reality in response to which the lion cub, like a writer, has to give the truth a 'petit coup de patte de l'imagination', mixing 'le vin du rêve avec l'eau amère de la vérité'.[57]

THE METAMORPHOSIS OF THE FAIRY TALE
Pierre Gripari's Anarchic Tales

Pierre Gripari's books for children portray the comic intrusion of fantasy into contemporary real life, in the manner of Claude Roy and Marcel Aymé. Unlike them, however, his colourful, often grotesque, tales employ a wide range of traditional fairy-tale motifs and devices, depicting the interaction of witches, fairies, and giants with human beings, animated talking objects and animals, transformations, and endless bizarre happenings in a manner that gently mocks the genre of the merveilleux itself. This self-conscious ironising of the material is very much in the tradition of Perrault but taken to an extreme. The reader's expectations of the merveilleux are repeatedly overturned by a giant who longs to be a family man, a little red devil who is the despair of his parents because he is virtuous, a witch who turns herself into a frog, and fairy gifts that become curses. Gripari produced several collections of tales for children—notably, the *Contes de la rue Broca* (1967), *Contes de la Folie Méricourt* (1983), and *Contes d'ailleurs et d'autre part* (1990) and also wrote a lengthy fairy tale (*L'Histoire de Prince Pipo*, 1976). In addition, he wrote collections of poetry and plays for children: *Pièces enfantines* (1977), *Marelles, poèmes pour enfants* (1988), and *Huit farces pour collégiens* (1989). The *Contes de la rue Broca*, in particular, have become a classic of children's literature and have been adapted for television.

For the 1967 edition of *Contes de la rue Broca*, Gripari takes the by now unusual step of providing a preface, but establishes his position vis-à-vis his readers and their expectations from the start, reversing the assumptions behind the provision of such apparatus in children's books in earlier times:

> Les enfants comprennent tout, cela est bien connu. S'il n'y avait qu'eux pour lire ce livre, l'idée ne me viendrait même pas d'y

écrire une préface. Mais je soupçonne, hélas, que ces contes seront lus également par des grandes personnes. En conséquence, je crois devoir donner quelques explications.[58]

To satisfy the most rational and sceptical adult reader Gripari goes to great lengths to establish the existence and exact whereabouts of the rue Broca, which is not evident on a two-dimensional map, because the street runs below ground level under the boulevard de Port-Royal. It therefore exists, he explains, in kind of different dimension from the rest of Paris and has its own special village atmosphere. The inhabitants are for the most part immigrants who, despite their diverse origins, have in common a love of stories, a predilection shared by Gripari, who asserts his preference for 'une histoire impossible' that paradoxically is likely to contain more profound truth than 'une histoire simplement plausible'.[59] His acquaintance with the children of the rue Broca and the origins of his stories are represented as a true story that nevertheless resembles a fairy tale, with himself cast as a strange visitor who haunts the cafés of the street and is seen by the children as a 'vieille sorcière', a role he readily assumes. Through this double transformation of writer into witch and vice versa, he becomes a narrator of fairy stories to a young, spellbound audience.[60] This collection is thus presented as the product of a project of oral improvisation and collaboration with the children and a testimony to their creative and imaginative powers, their talent for inventing dramatic and surprising situations, and their intuitive grasp of profound truths.

The children of the rue Broca and their families appear as themselves in many of the tales and their belongings (a doll, a piggy bank, a bowl of goldfish) are endowed with magical powers and play an active role, thus transforming reality into both fiction and the merveilleux. The merveilleux here coexists with the real world: witches read newspapers, and adults afflicted by magic consult their doctor, who charges them fantastic fees. The multiple fairy-tale motifs and mythical and literary allusions are imbued with a hyperbolic humour that is delightfully eclectic and ludic and frequently of the kind of dubious taste that appeals to children.[61] In 'La Sorcière de la rue Mouffetard', for example, a vain, wicked witch wishes to try a recipe for youth and beauty advertised in the *Journal des sorcières* by eating a little girl with tomato sauce. She accordingly targets Nadia, the daughter of Papa Saïd, the owner of the grocer's shop and bar in the rue Broca, but is forced to transform herself into all the 267 shopkeepers on the street in order to entice the child. In an extravagant denouement she is outwitted by Nadia's younger brother Bachir, and all the fake shopkeepers are left for dead with their heads cracked open and their brains spilling out; then the cash register in which she has imprisoned the girl falls on her own head. 'Scoubidou, la poupée qui sait tout' is a picaresque fantasy in which a doll belonging to Bachir, which can tell the past and the future when blindfolded, uses her magical powers to try to persuade Bachir's father to buy him a bicycle. Harassed by her magic so that every time he enters a shop he asks for a bicycle, Papa Saïd is advised by his doctor to get rid of the doll. The narrative draws on a familiar mythical and fairy-tale device and, more specifically, gestures towards Carlo Collodi's *Pinocchio*, when, after travelling around the world on a ship, Scoubidou is thrown into the sea and swallowed by a giant fish. Finding a large pearl in his belly, she persuades the reluctant fish to take her back to Paris by swimming up the Seine (an affront to his honour as a saltwater sea creature) and Bachir acquires his bicycle. Gripari's strong streak of irreverence towards the values of his society is apparent in 'Le Géant aux chausettes rouges', in which a giant, seeking to reduce his size so that he can marry a young human girl, is failed by wizards from China and Brittany and visits the pope, who calls the Virgin Mary on the telephone for advice. Miracles and magic are conflated when, adopting the role of a fairy godmother, she both reduces his size and grants him three wishes that enable him to fulfil his dream. His red socks, which have the magical power to build houses, enable him to earn a good living as a respectable husband and father.

The most intertextual tale is 'La Fée du robinet', which revises Perrault's 'Les Fées' in a comic, contemporary context. A pagan fairy living in a freshwater spring finds herself in a tap in a city kitchen when the water is diverted by engineers. (The narrator remarks that she was fortunate not to end up as 'la fée des cabinets'.[62]) The plot of Perrault's tale is followed closely, except that, through mistaking their motivations, the fairy's gifts to two sisters do not work out as she intends, although the ultimate results are appropriate. She rewards a cynical, opportunist girl with pearls falling from her lips at every word, a gift that leads to the girl's exploitation, first by her parents, who force her to say crude words because they produce larger pearls, and then by a young man who locks her in his flat and beats her if she does not produce her daily quantity of gems. The kind sister who is aware of the other's plight refuses to offer the fairy any jam, and is afflicted with spitting out snakes, a curse that, paradoxically, leads to her happiness as the wife of a doctor working on antivenom serum at the Institut Pasteur.

Gripari writes himself into the story 'La Sorcière du placard aux balais' as M. Pierre, the victim of a lawyer who sells him a house haunted by a witch and tells him the little refrain ('Sorcière, sorcière, prends garde à ton derrière') that will conjure her up—a refrain that, like many proscriptions in fairy tales, becomes an irresistible obsession and temptation.[63] Like many fairy-tale protagonists before him, M. Pierre is given three chances to free himself from her clutches by making a difficult demand of her and seeks advice from Bachir's magic goldfish. After two failed plans they tell him to ask for a hairy frog (her true persona) and, in a scene that is a cross between the scene in Perrault's 'Le chat botté' in which the cat tempts the vain ogre to turn himself into a mouse before pouncing on him, and the story of Samson and Delilah, M. Pierre seizes the vain witch when she has metamorphosed and, by shaving her hair, strips her of her powers.

French history itself is revised in 'Histoire de Lustucru', a tale allegedly inspired by hearing of Bachir's reply in class that the Roman general who conquered Gaul was called Lustucru. M. Pierre, struck by the amusing potential of this view, recounts the story of Lustucru, the son of a barbarian king blessed by a fairy with immortality but cursed with a ridiculous name, who, although responsible for all the major events in the history of France, is excluded from the history books and the credit given to others. His achievements include those attributed to, amongst others, Napoleon Bonaparte, Jeanne d'Arc, Julius Caesar, and Roland. It was Lustucru who conquered England in 1066 and, it is tentatively suggested, broadcast to the nation from London in June 1940. After two thousand years he is advised by the sorcière of the rue Mouffetard that the only way to fame is to have his name celebrated in a song, an aim he achieves when he kidnaps the cat of Mme Michel, a neighbour with whom he falls in love, and becomes the subject of a well-known children's song about their romance.

Gripari's Histoire du prince Pipo, de Pipo le cheval et de la princesse Popi (1976), a lengthy and elaborate fairy tale, is both an allegory of maturation involving separation from parents, the learning of new skills, and military service before attaining love, marriage, and adult responsibilities, as well as a reflection on the act of storytelling itself. He characterises the status of the tale as an autonomous entity spontaneously generated in a dream, which, forgotten by M. Pierre before he can write it down, is doomed, in a Pirandellian fashion, to seek another narrator who will give it narrative form. Rejected by a priest because of the lack of mention of God, by a journalist because of the lack of mention of socialism, and by many others who want to make changes to it, the tale returns weak and tired to M. Pierre who, in a parodic gesture towards the Catholic Mass, revives and nourishes it with his own flesh and blood and writes it down. The implied reader is, therefore, one who can accept and enjoy a fairy story for what it is. The tale contains many traditional fairy-tale features (dwarves, fairies, dragons, a beautiful princess, and a journey to a strange land beyond a volcano) but it also draws on the central structuring motif of the *Mille et une nuits*, for his escape from the enchanted 'Auberge des enfants perdus' depends upon his ability to tell a tale that the innkeeper does not know. At the third attempt, Pipo resolves to narrate to her the story of his own life up to this point, the first to be brave and honest enough to tell it, and procures his release. Gripari thus offers once again a validation of the originality of his own narrative and reveals the existential core of the tale as one of individual maturation. The power of the written word is exemplified when, after further trials, Pipo finds the book of his life in the Grande Bibliothèque, presided over by a white rat. He is disappointed not to find his future recorded there, for the book is being written only as the reader reads it, thus placing the reader in a dynamic relationship with both the text and Pipo's experience. He has, however, learnt a fundamental truth ('Ce qui est est, ce qui a été n'est plus, et ce qui sera n'est pas encore. Cela n'a l'air de rien, mais c'est toute la sagesse') and understands that he cannot recover the past and find his parents but must move onwards into his own future as king in his father's stead. In a final gesture of reader involvement (or perhaps entrapment), the reader curious to know the story of Pipo's son's life is invited to turn to the first chapter and reread the book 'car c'est à peu de chose près l'histoire de tous les fils de rois'.[64] The illusion of orality is maintained by direct address to the reader throughout, and Gripari encourages further involvement for young readers by suggesting that they draw pictures of the scenes that they liked most, even occasionally making suggestions for possible illustrations. Dedicated to real children, some of whom also feature in *Contes de la rue Broca*, the *Histoire du prince Pipo* is both traditional and highly original and, like the tales of Perrault, can be read on a number of levels.

Gripari's work is very reminiscent of that of Roald Dahl, whose novels, published between the 1960s and 1980s, have enjoyed immense popularity in France. In fact, four of Dahl's novels (*La Potion magique de Georges Bouillon, Matilda, Le Bon gros géant,* and *Les deux gredins*) are advertised in the back of the Folio Junior edition of *La Sorcière de la rue Mouffetard*.[65] Although frequently criticised (by adult readers and reviewers) as crude, cruel, and full of revolting details, the irreverent humour and fertile imaginativeness of Dahl's novels continue to appeal to children. Dahl's stories, like those of Gripari, involve the intrusion of witches, magic, and other fairy-tale ingredients in the lives of child characters who live in an imaginatively transformed version of reality. His *Revolting Rhymes* (1982), aimed at younger children, are metamorphoses of Perrault's classic fairy tales, including *Le Petit Chaperon rouge* and *Cendrillon*, into hilarious, subversive, and scatalogical versions in comic doggerel that, since much of the humour depends upon the reader's foreknowledge of the original, testify to the continuing interest in the potential and power of fairy tales.

Pef: The Magic of Words

La Belle lisse poire du prince Motordu (1980) by Pef (Pierre Elie Ferrier (1939–)), for readers aged four and upwards, is a further example of the appropriation of the fairy tale for a new purpose. Although based on the traditional model of a prince's quest for a bride, this tale is presented as 'pour se tordre de rire au royaume des jeux des mots et d'images'.[66] The humour derives from the highly inventive play on words that not only characterises the idiosyncratic speech of Prince Motordu and that of his parents but also the narrative itself, from the title onwards. The resulting linguistic felicities are reproduced in the large, brightly coloured images full of comic detail on every page, thus creating a surreal world in which language and concrete reality, as well as text and image, are mutually dependent. Thus, the opening statement that Motordu lives in 'un chapeau magnifique', above which flutter 'des crapauds bleu blanc rouge', is juxtaposed with an illustration of a large, pink, flower-trimmed hat with turrets topped with huge *tricolore* toads on the flagpoles.[67] The complicity between the text and image reinforces throughout the wittiness of the play on words. In a set-piece scene, the delights of a banquet, which consists of 'suisses de grenouille', 'purée de petit bois', and 'braises du jardin', are reproduced in both a written menu and in the dishes on the table. As in all the illustrations, there is a great deal of comic detail demanding lengthy or repeated perusal, including here a sprawling cat with an overstuffed belly and a wide-eyed mouse rushing off with a miniature shopping trolley full of goodies. Motordu's meeting with the princess Dézécolle, a school teacher who speaks in a conventional manner and offers to help him to talk like other children, provides much nonsense humour in the representation of his sums ('quatre et cinq = boeuf') and his compositions ('Napoléon déclara la guerre aux puces'). The text suggests a depiction of the fate of the child who is different, as his speech causes much hilarity in the classroom, but this is subverted when the other pupils find him less amusing as he progresses in his studies and his popularity is largely due to the kilos of candy he distributes every day. As in traditional tales, Motordu achieves assimilation into the dominant culture, but the tale ends with a neat reversal, for when he and Dézécolle marry she begins spontaneously to assume his former mode of speech, an unexpected denouement enhancing, in their eyes, the happy-ever-after ending. The disruption of the anticipated trajectory of the tale and a return to the beginning creates a satisfying sense of recognition that rounds off the humour.[68] A book best read aloud (as the reader quickly realises when attempting to decipher the enigmatic title), Pef's highly original tale, described in the publisher's blurb as 'le célèbre classique indispensable à tous les enfants', has much to delight the ear as well as the eye and is a splendid introduction for young children to the imaginative potential of language.[69] Although seemingly antididactic, Pef's games with words in fact not only invite the child reader to indulge in a different kind of reading, apparently anarchic but coherent on its own terms, but to consider the arbitrary nature of linguistic signs and of the rational ideas that convention invests in them.[70]

Other of Pef's works, notably those that deal with the conflicts of the twentieth century through images, have attracted criticism for treating sensitive issues lightly. In *Zappe la guerre* (1998), for example, a group of soldiers emerge from a war memorial eighty years after the First World War in order to see how the world they died to save has developed and are appalled to see on a television that images of continuing strife in Rwanda, Sarajevo, and all over the world are on every channel. The meeting between soldiers and a little boy suggests that future generations may work to avoid war and the tragedy that cut short the soldiers' own youth. Pef also seeks to explain the Second World War to children in *Je m'appelle Adolphe* (1994) in which a child born looking like Hitler suffers ostracism and exclusion, and learns of the reasons from an elderly woman who suffered Nazi atrocities firsthand. Although clearly open to criticism that such a bizarre plot and a simplified representation of the reality of concentration camps are inappropriate, Pef's work is based on the belief that children should be exposed to the truth in order not to grow up with a deformed view of the world in which they live and for which they will be responsible.[71]

A NEW AGENDA FOR THE BIBLIOTHÈQUE ROSE

As Hachette's Bibliothèque rose series celebrated its 150th anniversary in 2006, amongst the best-selling books on its list were the Witch, Winx Club, Cédric, Titeuf, and Totally Spies series, adapted from bandes dessinées or cartoon films. Charlotte Ruffault, the director of the fiction section of Hachette Jeunesse, has explained in a recent interview that this is where the future of the Bibliothèque rose lies:

La Bibliothèque rose est désormais un lieu de série et uniquement de série, qui viennent de plus en plus de la télé ou de la bande dessinée. Les grandes séries d'auteurs, même d'excellente qualité, tendent à se faire écraser par des séries plus fortes, nées de l'univers audiovisuel ou de la BD [bande desinée].[72]

The huge sales of these series have clearly validated this approach in economic terms. Totally Spies and Witch, aimed at girls ages seven and upwards, have sold over three quarters of a million copies. While conceding that the novelisation of existing material in a series signals a significant change in agenda for the Bibliothèque rose, Ruffault argues that it responds to a demand amongst young children for a fictional universe where 'on nage dans le connu'. Furthermore, she asserts that 'ce qui compte aujourd'hui, dans la littérature jeunesse, c'est la dichotomie masculin/féminin', arguing that girls now demand books addressed specifically to them and that cater to their interests. This does not mean, she hastens to add, 'des histoires à l'eau de rose' but 'du Bridget Jones junior, de la dérision, des histoires rigolotes', and the current trend reflects the policy that 'pour la Bibliothèque rose, les enfants sont prescripteurs à 100%'.[73] Clearly there are a number of issues worthy of debate here, not least the origins of such a demand, but the purpose here is to consider briefly an example of this new ethos for children's literature.

Fairies and other magical beings have now, it seems, joined the current trend in many children's books, with their associated merchandise, towards reflecting a materialistic trendiness in which even preteens are encouraged by media images of fashion and behaviour to see themselves as sexualised beings. In the Winx Club books, adapted from an American cartoon film series by Sophie Marvaud and aimed at readers age seven and upwards, the weak narratives feature a preoccupation with fashion and boys along with the magic. The plots focus on Bloom, a sixteen-year-old girl who discovers that she has magical powers and is transported to the kingdom of Magix, where, at a fairy university, she is to learn to hone her skills. Bloom and her three friends Stella, Flora, Musa, and Tecna, whose talents reflect both traditional magic and that of the technological age, are depicted in the illustrations—taken from the cartoons, as Bratz doll-like sirens, all legs, eyes, and hair—in skimpy, glamorous, and revealing outfits. With the assistance of four effetely handsome boys from the neighbouring university, the quartet work together to defeat the machinations of witches and grotesque monsters. These books, brightly coloured and dusted with glitter, are clearly remarkably popular and arguably offer empowering models of independence and endeavour to the young female reader, although it is impossible not to feel rather uncomfortable with such concluding remarks in a book for this age group as 'Il y a un temps pour tout dans la vie: un temps pour courir après les plus cruelles des sorcières, et un temps pour valser dans les bras du plus charmant des garçons.'[74] Reading a Winx Club volume after, say, *Les Malheurs de Sophie*, is an instructive experience in many ways, not least in revealing the definitive shift caused by the impact of the visual media on the balance between entertainment, instruction, and moral guidance in children's books.

FANTASY WORLDS AND THE CHILD AS SORCERER

The reintroduction of fantasy into children's books in France owed much to the 'English invasion' of the 1950s and 1960s. C. S. Lewis's Narnia novels, published from the 1950s, were highly successful in French translation. The series of seven novels, which chronicle the adventures of a family of ordinary children who gain access to the otherworld of Narnia, initially by entering through the back of a wardrobe, draws its appeal from the children's ability to move between two different worlds. *The Lion, the Witch and the Wardrobe* (1950), the best-known and most popular of the series, depicts the evacuation of the children during the war to an elderly professor's house in the country where they find the wardrobe, and their struggle against the White Witch in her battle for control of Narnia. The stories are Christian parables, and the children are enlisted in the cause of Aslan, the great lion, who, with his 'deep magic', succeeds—through sacrificing his own life and rising again—in defeating the forces of evil. The existence of other worlds is conceived here as a parallel universe to which only the privileged have access. Other fantasy texts, however, are set firmly in a different world, transporting the reader fully into an environment to which the only limits are those of the writer's imagination. The huge success throughout the 1960s of J. R. R. Tolkien's *Lord of the Rings* trilogy, first published in 1954–55, generated widespread interest in such 'High Fantasy' that has lasted to the present day and, indeed, received further impetus with the release of the film versions. The shelves in the children's section of bookshops in France, as in England, display a bewildering variety of tales of sorcery, dragons, and epic conflicts against supernatural forces.[75] These can be seen, for the most part, to adhere to the pattern of the epic or hero story and many accommodate the plot to the targeted audience by focussing on a youthful protagonist.

In more recent years, the phenomenal publishing success of J. K. Rowling's Harry Potter books, with its young protagonist who is himself a wizard, have had an enormous impact in France as in many other countries. *Harry Potter and the Philosopher's Stone* (1997) appeared in the Folio Junior series in 1998. The title was changed to *Harry Potter à l'école des sorciers*, perhaps to signal the content more clearly, and after an initial slow start, the book began to receive rave reviews, with sales rising to some 55,000 copies in 1999. The book won the Prix Sorcières (judged by librarians and specialist bookshops) for the best book in the ages nine to twelve category, and the back cover of the book carried quotations from reviews hailing it as 'une star de la littérature enfantine'.[76] A measure of its success is the advertisement at the back of a recent Fédération Nationale d'Achats pour Cadres (National Purchasing Federation for Managers) *200 romans jeunesse* guide advertising FNAC's active support for organisations combating illiteracy. Above a picture of a wizard's hat are the words 'Un enfant sur dix n'a pas su lire le best-seller de l'année 2003.'[77] Clearly, no further identification is needed. Ruffault asserts that 'sous l'influence de Harry Potter, la notion de fantaisie est devenue majeure. Sans doute parce qu'on vit dans un monde qui ne va pas si bien que ça.'[78]

Eric L'Homme's prize-winning fantasy trilogy *Le Livre des étoiles*, comprising *Qadehar le Sorcier* (2001), *Le Seigneur Sha* (2002), and *Le Visage de l'Ombre* (2003) are extremely readable, recent examples of this genre, and demonstrate a clear affinity with the Harry Potter series. The first book, *Qadehar le Sorcier*, in particular, replicates several aspects of the winning formula of Rowling's work.[79] In outline, the similarities are striking. The novel features a twelve-year-old protagonist, Guillemot, a boy with special magical powers of which, like Harry Potter, he is at first unaware. He becomes an apprentice under the care of Qadehar, a powerful sorcerer, and has a group of loyal friends, male and female, who share his adventures and have many encounters with monsters and supernatural occurrences. Like Harry, Guillemot is not a ready-made superhero: he is frequently afraid and lonely, suffers from bullying at school, and is tentative in his use of magic, although he is also brave and has a strong sense of justice. A salient feature of both books is that both Guillemot and Harry, the latter having survived when his mother and father were killed by the universally feared Voldemort, have close connections with the forces of evil through their parents. Guillemot, who has never known his father, also becomes the object of attention of an evil power known as 'l'Ombre', and of the mysterious Seigneur de Sha, who is seeking his son. The setting of L'Homme's book is significantly different from that in Rowling's work, however. Harry's world of wizards, although a fantasy environment where magical creatures and events are taken for granted, exists somewhere within but parallel to the real world to which the children must return at the end of each school year via 'platform 9¾' at London's King's Cross train station. The adventures take place mainly in the environment of the school, Hogwarts (*Poudlard* in the French version) although supernatural elements sometimes also invade the real world. The setting of *Qadehar le Sorcier* is the Pays d'Ys, an imaginary island with a quasi-medieval social structure halfway between the Monde Certain of which it was once a part (and which has similarities to modern-day Europe) and the strange Monde Incertain, home of unknown and dangerous forces. The island is linked with these other worlds by portals through which it is possible to pass by means of complex incantations known only to a few. In order to enhance the illusion of its reality for young French readers, the Pays d'Ys is said to have close connections with France, from which it imports films, television programmes, its education system, and Nutella, although the inhabitants of France are for the most part unaware of its existence.

Guillemot's adventures are not restricted like Harry's to a discrete environment, but range widely within his own country and the Monde Incertain. The structure in effect follows that of the traditional initiation narrative, with a departure from home, a number of encounters with dangerous adversaries, and a return home after a mission has been accomplished and lessons learnt. Like Harry Potter, Guillemot must first undergo an induction process into the world of magic and is initiated by his mentor Qadehar into the secrets of the *livre des étoiles* which allow him to control and implement his magical powers. The sorcery he learns is centred on the use of *graphèmes*, signs and words that must be summoned and invoked to produce a wide range of effects. Everything in the universe is connected in a kind of net called the *Wyrd*, a theory developed in the Monde Certain in chaos theory according to Qadehar, and the graphèmes are the keys that allow access to this network and the means to control it. A selection of these signs and the postures that must be adopted to replicate them are printed in Guillemot's notebook in the back of the Folio Junior edition as though initiating the reader, too, and—contrary to the usual practice in children's books—inviting the reader to try them at home!

The linear structure of the initiation plot is disrupted as the narrative follows the simultaneous fortunes of Guillemot and his friends in their mission to rescue a kidnapped school companion from the Monde Incertain. Because of Guillemot's inexperienced incantations, they land in separate places allowing for the depiction of fantastic locations (moving hills, floating villages, mysterious forests, a voracious desert, and sinister cities) and a variety of antagonists and helpers (orks straight out of Tolkien, giants, rapacious jellyfish, fearsome monsters known as Gommons, tribes of benign sea and desert dwellers, and a mysterious huntress who lives in a castle in a forest) before they are reunited and achieve their goal. After a climactic struggle between good and evil during which Qadehar, like Rowling's Dumbledore, arrives to save the day, they are able to return to Ys with the rescued Agathe. It is she who tells Guillemot of overhearing a conversation about the Seigneur Sha's search for his son, thus providing both a satisfactory closure to the first volume and, by introducing a new element, opens up the way for the second, a strategy used to good effect by Rowling and which has ensured L'Homme a following in France.[80]

Pierre Bottero, author of a number of books for young readers on sensitive subjects like the death of a parent (*Le Garçon qui voulait courir vite*, 2002), problematic friendships (*Amies à vie*, 2001), and social displacement (*Tour B2 mon amour*, 2004) as well as children's novels about horses (*Mon cheval, mon destin*, 2002), has contributed to the interest in fantasy worlds with his trilogy *D'un monde à l'autre*, which features a female protagonist. These novels are built upon the concept of parallel worlds and the narrative, like Camille, age thirteen in the first book *La Quête d'Ewilan* (2003), moves rapidly back and forth between the real world and Gwendalavir. Camille discovers her ability to enter the parallel world when she leaps out of the path of an oncoming lorry and finds herself in a strange place where she seems to be expected and is known as Ewilan, possessed of the magic power of bringing into being things she draws in her mind and destined to be the saviour of an empire menaced by evil monsters. The text playfully exploits the conventions of heroic fantasy (the first chapter involves a fight between a knight and a giant lizard) as Camille and her dreadlocked friend Salim, besieged by monstrous creatures in both worlds, pursue her quest with the aid of various helpers, including a ratlike creature with psychic powers. Bottero also explores the psychological impact on Camille of her discovery of her origins and immense responsibilities, and the development of her friendship with Salim. The first novel ends with her meeting with her brother Mathieu—who, like her, was placed in the real world for his safety—and after he declines to accompany her back to Gwendalavir, her return with Salim to try to save her world. Her further adventures there are the subject of the sequels *Les Frontières de glace* (2004) and *L'île du destin* (2005).

Judging by the prevalence and popularity of novels about fantasy worlds, magic, and the supernatural, once thought pernicious to children (and indeed still attracting criticism from adults anxious about the moral implications of the depiction of sorcery in children's books), this trend would seem to be set to fill a large place in the market for some time to come.

8

A LITERATURE FOR CHILDREN

In the second half of the twentieth century, books for young readers in the Western world were inevitably affected by the changing values and realities of contemporary life. After the postwar period of reconstruction, France had prospered economically and culturally in the late 1950s and 1960s, and, as elsewhere, the baby boom generated a cult of youth and the beginnings of an unprecedented youth culture in music, fashion, and film heavily influenced by British and American imports that has continued to escalate.[1] Television was beginning to have a significant, and in the eyes of some, unwelcome, influence on the nature and purveyance of culture.[2] But young people were also increasingly faced with the consequences of wide-ranging social changes—notably, the breakdown in traditional family structures, the 'sexual revolution', the effects of increased consumerism, and the uncertainties of a world overshadowed by nuclear threat. Along with new ideas, freedoms, and opportunities came new concerns and new existential dilemmas.

The May 1968 student protests in France against authority and traditional social structures that quickly spread to violent expressions of discontent in other sections of society 'sent shock waves through the educational, political and cultural institutions of France'.[3] These events—caused chiefly, according to John Ardagh, by the failure of economic change to be matched by social and structural change—brought to prominence a young, idealistic, and militant generation with very different attitudes, priorities, and needs from those of their parents and teachers, and 'dealt a permanent blow to the patterns of obedience to authoritarian rule, previously so marked in France'.[4] The mood of anti-establishment protest began to manifest itself in books for young readers in increased questioning of all traditional adult authority and a critical view of the world created by the older generations. The adult narrating voice was often displaced by the narrative perspective of the adolescent protagonist and adult characters were increasingly portrayed as unjust, narrow-minded, indifferent, or inadequate. The reader was thus invited to identify with an iconoclastic viewpoint and encouraged 'à ne pas accepter comme allant de soi les normes (respect automatique des parents et des autres détenteurs de l'autorité) d'une société jugée encore trop hiérarchisée'.[5] Conventional values were further overtaken by an unprecedented permissiveness in the media to which children were routinely exposed. After the economic slowdown of the mid-1970s, children's books began to reflect a harsher reality marked by increasing social instability, unemployment, delinquency, the problems of urban living, and conflict in a multicultural society and subjects that were formerly taboo in children's books (sexuality, violence, rape, murder, war) were soon being openly portrayed. The individualism characteristic of the postwar Western world and manifested in adult literature by existentialist writers is exemplified in children's books by a focus on the themes of identity and individual psychology, and the portrayal of new existential dilemmas. The adventure story became an exploration of the self.[6] Child or adolescent protagonists in books for young readers in the last quarter of the twentieth century tend to be portrayed as either more clear-sighted, unprejudiced, and courageous than the adults surrounding them (and thus empowered as representations of a better society) or as troubled and isolated, struggling to come to terms with themselves and who they are and their place in the environment of family, school, or society at large. Books for adolescents manifest a strong engagement with social issues such as poverty, urban blight, ethnicity, racism, and crime. The theme of initiation is still evident, but this is less a process of socialisation and the passive acceptance of contemporary values than one of self-realisation, a recognition of society's flaws and a desire to create a better future.

It is impossible within the parameters of this study to cover the stunning range of books written for children since the 1960s. This period has seen an unprecedented growth in the number of writers who, regarding themselves specifically and often solely as writers for the young, have expanded the boundaries of children's literature to encompass all the genres available to adults, and more. In respect of novels alone, publishers' catalogues indicate sections of adventure stories, school stories, fantasy and fairy tales, animal stories, historical tales, humour, detective stories, science fiction, horror stories, war stories, teenage stories, and narratives about the problems of immigration and cultural integration.[7]

This chapter identifies four major subgenres of the novel that have been and in most cases still are amongst the best-selling works: the detective novel, the novel about wartime experiences, teenage novels about the challenges of daily life and relationships, and works offering a comic portrayal of childhood. These texts have in common the focus on young protagonists engaged in situations in which they must act on their own initiative, often without the aid of adults, as they confront crime and social injustice, deal with difficult and distressing personal or family situations, or simply experience the physical and psychological effects of growing up. In several cases, the narrative is focalised through these protagonists, empowering the young reader with a view of the world that might strike a deep personal chord and offering reassurance and positive models for dealing with personal anxieties. The unqualified optimism of earlier children's books is often modified, however, by the realities of the modern world, and endings are by no means always happy nor problems always fully resolved.

THE CHILD AS RIGHTER OF WRONGS

The detective story, which has been seen as the product of the modern urban wilderness, is recognisably another form of the hero narrative model. A hero, superior in intellectual talents and often excelling in physical prowess, takes on the task of seeking out and defeating a villain, the equivalent of the ogre or wicked enchanter, who threatens to attack civilisation and destroy the social order.[8] The essential qualities of the adult (and in the early days, invariably male) detective hero like Arthur Conan Doyle's Sherlock Holmes or Georges Simenon's Inspector Maigret are logic and deductive powers and the ability to think on one's feet, thus highlighting the rational and empirical in the solving of a mystery. In thrillers or detective stories for children we find a variety of engagements in adventures, quests, and confrontations with disruptive and dangerous forces ranging from unsought and accidental involvement of the young protagonists to the exploits of the adolescent sleuth, and these engagements modify this pattern and the assumptions of the genre in interesting ways. Plots are generally less complicated and less overtly bloodthirsty (at least until relatively recently), the investigations come about more by chance than design, and action becomes a more important aspect of the story than the solving of a mystery through sophisticated deduction or interpretation of evidence based on experience and knowledge of the criminal mind.

The children's book that is credited with sparking an enthusiasm for the juvenile detective thriller was Erich Kästner's *Emil und die*

Detektive, first published in Germany in 1929. This novel achieved tremendous popularity in France and in the United Kingdom, although Kästner's works were banned by the Nazis in 1933 and publicly burned in Germany. It portrays the attempts by the ten-year-old Emil Tischbein, the son of a poor widow, to pursue the thief who steals his money while he is asleep on the train that takes him to visit relatives in Berlin. Together with a group of other Berlin schoolchildren he succeeds in tracking down the thief, a bank robber wanted by the police, and is duly rewarded. (A lighthearted moral advises the reader that one should always send one's money by postal money order.) This novel was innovative in foregrounding the children's energy, initiative, and determination in bringing the criminal to justice without the assistance of adults and influenced, amongst others, the works of Enid Blyton in the Famous Five and the Secret Seven series in which hardened criminals are routinely outwitted by a group of resourceful youngsters.

An English Influence and the Vogue for Series

The novels of Enid Blyton (1897–1968), which enjoyed immense popularity in France as at home in the United Kingdom were, in turn, a significant influence on the adventure story for young readers in the mid-twentieth century. Hachette bought the rights to Blyton's works in 1955 and many were published in the Bibliothèque rose series with new illustrations by French artists. While the Noddy books (translated into French as 'Oui Oui' and inaugurating a new collection for the very young, the *Minirose*, in 1962), now so castigated by critics for their political incorrectness, achieved a certain degree of popularity, it was the Famous Five stories that gripped the imagination of young French readers from the mid-1950s on under the name of the Club des cinq. The first to appear in France was, in fact, the second written by Blyton (*Five Go Adventuring Again*, 1942), thirteen years after its publication in the United Kingdom and titled simply *Le Club des Cinq* (1955). The order in which the books were published in France did not follow that of their publication in Britain; Blyton's first, *Five on a Treasure Island* (1942), in which the five children meet each other, did not, for some unaccountable reason, appear in France until 1962 as *Le Club des cinq et le trésor de l'île*. However, once launched, the titles appeared regularly, sometimes two or three a year, up until 1967.[9]

The innovative aspects of Blyton's stories in both the Famous Five and the Secret Seven series are the depiction of a group of children who are allowed to go about on their own on their bicycles, accompanied by their dog, and encounter all sorts of often dangerous adventures involving robbers, smugglers, gypsies, kidnappers, and other villains. The role of their parents in the stories is limited, and other adult characters are generally incompetent, stupid, or unscrupulous, allowing the children to assert their superior intelligence, initiative, and courage and outstrip the police in defeating the wicked. The self-assurance and solidarity of the group are signalled in the titles, and their relative freedom from adult intervention and control was enviable and empowering for the young reader of the time, as the present writer can testify. The novels underwent a process of acculturation in translation. Besides employing alternatives where names of places are mentioned, the children were given French names, with Julian, Dick, and Anne becoming François (thirteen), Mick (twelve), and Annie (eleven) Gauthier, the tomboy George (Georgina) becoming Claude (Claudine), and Timmy the dog was dignified with the magisterial name of Dagobert. The French titles often highlight the perilous nature of the situations in which the group find themselves, inserting the narrative in the tradition of the adventure mystery and the *roman policier*: *Le Club des cinq en péril* (*Five Get into Trouble*); *Enlèvement au club des cinq* (*Five Have Plenty of Fun*); *Le Club des cinq en embuscade* (*Five are Together Again*). Blyton has been much criticised for the insidious snobbery, sexism, and racism in her works, and it is a matter of debate as to whether child readers today, because of the deceptively contemporary feel of the novels, would be able to see these aspects and the paternalistic and gendered assumptions under-pinning the action and characterisation as simply outmoded features of their time. Blyton's fictional children belong to a middle-class privileged world and accept its values uncritically. Foreigners and outsiders are suspect and kept at a distance. The children's individual characteristics are largely traditionally gendered and reflect the respective roles in a family unit, the notable exception being the intriguing George / Claude, who is ill at ease with her female identity and wishes to be regarded as a boy. The potential for a sympathetic exploration of the effect of gender stereotyping on children is never exploited by the author, however, and the character does not evolve in the course of the series. Blyton excels as a creator of suspense, intrigue, and action, but her efforts to position the narrative at the level of the child reader often result in a uniformly bland and lexically impoverished discourse. Nevertheless, the involvement of the five children in extricating themselves from dangerous situations, solving mysteries, uncovering crimes, and impressing adults provides a new model of child-centred narrative for the postwar period.

The model of a series of stories based on the same set of characters and marked by predictability, familiarity, and an emphasis on action was taken up in France by Paul-Jacques Bonzon (1908–1978) in the 1960s and 1970s with his Les Six compagnons novels, published by

Hachette in the Bibliothèque verte. Like the Club des cinq novels, this lengthy catalogue of titles (thirty-eight by Bonzon himself and several more produced by other writers after his death) features a group of children who encounter exhilarating adventures wherever they go in tantalisingly improbable fashion and together solve all sorts of mysteries and crimes, earning the gratitude of the police and the government. The stories are more male-orientated than Blyton's books, for the six friends are all boys while one girl, Mady, and a dog, Kafi, are auxiliary, although by no means ineffective, members of the group. The first book in the series, *Les Compagnons de la Croix-Rousse* (1961), recounts the forming of the group when Tidou, who acts as narrator, comes to live in Lyon and is helped by some schoolfriends when his dog disappears. The titles thereafter, like those of the Club des cinq, indicate the variety of exotic places and remarkable situations in which they find themselves (*Les Six compagnons au gouffre Marzal*, 1963; *Les Six compagnons et l'avion clandestin*, 1967; *Les Six compagnons à Scotland Yard*, 1968; and *Les Six compagnons au village englouti*, 1976). Some of the adventures take place in Lyon and others during the school holidays, when camping trips and visits abroad are exploited to widen the scope of activities. No robber, hijacker, secret agent, or spy is safe once the group of children, fired by their love of adventure and desire to right wrongs, are on his trail: they prevent the murder of a new friend's father by his business partner in *Les Six compagnons et le château maudit* (1965); foil smugglers while on holiday near the border with Spain in *Les Six compagnons et la brigade volante* (1972), art thieves in *Les Six compagnons et la clef-minute* (1977), and saboteurs in *Les Six compagnons dans la ville rose* (1980); and uncover a spy ring in *Les Six compagnons et les skieurs de fond* (1979). *Les Six compagnons et le château maudit* is built upon the attempts of the children to solve a series of mysterious accidents in a large villa on the shores of Lake Geneva and contains, amongst many well-constructed and suspenseful scenes, an atmospheric pursuit of the villains on the lake in the mist. Despite the nature of the gang's opponents and the dangers they face, Bonzon's novels are, like Blyton's, remarkably free from the graphic violence and bloodshed that characterise much of today's children's literature. The Six compagnons series was translated into some sixteen languages and also appeared in the form of a *bande dessinée* that was published by Hachette in the 1980s.

Bonzon replicated this pattern in another series of the 1960s and 1970s featuring La Famille HLM (Habitation à loyer modéré) set in a high-rise housing estate (a *cité*) outside Paris. The four young adolescent protagonists—a brother and sister, their cousin, and the son of the concierge of their apartment block together with his dog Tic-Tac—uncover and solve all kinds of mysteries involving sinister strangers and disturbing events. With titles like *Les étranges locataires* (1966), *L'Homme à la valise jaune* (1967), *Le Marchand de coquillages* (1968), and *Rue des chats-sans-queue* (1968), these novels depict the environment of a new town cité in a time before such planned developments acquired the association with deprivation and crime that they have today.[10]

Three series by Georges Bayard (1918–) also enjoyed a wide readership. The Michel novels feature an idealised fifteen-year-old boy hero, his cousin Daniel, a young friend who works as a mechanic, and the pretty blonde girl Martine, a champion swimmer, who repeatedly find themselves embroiled in adventures and, as in the other series, bring their individual talents to the solving of mysteries in their home region near Amiens or in their holiday destinations. This series is enlivened by the presence of Michel's eleven-year-old twin siblings and features an impressive gallery of villains. Michel's dynamism and versatility are reflected in the books' titles: *Michel fait du cinéma* (1962), *Michel fait un rallye* (1975), and *Michel fait de la planche à voile* (1982). Bayard's Cécile series of the 1980s adapted the formula by featuring three girls whose activities always seem to involve them in adventures. Cécile and her friends Laure and Juju are sparky protagonists, each with their individual quirks (Cécile has a highly developed imagination, Laure likes eating, and Juju is devoted to astrology), and the appeal to female readers is enhanced by the involvement of Cécile's dynamic grandmother in their exploits. There is also a mild romance element in Juju's attraction to Cécile's brother. Cécile appears on television when she wins a visit to Florence in a competition run by Antenne 2 (and finds an occasion to solve a crime) in *Cécile et la panthère noire* (1982) and helps foil the enemy of a rock group in *Cécile et les rockers* (1984). For younger adolescents, the César series featured a twelve-year-old boy's family life with his father and two sisters, and his adventures with his cousin Victor in such less dramatic titles as *César fait du carting* (1964), *César fait du ski* (1978), and *César et la clef du mystère* (1979). A best-selling hero for older adolescent readers was Langelot, the eighteen-year-old super spy and member of SNIF (Service National d'Information Fonctionelle), an imaginary French secret service agency. Created by 'Lieutenant X' (Vladimir Volkoff) and surely influenced by Ian Fleming's James Bond novels, Langelot can be seen as the forerunner of Anthony Horowitz's Alex Rider. His exploits in forty novels involve foiling the dastardly plans of power-crazed villains, mad scientists, and an evil criminal organisation called Sphinx. Like the James Bond novels and films, the plots are far-fetched and violent and often involve a romantic though chaste attachment between the hero and a beautiful young girl.

Paul Berna (1913–1994): A Best-Selling Detective Mystery

Paul Berna's award-winning detective mystery *Le Cheval sans tête* (1955), seen as one of the few novels to match up to Kästner's and published the same year as Blyton's *Le Club des cinq*, differs from the latter's work in many respects.[11] The main characters, a gang of ten children of different ages and ethnic origins, live in the tenements of Louvigny, a working-class district of Paris that is close to the railway line and the shacks of ragpickers and bottle collectors. Their freedom of movement is limited to the streets, the large patch of waste ground where an old engine lies rusting, and the ramshackle and deserted industrial buildings near by. The children are not depicted as social victims, however; rather, Berna highlights the children's appropriation of their milieu and its transformation into a playground in 'ce petit univers assez laid qui était le leur, mais que leur joie de tous les jours transfigurait'.[12] Berna never condescends to the young reader and the characters' colloquial speech is colourfully realistic. The gang's main activity revolves around a large wooden horse on tricycle wheels, found by a rag-and-bone man on a bomb site and belonging to one of their number, Fernand Douin. The horse is lacking its head but has secured the children's devotion as a vehicle on which they take scrupulously organised turns to ride at great speed down the steep street, risking injury to both themselves and any unfortunate passersby, a dangerous game that occupies their days and is largely responsible for the cohesion of the group.

The children's troubles begin with the mutual antagonism between themselves and a market trader, one of a team of thieves, and they become involved with a train robbery of a hundred million francs when a suspect, pursued through the market by the local police inspector Sinet, drops the key to an abandoned factory where the money has been stashed inside the open neck of the horse. The narrative perspective is for the most part that of the children, although the reader is informed in a scene at the police station that the locality is implicated in the daring robbery. After finding the key, the children, ignorant of the real nature of the crime or the motives of the strangers who steal their precious horse, decide to explore the factory and revel in its redundant stock of carnival hats and toys. The juxtaposition of play and detection work preserves the sense of the youthfulness of the protagonists and underlines the difference between this novel and a roman policier. There follows a suspenseful and violent scene in which the children, aware that the robbers have an interest in the factory, lure them into a trap. As they lay siege to the children locked in the building, the dangerous men are cornered by the arrival of the neighbourhood dogs summoned by Marion, the enigmatic young girl who cares for the canine population of the area. The scene is endowed with an almost fantastic atmosphere, with the enumeration of the dogs (including their names and descriptions) filling several pages as they respond to Marion's whistle and converge on the factory. It is the light and noises emanating from the deserted building that alert the police, who arrive in time to save the crooks from being torn apart. The development of the relationship between the children and the policeman Sinet is interesting for it changes from antagonism to one of affection and respect. The children have, in effect, helped solve the mystery of the disappearing millions for the beleaguered and unsuccessful local police despite remaining unaware of what is at stake. In a conventional 'explanation' scene characteristic of the genre, Sinet joins the children in their den and fills in all the details of the robbery. Just as they are most interested in the fate of their horse, so, it transpires, the robbers were more embarrassed about confessing to the theft of the toy than to that of the hundred million francs. The plot comes full circle when the horse is found abandoned on a rubbish dump and returned to the delighted children. The head, too, has been discovered and affixed, but it is soon broken off again when the game recommences and the children decide that they prefer it headless.

The characters and interaction of the children are naturalistically depicted in this fast-moving novel, and the threat posed by the sinister villains is not undermined by the humour attached to the portrayal of their defeat. The solidarity of the group and the importance of friendship, symbolised by the role of the horse in their lives, is affirmed at the end when the leader, Gaby, confesses that at twelve he has exceeded the age limit originally established for membership of the gang: 'Nous grandirons ensemble, tout simplement … . ce n'est pas demain que nous nous arrêterons de rigoler.'[13] Translated as *A Hundred Million Francs* (the title thus foregrounding a different aspect of the story), Berna's novel was also a best-seller in the English-speaking world and was made into a film by Disney in 1963 as *The Horse without a Head*.

Contemporary Detective Fiction

The popularity of detective fiction is undiminished, and the influence of British authors in this field is still considerable. Publishers' catalogues feature, in their *littérature de jeunesse* lists, books by Blyton, Agatha Christie, Conan Doyle, and Anthony Horowitz's more recent Alex Rider novels, featuring the adventures of a juvenile recruit of the British Secret Service, beginning with *Stormbreaker* (2000). There are a large number of contemporary novels that feature child protagonists as victims or witnesses of a crime, as bystanders who become involved in a mystery, or as active investigators, although these are by no means mutually exclusive categories. The following and more feature in the Fédération Nationale d'Achats pour Cadres (National Purchasing Federation for Managers) catalogue *200 romans jeunesse. La bibliothèque idéale des 7/12 ans*. In Pierre Véry's *Les Disparus de Saint-Agil* (1987), a boys' secret society at a boarding-school becomes involved in sinister doings when the members begin to disappear. A school is also the setting for Marie-Aude Murail's *L'Assassin est au collège* (1992), a title that encapsulates the conjunction of two popular genres and evokes a shiver by its perversion of the familiar. In this story of poison-pen letters and mysterious, gory happenings, however, it is an adult detective acting as a teacher who leads the investigation rather than the pupils themselves. Bloodshed and murder are no longer thought inappropriate for a children's book—even those marketed at relatively young readers and featuring a young protagonist. A ten-year-old child is witness to events surrounding the murder of a neighbour in Béatrice Nicodème's *Y a-t-il un assassin dans l'immeuble?* (2000), and in Jean-Hugues Oppel's *Ippon* (2002), with a suggested age level of eleven and older, a boy who finds the babysitter with her throat cut has only his judo skills to protect him against the killer in the house. Jean-Loup Craipeau's *Gare au carnage, Amédée Petipotage!* (1994) depicts drug dealing and the attempted murder of a tramp, which leads a boy to risk his life to investigate the attack, yet surprisingly is marketed at seven- to eight-year-olds. A chance event or encounter often pitches the young protagonist into investigating a mystery: Jean Molla's chilling *Coupable idéal* (2002), in which the disappearance of a schoolboy and the murder of his father lead to a crisis of suspicion for a boy who has been in the wrong place at the wrong time, addresses pertinent questions of guilt and innocence. In Claude Klotz's *Drôle de samedi soir* (2001) a boy who is home alone watching television finds himself unexpectedly involved with a gang of burglars, while a young girl's discovery of a briefcase in a derelict car yard leads to intriguing complications in Henriette Bichonnier's *Kiki la Casse* (1986). Both boys and girls are portrayed as taking the initiative in investigating a crime: in Béatrice Nicodème's *Un détective de mauvais poil* (1998), a girl and her cat are drawn to investigate the fatal accident of which an outsider figure is accused, while in Thierry Crifo's *Le Vieil aveugle de Saint-Lazare* (2003) a group of boys take it upon themselves to investigate the murder of an old blind man in the Métro in opposition to the police.

One of the more interesting whodunnits is *Le Professeur a disparu* (1989) by Jean-Philippe Arrou-Vignod (1958–) illustrated with characteristically humorous images by Serge Bloch, and one of six novels featuring the same characters. Three children in their early teens, Mathilde Blondin, Rémi Pharamon, and Pierre-Paul Louis de Culbert (known to the others as P.-P. Cul-Vert), winners of a trip to Venice in a local schools competition, get mixed up with art forgers and a plot to steal a priceless painting for an unscrupulous private collector when their teacher-chaperone M. Coruscant disappears from their train during the night. The action, which takes place over three days, sees the youngsters alone in Venice at carnival time with very little money but determined to uncover the mystery of his disappearance by following clues found on a piece of paper in their compartment, tracking a suspicious man seen on the train, and spending a frightening night in an art gallery, during which P.-P. Cul-Vert is abducted by a gang of robbers. The narrative structure is more sophisticated than in many such novels, for the story is told through the eyes of the youngsters themselves in diary or letter form, thus revealing the very different and complex personalities of the three and their responses to their situation and to each other and offering different perspectives that allow the reader to feel implicated in their actions. P.-P. Cul-Vert is a highly intelligent boy whose self-conscious narrative shows him to be pompous, self-obsessed, and condescending to the others and pathetically comic in his fearfulness, desperation to impress, and lack of insight. It is he who gives away their presence in the gallery by screaming with fright and is thus kidnapped by the art thieves, but he is also capable of the brave and defiant gesture of threatening to throw the stolen painting overboard during a gondola chase that results in the capture of the villains. Rémi makes up in energy and bravery for what he lacks in academic prowess, but has little self-confidence and is burdened with a shameful secret alluded to at the start but only later revealed (his first words are 'Je ne m'aime pas').[14] Having cheated in the competition with prior knowledge of the essay topic supplied by his town-hall-official uncle, he is consumed with shame and guilt that he has deprived his close friend of his place amongst the winners. His narrative also reveals his sensitivities about his absent father, his grandiose surname, and his longing to be accepted by his brighter friends. The clever Mathilde, a newcomer at the school who misses her old friends, is often impatient with the boys but gradually drawn to Rémi and becomes the recipient of his secret during their night in the gallery (although he is unsure whether she has fallen asleep during his confession). She is loyal, sensitive, and persuasive and insists on equal involvement in their exploits.

It transpires that the disappearance of M. Coruscant is not connected with the strangers on the train, for he had simply alighted at a station to buy a drink during the night and then boarded the wrong train, and when he arrives back in Venice on the second morning with an Italian friend, the two adults join Mathilde and Rémi in the search for their abducted friend. The youngsters' powers of observation and deduction help to unmask the art thieves, capture the criminal art collector, and rescue P.-P., and they are able to resume their holiday, enjoying Venice for its treasures rather than as a place of isolation and fear. The novel conforms to the model of the initiation and maturation narrative, for the three are changed by their experience: in P.-P's final diary entry he admits that he has learnt humility and self-knowledge, respecting his companions, for his academic superiority did not help him to cope with the situation in which he found himself, and Mathilde writes of her appreciation of the boys and sense of integration. Rémi, who is given the last word, acknowledges his unfairness in mocking P.-P, and, because of his own role in the adventure, is able to accept Mathilde's sympathetic remark that he has earned his place in the group and feels more positive about himself. Jean-Philippe Arrou-Vignod has opined that books for young readers should offer a positive formative message: 'Les livres ne doivent pas être seulement un reflet fidèle: ils dépassent la simple réalité pour donner l'envie de vivre et de faire siens les enjeux de l'existence adulte.'[15] *Le Professeur a disparu* depicts such a process through the medium of an exciting and entertaining narrative that fully exploits the potential of its location and successfully maintains the suspense with rapid action that encourages the reader to engage in the recognition of clues and the solving of the mystery.[16]

Fantômette: A Superhero for Girls

Just as comic strips have their superheroes, the star of the modern adventure novel for young readers has to be Fantômette, the schoolgirl supersleuth and righter of wrongs invented by Georges Chaulet (1931–) in the 1960s. Her adventures run to forty-nine volumes published in Hachette's Bibliothèque rose series, and many are still in print today.[17] The novels feature three twelve-year-old schoolgirls, Boulotte, Ficelle, and Françoise, one of whom is suspected of being Fantômette, schoolgirl at Framboisy by day, dynamic masked crusader and detective by night.[18] In these stories, the hero model has been replaced by a young female character, although her age and gender do not affect in any respect her courageous battle against the forces of evil nor the efforts of her enemies to capture or kill her. It has been argued that female heroes are, in any case, simply portrayed as displaying traditionally 'male' characteristics, thus reinscribing the myth of heroism in a male sphere of action.[19] The comic-book figure of Wonder Woman, for example, who first appeared in America in 1941 and who rivals and even exceeds

her male counterparts in daring, comes to mind. Clearly, in the case of
Fantômette, the reader's willing suspension of disbelief has to go into
overdrive, but these texts are aimed at children and young adolescents
and depend upon an exhilarating wishful thinking on the part of the
reader coming into play. Fantômette's identity is kept secret from all,
including the reader, and, unlike Wonder Woman and Superman, her
transformation into her alter ego is never portrayed. There are clues to
who she is, however—not least the fact that, in many of the adventures,
Boulotte or Ficelle are in danger and are rescued by Fantômette. At the
end of the first story (*Les Exploits de Fantômette*, 1961), there is a strong
hint for the reader when it is remarked upon that a portrait of Françoise
bears a resemblance to the masked crusader. Like the superheroes of
American comics, Fantômette is instantly identifiable by her fantastic
costume, maintained from the first story onwards: she sports a yellow
tunic with a broad collar framing her face, a black cap with a pompon,
black tights and red shoes, a swirling black cape lined with red, and,
of course, a black mask. Dedicated to the fight against crime and the
pursuit of justice, she enjoys an international reputation and is often
summoned (sometimes by telephone) to save people in danger, to find
hidden treasure, or to investigate mysterious occurrences and dangerous situations that take her to many parts of the globe. The scope of
her exploits, like those of Jules Verne's adventurers, is infinite: readers
find her stranded in an African desert (in *Fantômette et le secret du
désert*, 1973), on an iceberg in the Atlantic (in *Fantômette brise la glace*,
1976), and travelling into space (in *Fantômette dans l'espace*, 1977). She
encounters not just petty thieves, swindlers, pirates, bandits, and art
thieves, but terrible adversaries with names like Sulfura (in *Fantômette
contre la main jaune*, 1971) and le seigneur Renard (in *Fantômette et le
secret du désert*, 1973) who all seem out to destroy her. She is repeatedly
pitted against her archenemies, Le Furet and his gang and Le Masque
d'Argent, a megalomaniac and inventor of deadly machines, from whose
clutches she escapes repeatedly and who, in turn, themselves evade capture. The adventures draw on disparate genres, involving her in investigating apparently supernatural occurrences and exposing the truth
(in *Fantômette contre le Géant*, 1963; *Fantômette et l'île de la sorcière*,
1964; and *Fantômette et la maison hantée*, 1971) as well as confronting
her with more modern and topical dangers like saving France from the
threat of attack by atomic rockets (in *Fantômette ouvre l'oeil*, 1984).

Unlike her comic-book counterparts, Fantômette has no supernatural powers, but depends upon her endless reserve of energy and staying
power, sharp intelligence, amazing powers of deduction, and physical
agility. With her school friends she shares typical teenage interests,

but she is in addition a mistress of disguise, an expert in martial arts, and has a photographic memory and other skills like lip-reading and the ability to speak several languages. Like the classic adult detectives, she uses her intellect to solve crimes, researching world affairs in her personal library and news archive, but her dangerous encounters also necessitate considerable physical skills like swimming, rowing, horse riding, parachuting, driving a car, and flying a plane. Like Wonder Woman she can call upon a range of gadgets to assist her (she carries on her person a dagger, a rope, a brooch containing a hidden blade, and a tear gas capsule in the pompom of her cap) and, of course, the conventions of the genre demand that she has immense powers of survival in order to extricate herself from potentially fatal situations and continue her crusade against evil. Her fearlessness and bravado in singlehandedly taking on so many dastardly villains are awesome and spiced with a nice humour (she leaves them tied up for the police to find, with her calling card pinned on their jackets). Although she generally works alone, she is occasionally aided by the police or by a young journalist who goes under the name of Oeil de lynx and is the only person to know her identity and telephone number. His journalistic talents and contacts and the pages of his newspaper *France-Flash* are frequently exploited by Fantômette in her sleuthing. With their endlessly inventive plots and handling of suspense and humour, the Fantômette novels are escapist fantasies but, despite the reservations of the type alluded to above, offer narratives of empowerment to young female readers accustomed to the homosocial world of the classic adventure story.

WRITING WAR AND THE HOLOCAUST

Although, for reasons discussed in earlier chapters, few fictional works for young readers were written during the Second World War about the war itself, from the 1970s onwards there appeared a number of retrospective novels that portray the French experience of this period. They aim not only to teach young readers about the past and events experienced perhaps by family members, but link with the theme of a search for identity common in the second half of the twentieth century and are often profoundly influenced by the author's own experience or memories of that period. Although the subject of the Holocaust in children's literature has recently attracted critical attention, little has been written about novels in French. For French writers, of course, France's position as an occupied country and the active cooperation of the Vichy regime in the deportation of Jews render an exploration of issues relating to the Holocaust more painful and poignant. The subject remains a highly sensitive one. France's difficulties in coming to terms with Vichy were revealed, for example, when in 1992 François Mitterand declared 16 July as a commemoration day for the Vél' d'Hiver roundup of Jews, but refused to accept blame for the persecutions on behalf of the French state, instead seeing Vichy as an aberration and an illegal régime.[20]

It has been argued that Holocaust literature can be distinguished by 'a combination of challenging subject matter, ethical responsibility and its position outside the normal boundaries of children's literature'.[21] Writing about the Holocaust for children poses a number of problems, not least that of infringing the rule of not frightening or upsetting the child reader and going against the long-established tendency to protect children from the harsher realities of life. The subject inevitably presents the young reader with a horror story beyond all fictional imaginings in which extreme and tangible evil really does happen and over which parents and other authority figures have no control because they, too, are victims. Moreover, no consolation is possible in a conventional happy ending to mitigate the horror. The problematics of telling the whole truth, 'speaking the unspeakable', are thus arguably even more acute in works addressing young readers.[22] Yet young people today are conditioned to see detailed images of real wars in newspapers and on television (sometimes even as events take place), so there is logically no reason why such events should not be explored in literature. Anne Frank's diary was published in France in 1950 and has been widely read by French schoolchildren. There is, however, also the danger inherent in writing novels about any historical period, and in particular one close to the time of writing, that fictionalising events will impede children's capacity to recognise and understand the factuality embedded in the texts;[23] as in any historical fiction, blurring the boundaries between truth and fiction can result in a skewed view of historical fact. This inevitably impacts upon the ethical stance of a work, the power of literature to affect children's attitudes and opinions. Most historical novels for young readers are centred on a child or adolescent and are similar, in effect, to narratives of initiation and maturation, depicting firsthand experience of a particular set of events. Ganna Ottevaere-van Praag objects that privileging the theme of initiation in historical novels and emphasising self-development and victory over difficulties runs the risk of inverting the significance of historical events such that even the most terrible can be read as a narrative akin to a *Robinsonnade*.[24] This potential problem is particularly relevant to the question of the legitimacy of providing an ending that will give some sort of psychological closure for the reader, even if this flies in the face of the implications of historical fact. There is, of course, also a fundamental ethical problem involved in creating a work about the Holocaust that children will want to read. Is an enjoyable book about the Holocaust, or indeed any humanitarian outrage, acceptable on any level?[25]

In the last few decades, however, a number of excellent novels have sought to keep the memory of this period alive and promote understanding and reflection via narratives of the experiences of children in wartime and narratives in which children learn about the events of the war. The theme of communication between generations and discussion about the war with grandparents is a common strategy employed to impart information and foregrounds the themes of memory and testimony. The use of a mediating adult figure, especially an adult who demonstrably has survived the horrors described, allows for both the communication of experience and a moderation of its effects on the listener. Such a relationship also encourages the fictional child, and through her the reader, to realise a personal link with the past and to think about the role of history in the life of an individual and the implications for the formation of identity. Different viewpoints on events may be offered that prompt the reader to adopt an evaluative position not only towards the past but in confronting issues of the present day. The initiatory role of an adult figure in such texts thus breathes new life into a device central to children's literature since the seventeenth century.[26] The relationship between child and grandparent figure is also portrayed as beneficial to both, encompassing aspects of the present experience of the survivors as well as the past—notably, anger, loneliness, isolation, and the need to talk and share memories.

In some novels this relationship comes about through a chance event or discovery that opens up new horizons or leads to life-changing experiences. Daniel Goldenberg's *Le Zaidé* (1988), for example, portrays the relationship between an eleven-year-old girl, believed orphaned when her parents disappear in a plane crash, and the old Jewish man who suddenly finds himself her guardian. Dragged out of his circumscribed existence and plunged into strange events that have him racing around Paris with the child, he also teaches her about the fate of Jews in the war and helps her to develop a sense of self. In the final weeks of his life he, too, is exposed to a different world and finds an unexpected solace in the relationship. The novels of Yaël Hassan are frequently based on the theme of the mutual benefit of cross-generational relationships. In *Un grand-père tombé du ciel* (1996), a novel that won the Prix du roman jeunesse (amongst other accolades), the young Leah gradually discovers the secret behind the bitterness and ill humour of a grandfather whom she did not know existed until he comes to live with them in Paris. A survivor of Auschwitz, he teaches her not only about the Holocaust and the loss of his first family but also about Jewish traditions, and through her youthful energy and enthusiasm he himself learns to live again. Such novels, while not shying from describing tragic events of the past, focus on the positive effects of sharing memories and creating new bonds.

Experiencing the Holocaust

Claude Gutman's novel *La Maison vide* (1990), which won the Prix Européen de la Littérature de Jeunesse, represents an interesting response to the questions raised above. *La Maison vide* is the fictional testimony of a fifteen-year-old Jewish boy, David Grunbaum, living in Paris at the time of the Occupation, but interweaves fact with fiction, drawing on the experiences of the author's own Jewish family and incorporating real events of 1942–44. Although Gutman was born in 1946, he has explained that he heard stories from his militant communist father about the fate of his grandparents during the pogroms against the Jews in Poland in the 1920s, the deportations, and his father's own escape from a roundup of Jews in Lyon in 1943, and was aware that their experiences, and David's, could easily have been his own.[27] He recounts that the trial of Klaus Barbie (the 'Butcher of Lyon') in 1987 and the revelation of the planned extermination in 1944 of the children at the *Maison d'Izieu*, an orphanage run by Sabine Zlatin in a village between Lyon and Chambéry where refugee Jewish children were hidden, prompted the writing of the novel as a testimony 'de quelque chose de vrai, d'un point de vue émotionnel'.[28] Gutman clearly felt that the power of fiction to communicate the truth and the emotion of an experience was potentially greater than that of a work of nonfiction. He addresses the problem of the withholding of full information from the young reader by presenting an adolescent's limited view of events, with the narrative capturing the incomprehension, rage, grief, and sense of helplessness of the young in the face of the unspeakable. Gutman claims that he wanted to write not about the deportation of the Jews from France but about the consequences for a child left behind, the absence and loss of family.[29] This sense of absence, already suggested by the title, in effect pervades the whole of the book. His protagonist David is moved to write about what has happened almost immediately after the catastrophe of the raid on the orphanage where he has lived happily for months and still lacks knowledge at this point of the full horror behind events and of the fate of his family. This strategy of providing an intimate viewpoint, with its consequent limitation of perspective, creates a powerful sense of the time depicted without any benefit of hindsight. David's anger and emotions are still raw and spill over onto the retrospective narrative, which is interspersed with anguished questions. The time sequence is dislocated with references to *avant* and *après*, and past events are juxtaposed with passages describing his present feelings as, in a location unknown to the reader for some time, he writes frantically to try to make sense of what has happened.

The novel begins with the first intrusion of disruption and violence into the life of David, then age thirteen and the son of a tailor, when he is exiled from his own bedroom without explanation to sleep in the apartment of a non-Jewish neighbour, Mme Bianchotti, whose only son has already been killed in the war. His resistance earns him an unexpected slap from his father, only now understood as a 'gifle d'amour'. The repeated 'Pourquoi? Pourquoi me chassaient-ils?' is symptomatic of his lack of comprehension, sense of injustice, and impotent fury throughout the events that destroy his childhood.[30] He learns about the evil of anti-Semitism from his father's story of the massacre of his first family in Poland and his flight to France, a journey as eventful as a novel of adventure, but only later realises the full significance of his father's injunction to 'Vivre, à tout prix'.[31] Despite his experiences, his father, delighted to be in a free country, is blinded to the realities around him by his gratitude to France, which gave him a new family and life, refusing to believe newspaper reports at the start of the war and obstinately dismissing the risks even when the Germans enter Paris. For the young David it seems that 'Les Ogres arrivent. Les vrais. Pas ceux qui faisient déjà vraiment trembler dans *Le Petit Poucet*. Les vrais Ogres à canons, gueules béantes.'[32] The rapid changes in the family's life caused by the measures taken by the Germans and the Vichy government between September 1940 and 1942 to exclude Jews from society are recorded as the neighbours start to leave, his parents' shop is closed, and they are forced to wear the yellow Star of David on their sleeves. David watches from the window as his parents are taken away as part of the infamous arrest of 12,884 Jews in Paris (known as 'le Grand Rafle') on 16 and 17 July 1942. (The victims were held temporarily in a sports stadium, the Vélodrome d'Hiver, before being deported, many of them to die in Auschwitz.) For the young reader who already has knowledge of these events and can fill in the gaps, the poignancy of David's ignorance of his parents' fate is intensified, while his desperation to know and understand encourages the reader who knows little or nothing of the truth to ask questions and learn.

David's confusion about what is happening and whom he should trust spill over into fury and rebellion against the people who, he later realises, have endangered themselves to save him—actions that he retrospectively strives to explain and atone for in his narrative. At the

Catholic boarding school where he is hidden under a false identity, the loss of selfhood is exacerbated by his enforced inclusion in the Catholic rituals and teaching, which he feels threaten his identity, and this leads to the defiant but dangerous gesture of proclaiming his Jewishness before the whole school—ironically, by displaying on his chest the yellow Star of David, the iconic image of the Holocaust. The orphanage and safe house for Jewish children to which he is subsequently sent, run by surrogate mother figure and communist sympathiser Mme Lonia, is based on the real-life Maison d'Izieu, from which forty-four Jewish children and seven adults were forcibly removed on 6 April 1944, the majority to be gassed at Auschwitz. David's description of how he began to overcome his sense of alienation and to find enjoyment in friendship and shared activities under the benign supervision of Lonia is juxtaposed with indications that he is now alone in the empty house, although the manner of the departure of the others is withheld until the last pages of the book.

Gutman explains that the invention of Claire, the young girl whom David meets through his piano lessons and with whom he experiences first love, is a matter of narrative expediency in order to remove David from the orphanage at a critical moment, for it is the morning after he has spent a chaste night with Claire in the woods, having lied to Lonia about his whereabouts, that he returns in time to see the children being loaded on to lorries by armed SS men.[33] When he is forced to stay hidden by M. Rigal, the gamekeeper, the torment underpinning David's urge to write becomes clear: at fifteen, he is consumed by the guilt of the survivor, a sense that he is a coward and a betrayer, distraught that he was not with his friends, singing the 'Marseillaise' as they were driven away. His narrative, which in the last stages becomes rushed and fragmented, is not just a testimony but an attempt to unburden himself and a cry for pardon for a crime that was not his: 'La maison est vide. Papa, maman, Lonia, je ne l'ai pas fait exprès. Je le jure.'[34] His final words are a paradoxical reproach to Lonia for abandoning him to survival, but there is also an invocation of the name of his girlfriend, Claire, a suggestion, perhaps, of hope for the future if love also survives. Lonia's advice to David to work hard at school ('Il faut être armé pour la vie et pas seulement avec des pistolets et des mitraillettes. La parole est une arme aussi terrible contre les exploiteurs') reflects Gutman's desire to transmit to young readers the memories that are not actually his but were transmitted to him by his father in order to help his own children and his readers understand something of what lies behind the injunction 'Il ne faut jamais oublier'.[35] The paratextual elements in the book's 'Supplément' (a chronology of the period, extracts from the ordonnances requiring

Jews to wear the yellow star, extracts of the laws issued by Vichy to exclude Jews from social roles and activities, and a list of instructions for the personnel responsible for arresting Jews in July 1942) help the older child reader to contextualise David's experiences and interpret the distinction between fact and fiction in the text. David's story is continued in the sequels *L'Hôtel du retour* (1991) and *Rue de Paris* (1993) as he discovers the truth about the deportation of Jews and the fate of his parents and struggles to live despite this knowledge—a journey that eventually takes him to a kibbutz in Palestine.

The events of 1942 as seen from the perspective of Jewish victims are also explored for readers age six and older by Yaël Hassan in *A Paris sous l'Occupation* (2000; in the Des enfants dans l'histoire series published by Casterman). This short text relates the experiences of the young Jewish girl Clara and her friend Julien, who helps and supports her when her mother is taken off to the Vél' d'Hiver. Julien's father is a policeman and reluctantly involved in the rounding up of Jews, and the family helps hide Clara before she is sent to a safe house for Jewish children. Through a close focus on the implications of events for the two children and their parents, Hassan evokes the climate of fear, grief, and despair pervading daily life, but manages to effect a relatively happy ending when Clara's mother returns from the labour camp. Each short chapter of the fictional narrative is juxtaposed with a brief outline of historical facts that set out the reality behind Clara's story, presenting events in a simple, straightforward language. In her account Hassan does not seek to gloss over the truth of the involvement of the French people in events: Clara and her mother are betrayed to the Nazis by a neighbour, and Hassan insists that the Vichy government adopted the anti-Semitic policies encapsulated in the Statut des Juifs 'de sa propre initiative'.[36]

Nicole Ciravégna's *La Rue qui descend vers la mer* (1971), a novel for adolescent readers, also blends fact and fiction in its portrayal of the burgeoning love between an adolescent boy Aldo and a Jewish girl against the background of events of the winter of 1943, which saw the destruction by the Germans of the Vieux Port in Marseilles and the displacement of the population. The dedication informs the reader that '45,000 Marseillais ont vécu cette tragédie en janvier 1943. Ce roman a été écrit en témoignage de l'injustice qui leur fut faite en ce temps-là.'[37] At the centre of the novel is the great Vieille Charité, built as a home for mendicants in the reign of Louis XIV and in 1943 housing poor and largely immigrant families in cramped, dark, and damp rented tenements.[38] Much of the action takes place within its walls and in the once splendid courtyard surrounded by arcaded galleries and with an imposing chapel in the centre, now a fetid open space filled with detritus where children play and inhabitants queue to get water from a pump. The oppressive atmosphere of lives spent in squalor, deprivation, and fear in the tenement dwellings is movingly evoked through images of the overpowering smells of cooking, sweat, and urine; the constant clamour of arguing voices; and physical details like the 'coffee' made of roasted acorns, chicory, and barley; the carefully hoarded food coupons; the dim lightbulbs and blackened walls; the snails gathered by an old woman in a cemetery to sell in the street; and the matted hair, snotty noses, and filthy rags of the children. The novel is also a celebration of the resilience and altruism amidst such hopelessness of people for whom the future is uncertain and the present lived in the shadow of enemy occupation. The reactions to their plight of a large and varied cast of characters (including Aldo's feisty old soldier grandfather; the hot tempered but loyal and generous Rita, owner of a restaurant in the rue Mayousse; and Pi, the young boy who works in the black market) reveal a gamut of tensions, conflicts, hopes, and anxieties born of a critical situation over which they have no control.

The protagonist Aldo is an exuberant fifteen-year-old who lives with his widowed mother in the Vieille Charité and is involved with a local schoolmaster in a Resistance network, relishing what he sees as his heroic role as a messenger. His love for Lila, a young waitress in a small restaurant, changes his life when, as scores of German troops surround the area unexpectedly one January night, he discovers that she is really Sarah, the daughter of a wealthy Jewish doctor. When the Germans round up the inhabitants of the old quarter prior to evacuating them to a camp while their homes in the Vieux Port are destroyed, Aldo takes it upon himself to protect her and, after they are returned to Marseilles, to organise lodgings at the Vieille Charité for his dispossessed friends from the street. His love of weaving stories to entertain his friends and his tendency to construct himself as a hero derived from films find fulfilment in the drama into which they are all thrust. Sarah, with her beauty and refined manners and sensibilities is an anomaly in this ghetto, and Aldo must not only protect her identity but prevent her from denouncing herself to protect those, in turn, who have sheltered her. Although Sarah remains a rather enigmatic figure for the reader because the action is largely focalised through Aldo, the sporadic shifting of the point of view in later chapters allows the reader to share her efforts to overcome her instinctive disgust at her environment and to join Aldo's world. Her loyalty and love are demonstrated by her refusal of the offer of an alternative existence with Rita in her new restaurant in an idyllic country setting in Aubagne, and her assumption of the role of teacher, in Aldo's absence, to the children of the Vieille Charité. The novel evokes the implications of a life of daily fear in the depiction of the risks Aldo and Sarah run in their work in a hospital and are symbolised by the sombre building in a sunlit street in which are crammed Jewish prisoners guarded by German soldiers with machine guns and a huge dog, an intimation of the unspoken fate of Sarah's parents and of what has been happening in the world beyond their city.

The cataleptic state into which Sarah sinks when, while others are celebrating the liberation of Marseilles she learns of the arrest of her parents, leads to the revelation that she and her brother had long known of the real situation in the extermination camps, but had vowed not to burden others with this knowledge. Ciravegna provides a happy (and arguably highly sentimental) ending, however, that exemplifies the problematic nature of providing a consoling form of closure in a novel on this subject. Having returned from achieving his dream of fighting for the *maquis*, Aldo takes Sarah to a friend's farm in the countryside to help with the grape harvest; there she is moved by helping care for their hosts' baby and by Aldo's interpretation of her parents' death as a triumph of dignity and humanity to begin to overcome her crippling grief and sense of guilt at surviving and to embrace her own desire to live. The novel ends on a kiss that marks the end of adolescence and a new life of hope. Whether this is read as a contrived and idealised ending, privileging the victory over adversity of two (fictional) individuals in a manner that deflects the reader's attention from the wider-scale human catastrophe or as an assertion of the resilience of human nature that instinctively seeks for happiness and prevails despite the most dehumanising events is a matter for the individual reader to decide.

These novels have in common the themes of solidarity and resistance against oppression and present the evils of anti-Semitism in simple but vivid terms. Although not shirking the responsibility of portraying the role of Vichy and the French in events, they also emphasise humanitarian actions and the work of those who risked their lives for their beliefs. As Mme Bianchotti tells David in *La Maison vide*, 'Il existe de braves gens, encore, en France.'[39] Not surprisingly, children's books tend not to represent arguments from the other side, nor feature fascists or collaborators as protagonists whose position the young reader is invited to understand. On the contrary, the Nazis are invariably portrayed as ogres or bogeymen, which underlines the monstrous nature of their actions and dehumanised through an emphasis on their uniforms, the sound of their boots, and of abrupt, shouted orders. Sometimes, like bogeymen, they are represented more by the fear their ubiquity generates rather than by their physical presence. Such strategies provide the young reader with a 'permission to hate', which is not deemed transgressive or racist in its turn, but which can be indulged in without forfeiting the approval of adults.[40]

The Algerian War and Children's Books

Young French readers may be less acquainted with the events of the Algerian War than with those of the Second World War, for, characterised as 'the war without a name', this conflict was, until the 1990s, all but submerged in silence.[41] Events in the late 1950s and early 1960s came to symbolise the painful process of decolonisation and the demise of the colonial myth, generating much bitterness and mutual resentments that had far-reaching implications that still impinge on the relationships between the indigenous population of France and the large ethnic group of North African origin. Philip Dine's examination of images of the Algerian War in French literature and cinema between 1954 and 1992, does not, however, include works written for young readers. Since the 1990s, several novels have appeared that portray aspects of the conflicts in Algeria and stand in stark opposition to the celebration of imperialist and colonialist values that permeated children's books from the last third of the nineteenth century. Un Eté algérien (1990) by Jean-Paul Nozière (1943–) tackles the sensitive issues involved in the story of two fifteen-year-old boys, Selim Bellilita, an Algerian Muslim, and Paul Barine, a French Christian, who have grown up as close friends on Paul's father's farm. The summer in question is that of 1958, when rebel activists of the Front de Libération Nationale (FLN) are attacking and burning farms and killing French colonials in the streets and Muslims are being executed in military reprisals. Events are narrated by Salim, thus giving the young reader of Metropolitan France the opportunity to see events from the other side, and the text begins with a brief account of 5 July 1962 when, as a soldier, he witnesses the celebrations of the declaration of independence of his country. The main part of the book is a retrospective account of the journey of this young boy from a law-abiding labouring family, loyal to their French masters, to becoming involved in the bloody struggle. 'A quel moment le destin a-t-il posé son doigt sur moi?' he asks in an italicised passage at a critical moment in the text.[42] The reader is immersed in Salim's viewpoint as he sees his boyhood friendship change and disintegrate. His awareness of being perceived as other, and indeed as a potential enemy, begins with the shock of being removed from the school where he has been educated alongside Paul by M. Barine in order to work on the farm with the other workers. This is a seminal moment in his psychological, and eventually political, development as he indicates in the opening section that precedes the retrospective narrative, 'Ma guerre, je l'avais gagnée et perdue durant l'été 1958.'[43]

In this text the young protagonist is an active participant, as well as victim, of events. It is because of his education and intelligence that Salim is recruited as a spy for the FLN, recording and passing on information about troop movements and information gleaned on the farm. The ability to read and write and the symbolic importance of words are seen as crucial issues in the struggle against oppression. Lakdar, the fellow worker who recruits Salim, finds it expedient to conceal his literacy from his masters and hence his access to knowledge and ideas that nourish insurgency. He quotes Albert Camus's *La Peste* ('Il faut être fou, aveugle ou lâche pour se résigner à la peste') to persuade Salim, already reeling from the injustice and humiliation of his exclusion from school, to join the resistance fighters.[44] The use of Arabic or French on the farm (the former is spoken in the fields but forbidden in the house), and in the confrontations with soldiers where Arabic is used to insult and demean, are symptomatic of the oppression of the colonial situation and the attitudes of the different characters. After independence is achieved, the rebaptising of the country as Al-Djezaïr is seen as symbolic of triumph over the colonial yoke. Salim's attitude towards his role as a spy is, however, ambivalent, swinging between shame and exultation at the exciting challenges presented by the clandestine writing down and passing on of his observations, and the reader is confronted with the complexity of the question of where betrayal lies.

The development of tensions between the two families on the farm is traced through the events of the hot summer. Although M. Barine seems a benign and paternalistic master, his actions are motivated ultimately by his concern for the land his family has farmed since 1848 and his resentment of any threat to what he blindly regards as his right to it. In Paul, the reader witnesses the perversion of childhood instincts by fear and insecurity, the internalisation of the prejudices of the white ruling class manifesting itself in his insults towards Arabs in front of his friend. Salim's growing anger at the habitual submissive attitude of his father, Tayeb, towards M. Barine and his witnessing of the sadistic behaviour of the French soldiers fuel his resentment, and it is his information that the farm will be left unguarded for a night that leads to the rebel attack followed by the arrival of the military, which leave both Paul's father and his own dead. This shocking culmination of events is presented through a third-person narrative, offering a factual account that distances Salim from a situation that has moved beyond his control. The account of the attack in an official dispatch that presents Tayeb, who is summarily shot, and Lakdar, who has been tortured

by the soldiers, as victims of a rebel massacre defending the farm alongside their master exemplifies the convenient manipulation of words in
the rewriting of events by those in charge. An epilogue, which gives a
rapid survey of the political events of 1962 that preceded the declaration of independence, is followed by a brief paragraph informing the
reader that, five years later, Paul has achieved his goal of becoming a
teacher at his old school and that Salim now occupies an important
place in a ministry. The tragedy of the situation is encapsulated in a
footnote to their friendship that explains that although both have frequently visited the site of the farm, they have never met again. As with
Gutman's novel, the Folio Junior edition contains a dossier of facts
to help orientate the young reader and provide background information concerning the war in Algeria. The focus in the novel, however, is
once again on the individual and intimate, mediating history through
the personal experience of a young person faced with a life-changing
choice in a situation not of his making. That the protagonist and his
family here are portrayed as victims of recent French oppression makes
for challenging reading for those of age eleven and upwards, at whom
the book is targeted.

Other writers, too, have chosen to present the Algerian war through
the eyes of an Algerian child protagonist: Jacques Delval's *Le Train
d'El-Kantara* (1998) features a thirteen-year-old boy who sells water to
the French soldiers who pass through his village by train and, when he
jumps onto a convoy, he is plunged into events that allow him to witness the war firsthand. *Quand ils avaient mon âge . . Alger 1958–1962*
(2002), by Gilles Bonotaux and Hélène Lasserre, a book designated for
those ages nine and older, aims to present the war through the eyes
of children whose ordinary childhood preoccupations and lives were
changed dramatically by the outbreak of war, thus eliciting identification and empathy.

TEENAGE FICTION

The youth culture that developed in the 1960s led to the development
of a genre aimed specifically at young people on the threshold of adult
life in an uncertain world where traditional values and authorities were
seen as inadequate and where they would have to learn to make their
own decisions. Beginning in America, the concept of 'teenage fiction'
aimed at a new, more sophisticated market of young readers for whom
the social and sexual freedoms of the second half of the century posed
new dilemmas soon took hold in France as in Britain. Teenage fiction
has been seen as overly introspective and narcissistic because of its

focus on the emotions and conflicts of adolescent years, as writers for this market sought to acknowledge the complexities of growing up in the modern age and to portray choices and their consequences without overt moralising.[45] Many novels for teenagers or young adults have taken the approach of portraying adolescent experience humorously, on the grounds that young readers simply want to read amusing stories about the daily experience of characters like themselves, but increasingly in the last quarter of the twentieth century and into the twenty-first, teenage fiction has sought to widen their readers' horizons and to encourage reflection on serious social and personal issues like sexual relationships, feminism, homosexuality, racism, divorce, bereavement, delinquency, drugs, unemployment, and child abuse.

Susie Morgenstern: 'C'est la vie'

Susie Morgenstern (1945–) is an American living in France whose some sixty books, aimed for the most part at young adolescents, have been widely translated and have won numerous literary prizes since the 1980s. On her website she tells us that 'j'aime espionner la vie de tous les jours', and her funny, optimistic books show her young protagonists confronting many of the crises experienced by the modern teenager at home and at school.[46] Her novels are firmly grounded in the quotidian. Amongst her favourite themes are the minutiae of the school day, the relationship between child and parents, teachers, or *au pairs*, and young teenage love, and the popularity of her books amongst young readers suggests that she succeeds in striking a chord in her portrayal of an adolescent viewpoint. The world of fast food, television, and homework with its anxiety about grades, self-image, and friendships as well as childhood feuds and frustrations is an instantly recognisable one for today's readers. Morgenstern informs us that she has drawn heavily on her own experience and that of her daughters who, in a few cases, have collaborated with her in the writing of the work. Like much contemporary fiction for young readers, her novels are essentially optimistic, and anxieties, pain, and distress, while not absent, are modified by the humour and the invariably cheerful and upbeat endings in which renewed joy is brought into the lives of the protagonists and problems are resolved.

The role of school in young lives in both an academic and a personal sense is explored in several of Morgenstern's books for the younger teenager. *La Liste des fournitures* (2002), advertised as for the seven- to eight-year-old age range, takes an original approach, portraying humorously the havoc caused in the weeks before the *rentrée* for four children trying to fulfil all the requirements on the book and stationery lists issued by four different teachers. In *Le fiancé de la maîtresse* (1997), for the same age range, Morgenstern depicts the growing awareness amongst a group of children that their teacher has a life outside school and, in a far more subtle way than in Hachette's Titeuf series, the beginnings of an interest in the subject of relations between the sexes. In *Même les princesses doivent aller à l'école* (1991), she blends fantasy with reality in the entertaining story of the tribulations of the daughter of an impoverished king when the family are forced to move from their castle to a new home in a cité HLM and she goes to school for the first time. Despite her enthusiasm, things do not turn out as she expects, as is often the case with Morgenstern's young protagonists, for, as the publicity blurb explains, 'l'école de la République implique pas mal de bouleversements pour une famille princière'.[47]

One of her most successful novels, *La Sixième*, published in 1984 and based on her daughter Mayah's experiences, recounts the problems of the first year at senior school for the eleven-year-old Margot Melo from the moment of the arrival of the official letter of notification. The novel captures her excitement and enthusiasm, but also the fear of the unknown and all the anxieties generated by the need to obtain the right documentation and equipment, anxieties exacerbated by her mother's disorganisation and her elder sister's unhelpful and (maliciously?) erroneous advice about what she must do to avoid humiliation (above all, not wear a skirt or carry a satchel). *La Sixième* takes what today might be seen as the potentially problematic step of encouraging reader identification with a conscientious and responsible student, one who not only strives to do her best but invests her energies in trying to improve the motivation and diligence of her classmates and the class's standing in the eyes of the teachers who see them as academically hopeless, undisciplined, and disruptive. Margot's disappointments and frustration when her plans fail are convincingly and unsentimentally depicted: her classmates welcome her offers to help them with their studies as an opportunity simply to copy her work, and, predictably, no one turns up to the class solidarity meeting she organises. Her good intentions often rebound on her personally, her enthusiasm dented by slipping grades and detentions. Because the narrative is focalised through the child, the teachers seem remote, harassed, and in some cases even hostile. Margot's parents impinge little on the crises she undergoes, her mother offering only anodyne reassuring remarks and her father remaining relatively uninvolved until the memorable moment when he stages a protest by taking Margot's place at a class detention. A class trip to Rome and a strike by the teachers allow friendships to flourish outside the school environment. The latter, a day when the pupils demonstrate their independence and, at last, solidarity, by pooling their resources and going on a group outing to the beach and the cinema, is a positive step in Margot's socialisation. The novel ends conventionally with the end of the school year but also on an unexpectedly poignant note when the young boy who has a crush on her purloins her satchel in a moment of jealous rage and empties her work files into the windy, wet playground. Margot's silent, helpless despair as she watches her year's work disintegrate is movingly evoked (even if the tenor of her thought 'Où va ma culture?' seems a shade improbable), but the novel ends on a ruefully optimistic note as Margot remarks of her satchel, 'Au moins, c'est léger maintenant.'[48] *La Sixième* reiterates many of the conventions of the school novel in the portrayal of the relationships amongst the pupils and between the pupils and teachers, but the narrative faithfully reproduces the everyday hassles of school life and the plot is simply the steep learning curve that Margot undergoes. What she learns about human nature and herself is ultimately more significant than the maths tests and historical dates over which she agonises and initially deems to be the key to success.

Relationships within the family are a central theme in much teenage fiction, and feature to different extents in most of Morgenstern's works. In *L'Amerloque* (1992), Morgenstern exploits her own early experience as an American in France and her interest in cultural exchange in a humorous story of the relationship between twelve-year-old Mathilde and a new au pair Elsie, an ebullient and energetic black American, recounted by Mathilde herself. Mathilde's home life is different from Margot's: she lives in a large Parisian apartment crammed with valuable objects along with her socialite mother and stepfather and has spent her life with a succession of au pairs. The arrival of Elsie, the thirteenth au pair, brings an unexpected breath of the merveilleux into her life. Although disposed toward resenting the new arrival, she is gradually won over by Elsie's irrepressible appetite for life, summed up in her favourite phrase, 'Let's go!' Elsie asserts her dominance over the household on her arrival by going straight to bed and sleeping for three days, and intrigues Mathilde with her vast trunk that contains apparently endless resources of food and other necessities from America. Prefigured before her arrival as a 'treizième fée porte-malheur', Elsie is in fact more like a good fairy, effecting positive transformations in everything and everybody around her, even breaking through the cool reserve of the neighbours to befriend and enchant them all.[49] Her brash effervescence often embarrasses the child and her behaviour is eccentric (she borrows precious objects from the apartment for her art student friends to copy although, to general consternation, she returns both originals and copies) but Mathilde soon succumbs to her human-ity and goodheartedness ('c'est qu'elle m'a appris que nous sommes des êtres humains parmi d'autres êtres humains, et que si nous ne nous touchons pas, la vie ne sert à rien').[50]

The bizarre turn that Mathilde's life takes when Elsie disappears after being attacked on the Métro and is replaced by two male Norwegian dressmakers, both called Tomas, develops into a hilariously anarchic scenario characteristic of Morgenstern's work. The chaos caused by the reappearance of Elsie and the installation of her family in the apart-ment when her brother is brought to Paris for a kidney transplant is sealed by the return of Mathilde's mother from holiday with the unwel-come news that she is pregnant. Mathilde is forced by Elsie to confront her childish self-absorption and egotism ('ce MOI géant qui envahit tout l'univers') and to overcome her disgust and rage at this news, and from Elsie's family she learns about a kind of family feeling and soli-darity that she has never known.[51] As in fairy tales, Mathilde is enabled to move forward into young adulthood by beginning to think of oth-ers, and a happy ending is arranged with the news that she is to spend the summer as an au pair herself with Elsie's family in New Jersey and that Elsie is to return to help care for the new baby. The number of issues that Morgenstern packs into this novel is considerable: not only the psychological development of a lonely and self-absorbed child in a wealthy but emotionally dysfunctional family and the cultural shock (for both parties) upon Elsie's arrival, but school rivalries, the spectre of being displaced as a spoilt, only child by a new sibling, and nascent sex-uality in the friendship between Mathilde and a boy in her class, whose chaste hand holding contrasts with the messages on the T-shirts ('Sex', and 'Be bad while you're young!') that Elsie gives her. Over all presides the presence of Elsie, a modern day *sorcière* who, with her 'magic' trunk and her ability to make everyone happy, must rate as one of the most attractive characters in contemporary children's books.

The majority of Morgenstern's works deal with the young teenager's struggle with self-image, the turmoil of unfamiliar emotions, thwarted expectations, and conflicting demands and choices about how to behave in unprecedented situations. *La Grosse patate* (1979), for example, con-fronts a still deeply relevant issue in depicting sympathetically the dilemma of a young girl torn between her longing to be slender and her love of eating. Morgenstern fully understands the importance of peer relationships in a child's self-image and development and both the anxi-eties that efforts to make friends can generate and the empowering ben-efits of friendship are frequent topics in her novels. In *Lettres d'amour de 0 à 10* (1996), a novel for the nine- to twelve-year-old age range that won

Morgenstern an array of literary prizes, the protagonist is the ten-year-old Ernest who, after the death of his mother and the disappearance of his father, lives a lonely and boring existence with his grandmother. The only significant point of contact between them is an indecipherable letter sent by his great-grandfather in the First World War. Ernest's life and, eventually, that of his grandmother too, are transformed by the friendship and affection of Victoire, a young girl in his class, and her thirteen brothers. The ending is heartwarmingly optimistic and reassuring, for Ernest also finds his father and the family is reunited. The love letters of the title turn out to be the unsent letters his father has written to him every day of his life while the great-grandfather's letter that symbolised the past lives of Ernest and his grandmother is revealed to be not a love letter but a cursory request for warm socks.

The nascent stirrings of physical attraction to another person and the difficulties of coping with the first throes of a romantic relationship were themes that began to invade books for adolescent readers from the 1970s on and feature in several of Morgenstern's works, notably *L'Amerloque* and the series of brief texts that trace the efforts of Mina to find a boyfriend (*Je t'aime*, 2003; *Je te hais*, 2004; and *Je t'aime encore [quand même]*, 2006). After selecting a new boy in her class as the object of her attentions, Mina's efforts meet with little success until, when he eventually gives her a Valentine Day's gift, she decides to return it and grow up a bit more before embarking on the search for love. *Premier amour, dernier amour* (1987) is an autobiographical novel recounting the love at first sight of an eighteen-year-old American exchange student for a young French mathematician, and it is perhaps symptomatic in the changes in perception of suitable topics for children's books that this text is now targeted at the nine- to twelve-year-old age group. Finally, Morgenstern brings together the two subjects of cultural exchange and love in *Les Deux moitiés de l'amitié* (1983), which focuses on a highly sensitive topic for the time of publication (and indeed since): the developing affection between a Jewish girl and an Arab boy. This text perhaps best displays Morgenstern's desire to push out the boundaries of conventional teenage fiction to embrace topics that alert her readers to the realities of the outside world.

Valérie Dayre: The Darker Side of Adolescence

Valérie Dayre (1958–) has written books for younger children, notably the Gaspard series, based on a day in the life of a small boy and a picture album *L'Ogresse en pleurs* (1996), which can in fact be read on different levels, but it is her novels for adolescent readers with which the present discussion is concerned.[52] With her highly original plots and innovative stylistic strategies, she immerses the reader in the psychology of her complex and sometimes disturbed adolescent protagonists as they confront anxieties, dilemmas, and traumas in an everyday life that is both ordinary and full of cruelty, injustice, violence, lies, and betrayal. The themes of rebellion against parents and teachers, the conflicting emotions of resentment and a desire to be loved, and the sense of alienation and uniqueness characteristic of much teenage fiction are deployed here in sophisticated narratives that allow the reader to share the protagonist's view of the world coloured by their conflicting and ambivalent emotions. Although like most fiction for adolescents Dayre's novels are structured on the pattern of initiation and maturation that involves an understanding and acceptance of oneself and other people, the experiences that her protagonists undergo are often extremely painful and their own actions disconcerting. She refuses in several of her novels to provide a clear-cut or conventionally happy ending, with issues left unresolved or the reader disorientated by surprise revelations that alter the perception of what has been read. In effect, the reader is frequently manipulated by Dayre's use of flashbacks and flashforwards and, in first-person narratives, an inbuilt uncertainty about the status of the events described. The tendency of her protagonist narrators to re-create reality in the image of their own desires or frustrations destabilises the narrative and forces the reader to participate proactively in untangling the 'truth'.

In *C'est la vie, Lili* (1991), for example, a young girl going on holiday with her parents sees a dog being abandoned by its owners at a motorway service station and imagines herself in his place, left behind by her parents. Events are recorded in diary form as though they were true, and only when the reader interrogates the sequence of dates at the head of each entry does uncertainty begin to creep in. Lili's description of her days spent at the service station, sleeping rough with the dog and thinking up ruses to obtain food, is a Robinsonnade transplanted into a very contemporary context. The service station is like a desert island and her adventure fulfils a fantasy of isolation, self-sufficiency, danger, and survival. The relationship of Lili with her parents is a complex one: an only child who lives in her mind, she is aware that her parents have their own fantasies of escape from mundane reality (apparent in their dream of visiting Venice, which keeps arguments at bay) and dimly senses that she might be an impediment to them. She is confused about her feelings, which vary between exasperation, antagonism, and affection, and the story of her abandonment can be seen as a sublimation of her anxieties, a manifestation of every child's fear—or, perhaps, every child's fantasy.

The reader's relief when it is revealed in the second half of the book that the adventure is a story written by Lili while sitting on the beach is short-lived, for Lili goes on to record that, after discovering and reading her notebook, her horrified parents do leave her at a service station and lie to the police to teach her a lesson. She is forced to confront the question of betrayal, not just that of her parents but her own, for she is aware that her parents would see her writing as a treacherous act ('Elle comprit qu'elle s'était trahie, qu'on l'avait trahie, qu'elle avait trahi').[53] Dayre complicates further the manipulation of the reader through false trails, however, for in fact Lili's parents never find out what she has written, nor take any such revenge, and on the last morning of the holiday, Lili is consumed with guilt and anger at herself for creating such a lie about them. She is now able to understand and accept her parents' own need for a dream of escape, realising that she will be an adult, and perhaps a parent, one day. This epiphanic moment allows her to discard her fears of rejection, and declare her love and need for them and her happiness at the continuation of her familiar everyday life ('Elle avait l'impression d'être redevenue un bébé. Ou au contraire une très grande personne. Elle s'en fichait').[54]

The theme of betrayal also underpins *Les Nouveaux malheurs de Sophie* (2001) in which the protagonist is seduced by the glamour of her wealthy aunt Cora and her family when she spends a holiday with them in their mountain villa near Nice and betrays her mother in her thoughts by feeling ashamed and irritated by her. Sophie is one of six children in a relatively poor family, and close to her mother, who detests Cora's patronising of her family from afar by sending parcels of second-hand clothes. Sophie is an affectionate and impressionable child of indeterminate age but still young enough to enjoy playing elaborate games with her cousins, and she is immediately attracted to Cora's beautiful home full of luxurious objects, her expensive clothes and scent, and her elegant manners—with whom Sophie compares unfavourably her own mother with her plain dresses, cigarettes, modesty, and strict principles. Enchanted by her environment and the freedom enjoyed by her spoilt cousins, Sophie is drawn into their elaborate fantasy game, which is, in fact, a mask for the psychological torture of another visitor, the young boy Félix, with the apparent complicity of Cora. Sophie is too happy at being included on her cousins' side in the game to feel much sympathy for Félix, until, on a return visit alone during the next holidays, she finds herself the outsider and terrorised victim. Her aunt now turns her back on her, her bedroom is a windowless cupboard, and her hair is hacked off by her cousin when Sophie seeks to emulate her style, a gesture perhaps towards the scene in which another Sophie hacks off her own hair in Segur's *Les Malheurs de Sophie* (1859).

Unlike the Comtesse de Ségur, however, Dayre incorporates a sharp critique of bourgeois provincialism and snobbery with a sinister edge. Sophie's epiphany comes when her mother comes to take her away and she sees Cora and her family in a different light. Her aunt, whose perverted character is symbolised by the stale stink of her perfume pervading the garage to which the secondhand clothes are relegated, has condoned and encouraged her children's sadistic exploitation of a vulnerable child in order to harden them up ('N'était-ce pas elle, d'ailleurs, qui fournissait leurs proies à ses petits ogres?').[55] For the disabused Sophie, who has lived the common childhood fantasy of displacing her real family with a more exotic one, the experience leads to a revaluation and happy acceptance of her own life, but for Félix, who has no supportive family to rescue him, there is no such happy ending. This novel, which explicitly rejects any romantic notions of childhood by showing the young to be capable of viciousness and treachery, is framed by a brief narrative in which the narrator's son asks her whether she has ever had an experience that caused her to grow up quickly and Sophie's story, her own, is the response to his question. Returning to the present at the end, she reveals that her son is called Félix after the unfortunate child who has remained, for her, 'une honte, une leçon et une reconnaissance' and that her story is intended to save him from the kind of pain she suffered.[56]

Comme le pas d'un fantôme (2002), the story of the lonely and sensitive boy Gabriel, who is sent by his constantly absent parents to stay in an isolated country house with a cold and unsociable middle-aged cousin he has never met, is very different in style and content. A retrospective first-person narrative, the opening words of the prelude ('Un jour, peut-être, je reviendrai à Quatre-Rives, lorsque le temps aura fait son oeuvre, quand il aura éteint les amours mortes comme les haines vives') evoke the favourite themes of romantic novels: solitude, doomed love ,and past pain that has left lingering traces in the present.[57] The setting and mood recall, for example, the novels of George Sand with an isolated, gloomy house surrounded by trees and undergrowth and an abandoned village attached to a long extinct factory in the valley that Gabriel is discouraged from visiting, the mystery of the footsteps of a shadowy figure haunting the grounds at night, and an old love letter he discovers hidden in a drawer. But the ghost hovering over this novel is that of Alain-Fournier's *Le Grand Meaulnes*, for Gabriel becomes obsessed with the clandestine love affair he constructs in his mind from further letters discovered between a local girl, Marianne, and Romain, whom he imagines to be his host's absent son. Like Alain-Fournier's François Seurel, Gabriel has a heightened sensibility and susceptibility to romance, and, half in love with the elusive Marianne himself, identifies himself with their secret relationship. Convinced by the letters and red ribbons tied to bushes that she is expecting a rendezvous on an imminent date and believing that his cousin's expected guest is Romain, he contrives to take her the news of her lover's impending arrival by keeping the appointment by a bridge in the village himself. The discovery that Marianne is an old madwoman devastates him only a little less than the discovery on the arrival of his cousin not with his son, as Gabriel had expected, but his old father, that the Romain of his imaginings is his cousin himself, whose love affair with the village girl ended abruptly thirty-three years earlier when he was forcibly sent away from home. Gabriel's disillusionment and anguish are exacerbated at the end of the novel by the destruction of the village in a fire set by Marianne, a scene also watched by his cousin, whose icy eyes are filled by the colour 'du renoncement et de l'abdication de toute une vie' and the old man whose eyes 'contemplaient la vallée avec la fièvre que procure une ultime victoire'.[58] There is no comforting happy ending here: the recognition of the indifference and treachery of which adults are capable and the complexity of human relationships provide a brutal awakening for Gabriel, as he forewarns the reader at the beginning of the narrative ('Les flammes ont dévoré mes illusions d'adolescent').[59]

The narrative approach employed in *Je veux voir Marcos* (1998) demonstrates Dayre's versatility and innovativeness. The entire text takes the form of a broadcast of a weekly reality TV show, titled *Où es-tu*, which tracks down missing people. The jocular but self-promoting and patronising tone of the presenter JIB alerts the reader to the artificiality and cynicism of a project that treats people's misery as spectacle. Cases are clearly chosen for their dramatic value, and his oblique criticisms of the dress, mannerisms, and attitude of the mother of the missing boy, and his condescending treatment of the witnesses, sit uncomfortably with his protestations of sympathy, revealing his greater concern with what makes good television. The personality of the absent protagonist, Pablo Santos, a troubled teenager who has evaded the caretakers who were taking him on a trip round France as part of a programme of reeducation for delinquents, is reconstructed through the viewpoints offered by those who knew him (or at least, those who agree to be filmed) and the circumstances of his disappearance are accumulated in the manner of a treasure hunt. The reports and interviews of the roving presenter who follows the trail (in this case to South America, where it transpires that Pablo has gone to meet Marcos, the leader of the rebel army of *zapatistes* living in the forest in Mexico) are presented as live, but her findings—and hence, eventually, Pablo's whereabouts—are obviously known in advance of the weekly broadcast revealing the news to viewers. This fact, and the delays caused by the interventions of historians and sociologists who are called in to explain things to the viewers, are the source of distress and resentment to the boy's mother who is kept waiting to know of her son's fate. The outcome of the quest, that Pablo has either been taken away to prison or is already dead brings the show to an abrupt end, the camera focussing on the devastated face of Mme Santos. An epilogue, narrated in the third person, throws a deeply cynical light on the whole scenario, however: after the broadcast, the party celebrating the two hundredth episode of the show goes ahead and JIB is delighted with the result: 'Cette fin de transmission était terriblement émouvante, télégénique'. The validity (and perhaps even the veracity) of the whole enterprise is then brought into question by his reflection on Mme Santos's 'performance':

> Mme Santos a gagné en présence d'une semaine sur l'autre. Elle a acquis, presque … . Il se sent un peu audacieux d'avoir laissé ce mot lui venir à l'esprit: elle a acquis du métier. Elle a très bien pleuré. C'était très vrai.

The text finishes on a bitter comment on real life (after the television has been switched off) that is intended to provoke reflection on the difference between reality and its presentation in the media: 'En France, c'est la nuit, et presque tout va bien. N'est-ce pas? Au Méxique, c'est une autre nuit.'[60]

Dayre contravenes many of the traditional taboos of children's literature in terms of content and narrative approach. The awareness that situations and relationships in life cannot be constrained within the convenient conventions invented in fiction nor always produce satisfying resolutions can be clearly seen in *Sale gamine* (1999). The relationship between a young girl, Ninon, and a reclusive elderly woman, Marguerite, develops through a network of lies and deceit after Ninon has appeared at Marguerite's door one night in distress after her father's car has been involved in an accident. The focalisation switches repeatedly from Marguerite to Ninon, and the register of speech employed both here and in the dialogue is highly informal and colloquial. The truth of Ninon's father's death (he is a businessman murdered because of the shady deals that have kept his family in luxury) exemplifies once more Dayre's interest in the theme of the dark secrets underlying family life. The surprise revelation in this text comes when Marguerite's past history of terrorist activities against her employers emerges, throwing light on her self-imposed isolation and reluctance to be involved with the police. Dayre invokes an ironic awareness of the tradition of a moral outcome and a happy ending to a story when, after Ninon has turned up again and exonerated Marguerite of any involvement in the crime, the woman reflects upon the possible outcomes of her undesired adventure: she imagines Ninon and her mother living a much reduced but still comfortable lifestyle (the moral), Ninon paying her a joyful visit (the emotion of a happy ending), and a letter from the child suggesting that their friendship will continue (a note of hope). But these are all in Marguerite's imaginings and, despite the mutual influence they have undergone, there is no guarantee that the changes wrought in the lives of the troubled child and the troubled elderly woman by their brief relationship will bear further fruit.

A CHILD'S VIEWPOINT: SEEING THE FUNNY SIDE

As has already been seen, two of the most significant developments in the twentieth century in writing for the young were the eschewing of an adult narrative viewpoint in favour of capturing the child's view of the world and even (with varying degrees of success) the child's voice, and the increasing and changing role of humour.[61] The latter, sometimes sophisticated, ironic, or playful, has also occasionally been of a tasteless, crude, and scatalogical kind. Two series that encapsulate both these approaches in radically different ways are René Goscinny and Jean-Jacques Sempé's Le Petit Nicolas books and the Titeuf cartoon strips and their adaptations. Both seek to capture the everyday experiences of a small child (both Nicolas and Titeuf are under ten) and both have a history of a dual readership.

The Petit Nicolas stories, with text by Goscinny and images by Sempé, were initially serialised in the paper *Sud-Ouest Dimanche* in 1959, then in *Pilote,* and appeared in book form in 1961. Since then, the five volumes have sold more than eight million copies in more than thirty different languages. Although often seen as an innovative landmark approach in children's books, it is debatable whether the appeal of the stories is not greater for adults than for the young themselves. The narrative is given over entirely to the child as Le Petit Nicolas himself narrates trivial excitements and disasters of his daily life at home and at school such as are familiar to any young or adult reader: the school photograph, a game of football, a new bicycle, being ill, fighting with friends, having to write thank you letters, and so on. Each chapter recounts a discrete incident, so that the effect is similar to that of the treadmill plots of early books for the young, as, for example, the comtesse de Ségur's *Les Malheurs de Sophie*. Unlike the moral and didactic works, however, all the childhood experiences depicted here are rendered humorous. Despite his disappointments and accidents, Nicolas suffers no real lasting pain or anguish, and the stories are not concerned with the impact of personal and environmental factors on the child's psychological development. Rather, they are a celebration of childhood, and, to an extent, a celebration of transgression, for Nicolas and his schoolfriends have scant regard for rules and the conventions of good behaviour, and are constantly arguing, fighting, getting into trouble, and causing chaos in the classroom.

The popularity of the books with adults clearly rests on an element of nostalgia that makes the reader complicit with the narrative's amusing depiction of childhood preoccupations and responses. The use of a child's voice not only evokes the personality of Nicolas, but encourages reader identification, a strategy reinforced by the frequent use of *nous* and *on* ('On a décidé d'être drôlement sages', 'On a eu l'inspecteur') and by the occasional direct address to the reader ('C'est chouette de savoir s'amuser tout seul, comme ça').[62] The humour mainly resides in the narrative itself, which both captures the child's self-orientated and naïve view of events and creates a colloquial, childish mode of expression that is both believable and manipulated. The written text reflects the oral in its employment of the vocabulary and the recognisable patterns of children's speech but exaggerates these for comic effect. The most immediately striking example of this is the use of repetition: references to Nicolas's friends are accompanied by an identifying tag; thus we find Alceste, his best friend, 'qui est très gros et qui mange tout le temps'; Agnan, 'qui est le premier de la classe et le chouchou de la maîtresse'; and Eudes, 'qui est très fort et il aime bien donner des coups de poing sur le nez des copains'. The narrative and the characterisation are thus both realistic and caricatural, a dual effect matched by Sempé's simple, witty line drawings that illustrate the narrative.

Although intensely focalised through Nicolas, the narrative offers different levels of inference through throwaway remarks or blatant omissions, however, encouraging the reader to fill in the gaps between what is being narrated and Nicolas's interpretation, and glean an interpretation of events and situations unrealised or misinterpreted by Nicolas, which increases the humorous effect. In such incidents, the humour is clearly directed at Nicolas and his naïveté by the adult author, which, arguably, suggests that the text is targeting an adult reader rather than a child whose inexperience might align him more closely with Nicolas's point of view. However, in presenting the world through the eyes of an innocent, the text reveals an ironic view of human relationships and an implicit criticism of social pretensions or hypocrisy. Many incidents involve Nicolas's puzzled or disgruntled view of adult behaviour, like the rivalry between his father and their neighbour, his father's syco-phantic attitude towards his boss, and the tensions between his parents over money that often result in Nicolas being sent to his room while they argue. The actions and responses of the child characters are, more-over, privileged over that of adult authority, which is often represented as ridiculous and is joyously, even when unconsciously, undermined or thwarted. In Le Petit Nicolas the school inspector who patronises the schoolmistress with his demonstration of the effects of simple child psychology and the photographer who boasts that he knows how to talk to children are both overwhelmed by the children's anarchic obtuseness and inability to adapt their instinctive reactions. Although the reader (and certainly the adult reader) cannot help but sympathise with the attempts of the long-suffering teacher to control the boisterousness of her pupils, the episode in which the whole class is locked away during the visit of the minister because they are deemed to be irredeemably dissipated can be seen as a satirical comment on an overrigid and fail-ing school system.

Much of the humour of the anecdotes derives from the deconstruc-tion of the familiar and the upsetting of the reader's expectations, and indeed, those of the characters, demonstrating the underlying sophis-tication of the narrative. Thus a general brawl that breaks out over the organisation of a football match is deemed to be a great day's fun, even though the episode ends with the realisation that they have forgotten to bring a ball. In the same volume, the shopping trip to the market when Nicolas's father decides to give a lesson in domestic economy to his wife ends in disaster, much to Nicolas's delight. Situations rarely work out as Nicolas expects: he is often punished for the results of good inten-tions and not punished when he expects to be, as when his father is too preoccupied with the cost of a joint of lamb to notice the comments on his school report. On this occasion, the outcome involves a double sur-prise, for Nicolas, sent to bed while his parents argue, is upset because 'si mon papa et ma maman m'aimaient, ils s'occuperaient un peu de moi!'[63] His anticipation of a boring afternoon spent with a visiting little girl turns to surprise when she turns out to hate books and flowers and breaks the garage window with a football ('elle est chouette, Louisette, et quand on sera grands, on se mariera. Elle a un shoot terrible!').[64]

The humour of the Le Petit Nicolas series is diverse enough to appeal to readers of all ages, and, despite its anarchic elements, is unproblem-atic in its content. The Titeuf phenomenon, which has swept through the world of comic strips in more recent years and also appears in adapted form in the Bibliothèque rose, is an entirely different approach to the representation of childhood. The adventures of the eight-year-old practical joker Titeuf, a cartoon figure of grotesque appearance, with a yellow ostrich plume of hair on his otherwise bald head, was created by Philippe Chappuis (Zep) and first appeared in 1993 in *Dieu, le sexe et les bretelles*, a comic-strip album aimed at adults. The character quickly found a ready audience amongst the young, however, and his exploits are now hugely popular playground reading. Apart from a series of albums, he is the star of the popular comic *Tchô!* named after one of his favourite expressions, along with such bizarre characters as Captain Biceps (the ultimate superhero), Samson and Néon (a boy and an alien), Tony and Alberto (a boy and his dog), and Malika Secouss, a tough and enterprising young girl. The strips have also been adapted for the Bibliothèque rose by Shirley Anguerrand (pseudonym of Hélène Bruller) as illustrated tales that incorporate cartoon frames with speech balloons and are recommended for those nine years old and over. According to the website celebrating 150 years of the series, these novelised versions came to the financial rescue of the Bibliothèque rose at a critical point in the 1990s, selling more than five million copies in six years.[65]

The content of the Titeuf strips and their adapted versions is scatalogical in the extreme: the gags nearly always involve bodily functions, and Titeuf's pranks include putting dog turds on people's doormats wrapped in newspaper which he then sets alight so that when they try to stamp out the flames, they are covered in excrement. They also break what has been until very recently one of the major taboos in children's literature in not just talking openly about sex, but using sexual activity overtly as a subject for humour. Titeuf is preoccupied with girls and perpetually curious about sex. In the one-page cartoon strip stories of the albums, his questions to his horrified parents and teachers and his wildly ill-informed discussions with his friends about condoms, pregnancy, pornography, and AIDS may shock adult readers but, after all, do reflect the curiosity and embarrassed hilarity that such subjects trigger in young children. It is, however, difficult to see such albums as *L'Amour, c'est pô propre* (1993), with its intense focus on sexual activity, as a book for child readers. In one strip, Titeuf walks in on his parents having sex on the floor and the humour derives from their frantic attempts to make him believe they are doing gymnastics. In the last frame we see him self-importantly explaining to his friend that he now knows what characters in films are doing when they are naked together. His fascination with the subject recurs in episodes where he watches dogs having sex, startles a pregnant woman with his comments, believes that possessing a condom will save him from AIDS, and speculates with his friends about the number of sexual acts needed to produce four children. His curiosity and anxieties may help, arguably, to 'dédramatiser le sexe' by allowing the better informed reader to laugh at his naïveté.[66] In this respect, the Titeuf strips could be seen to reflect and challenge what Michel Foucault has described in his *Histoire de la sexualité* (1976) as the long-established repression of talk about sex, a product of the nineteenth century and ostensibly intended to protect children, but which, by means of different discourses that focus on secrecy, forbidding, and denial, has paradoxically foregrounded the subject as dangerous and thus created a climate of greater fascination.[67]

The sexual content of the albums has been removed and the content generally toned down for the Bibliothèque rose versions (although the 'F-word' appears in one of the accompanying cartoons in *Les Filles, c'est nul*). The focus is more on Titeuf's misadventures and misfiring pranks, although the obsession with excrement and vomit remains. In *Les Filles. C'est nul*, for example, we see him both bullied and bullying on the way to school through rough urban streets, causing mayhem at guitar lessons, playing at spacemen and football with his group of colourful friends (one of whom ends up with a goldfish bowl of vomit on his head), and being taken to visit a psychiatrist. His fancy for a school friend Nadia and his attempts to kiss her replace the sexually explicit jokes of the albums. As in the Le Petit Nicolas stories, the behaviour of adults is mocked, whether the violent quarrels of fathers at football matches, the repressiveness of teachers, or the mind-blowing slowness with which his grandparents play Scrabble, and they are frequently seen as aliens. Titeuf, like Nicolas, recounts his own adventures in the novelised versions, and his highly colloquial language is highlighted in the titles of the volumes (*C'est pô une vie ...* , *C'est pô croyab'*, *Même pô mal ...*). In the albums, the children's speech in the comic strips is even more colourful and expressively crude, which undoubtedly reflects contemporary standards of playground interaction if it does little to raise children's expectations of themselves and others.

Like Le Petit Nicolas, Titeuf is enjoyed by a dual audience. His adventures have been translated into some fifteen languages (although not, to date, into English) and are the subject of extensive franchising in France, his face appearing on a huge range of products. Zep has been quoted as describing Titeuf as 'punk, in a gentle easy way', and although he may not be every parent's idea of desirable reading material, he is clearly a big hit with the young.[68] The success of Titeuf in the Bibliothèque rose illustrates the way in which agendas in the production of children's literature have changed in the latter half of the twentieth century. Titeuf is hardly a positive role model, yet the reader is encouraged to laugh at the failure of his backfiring plans. Of course, his curiosity and obsessions could be said to help child readers to understand their own anxieties, as he articulates thoughts and questions that they might not dare to voice and indulges in activities that they might not dare to try, as well as entertaining them with words and images that only a decade or so ago would have been anathema in children's literature.

CONCLUSION

In one *Titeuf* cartoon strip, Titeuf's father is shown reading *Le Petit Prince* to Titeuf at bedtime. The boy is patently bored until they come to the passage where the fox explains to the little prince that *apprivoiser* means *créer des liens*. Titeuf springs into life: 'Et il l'attache à l'arbre avec une chaîne en acier! Et après!? Le renard, il le décapite?! Ou c'est le petit prince qui le napalmise?!' His demoralised father is seen in the last frame buying 'Destroy-Mag', 'Megadrive Junior', and 'Captain Superkill' instead.[1] This episode highlights a central problem in writing or buying books for children and, indeed, in trying to assess from the standpoint of an adult the effect of texts on young readers and therefore the success or otherwise of a writer's attempts to communicate a message. The *Titeuf* strips themselves are in fact an excellent example of the disparity that may exist between the reading chosen and approved by adults and the preferences of children themselves, a factor not addressed or perhaps not even envisaged by early writers of books for the young. As has been seen, a large part of the market of children's reading material has now shifted from one controlled by adults with a more-or-less clear pedagogical agenda to one dominated by the desire to amuse young readers, or by a child-driven demand. Many magazines include comments and requests from readers about content that clearly influence publishers' decisions. In many areas, as in the case of the Bibliothèque rose, French children's books are now inextricably linked with other media, and profoundly influenced by imports from the English-speaking world.

The aim of creating an ideal child reader in narratives that would assume the sharing of a common viewpoint or persuade the reader to take on board the values promoted in the text has been replaced in many cases by a reflection of what are perceived to be children's own interests, preoccupations, or desires. In fictional works like *The Winx Club* or the cartoon strips in *Tchô!* the amusement imperative is uppermost, and realistic role models have been superceded by a humorous or fantastic alter ego or a commercialised model of modern childhood. The concept of influencing child readers, which has been fundamental to children's literature since its early beginnings, has become in such instances a problematic one.

Yet, there is also a huge amount of original, stimulating literature of a very high quality being produced in France today. As well as writers like Daniel Pennac and Michel Tournier who have produced books for the young, there are large numbers of authors specialising in children's books that it has not been possible to include in this study: Marie Desplechin (novels about dilemmas in everyday life), Gudule (Anne Duguël) (challenging novels touching on issues like racism and poverty, and fantasy), Michel Honaker (detective novels and fantasy), Thierry Lenain (outspoken novels on contemporary topics like drugs, racism, and child abuse), and Brigitte Smadja (novels about adolescence and love), amongst many others. In this respect, the second half of the twentieth century and the start of the twenty-first can be seen as another 'golden age' in children's books, even exceeding that of the second half of the nineteenth century. In fiction, the foregrounding of child or adolescent protagonists and attempts to capture a young narrative voice have resulted in a child-centred literature that explores the physical, psychological, and social experiences of growing up in a complex world and offer the reader reassurance, positive images of selfhood, and a wider perspective. Young protagonists are given autonomy and power to cope with difficulties and improve their own lives and the lives of others.

Fiction for young readers now also opens up the reading child's experience to wider (social, political, and ecological) topics, exploring and debating issues and viewpoints about the world in which they live, rather than just mediating facts. In an interview, Marie-Aude Murail, author of *L'Assassin est au collège*, *Baby-sitter Blues*, and *Oh Boy!* defends exposing children to topics previously deemed to be taboo on the grounds that children are now far more aware of what she calls 'les dures réalités' and are likely to have questions they would like to ask, although she deplores fictional works in which the 'message' is too visible because overt didacticism intrudes upon the pleasure that a book should provide. She articulates the choice facing a writer between keeping young readers in a cocoon or looking at the world with them 'tel qu'il est, mais en les accompagnant dans cette découverte. Ce qui s'appelle éduquer, et les livres de jeunesse sont alors un fameux relais.'[2] Although virtually all taboos in terms of subject matter have been lifted, responsibility and sensitivity are still exercised, particularly in fictional works and picture books for the very young, and narrative strategies are employed that enlighten, reassure, and empower the reader. In Lenain's *La Fille du canal* (1992), for example, a short novel targeted by the publishers at eleven-year-olds and over and a winner of several literary prizes, the theme of the sexual abuse of a young girl by her male drawing teacher is presented through a juxtaposition of a third-person narrative of Sarah's emotional turmoil and the first-person narrative of her class teacher, who was herself abused when young. The image of the frozen canal symbolises the child's blocked emotions as a consequence of the abuse by a man who has stolen her childhood. The female teacher, recognising something of her past self in Sarah's odd behaviour but fearing that she is in danger of imposing her own story on the child, realises what is happening and rescues her, and both she and Sarah are able to begin to confront the trauma they have experienced and find closure. The novel deconstructs the child's feelings of isolation and imparts to the reader a comforting message that pain should not be interiorised in solitude and that help is always at hand.

The history of literature for young readers since the mid-nineteenth century has continued to be one of appropriation of traditional stories and of innovation. Children's books continue to rewrite existing narratives and exploit the potential of intertextual practices. We have seen how the initiation and maturation model of fairy tales has been reworked in different ways in the novel of domestic realism, the novel of adventure, and the novel of daily life in the new millennium. The hero story, one of the oldest forms of narrative, has found fertile ground in recent years in the fantasy novel, the structure and content of which have much in common with chivalric romance. The conventions of fairy tales have also been exploited, because of their very familiarity, to provide humour and subvert both social and literary values. Other narrative models have also been manipulated in this way. The *Robinsonnade*, for example, has survived from the eighteenth century to the present day in different guises. Michel Tournier's *Vendredi, ou la vie sauvage* (1971), however, is a radical reworking of both Daniel Defoe's *Robinson Crusoe* and the traditional Robinsonnade. The novel, which is itself a rewriting especially for young readers of Tournier's earlier work *Vendredi ou les limbes de la Pacifique* (1967), conforms to the model of an initiation narrative, but with an innovative reversal of conventions. The initiation his Robinson undergoes into his exotic surroundings and cultural otherness through his relationship with Vendredi leads to a personal transformation in which he rejects the oppressive civilised organisation he has tried to install on the island in favour of a free, joyful, and self-determined existence.[3] This novel thus not only subverts the codes of civilised society and confounds the informed reader's expectations but interrogates the premises of the Robinsonnade model itself.

Although the formal experimentations of the postwar *Nouveau roman* writers did not noticeably affect the aesthetics of children's books, experimentation in style and structure has not been absent. The most extreme example of this is perhaps the series of Les Livres dont vous êtes le héros, fantasy novels in which the reader is engaged dynamically in the plot. The work of British writers, these hybrid game books fall into different subseries with titles like *Défis fantastiques, Sorcellerie, La Quête du Graal,* and *Astre d'Or.* In these texts, the first of which, *Le Sorcier de la montagne de feu,* was published in 1982, the reader assumes the role of the protagonist and is required to make choices among various courses of action on almost every page that direct them towards different outcomes, thus creating the illusion of contolling (within limited parameters) the trajectory of the plot.

Rather than a shortage of stimulating, innovative reading material, then, the problem facing children's literature today is instead persuading children to read when there are so many other less time-consuming and more effortless modes of entertainment. There is a huge range of comics and magazines now available, many of which still maintain an educational agenda with factual material and discussion pages on contemporary topics: *Okapi, le magazine des années collège,* for example, carries pieces on science, history, geography, and nature as well as topics of interest to adolescents (school, sport, relationships with the opposite sex); *Youpi,* for children from age five, presents information about nature and history in an easily digestible illustrated form; *Pomme d'Api,* for children of three to seven, combines illustrated tales, games, and the exploits of fictional characters like Petit Ours Brun with a special section for parents; while *Pomme d'Api Soleil* introduces readers of four to eight to moral issues, religious topics, and Bible stories. Magazines like *Je Bouquine,* for ages ten to fifteen, and *J'aime lire,* for younger readers of seven to ten, both published like those above by Bayard Presse, help and encourage young readers to enjoy reading and to engage with literature. *Je Bouquine* includes in each issue a story by a well-known author, extracts from novels in bande dessinées form to whet the reader's appetite, a dossier and illustrated strip on the life and work of a contemporary writer, interviews, and news features about other books, films, and music. As in the compilation texts of the eighteenth century, the young reader is thus initiated into the world of culture, although new strategies are used to stimulate and entice.

Children's literature has until relatively recently been regarded by literary critics as a marginal or inferior genre with a limited, undemanding audience, and one in which aesthetic concerns are subordinated to pedagogical imperatives. The variety and quality of reading material for the young now produced in France and the status of specialist children's authors who are no longer regarded as second-class writers suggest that a more appropriate view is now that 'la littérature pour la jeunesse devient de la littérature "tout court"'.[4]

NOTES

INTRODUCTION

1. Emer O'Sullivan, *Comparative Children's Literature*, trans. Anthea Bell (London: Routledge, 2005), 54.
2. Michelle Perrot, 'Roles and Characters', in *A History of Private Life*, ed. Philippe Ariès and Georges Duby, vol. 4, *From the Fires of Revolution to the Great War*, ed. Michelle Perrot (Cambridge, Mass.: Belknap Press of Harvard University Press, 1990), 196.
3. See Rosemary Lloyd, *The Land of Lost Content: Children and Childhood in Nineteenth-Century French Literature* (Oxford: Clarendon, 1992). It has been claimed that 'autour de 1850, le personnage de l'enfant entre massivement dans la littérature'; see M. J. Chambert de Lauwe, *Un monde autre: L'Enfance* (Paris: Payot, 1971), 18.
4. See Colin Heywood, *Childhood in Nineteenth-Century France: Work, Health and Education amongst the 'Classes Populaires'* (Cambridge: Cambridge University Press, 1988).
5. Isabelle Nières-Chevrel, 'Lisières et chemins de traverse. Avant-propos', in *Littérature de jeunesse, incertaines frontières*, ed. Isabelle Nières-Chevrel (Paris: Gallimard, 2005), 9–10. See also my discussion of this issue in the introduction to the present study's volume 1, *The Beginnings: 1600–1830*.
6. Wolfgang Iser, *The Act of Reading* (London: Routledge and Kegan Paul, 1978), 34.
7. John Stephens, *Language and Ideology in Children's Fiction* (London: Longman, 1992), 86.
8. John Stephens and Robyn McCallum, *Retelling Stories, Framing Culture: Traditional Stories and Metanarratives in Children's Literature* (New York: Garland, 1998), 3.
9. See the different categories of intertextuality proposed in Gérard Genette, *Palimpsestes. La Littérature au second degré* (Paris: Seuil, 1982).

10. These issues are discussed in Christine Wilkie, 'Intertextuality', in *International Companion Encyclopedia of Children's Literature*, ed. Peter Hunt and Sheila Ray (London: Routledge, 1996), 131–37.

11. There have been several broad surveys of the field—by Latzarus (1924), Hazard (1932), Trigon (1950), Caradec (1977), Escarpit (1981), Jan (1973), Soriano (1974), and Ottevaere–van Praag (1987)—that are limited in scope chronologically or include French books in a wider European context; these are listed in this volume's bibliography. In recent years, modern theoretical approaches to the study of children's literature have informed the work of Isabelle Nières Chevrel, Francis Marcoin, Ganna Ottevare–van Pragg, Jean Perrot, and others. Francis Marcoin's *Librairie de jeunesse et littérature industrielle au XIXe siècle* (Paris: Champion, 2006) was regrettably not yet available at the time of the writing of this volume.

CHAPTER 1

1. See the first volume of the present study: Penny Brown, *A Critical History of French Children's Literature*, vol. 1, *The Beginnings, 1600–1830* (New York: Routledge, 2007).

2. Robert J. Bezucha, 'An Introduction to the History', in *The Art of the July Monarchy: France 1830 to 1848*, exhibition catalogue, (Columbia: University of Missouri Press, 1990), 20–33.

3. François Furet and Jacques Ozouf, *Reading and Writing: Literacy in France from Calvin to Jules Ferry* (Cambridge: Cambridge University Press, 1982), 121–22.

4. Laura Strumingher, 'Square Pegs into Round Holes: Rural Parents, Children and Primary Schools, France 1830–1880', in *Popular Traditions and Learned Culture*, ed. Marc Bertrand; Stanford French and Italian Studies 35 (Saratoga, Calif.: Anma Libri, 1985), 134–35.

5. Furet and Ozouf, *Reading and Writing*, 146. On the Falloux Law, see R. D. Anderson, *Education in France 1848–1870* (Oxford: Clarendon, 1975), 45–50.

6. Furet and Ozouf, *Reading and Writing*, 122.

7. Anderson, *Education in France*, 116.

8. Robert J. Bezucha, 'The Renaissance of Book Illustration', in *The Art of the July Monarchy: France 1830 to 1848*, exhibition catalogue, (Columbia: University of Missouri Press, 1990), 192–213.

9. As one author commented, 'Is there anyone amongst us who in youth did not receive it as a New Year's gift?' See Henri Beraldi, author of *Estampes et livres 1872–1892* (Paris, 1892), quoted in Gordon N. Ray, *The Art of the French Illustrated Book 1700–1914* (New York: Pierpont Morgan Library/ Cornell University Press, 1982), 272.

10. Ségolène Le Men, *Les Abécédaires français illustrés du XIXe siècle* (Paris: Promodis, 1984).

11. For details of the factual information reproduced here, see Martyn Lyons, *Le Triomphe du livre: une histoire sociologique de la lecture dans la France du XIXe siècle* (Paris: Promodis, 1987), 77–103.

12. Marie-Thérèse Latzarus, *La Littérature enfantine dans la seconde moitié du XIXe siècle* (Paris: Presses universitaires de France, 1924), 80.

13. Ganna Ottevaere–van Praag, *La Littérature pour la jeunesse en Europe occidentale (1750–1925)* (Bern, Switzerland: Peter Lang, 1987), 350.

14. Jean Glénisson, 'Le Livre pour la jeunesse', in *Histoire de l'édition française*, ed. Henri Martin and Roger Chartier, vol. 3, *Le Temps des Editeurs, du romantisme à la Belle Epoque* (Paris: Promodis, 1986), 417–22.

15. Ibid., 424. Glénisson states that the livres de prix industry was 'un des principaux moteurs de la librairie française' at this period (424).

16. Ibid., 423; no dates are indicated for these texts.

17. Latzarus, *La Littérature enfantine*, 84. Latzarus follows a brief discussion of Berquin and Bouilly with a chapter headed 'Livres édifiants: livres ennuyeux 1840–1860'; Trigon is reluctant to discuss such livres de prix at all.

18. Glénisson, 'Le Livre pour la jeunesse', 425.

19. For a discussion of exemplary lives narratives, see Brown, *A Critical History*, vol. 1, chap. 6.

20. Jean Mistler, *La Librairie Hachette de 1826 à nos jours* (Paris: Hachette, 1964), 50.

21. Ottevaere–van Praag, *La Littérature pour la jeunesse*, 186.

22. Mistler, *La Librairie Hachette*, 56.

23. 'Prospectus', Bibliothèque des chemins de fer, quoted in Francis Marcoin, *La Comtesse de Ségur, ou le Bonheur immobile* (Arras, France: Artois Presses Université), 25.

24. Pierre-Jules Hetzel, "Letter to Francisque Sarcey (n.d.),", quoted in A. Parménie and C. Bonnier de la Chapelle, *Histoire d'un éditeur et de ses auteurs. P.-J. Hetzel (Stahl)* (Paris: Albin Michel, 1953), 596.

25. The collection was later bought by Hachette and reissued in four volumes in 1860. See Etienne Dennery, in *De Balzac à Jules Verne: un grand éditeur du XIXe siècle*, exhibition catalogue (Paris: Bibliothèque Nationale), 18.

26. Pierre-Jules Hetzel, 'Notice', in *Les Fables de Florian* (Paris: Hetzel, 1842); quoted in Dennery, *De Balzac à Jules Verne*, 18.

27. P.-J. Stahl, 'Sur les contes de fées', preface to Charles Perrault, *Contes* (1861), facsimile ed. (Paris: Hachette, 1978), 15.

28. This view, best embodied in William Wordsworth's 1807 poem 'Ode on the Intimations of Immortality', is also found in the poems of Marceline Desbordes-Valmore and Victor Hugo.

29. Ottevaere–van Praag, *La Littérature pour la jeunesse*, 145–46.

30. Bezucha, 'The Renaissance of Book Illustration', 200; Ray, *The Art of the French Illustrated Book*, 247–51.

31. Charles Nodier, 'Des fées et de leur littérature en France', in *Revue des Deux Mondes*, April 1862 p 648 + quoted in Pierre-Georges Castex, *Le Conte fantastique en France* (Paris: José Corti, 1951), 121.

32. Charles Nodier, *Conte*, and Garneir ed. Pierre-Georges Castex (Paris: Garneier, 1961), 581.

33. George Sand, *Histoire du véritable Gribouille* (Paris: Gallimard, 1978), 64.

34. Ibid., 59.

35. Stahl, 'Sur les contes de fées', 40–41.

36. I am indebted to the website http://www.roman-daventures.com and to Roger Mathé, 'L'Image de l'Indien emplumé et du trappeur dans la littérature populaire au dix-neuvième siècle', in *Popular Traditions and Learned Culture*, ed. Marc Bertrand; Stanford French and Italian Studies 35 (Saratoga, Calif.: Anma Libri, 1985), 179–209, for invaluable information on French writers in this genre.

37. See Brown, *A Critical History*, vol. 1, chap. 4.

38. Gérard Genette, *Palimpsestes. La Littérature au second degré* (Paris: Seuil, 1982), 10.

39. Louis Desnoyers, preface to *Les Mésaventures de Jean-Paul Choppart*, quoted in François Caradec, *Histoire de la littérature enfantine en France* (Paris: Albin Michel, 1977), 117.

40. Ibid., 118.

41. Pierre-Jules Hetzel, preface to Louis Denoyers, *Les Mésaventures de Jean-Paul Choppart* (1864), vi, cited in Ottevaere–Van Praag, *La Littérature pour la jeunesse*, 154.

42. Ibid.

43. *L'Abeille*, 1839, quoted in Alain Fourment, *Histoire de la presse des jeunes et des journaux d'enfants (1768–1988)* (Paris: Editions Ecole, 1987), 44.

44. Fourment, *Histoire de la presse*, 48.

45. *Journal des jeunes persones*, 1846, quoted in Fourment, *Histoire de la presse*, 66.

46. Fourment, *Histoire de la presse*, 58.

47. Ibid., 79.

48. *La Mode des demoiselles* and *Moniteur des demoiselles*, 1848, both quoted in Fourment, *Histoire de la presse*, 70.

49. *L'Image*, 1847, quoted in Fourment, *Histoire de la presse*, 74.

CHAPTER 2

1. See Jean Calvet, *L'Enfant dans la littérature française. Des origines à 1870* (Paris: Lanore, 1930), 193–95.

2. Marie-Thérèse Latzarus, *La Littérature enfantine dans la seconde moitié du XIXe siècle* (Paris: Presses universitaires de France, 1924), 92.

3. Paul Hazard, *Les Livres, les enfants et les hommes* (1932; reprint, Paris: Hatier, 1967), 105; Ganna Ottevaere–van Praag, *La Littérature pour la jeunesse en Europe occidentale (1750–1925)* (Bern, Switzerland: Peter Lang, 1987), 213–15.

4. Ottevaere van Praag, *La Littérature pour la jeunesse*, 418–19, holds this to be true of most children's literature, with some exceptions, between 1750 and 1890.

5. Jean Mistler, *La Librairie Hachette de 1826 à nos jours* (Paris: Hachette, 1964), 151.

6. Ibid., 150. The journal was to merge with Hetzel's *Magasin d'éducation et récréation* in 1876.

7. Rosemary Lloyd, *The Land of Lost Content: Children and Childhood in Nineteenth-Century French Literature* (Oxford: Clarendon, 1992), 21, asserts that 'most students of children's literature acknowledge that the real birth of books for children in France comes with the signing of the contract between Hachette and Mme de Ségur in 1855 and the associated development of the *Bibliothèque rose*'.

8. See, for example, Hortense Dufour, *La comtesse de Ségur, née Rostopchine. Biographie* (Paris: Flammarion, 2000), 93.

9. Comtesse de Ségur to Emile Templier, 5 July 1860, cited in Mistler, *La Librairie Hachette*, 216. Apart from a chapter on Ségur, Mistler says little about the Bibliothèque rose.

10. See Pierre Bléton, *La Vie sociale dans le second Empire, un étonnant témoignage de la Comtesse de Ségur* (Paris: Editions ouvrières, 1963).

11. For a discussion of this issue, see Laura Kreyder, *L'Enfance des saints et des autres. Essai sur la comtesse de Ségur* (Paris: Schena-Nizet, 1987), 138–48.

12. Ottevaere–van Praag, *La Littérature pour la jeunesse*, 245; Marc Soriano, *Le Monde de l'Education* 12 (1975), cited in François Caradec, *Histoire de la littérature enfantine en France* (Paris: Albin Michel, 1977), 147.

13. See Kreyder, *L'Enfance des saints et des autres*, 118–19; and Jacques Chupeau, 'Instruire en amusant: théorie et pratique du récit éducatif à l'époque de la comtesse de Ségur', in *La Comtesse de Ségur et ses alentours*, ed. Isabelle Nières-Chevrel, *Cahiers Robinson* 9 (Artois, France: Université d'Artois, 2001), 57–65; the latter volume contains many useful papers on aspects of the work of Ségur and her contemporaries.

14. Dufour, *La comtesse de Ségur*, 550, cites evidence of Ségur's anti-Semitism.

15. Comtesse de Ségur, *Les Bons enfants* (1862; reprint, Paris: Hachette, 1921), 29.

16. See Penny Brown, 'Gustave Doré's Magical Realism: The Nouveaux contes de fées of the Comtesse de Ségur', *Modern Language Review* 95, no. 4 (2001): 964–77.

17. See Penny Brown, 'La Comtesse de Ségur et les contes de fées', in Nières-Chevrel, ed., *La Comtesse de Ségur et ses alentours*, 139–44.

18. The illustrations depict Ourson with a dark skin, so the tale can be seen as a general comment on 'difference'. The ending, however, although conforming to fairy-tale tradition, undermines the theme of acceptance.

19. Comtesse de Ségur, *Les Malheurs de Sophie* (1859; reprint, Paris: Gallimard, 1977), 9.

20. On the role of dolls, see Alison Finch, *Women's Writing in Nineteenth-Century France* (Oxford: Oxford University Press, 2000), 113; and Marie-Christine Vinson, *L'Education des petites filles chez la comtesse de Ségur* (Lyon: Presses universitaires de Lyon, 1987), 54–58.

21. For a discussion of punishments and discipline in Ségur's novels, see Vinson, *L'Education des petites filles*, 181–221.

22. Comtesse de Ségur, *Les Petites filles modèles* (1858; reprint, Paris: Gallimard, 1980), 123.

23. The family names of Ségur and Pitray are only lightly hidden in the anagrams.

24. Contrary to the expectations, perhaps, of readers who have enjoyed the development of the relationship between Sophie and Paul throughout the trilogy, Sophie is said to marry Jean, and Paul marries Marguerite.

25. Dourakine is widely considered to be based on Ségur's father, Fédor Rostopchine. Articles covering a range of aspects of these two texts can be found in *Les Cahiers de la Comtesse* 1 (2000) and *Les Cahiers séguriens* 2 (2001), the latter being a newer name for the same journal.

26. Kreyder, *L'Enfance des saints et des autres*, 89, calls Dourakine a 'Sauveur obscène, en qui s'allient le grotesque et le sublime'.

27. See Penny Brown, 'Le Paradoxe de l'Ange gardien, ou les Malheurs du Général Dourakine', *Les Cahiers de la comtesse* 1 (2000): 28–30.

28. Serfdom had in fact been abolished in Russia in 1861.

29. See Bénédicte Le Ru, 'L'Image de la Russie chez la comtesse de Ségur', in Nières-Chevrel, ed., *La Comtesse de Ségur et ses alentours*, 155; and *Les Cahiers séguriens* 2 (2001), an issue devoted to *Le Général Dourakine*.

30. The *Souvenirs d'un sibérien*, by Rufin Pietrowski, appeared in the *Revue des deux mondes* in April and May 1863. Ségur was being very topical here, as Poland was seeking independence from Russia in 1863.

31. See Penny Brown, 'La chute de l'homme (et de la femme) dans un livre pour les enfants', *Les Cahiers Séguriens* 2 (2001): 55–58.

32. Kreyder, *L'Enfance des saints et des autres*, 90.

33. The first part of Lesage's *Histoire de Gil Blas de Santillane* was published in 1715, the second part in 1725, and the third part in 1735.

34. According to Mistler, *La Librairie Hachette*, 216, Ségur was persuaded by Emile Templier to make Cadichon repent in this manner. Dufour, *La comtesse de Ségur*, 523–24, sees Cadichon as representative of a bitter and rebellious side of the comtesse herself.

35. Comtesse de Ségur, *Jean-qui-grogne et Jean-qui-rit* (1865; reprint, Paris: Hachette, 1931), 112–13.
36. Comtesse de Ségur, *La Fortune de Gaspard* (1866; reprint, Paris: Hachette, 1931), 5.
37. See the discussion of this in Marc Soriano, 'Bibliothèque rose ou série noire?' preface to *La Fortune de Gaspard* (Paris: Pauvert, 1972); and Kreyder, *L'Enfance des saints et des autres*, 194–201.
38. Kreyder, *L'Enfance des saints et des autres*, 113–14, argues that Ségur believed that 'non seulement l'instruction n'est pas utile pour le peuple, mais qu'elle peut lui être profondément nocive, en le mettant en contact avec un savoir qui l'éloignera de ses croyances, le déracinera, l'aigrira.'
39. R. D. Anderson, *Education in France 1848–1870* (Oxford: Clarendon, 1975), 137–41.
40. See Penny Brown, 'Savoir lire: pouvoir ou perversion? La Fortune de Gaspard et le problème de savoir lire dans la littérature enfantine', *Les Cahiers Séguriens* 3 (2002): 31–37.
41. Ségur, *La Fortune de Gaspard*, 253.
42. Francis Marcoin, *La Comtesse de Ségur, ou le Bonheur immobile* (Arras, France: Artois Presses Université, 1999), 228.
43. Ségur, *La Fortune de Gaspard*, 5.
44. Ségur, *Après la pluie, le beau temps* (1871; reprint, Paris: Hachette, 1930), 241, 244.
45. Soriano, *Le Monde de l'Education* 12 (1975), cited in François Caradec, *Histoire de la littérature enfantine*, 147, asks, 'comment expliquer que la comtesse de Ségur continue de sévir dans les collections très répandues, malgré son racisme, son féodalisme et son ultramontanisme militants que son indisputable talent rend encore plus nocifs?'
46. François Mauriac, *La Robe prétexte* (Paris: Grasset, 1914), 12, 20, cited in Kreyder, *L'Enfance des saints et des autres*, 217–19.
47. See the Comtesse de Ségur website at http://comtessedesegur.ifrance.com.
48. Marcel Bouteron, ed., *Correspondance avec Zulma Carraud* (Paris: A. Colin, 1934), 218.
49. Francis Marcoin, 'Autour de la comtesse', in Nières-Chevrel, ed., *La comtesse de Ségur et ses alentours*, 27.
50. See the discussion of Carraud's works in Laura Strumingher, *What are Little Girls and Boys Made of? Primary Education in Rural France 1830–1880* (Albany: State University of New York Press, 1983), 48–59.
51. Latzarus, *La Littérature enfantine*, 85.
52. See the discussion of this novel in Christa Delahaye, 'Le Joueur et le colporteur: rencontre de deux figures de voyageurs européens de la seconde moitié du XIXème siècle dans les villes d'eaux', in Nières-Chevrel, ed., *La Comtesse de Ségur et ses alentours*, 49–56.
53. Marcoin, 'Autour de la comtesse', 31.

54. Julie Gouraud, *Lettres de deux poupées* (1864; reprint, Paris: Hachette, 1881), 28.
55. Latzarus, *La Littérature enfantine*, 128.
56. Ottevaere–van Praag, *La Littérature pour la jeunesse*, 240. Latzarus's description of Fleuriot as 'idéaliste' while Ségur is a 'réaliste' is an extremely oversimplified one.
57. Zénaïde Fleuriot, *Tranquille et Tourbillon* (1880; reprint, Paris: Hachette, 1914), 303, 209.
58. The greater complexity of her character and her rapid changes of mood have, in effect, drawn comparisons with the Comtesse de Ségur's Sophie; see Latzarus, *La Littérature enfantine*, 134.
59. Raoul's story is continued in the sequels *Plus tard, ou le jeune chef de famille* (c. 1879) and *Raoul Daubry, chef de famille* (1879).
60. This view is shared by Ottevaere–van Praag, *La Littérature pour la jeunesse*, 240.
61. Olga de Pitray, *Robin des bois* (Paris: Hachette, 1889), 91.

CHAPTER 3

1. Hetzel also published books for adult readers—notably, works by Juliette Adam, Emile Erckmann and Alexandre Chatrian, Victor Hugo, Ivan Turgenev, and the early works of Alphonse Daudet and Émile Zola. After his death in 1886, his son Louis-Jules Hetzel continued to specialise in children' books.
2. Pierre-Jules Hetzel, editorial comment in *Magasin d'éducation et de récréation* 26, 2e semestre, 320, cited in Jacques Chupeau, 'Le Moraliste des enfants: P.-J. Stahl', in *Un Editeur et son siècle. Pierre-Jules Hetzel (1814–1886)*, ed. Christian Robin (Saint-Sébastien, France: ACL Edition Société Crocus, 1988), 207.
3. Hetzel in fact produced different series, with and without illustrations, see Etienne Dennery, 'Préface', in *De Balzac à Jules Verne: un grand éditeur du XIXe siècle*, exhibition catalogue (Paris: Bibliothèque Nationale, 1966), 58.
4. Catalogue, bound in the edition of X. B. Saintine, *Picciola* (Paris: Hetzel, 1887), 5.
5. Roger Bellet, 'L'Aventure didactique dans le *Magasin d'Education et de Récréation* (1864–1869)', in *L'Aventure dans la littérature populaire au XIXe siècle*, ed. Roger Bellet (Lyon, France: Presses Universitaires de Lyon, 1985), 89.
6. Pierre-Jules Hetzel, 'A nos lecteurs', *Magasin d'education et de récréation* 1 (1864), quoted in Guy Gauthier, 'Une morale laïque sous le Second Empire: la morale de Stahl dans le *Magasin d'éducation*', in Robin, ed., *Un Editeur et son siècle*, 189–204.

7. Karin Lesnik-Oberstein, *Children's Literature, Criticism and the Fictional Child* (Oxford: Clarendon, 1994), 39, suggests that this is true of most children's books of this period.

8. Pierre-Jules Hetzel, 'Préface', in Louis Ratisbonne, *La Comédie enfantine*, 1860–61, quoted in Dennery, 'Préface', 59.

9. P.-J. Stahl, 'Préface', in P.-J. Stahl, *La Morale familière* (Paris: Hetzel, 1868), cited in Dennery, 'Préface', 65.

10. Hetzel, 'A nos lecteurs', quoted in Gauthier, 'Une morale laïque sous le Second Empire', 190.

11. Gauthier, 'Une morale laïque sous le Second Empire', 195.

12. Ibid., 198.

13. Pierre-Jules Hetzel, Letter to Cuvillier-Fleury, Dec. 1874, quoted in A. Parménie and C. Bonnier de la Chapelle, *Histoire d'un éditeur et de ses auteurs. P.-J. Hetzel (Stahl)* (Paris: Albin Michel, 1953), 595.

14. Ibid.

15. Daniel Compère, 'Le Robinson Suisse relu et récrit par Hetzel', in Robin, ed., *Un Editeur et son siècle*, 223–232.

16. Pierre-Jules Hetzel, 'Préface', in his adaptation of Johann David Wyss's, *Le Robinson suisse*, quoted in Compère, 'Le Robinson Suisse', 224.

17. Pierre-Jules Hetzel, 'Avertissement de l'éditeur', in Jules Verne, *Voyages et Aventures du capitaine Hatteras* (Paris: Hetzel, 1867), 1–2.

18. François Furet and Jacques Ozouf, *Reading and Writing: Literacy in France from Calvin to Jules Ferry* (Cambridge: Cambridge University Press, 1982), 45.

19. Pierre-Jules Hetzel to Charles Augustin Sainte-Beuve, 16 December 1861, quoted in Parménie and Chapelle, *Histoire d'un éditeur et de ses auteurs*, 378.

20. Bellet, 'L'Aventure didactique', 96.

21. This idea was based on the experiments with hot air balloons of Verne's friend Nadar (Félix Tournachon).

22. See Simone Vierne, *Jules Verne et le roman initiatique* (Paris: Editions du Sirac, 1973).

23. Hetzel, 'Avertissement de l'éditeur' in *Magasin d'éducation et de récréation* 1, March 1864, 1–2.

24. Timothy Unwin, *Jules Verne: Journeys in Writing* (Liverpool, England: Liverpool University Press, 2005), 158. Verne's interest in the travel narrative also informed his three-volume *Histoire des grands voyages et des grands voyageurs* (1880).

25. Jean Chesneaux, *The Political and Social Ideas of Jules Verne*, trans. Thomas Wikeley (London: Thames and Hudson, 1972), 21.

26. Andrew Martin, *The Mask of the Prophet* (Oxford: Clarendon, 1990), 19.

27. See Chesneaux, *The Political and Social Ideas of Jules Verne*, 116.

28. See, for example, Chesneaux, *The Political and Social Ideas of Jules Verne*, 11–22.
29. Richard Phillips, *Mapping Men and Empire: A Geography of Adventure* (London: Routledge, 1997), 117.
30. See Chesneaux, *The Political and Social Ideas of Jules Verne*, chap. 6.
31. See Peter Aberger, 'The Portrayal of Blacks in Jules Verne's *Voyages extraordinaires*', *French Review* 53 (1979): 199–206.
32. Phillips, *Mapping Men and Empire*, 135.
33. Ibid., 137.
34. Chesneaux, *The Political and Social Ideas of Jules Verne*, 76, sees this as typical of the vision of the followers of Saint-Simon.
35. This echoes the view of Mme de Genlis in *Les Veillées du château* (1784) that in fictional narratives, the marvellous element is only interesting if it is also true. In 'Alphonse et Dalinde, ou la féerie de l'art et de la nature', the tale told by the mother, who is shocked to find her children reading a fairy story by Mme d'Aulnoy, all the marvels have a scientific explanation in order to show that truth is stranger, and more educational, than fiction.
36. Unwin, *Jules Verne: Journeys in Writing*, chap. 2, discusses the issue of Verne's reputation as a 'techno-prophet' at length.
37. *Nautilus* was the name given to the submarine invented by Robert Fulton at Napoleon's behest in 1800, but it was never used. *Vingt mille lieues sous les mers* also owes much to the work of Verne's friend Jacques-François Conseil (whose name Verne uses for Arronax's servant in the novel) and to the French experimental submarine *Le Plongeur*, abandoned after tests in 1864.
38. See, for example, Chesneaux, *The Political and Social Ideas of Jules Verne*, 30; and François Caradec, *Histoire de la littérature enfantine en France* (Paris: Albin Michel, 1977), 170–71. One enthusiastic reader, Jean-Paul Sartre, recalls that as a child he always jumped over these passages but found himself imitating Verne in his own early writing; see Sartre, *Les Mots* (Paris: Gallimard, 1964), 18–19.
39. Chesneaux, *The Political and Social Ideas of Jules Verne*, 44.
40. Unwin, *Jules Verne: Journeys in Writing*, chap. 4, attributes this stereotyping to Verne's interest and experience in theatre.
41. Unwin, *Jules Verne: Journeys in Writing*, 171.
42. William Golding, 'Astronaut by Gaslight', *Spectator*, 9 June, 1961, 841, quoted in Martin, *The Mask of the Prophet*, 70.
43. Jules Verne, *L'Île mystérieuse* (1874–75; reprint, Paris: Hachette, 1996), 15.
44. See Vierne, *Jules Verne et le roman initiatique*, 155 and passim, for a discussion of Verne's fascination with the 'monstre/génie' dichotomy.
45. *Les Cinq cents millions de la Bégum* was Verne's rewriting of a text originally drafted by Paschal Grousset (André Laurie).

46. Jules Verne, *Souvenirs d'enfance et de jeunesse* (1890), quoted in Daniel Compère, *Jules Verne. Ecrivain* (Geneva: Droz, 1991), 33.

47. Unwin, *Jules Verne: Journeys in Writing*, 207, describes this process as turning 'the genre of exploration into an exploration of genre'.

48. Jules Verne, *Un capitaine de quinze ans* (Paris: Hachette, 1967), 525. To Hetzel's objection that Dick was too serious for his age, Verne replied that 'je n'aurais pu voir dans ce petit Américain, tel que je le concevais, un gamin de Paris!' Jules Verne to Pierre-Jules Hetzel, 14 May 1878, quoted in Vierne, *Jules Verne et le roman initiatique*, 338.

49. It has been suggested that the obsession with the theme of the 'père initiatique' relates to Verne's feelings about his relationship with Hetzel. See Marcel Moré, *Le Très curieux Jules Verne* (Paris: Gallimard, 1960), 21–53.

50. F. J. Harvey Darton, *Children's Books in England: Five Centuries of Social Life* (Cambridge: Cambridge University Press, 1982), 247.

51. Caradec, *Histoire de la littérature enfantine en France*, 168.

52. Verne, *Un capitaine de quinze ans*, 427.

53. Jules Verne to Pierre-Jules Hetzel, 3 December 1883, quoted in Compère, *Jules Verne. Ecrivain*, 28.

54. Martin, *The Mask of the Prophet*, 11; Arthur B. Evans, *Jules Verne Rediscovered: Didacticism and the Scientific Novel* (New York: Greenwood, 1988), 4.

55. Arthur B. Evans, 'Jules Verne and the French Literary Canon', in E.J. Smyth (ed.), *Jules Verne: Narratives of Modernity* (Liverpool, England: Liverpool University Press, 2000), 14, claims that Verne was 'systematically shunned by the French literary and university establishment as being a "mere" writer of children's stories'.

56. Émile Zola, 'Les romanciers contemporains', in *Les Romanciers naturalistes* (Paris: Charpentier, 1890), 356–57.

57. Martin, *The Mask of the Prophet*, 9.

58. Jules Verne to Pierre-Jules Hetzel, 1870, quoted in Compère, *Jules Verne. Ecrivain*, 28.

59. Kiera Vaclavik, 'Jules Verne écrivain . . . de jeunesse: The Case of *Voyage au centre de la terre*', *Australian Journal of French Studies* 42, no. 3 (2005): 276–83, argues the case for the significance of considering Verne as a writer for the young.

60. Jules Verne, 'Jules Verne at Home', interview, *Strand Magazine*, February 1895, cited in Compère, *Jules Verne. Ecrivain*, 11; Unwin, *Jules Verne: Journeys in Writing*, 182.

61. Phillips, *Mapping Men and Empire*, 129.

62. Paschal Grousset (André Laurie), 'Jules Verne vu par André Laurie', *Le Temps*, 26 March 1905, quoted in Francis Lacassin, ed., *Des Enfants sur les routes* (Paris: Laffont, 1994), 1138–41.

63. Anonymous, *L'Humanité*, 3 April 1905, quoted in Lacassin, ed., *Des Enfants sur les routes*, 1142.

64. Jean Marie Gustave Le Clézio, 'J'ai grandi avec ses livres', *Jules Verne. L'Odyssée de la terre, Géo*, hors-série, 2003, 6–11.

65. The first collection, titled *Le Château de Pictordu*, contained, after the title story, 'La Reine Coax', 'Le nuage rose', 'Les Ailes du courage', and 'Le Géant Yéous', and the second, titled *Le Chêne parlant* contained the title story, 'Le Chien et la fleur sacrée', 'L'Orgue du Titan', 'Ce que disent les fleurs', 'Le Marteau rouge', 'La Fée Poussière', 'Le Gnome des huîtres', and 'La Fée aux gros yeux'.

66. George Sand, *Histoire de ma vie*, ed. Damien Zanone (Paris: Flammarion, 2001), vol. 2, 2e partie, 146.

67. George Sand, *Contes d'une grand-mère*, ed. Philippe Berthier (Meylan, France: Les Editions de l'Aurore, 1982), 2:32. The tales were initially published separately in the adult papers *Le Temps* and the *Revue des deux mondes*.

68. Gillian Beer, *Darwin's Plots: Evolutionary Narratives in Darwin, George Eliot, and Nineteenth-Century Fiction* (London: Routledge and Kegan Paul, 1983).

69. Ibid., 114.

70. See Pietro Corsi and Paul J. Wendling, 'Darwinism in Germany, France and Italy', in *The Darwinian Heritage*, ed. David Kohn (Princeton, N. J.: Princeton University Press, 1985), 683–729.

71. George Sand, 'Le Marteau rouge', in *Contes d'une grand-mère*, 2:150.

72. A new edition of this tale published in 1977, with the title 'Brise et rose' and illustrated with sensual images by Nicole Claveloux, underlines the motif of the transformation of the destructive male force and the celebration of the feminine by depicting the breeze as a naked female with butterfly wings, George Sand, *Brise et rose* (Paris: Editions des femmes, 1977).

73. George Sand, 'La Fée Poussière', in *Contes d'une grand-mère*, 2:155.

74. Ibid., 157.

75. Ibid., 160.

76. Phillips, *Mapping Men and Empire*, 3, notes that 'European empires and European masculinites were imagined in geographies of adventure'.

77. Anne Hugon, 'Conquête et exploration en Afrique noire' in *Images et colonies. Iconographie et propagande coloniale sur l'Afrique française de 1880 à 1962*, ed. Nicolas Bancel, Pascal Blanchard, and Laurent Gervereau (Paris: BDIC-ACHAC, 1993), 19.

78. Gilles Manceron, 'Le Missionaire à barbe noire et l'enseignement laïque' in Bancel, Blanchard, and Gervereau, eds., *Images et colonies*, 70.

79. I am indebted to the website http://www.roman-daventures.com for some of the factual information in this section.

80. See http://www.roman-daventures.com.

81. Ganna Ottevaere–van Praag, *La Littérature pour la jeunesse*, 283.
82. Jean de Trigon, *Histoire de la littérature enfantine de ma Mère l'Oye au roi Babar* (Paris: Hachette, 1950), 108.
83. Examples can be viewed at http://www.roman-daventures.com.
84. They were published by Talladier until 1960 and in the J'ai Lu series in the early 1980s.
85. Alphonse Daudet, *Tartarin de Tarascon* (1872; reprint, Paris: Gallimard, 1987), 24.
86. Daudet followed up on the success of *Tartarin de Tarascon* with the sequels *Tartarin sur les Alpes* (1885) and *Port-Tarascon* (1890).

CHAPTER 4

1. Michelle Perrot, 'The Family Triumphant', in *A History of Private Life*, ed. Philippe Ariès and Georges Duby, vol. 4, *From the Fires of Revolution to the Great War* (Cambridge, Mass.: Belknap Press of Harvard University Press, 1990), 144; Rosemary Lloyd, *The Land of Lost Content: Children and Childhood in Nineteenth-Century French Literature* (Oxford: Clarendon, 1992), 14–16.
2. Lloyd, *The Land of Lost Content*, 16.
3. For a detailed discussion of child labour and legislation, see Colin Heywood, *Childhood in Nineteenth-Century France: Work, Health and Education amongst the 'Classes Populaires'* (Cambridge: Cambridge University Press, 1988).
4. Heywood, *Childhood in Nineteenth-Century France*, 249.
5. Ibid., 265.
6. See, for example, Marie-Thérèse Latzarus, *La Littérature enfantine dans la seconde moitié du XIXe siècle* (Paris: Presses universitaires de France, 1924), 230; François Caradec, *Histoire de la littérature enfantine en France* (Paris: Albin Michel, 1977), 181–82. Dickens also acted as an advisor to Hachette on English works appropriate for translation.
7. Valentin Jamerai Duval (1695–1775), abused by his stepfather, went to work as a shepherd and, after contracting smallpox, educated himself and became librarian to the Duc de Lorraine and a professor of history at the University of Lorraine; William Hutton (1723–1815) worked in a silk factory from the age of seven and went on to acquire a large fortune in the book trade; Henri Stilling (1740–1817), an orphan at two, worked in the fields but became a doctor and literary man. See Latzarus, *La Littérature enfantine*, 237–38.
8. It was not until the last decade of the century that firm legislation came into force to protect children from abuse at home and at work. See Michelle Perrot, 'Roles and Characters' in *A History of Private Life*, ed.

Philippe Ariès and Georges Duby, vol. 4, *From the Fires of Revolution to the Great War*, 179; Lloyd, *The Land of Lost Content*, 19; Heywood, *Childhood in Nineteenth-Century France*, 318–19.

9. Ganna Ottevaere–van Praag, *La Littérature pour la jeunesse*, 213–17.

10. See, for example, Hesba Stretton's *Alone in London* (1869) and George Eliot's *Silas Marner* (1861).

11. Latzarus, *La Littérature enfantine*, 233, gives neither dates nor much detail of most of the texts, but their number suggests a considerable fashion for this sort of tale.

12. For a detailed discussion of *Sans famille*, see David Steel, 'Hector Malot, *Sans famille* and the sense of adventure', *New Comparison* 20 (1995): 75–95; and Lloyd, *The Land of Lost Content*, 138–45.

13. 'J'ai cherché à amuser ceux qu'on ennuyait, j'ai voulu leur donner le goût de la lecture et aguiser leur curiosité au lieu de l'émousser; j'ai voulu aussi provoquer leur intérêt, émouvoir leur coeur, les attirer, les retenir, les amener à demander aux livres leurs joies ou leurs consolations'; Hector Malot, *Le Roman de mes romans* (1895), quoted in Agnès Thomas-Maleville, *Hector Malot. Ecrivain au grand coeur* (Monaco, Rocher, 2000), 122.

14. Malot's novel *Le Mousse*, dedicated to his granddaughter Perrine, deals with a similar theme, but less obviously targets a young readership. It was Malot's last novel and, for reasons unknown, was not published until 1997. See Yves Pincet, 'Préface', in Hector Malot *Le Mousse* (Monaco, Rocher, 1997), 16–19.

15. Hector Malot, *Romain Kalbris* (1869; reprint, Paris; Hetzel, 1895), 55.

16. Ibid., 58.

17. See Steel, 'Hector Malot, *Sans famille*', 91.

18. Thomas-Maleville, *Hector Malot. Ecrivain au grand coeur*, 170–71.

19. Steel, 'Hector Malot, *Sans famille*', 84.

20. Malot had visited England and wrote *La Vie moderne en Angleterre* (1862), a collection of articles including sections on the East End of London. In 1876, Jules Vallès also told him of his plans to write a book about the seamier sides of London life. See Steel, 'Hector Malot, *Sans famille*', 86.

21. Steel, 'Hector Malot, *Sans famille*', 89–90, suggests many possible interpretations of this issue, including that it is a comment on the dysfunctional nature of French families, although the Driscolls and the Milligans are equally so.

22. Thomas-Maleville, *Hector Malot. Ecrivain au grand coeur*, 219.

23. This is based on a real place, Flixécourt, in the Somme region. See Thomas-Maleville, *Hector Malot. Ecrivain au grand coeur*, 220.

24. Thomas-Maleville, *Hector Malot. Ecrivain au grand coeur*, 222.

25. Hector Malot, *En famille* (1893; reprint, London: Nelson, 1932), 286.

26. Antoine Prost, *Histoire de l'enseignement en France, 1800–1967* (Paris: Armand Colin, 1968), 335–36.

27. Pierre-Jules Hetzel, editorial comment in *Magasin d'éducation et de récréation* (July 1871), n.p., quoted in Alain Fourment, *Histoire de la presse des jeunes et des journaux d'enfants (1768–1988)* (Paris: Editions Ecole, 1987), 124.

28. Fourment, *Histoire de la presse*, 124.

29. See Jacques and Mona Azouf, 'Le Tour de la France par deux enfants. Le petit livre rouge de la République', in *Les Lieux de mémoire*, ed. Pierre Nora, vol. 1, *La République* (Paris: Gallimard, 1984), 291–321.

30. After the loss of this territory to Prussia, the inhabitants were forced to move to other areas of France if they wished to retain their French citizenship but orphans were refused permission to leave and were thus considered as German.

31. G. Bruno, *Le Tour de la France par deux enfants* (Paris: Belin, 1994), 4. This edition is a facsimile reprint of the 1906 expanded edition.

32. Ibid., 4.

33. Ibid., 102.

34. See John Strachan, 'Romance, Religion and the Republic: Bruno's *Le Tour de la France par deux enfants*', *French History* 18, no. 1 (2004): 96–118.

35. Ibid., 111.

36. Ségolène Le Men, 'La Pédagogie par l'image dans un manuel de la Troisième République', in *Usages de l'image au XIX siècle*, ed. Stéphane Michaud, Jean-Yves Mollier, and Nicole Savy (Paris: Editions Créaphis, 1992), 122.

37. Ibid., 126.

38. Bruno, *Le Tour de la France*, 296.

39. Strachan, 'Romance, Religion and the Republic', 114–15.

40. Bruno, *Le Tour de la France*, 318.

41. L. Schoumacker, *Erckmann-Chatrian, étude biographique et critique d'après des documents inédits* (Strasbourg, France: Université de Strasbourg, 1933), 5.

42. See Jean Bastaire, 'Pour une "lecture-enfant" d'Erckmann-Chatrian', in *Erckmann-Chatrian, entre imagination, fantaisie et réalisme: du conte au conte de l'histoire*, ed. François Marotin (Phalsbourg, France: Editions de la Musée de Phalsbourg, 1999), 19–25.

43. Yves Pincet, 'Erckmann-Chatrian à travers les morceaux choisis dans les manuels scolaires' in Marotin, ed., *Erckmann-Chatrian*, 353.

44. Ibid., 344.

45. See Charles Grandhomme, 'Le Conteur dans les *Romans nationaux*', in Marotin, ed., *Erckmann-Chatrian*, 273–89.

46. Bastaire, 'Pour une "lecture-enfant" d'Erckmann-Chatrian', 25.

47. Emile Erckmann to Pierre-Jules Hetzel, 15 March 1871, quoted in Etienne Dennery, *De Balzac à Jules Verne: un grand éditeur du XIXe siècle*, exhibition catalogue (Paris: Bibliothèque Nationale), 75.

48. Jean-François Chanet, 'Erckmann-Chatrian dans les revues d'enseignement primaire sous la Troisième République', in Marotin, ed., *Erckmann-Chatrian*, 335.

49. Emile Erckmann and Alexandre Chatrian, *Histoire d'un paysan*, reprinted in *Gens d'Alsace et de Lorraine* (Paris: Verso, 1999), Présentation de J .P. Rioux, 181.

50. Chanet, 'Erckmann-Chatrian dans les revues', 336; Yves Pincet, 'Erckmann-Chatrian', 341–65.

51. Fourment, *Histoire de la presse*, 127.

52. See Penny Brown, *A Critical History of French Children's Literature*, vol. 1: *The Beginnings 1600–1830* (New York: Routledge, 2007).

53. Latzarus, *La Littérature enfantine*, 204.

54. I am indebted to the website http://www.roman-daventures.com for the factual information in this section.

55. Danrit's novels are described on http://www.roman-daventures.com as imbued with 'pas un bellicisme conquérant, mais paniqué, paranoïque' in this respect.

56. See http://www.roman-daventures.com.

CHAPTER 5

1. Ganna Ottevaere–van Praag, *La littérature pour la jeunesse*, 298; Laura Noesser, 'Le Livre pour enfants', in *Histoire de l'édition française*, ed. Henri Martin and Roger Chartier, vol. 4, *Le Livre concurrencé 1900–1950* (Paris: Promodis, 1985), 457.

2. Marc Soriano, *Guide de la littérature pour la jeunesse* (Paris: Flammarion, 1974), 70.

3. Isabelle Jan, *La Littérature enfantine* (Paris: Editions Ouvrières, 1969), 12.

4. Jean-Alexis Néret, *Histoire illustrée de la librairie et du livre français* (Paris: Lamarre, 1953), 231.

5. Noesser, 'Le Livre pour enfants', 457–58.

6. Judith Proud, *Children and Propaganda. 'Il était une fois. . . ': Fiction and Fairy Tale in Vichy France* (Oxford: Intellect, 1995), 13.

7. Jean-Paul Sartre, *Les Mots* (Paris: Gallimard, 1964), 57–58.

8. Simone de Beauvoir, *Mémoires d'une jeune fille rangée* (Paris: Gallimard, 1958), 70–71.

9. Ottevaere–van Praag, *La Littérature pour la jeunesse*, 339–40; Marie-Thérèse Latzarus, *La Littérature enfantine dans la seconde moitié du XIXe siècle* (Paris: Presses universitaires de France, 1924), 287.

10. Maurice Crubellier, *L'Enfance et la jeunesse dans la société française 1800–1950* (Paris: Armand Colin, 1979), 362–63.
11. Louis Pergaud, *La Guerre des boutons* (Paris: Mercure de France, 1963), 9.
12. These figures are taken from Annie Renonciat, *Livre mon ami. Lectures enfantines 1914–54* (Paris: Mairie de Paris, 1992), 11.
13. Emile Moselly, 'L'Ogre et le Petit Poucet', quoted in Renonciat, *Livre mon ami*, 12.
14. Mission statement of Larousse's *Livres roses series*, quoted in Renonciat, *Livre mon ami*, 12.
15. Laura Noesser, (ed), *Fonds ancien de littérature pour la jeunesse. Catalogue de livres imprimés avant 1914.* (Paris: Bibliothèque de l'Heure Joyeuse, 1984), 66.
16. Renonciat, *Livre mon ami*, 12.
17. Ibid, 16. *Flambeau, chien de guerre*, is discussed in more detail in chapter 6.
18. Renonciat, *Livre mon ami*, 57.
19. Latzarus, *La Littérature enfantine* was published in 1924; and Paul Hazard *Les Livres, les enfants et les hommes* was published in 1932.
20. Noesser, 'Le Livre pour enfants', 463.
21. The Bibliothèque de l'Heure Joyeuse is situated in the rue des Prêtres Saint-Severin on the Left Bank. Its holdings are a major resource for the study of children's literature.
22. The theme appears most notably in *Genitrix* (1923) and *Le Sagouin* (1951).
23. Renonciat, *Livre mon ami*, 69.
24. Mathilde Leriche, *Cinquante ans de littérature de jeunesse, quatre conférences sur la littérature pour les enfants en France en 1939* (Paris: Magnard et L'Ecole, 1939), 29, quoted in Renonciat, *Livre mon ami*, 69–70.
25. Jean Perrot, 'Patapoufs et Filifers: une aubaine pour la théorie', in *Littérature de jeunesse, incertaines frontières*, ed. Isabelle Nières-Chevrel (Paris: Gallimard Jeunesse, 2005), 229, suggests that Maurois and Bruller were influenced by Grandville's *Un autre monde* (1844), in which class distinctions are ridiculed by the portrayal of the relationships between grotesquely tall and thin and short and fat people.
26. This is an example of Jean Giraudoux's argument, dramatised in *La Guerre de Troie n'aura pas lieu* (1935), that relatively insignificant places or people can easily become the catalyst for war.
27. See Judith Proud, 'Introduction', in *Children and Propaganda: 'Il était une fois': Fiction and Fairy Tale in Vichy France* (Oxford: Intellect, 1995), 13–14.
28. Renonciat, *Livre mon ami*, 93.
29. Proud, *Children and Propaganda*, 13. Renonciat, *Livre mon ami*, lists few new works in this period.

30. Proud, *Children and Propaganda*, 14.

31. Ibid., 16–17.

32. W. D. Halls, *The Youth of Vichy France* (Oxford: Clarendon, 1981), 168.

33. Youki Desnos, *Avant-Propos* in *Chantefables et Chantefleurs* (Paris: Gründ, 1955), quoted in *Chantefables et Chantefleurs de Robert Desnos* (Paris: Gründ, 1995), illustrated by Zdenka Krejcová, n.p.

34. Halls, *The Youth of Vichy France*, 439, n.32; 148.

35. Serge Dalens is the pseudonym of Yves de Verdilhac, who was one of the founder members of the Signe de Piste collection.

36. See the websites http://www.sdp-livres.com and http://www.signe-de-piste.com.

37. Serge Dalens, quoted on http://www.sdp-livres.com.

38. Serge Dalens, *La Mort d'Eric* (1943; reprint, Paris: Fleurus, 1996), 200.

39. Ibid., 200–201.

40. Ibid., 204.

41. Ganna Ottevaere–van Praag, *Histoire du récit pour la jeunesse au vingtième siècle* (Bruxelles: Peter Lang, 1999), 23.

42. Colette Vivier, *La Maison des petits bonheurs* (1939; reprint, Paris: Casterman, 2004), 267.

43. Danièle Henky, *L'Art de la fugue en littérature de jeunesse. Giono, Bosco, Le Clézio, maîtres d'école buissonnière* (Bern, Switzerland: Peter Lang, 2004), 6. The publishing ethos of the Bibliothèque blanche, to prove a library for juvenile readers 'd'une valeur littéraire certaine' is stated inside each volume.

44. R. T. Sussex, *Henri Bosco, Poet-Novelist* (Christchurch, New Zealand: University of Canterbury Press, 1966), 17.

45. Ibid., 60.

46. Henky, *L'Art de la fugue en littérature de jeunesse*, 6. The frequent presence of this text in school syllabuses may however account for its sales.

47. Ibid., 125–26.

48. Henri Bosco, *L'Enfant et la rivière* (1945; reprint, Paris: Gallimard, Folio Junior, 1979), 84.

49. Henky, *L'Art de la fugue en littérature de jeunesse*, 149.

50. Bosco, *L'Enfant et la rivière*, 116. Henky, *L'Art de la fugue en littérature de jeunesse*, 136–45, makes extensive comparisons between this scene and that of the fête étrange in *Le Grand Meaulnes*.

51. Jean Giono, *Oeuvres romanesques complètes*, ed. Robert Ricatte (Paris: Gallimard, 1980), 5:1402–7.

52. Henky, *L'Art de la fugue en littérature de jeunesse*, 63–64.

53. Giono, 'L'Homme qui plantait des arbres' *Oeuvres romanesques complètes*, 762.

54. Henky, *L'Art de la fugue en littérature de jeunesse*, 71.

55. Ibid., 50–54.

56. Ibid., 61.

CHAPTER 6

1. Laura Noesser, 'Le Livre pour enfants', in *Histoire de l'édition française*, ed. Henri Martin and Roger Chartier, vol. 4, *Le Livre concurrencé 1900–1950* (Paris: Promodis, 1985), 457.

2. Maurice Crubellier, *L'Enfance et la jeunesse dans la société française 1800–1950* (Paris: Armand Colin, 1979), 336.

3. Marie-Thérèse Latzarus, *La Littérature enfantine dans la seconde moitié du XIXe siècle* (Paris: Presses universitaires de France, 1924), 140–50, gives an account of the content and popularity of the *Images d'Epinal*. The publication of Epinal prints in America from 1888 have been seen as an influence on the beginnings of American newspaper comic strips. See Dennis Gifford, 'Popular Literature: Comics, Dime Novels, Pulps and Penny Dreadfuls', in *International Companion Encyclopedia of Children's Literature*, ed. Peter Hunt and Sheila Ray (London: Routledge, 1996), 253.

4. Ségolène Le Men, 'Les Abécédaires à figures en France au XIXe siècle' in Glénisson, 'Le Livre pour la jeunesse', in *Histoire de l'édition française*, ed. Henri Martin and Roger Chartier, vol. 3, *Le Temps des Editeurs, du romantisme à la Belle Epoque* (Paris: Promodis, 1986), 418–19; 418–19; Le Men, *Les abécédaires français illustrés du XIXe siècle* (Paris: Promodis, 1984).

5. See Geneviève Lacambre, 'Les milieux japonisants à Paris (1860-80)', in *Japonisme in Art: An International Symposium*, ed. Society for Study of Japonisme, (Committee of Year 2001 and Kodanska International, Tokyo, 1980), 43–55.

6. See Isabelle Nières-Chevrel, 'In and Out of History: *Jeanne d'Arc* by Maurice Boutet de Monvel', 33–40, and Penny Brown, 'Reinventing the Maid: Images of Joan of Arc in French and English Children's Literature', 41–52, both in *The Presence of the Past in Children's Literature*, ed. Ann Lawson Lucas (Westport, Conn.: Praeger, 2003).

7. For a full discussion of different interpretations of Jeanne d'Arc, see Marina Warner, *Joan of Arc: the Image of Female Heroism* (Harmondsworth, England: Penguin, 1983).

8. For other examples, see Roger Odin, *Jeanne d'Arc à l'école: Essai sémiotique* (Paris: Editions Klincksieck, 1980).

9. Maurice Boutet de Monvel, *La Vie de Jeanne d'Arc* (Paris: Plon, Nourrit, 1896), 4.

10. Nières-Chevrel, 'In and Out of History', 33.

11. See http://www.benjaminrabier.com.

12. Hergé claimed he had not consciously modelled his creation on Rabier's character; see Matthew Screech, *Masters of the Ninth Art: Bandes dessinées and Franco-Belgian Identity* (Liverpool, England: Liverpool University Press, 2005), 18.

13. The success of Rudyard Kipling's *The Jungle Book* (1894), *The Second Jungle Book* (1895), and *Just So Stories for Little Children* (1902) contributed to a large extent to the popularity in France as in Britain of stories in which animals played a central or allegorical role.

14. Annette Becker, 'Postface', in Benjamin Rabier, *Flambeau, chien de guerre* (Paris: Tallandier, 2003), 70. The text was originally published by Tallandier in 1916.

15. Rabier, *Flambeau*, 63.

16. Becker, 'Postface', 66.

17. I am indebted to the discussion by François Robichon at www.benjaminrabier.com for some of the information in this section.

18. The allusions here are to the 1936 and 1938 elections and the gains of the Popular Front leading to the premierships of Léon Blum and Edouard Deladier, respectively.

19. Ganna Ottevaere–van Praag, *La Littérature pour la jeunesse*, 362.

20. Noesser, 'Le Livre pour enfants', 458.

21. Ottevaere–van Praag, *La Littérature pour la jeunesse*, 363.

22. See Thierry Groensteen and Benoît Peeters, *Töpffer: L'Invention de la bande dessinée* (Paris: Hermann, 1994).

23. Christophe referred to Töpffer as 'mon maître et mon modèle'; cited in François Caradec, *Histoire de la littérature enfantine en France* (Paris: Albin Michel, 1977), 198.

24. Marjorie Alessandrini, *Encyclopédie des bandes dessinées* (Paris: Albin Michel, 1986), 60.

25. Caradec, *Histoire de la littérature enfantine en France*, 196.

26. We read, 'une trajectoire parabolique d'un mouvement uniformement accélérée, selon la loi très connue de la chute des corps'. This strip can be viewed at http://www.chez.com/aws2/fenou3.htm.

27. The series are *Les Facéties du Sapeur Camember* (1890–96), *Le Savant Cosinus* (1893–99), and *Les Malices de Plick et Ploc* (1894–1904).

28. *L'Idée fixe du savant Cosinus*, quoted in Caradec, *Histoire de la littérature enfantine en France*, 198.

29. A survey of magazines published during this period can be found in Alain Fourment, *Histoire de la presse des jeunes et des journaux d'enfants (1768-1988)* (Paris: Editions Ecole, 1987).

30. Ibid., 196.

31. J. P. Gourevitch, at http://jpgour.club.fr/presse.html, gives the number of magazines that began in or after 1919 as a staggering ninety, many of which were very shortlived, and only twenty lasted more than ten years.

32. *Mon Camarade*, quoted in Fourment, *Histoire de la presse*, 176.

33. *Benjamin*, quoted in Fourment, *Histoire de la presse*, 186.

34. No direct source stated, quoted in Fourment, *Histoire de la presse*, 186.

35. Judith Proud, *Children and Propaganda. 'Il était une fois. . . ': Fiction and Fairy Tale in Vichy France* (Oxford: Intellect, 1995), 23.

36. Ibid., 24.
37. For a full discussion of *Le Téméraire*, see Pascal Ory, *Le Petit Nazi illustré* (Paris: Editions Albatross, 1979).
38. Ibid., 36.
39. Proud, *Children and Propaganda*, 14.
40. *Siroco*, quoted in Annie Renonciat, *Livre mon ami. Lectures enfantines 1914–54* (Paris: Mairie de Paris, 1992), 95.
41. *Le Jeune Patriote* eventually became *Vaillant*. See Laurent Marie, '*Le Grêlé 7/13*, a (Communist) Children's Guide to the Resistance', in *The Francophone Bande Dessinée*, ed. Charles Forsdick, Lawrence Grove, and Libby McQuillan (Amsterdam: Rodopi, 2005), 74–82.
42. Marie-Anne Couderc, *Bécassine inconnue* (Paris: CNRS Editions, 2000), 27. Couderc gives a full account of the origins and development of the *Bécassine* albums.
43. Ibid., 31. An exhibition of dolls and their accessories associated with *La Semaine de Suzette* was held at the Musée de la Poupée in the spring of 2005.
44. Her appearance was modified slightly by the various artists responsible at different times for the strip. See Couderc, *Bécassine inconnue*, for full details.
45. Francis Lacassin, *Pour un 9ème art, la bande dessinée* (Paris: U.G.E., 1971), 131.
46. Caumery and J.-P. Pinchon, *Bécassine fait du scoutisme* (1931; reprint, Paris: Gautier-Languereau, 1993), 1. See the discussion of the different narrative strategies in Couderc, *Bécassine inconnue*, 249–54.
47. Fourment, *Histoire de la presse*, 195, relates that these three albums were seized by German occupying forces in June 1940.
48. Caumery and J.-P. Pinchon, *Bécassine pendant la Grande Guerre* (Paris: Gautier-Languereau, 1915), 61.
49. Couderc, *Bécassine inconnue*, 54, attributes this change to the birth of Maurice Languereau's own daughter in 1922.
50. Charles Forsdick describes this as the creation of a 'temporal alterity which forces Breton culture into the past' and a 'fixity and denial of coevalness'; see Forsdick, 'Exoticising the *Domestique*: Bécassine, Brittany and the Beauty of the Dead', in *The Francophone Bande Dessinée*, ed. Charles Forsdick, Lawrence Grove, and Libby McQuillan (Amsterdam: Rodopi, 2005), 34.
51. Examples of the covers of the Lili albums can be seen at http://membres-lycos.fr/tweetiz. On the covers of the earlier albums, Lili is depicted as a young girl wearing a white blouse and red checked skirt or red trousers.
52. Marjorie Alessandrini, *Encyclopédie des bandes dessinées*, 206. Examples of the album covers can be viewed at http://matthieu.chevrier.free.fr/.

53. Examples of *Bibi Fricotin* covers can be seen at http://www.coolfrench-comics.com/bibifricotin.htm and http://membres.lycos.fr/starmars/bibi-fricotin2.html.

54. Ottevaere–van Praag, *La Littérature pour la jeunesse*, 308.

55. Alessandrini, *Encyclopédie des bandes dessinées*, 226.

56. Ibid.

57. Crubellier, *L'Enfance et la jeunesse*, 368–69.

58. Latzarus, *La Littérature enfantine*, 158.

59. Georges Sadoul, *Ce que lisent les enfants* (Paris: Bureau d'Editions, 1938), 15.

60. Jean de Trigon, *Histoire de la littérature enfantine de ma Mère l'Oye au roi Babar* (Paris: Hachette, 1950), 175.

61. The full text of this law can be viewed at http://homoedu.free.fr.

62. Paul Faucher founded the Bureau Français d'Education Nouvelle and wrote a 'manifesto' explaining these concepts in 1926. See http://ecoles-differentes.free.fr/art4j.htm.

63. Noesser, 'Le Livre pour enfants', 458.

64. The wild animal books were acclaimed in the English translations for their realistic and unsentimental approach to nature study, the title pages describing the books as having 'that delicate gaiety which shows that they come from the French'. See *Père Castor's Wild Animal Books*, translated by Rose Fyleman (London: George Allen and Unwin, n.d).

65. Marc Soriano, *Guide de la littérature pour la jeunesse* (Paris: Flammarion, 1974), 236.

66. See http://www.flammarion.com.

67. Bettina Hürlimann, *Three Centuries of Children's Books in Europe* (London: Oxford University Press, 1967), 195.

68. Caradec, *Histoire de la littérature enfantine en France*, 213. The last two albums, published after Jean de Brunhoff's death, contained separately published and/or unfinished episodes.

69. Caradec, *Histoire de la littérature enfantine en France*, 214; Hurlimann, *Three Centuries of Children's Books*, 196. The Babar stories were first translated into English in 1933 with a preface by A. A. Milne.

70. See www.signe-de-piste.com/page125.

71. Screech, *Masters of the Ninth Art*, 53.

72. A full list of titles of Spirou albums and their creators can be found at http://www.en.wikipedia.org/wiki/Spirou.

73. Screech, *Masters of the Ninth Art*, 70, suggests that this is intended to reflect Gaston's mind.

74. It has been argued that France and Belgium have a sense of shared cultural identity that is particularly manifest in the bande dessinée and in Tintin in particular; see Screech, *Masters of the Ninth Art*, 2–4.

75. Harry Thompson, *Tintin, Hergé and His Creation* (London: Hodder and Stoughton, 1991), 10.

76. Michael Farr, *Tintin: Le Rêve et la Réalité* (Brussels: Moulinsart, 2001), 17. See also Thompson, *Tintin, Hergé and His Creation*, 217–18, for publication details.

77. See Alessandrini, *Encyclopédie des bandes dessinées*, 113–14; and Screech, *Masters of the Ninth Art*, 27–28.

78. It was included in the first volume of the *Archives Hergé* published in 1973, and a facsimile of the black-and-white original appeared in album form in 1999, to celebrate Tintin's 70th anniversary. Hergé's portrait of the Soviet Union was based almost entirely on Joseph Douillet's *Moscou sans voiles* (Paris: Editions Spes, 1928). See Farr, *Tintin: Le Rêve et la Réalité*, 13.

79. Interview with Hergé in Numa Sadoul, quoted in Numa Sadoul, *Entretiens avec Hergé* (Tournai, Belgium: Casterman, 1989), 74.

80. Arguments for and against the view of Hergé as a collaborator and an anti-Semite were reviewed in Tim Judah, 'Tintin in the Dock', *Guardian Weekend*, 30 January 1999, 8–18.

81. Judah, 'Tintin in the Dock', 14.

82. Gaston Leroux (1868–1927) was the author of *Le Fantôme de l'Opéra* (1910) and a number of novels featuring the amateur detective Rouletabille.

83. Screech, *Masters of the Ninth Art*, 23.

84. Ibid., 25.

85. Farr, *Tintin: Le Rêve et la Réalité*, analyses this realism album by album.

86. Hergé himself had a close Chinese friend of the same name, who was missing for many years after the Cultural Revolution of the 1960s and with whom he was reunited only in 1981. Judah, 'Tintin in the Dock', 18.

87. On the occasion of the first American landing on the moon, a cartoon appeared depicting Tintin welcoming astronaut Neil Armstrong as he stepped from the lunar landing craft.

88. Hergé is reported to have urged his publisher to print *Le Sceptre d'Ottokar* quickly for maximum impact as it was based on the imminent invasion of Albania; Judah, 'Tintin in the Dock', 14.

89. Screech, *Masters of the Ninth Art*, 45.

90. Hergé, *Tintin et les Picaros* (Tournai, Belgium: Casterman, 1976), 11, 62.

91. Judah, 'Tintin in the Dock', 18.

92. See, for example, http://www.tintin.com and http://www.tintin.free.fr.

93. Screech, *Masters of the Ninth Art*, 86.

94. Ibid., 88.

95. In the English translations by Anthea Bell and Derek Hockridge the names are equally inspired: Idéfix becomes Dogmatix, the Druid Panoramix is named appropriately Getafix, the bard Cacofonix, and amongst the Britons are Dipsomaniax and Hiphiphurrax.

96. René Goscinny and Albert Uderzo, *Astérix gladiateur* (Paris: Dargaud, 1964), 42.

97. Screech, *Masters of the Ninth Art*, 81.

CHAPTER 7

1. See, as examples of the merveilleux used for a didatic purpose, Mme Le Prince de Beaumont, *Magasin des enfans* (1756); and Mme de Genlis, *Les Veillées du château* (1784).
2. Ottevaere–van Praag, Ganna, *Histoire du récit pour la jeunesse au XXe siècle (1929-2000)* (Brussels: Peter Lang, 1999), 23.
3. P.-G. Castex, *Le Conte fantastique en France* (Paris: José Corti, 1951), 8; Tzvetan Todorov, *Introduction à la littérature fantastique* (Paris: Editions du Seuil, 1970), 29.
4. Todorov, *Introduction*, 59.
5. Charles Vildrac, *L'Ile rose* (1924; reprint, Paris: Albin Michel, 1929), 93.
6. Ibid., 170.
7. André Maurois, *Le Pays des 36,000 volontés* (1928; reprint, Paris: Hachette, 2003).
8. See Martin Steins, *Blaise Cendrars: bilans nègres*. Archives des Lettres Modernes. Etudes de critique et d'histoire littéraire 169 (Paris: Minard, 1977), 5–12.
9. Blaise Cendrars, *Petits contes nègres pour les enfants des blancs* (1928; reprint, Paris: Gallimard, 1998), 5.
10. Steins, 16–18. The title of Cendrars's *Comment les blancs sont d'anciens noirs* (1930) suggests a view that white people represented a higher level of evolution.
11. Cendrars, *Petits contes nègres*, 94.
12. Ibid., 14.
13. Ibid., 36.
14. Marcel Aymé, 'Préface' in *Les Contes du chat perché* (1939; reprint, Paris: Gallimard, 1973), 7.
15. Marcel Aymé, unnamed source, quoted in François Caradec, *Histoire de la littérature enfantine en France* (Paris: Albin Michel, 1977), 219.
16. Aymé, 'Préface', 7.
17. Jean-Louis Dumont, *Marcel Aymé et le merveilleux* (Paris: Nouvelles Editions Debresse, 1967), 93.
18. Aymé, 'Préface', 13.
19. Dumont, *Marcel Aymé et le merveilleux*, 88.
20. Judith Proud, *Children and Propaganda. 'Il était une fois. . . ': Fiction and Fairy Tale in Vichy France* (Oxford: Intellect, 1995), 27.
21. Jack Zipes, *Fairy Tales and Fables from Weimar Days* (Madison: University of Wisconsin Press, 12). Zipes's introduction charts the development of the politicising of fairy tales in Germany during this period. Whereas before the war, the tales of the Brothers Grimm were standard reading in German schools, they were banned by the Allied Occupation forces after 1945 because they were felt to have contributed to Nazi barbarity.

22. I am indebted to Judith Proud for the reproduction and discussion of these tales in *Children and Propaganda*. Proud analyses these two tales in detail and discusses their shortcomings as propaganda allegories.

23. Proud, *Children and Propaganda*, 79–84.

24. This tale is associated directly with the Germans as censorship inscriptions link it with *Propaganda Abteilung* that was operating in Paris; Proud, *Children and Propaganda*, 26.

25. This is noted by Proud, *Children and Propaganda*, 36, to be inspired by the discovery of murdered Polish officers in the forest of Katyn in 1943.

26. Proud, *Children and Propaganda*, 86–87.

27. Ibid., 55.

28. Ibid., 8, 40.

29. It is interesting to note that an external force (a storm) is blamed for wreaking havoc, thus avoiding apportioning of blame to any internal element (the Vichy régime).

30. For a discussion of such biographies, see Proud, *Children and Propaganda*, chap. 4.

31. Jean Perrot, 'Préface' to Danièle Henky, *L'art de la fugue en littérature de jeunesse* (Bern, Switzerland: Peter Lang, 2004), xvii.

32. Brian Masters, *A Student's Guide to Saint-Exupéry* (London: Heinemann, 1972), 90.

33. Antoine de Saint-Exupéry, *Le Petit Prince* (Paris: Gallimard, 1997), 5.

34. Masters, *A Student's Guide*, 6. Saint-Exupéry had also worked as a pilot for the mail courier firm Latécoère in South America in the late 1920s.

35. It is tempting to wonder whether Saint-Exupéry may have been inspired by an episode in some versions of the *Robinson suisse* in which the family watch a huge boa consume their donkey whole.

36. Saint-Exupéry, *Le Petit Prince*, 20.

37. Caradec, *Histoire de la littérature enfantine en France*, 222, is of the opinion that these are 'pastiches de dialogues d'instruction, qui peuvent faire sourire les adultes, mais désorientent inutilement de jeunes lecteurs'.

38. Saint-Exupéry, *Le Petit Prince*, 72.

39. Caradec, *Histoire de la littérature enfantine en France*, 222, suggests that it is not a successful book for children but 'un conte pour adultes qui refusent de grandir, écrit en un faux style de littérature enfantine'.

40. Maurice Druon, *Tistou les pouces verts* (1957; reprint, Paris: Livre de Poche, 1968), 9.

41. Ibid., 162.

42. Ibid., 184.

43. J. M. G. Le Clézio, *L'Inconnu de la terre* (Paris: Gallimard, 1978), 240.

44. Ibid., 226, 225. See also Jean Onimus, *Pour lire Le Clézio* (Paris: Presses Universitaires de France, 1994), 127.

45. Henky, *L'Art de la fugue en littérature*, 170.

46. Ibid., 162–63. Le Clézio has stated that his desire from childhood was to write a novel like Jules Verne. See Pierre Lhoste, *Conversations avec J. M. G. Le Clézio* (Paris: Seghers, 1971), 61.

47. J. M. G. Le Clézio, *Voyage au pay des arbres* (Paris: Gallimard, 1978), 8, 22.

48. Henky, *L'art de la fugue*, 162–63, argues that the effect of Le Clézio's portrayal of his child characters is to 'envelopper . . . son lecteur dans le tissu de la réalité'.

49. Claude Roy, *La Maison qui s'envole* (1977) (Paris: Gallimard, 1997), 53, 67.

50. Ibid., 32.

51. Jacques Prévert, 'L'Enfant abandonné', in *Spectacle*, in Jacques Prévert, *Oeuvres complètes*, ed. Danièle Gasiglia-Laster and Arnaud Laster (Paris: Gallimard, 1992), 2:298.

52. Jacques Prévert, 'Le Cancre', in *Paroles*, in Prévert, *Oeuvres complètes*, 2:43.

53. The original edition is reproduced in Jacques Prévert, *Oeuvres complètes*, 1:901–66.

54. Jacques Prévert, *Contes pour enfants pas sages* (Paris: Gallimard, 2005), 13.

55. Prévert, *Contes pour enfants pas sages*, 28.

56. See Prévert, *Oeuvres complètes*, 1:1382.

57. Ibid., 1:176.

58. Pierre Gripari, *La Sorcière de la rue Mouffetard, et autres contes de la rue Broca* (Paris: Folio Junior, 1997), 9.

59. Ibid., 12.

60. Ibid., 15.

61. See, for example, the successful series in English of rewritings of classic fairy tales titled *Seriously Silly Fairy Stories*, with their scatalogical humour and mocking of fairytale conventions.

62. Gripari, *La Sorcière*, 88.

63. Ibid., 106.

64. Pierre Gripari, *Histoire du prince Pipo, de Pipo le cheval et de la princesse Popi* (Paris: Hachette, 1997), 190.

65. *George's Marvellous Medicine* (1981), *Matilda* (1988), *The B.F.G.* (1982), *The Twits* (1980).

66. Publisher comments, in Pef, *La Belle lisse poire du prince Motordu* (Paris: Gallimard, 1980), back cover.

67. Pef, *La Belle lisse poire du prince Motordu*, n.p.

68. Jean Perrot, *Du jeu, des enfants et des livres* (Paris: Editions du Cercle de la Librairie, 1987), 148.

69. Prince Motordu appears in other titles such as *Motordu: champignon olympique* (2000), *Motordu et le fantôme du chapeau* (1999), and *Motordu et les petits hommes vers* (1998), which gesture humorously towards the typical plots of adventure stories.

70. Pef also wrote an *Encyclopefdie* (1997) that turns the traditional formal dictionary into a source of linguistic fun.

71. Jean Perrot, *Jeux et enjeux du livre d'enfance et de jeunesse* (Paris: Editions du Cercle de la Librairie, 1999), 338, describes Pef's work as 'cette dramatisation de l'absurde qui place la morale même à la limite de ce qui peut être toléré'. This issue is discussed in relation to these two texts in Julie Parizot, 'Entre humour et l'amour des images: Pef et son univers des mots rordus', available online at http://jeunet.uni-lille3.fr.

72. Charlotte Ruffault, 'La Bibliothèque rose souffle ses 150 bougies!' interview, available online at http://cultureetloisirs.france2.fr/livres/dossiers/18797459-fr.php?page=5.

73. Ibid.

74. *Winx Club. L'Université des fées*, adapted by Sophie Marvaud (Paris: Hachette, 2005), 84.

75. Note also the popularity of the Dungeons and Dragons board and computer games, and the Chair de poule (Goosebumps) series, a collection of novels published in the mid-1990s that feature the supernatural.

76. J. K. Rowling, *Harry Potter à l'école des sorciers*, trans. Jean-François Ménard (Paris: Gallimard, 1998).

77. *Guide FNAC. 200 romans jeunesse: La bibliothèque idéale des 7/12 ans* (Paris: FNAC, 2004), 139.

78. Ruffault interview.

79. Eric L'Homme, *Qadehar le Sorcier* (Paris: Gallimard, 2001).

80. The sequels are *Le Seigneur Sha* (2002) and *Le Visage de l'Ombre* (2003).

CHAPTER 8

1. See John Ardagh, *France Today* (London: Penguin, 1995), 16; see various useful articles in Malcolm Cook, ed., *French Culture since 1945* (Harlow, England: Longman, 1993).

2. Alan Pedley, 'The Media', in Cook, ed., *French Culture since 1945*, 171–74, discusses the influence of television as 'panacea or monster'.

3. Alex Hughes, 'Gender Issues', in Cook, ed., *French Culture since 1945*, 247.

4. Ardagh, *France Today*, 19–20.

5. Ganna Ottevaere–van Praag, *Histoire du récit pour la jeunesse au XXe siècle (1929-2000)* (Brussels: Peter Lang, 1999), 167.

6. Ottevaere–van Praag, *Histoire du récit*, 219.

7. See *Guide FNAC. 200 romans jeunesse. La bibliothèque idéale des 7/12 ans* (Paris, France: FNAC, 2004).

8. Marjorie Hourihan, *Deconstructing the Hero: Literary Theory and Children's Literature* (London: Routledge, 1997), 92.

9. Details of dates and titles of publication of the French translations can be found at http://perso.orange.fr/lebrunf9/bd/bverte/cinq.html.

10. See the website http://perso.orange.fr/lebrunf9/bd/bverte for many fascinating details of the series discussed in this section.

11. Humphrey Carpenter and Mari Prichard, *The Oxford Companion to Children's Literature* (Oxford: Oxford University Press, 1984), 166. *Le Cheval sans tête* won the Salon de l'enfance award in 1955. Berna, like Blyton, devoted himself to writing for the young and produced novels about space travel as well as mystery thrillers.

12. Paul Berna, *Le Cheval sans tête* (1955; reprint, Paris: Hachette, 2005), 215.

13. Ibid., 216.

14. Jean-Philippe Arrou-Vignod, *Le Professor a disparu* (Paris: Gallimard, 1989), 10.

15. Jean-Philippe Arrou-Vignod, quoted in *Guide FNAC*, 218.

16. The six other novels involving the same characters are *P. P. Cul-Vert, détective privé*, 1993; *P.P. et le mystère de Loch Ness*, 1998; *Sur la piste de la salamandre*, 1995; *Enquête au collège*, 1991; and *Le Club des inventeurs*, 2000.

17. A list and brief description of the Fantômette novels and other associated information can be found at http://millepompons.free.fr. In 2006, Chaulet produced *Le Retour de Fantômette* to celebrate the 150th anniversary of the Bibliothèque rose.

18. There are four friends in the first book, but the fourth, Isabelle, does not appear in subsequent books.

19. Hourihan, *Deconstructing the Hero*, 206.

20. Nicholas Atkin, *The French at War 1934–1944* (London: Longman, 2001), 98. In June 2006, a landmark ruling ordered the SNCF and the French Government to pay damages of 60,000 Euros to claimants as compensation for the deportation of Jews during the Second World War.

21. Lydia Kokkola, *Representing the Holocaust in Children's Literature* (New York: Routledge, 2003), 11.

22. Ibid., 16.

23. Ibid., 2.

24. Ottevaere–van Praag, *Histoire du récit*, 205.

25. The final chapter of Kokkola, *Representing the Holocaust*, considers this problem.

26. Ottevaere–van Praag, *Histoire du récit*, 207. See also, for example, Charles Perrault's Mère l'Oye (1697), as well as Mentor, the tutor of the young Télémaque in François Fénelon's *Les Aventures de Télémaque* (1699).

27. Claude Gutman, interview, in supplement to *La Maison vide* (Paris: Gallimard, 1993), 107.

28. Ibid., 107.
29. Ibid., 108.
30. Gutman, *La Maison vide*, 23.
31. Ibid., 22.
32. Ibid., 31.
33. Gutman interview, 112.
34. Gutman, *La Maison vide*, 102.
35. Gutman, *La Maison vide*, 92, Gutman interview 108.
36. Yaël Hassan, *A Paris sous l'Occupation* (Paris: Casterman, 2000), 17.
37. Nicole Ciravegna, *La Rue qui descend vers la mer* (1971; reprint, Paris: Magnard, 2005). The 2005 edition contains the second part, originally titled *Aldo et Sarah*.
38. The Vieille Charité now houses a museum and is an important historical landmark in Marseilles.
39. Gutman, *La Maison vide*, 56.
40. Kokkola, *Representing the Holocaust*, 134.
41. John Talbott, *The War Without a Name: France in Algeria, 1954–1962* (London: Faber and Faber, 1981), cited in Philip Dine, *Images of the Algerian War: French Fiction and Film, 1954–1992* (Oxford: Clarendon, 1994), 6–7.
42. Jean-Paul Nozière, *Un été algérien* (1993; reprint, Paris: Gallimard, 1998), 84.
43. Ibid., 10.
44. Ibid., 66.
45. Julia Eccleshare, 'Teenage Fiction: Realism, Romances, Contemporary Problem Novels', in *International Companion Encyclopedia of Children's Literature*, ed. Peter Hunt and Sheila Ray (London: Routledge, 1996), 387.
46. See the website http://susie.morgenstern.free.fr/siteweb/AE.htm.
47. *Guide FNAC*, 41.
48. Susie Morgenstern, *La Sixième* (Paris: L'Ecole des loisirs, 1984), 140, 141.
49. Susie Morgenstern, *L'Amerloque* (Paris: Médium, 1992), 14.
50. Ibid., 75.
51. Ibid., 123.
52. Valérie Dayre, *Lundi, Gaspard prend le train* (1999), *Mardi, Gaspard va à l'école* (2000), *Mercredi, Gaspard est amoureux* (2000), *Jeudi, Gaspard a mal aux dents* (2001), *Vendredi, Gaspard dans la nuit* (2002), *Samedi, Gaspard fait l'andouille* (2002), and *Dimanche, Gaspard s'amuse* (2003), are all published by L'Ecole des Loisirs in Paris.
53. Valérie Dayre, *C'est la vie, Lili* (Paris: L'Ecole des Loisirs, 2002), 116.
54. Ibid., 152.
55. Valérie Dayre, *Les Nouveaux malheurs de Sophie* (Paris: Médium, 2001), 164.

56. Ibid., 163.
57. Valérie Dayre, *Comme le pas d'un fantôme* (Paris: L'Ecole des Loisirs, 2002), 7.
58. Ibid., 153.
59. Ibid., 8.
60. Valérie Dayre, *Je veux voir Marcos* (Paris: L'Ecole des Loisirs, 1998), 175.
61. For various essays on this topic, see Jean Perrot, ed., *L'Humour dans la littérature de jeunesse* (Paris: Editions In Press, 2000).
62. Sempé-Goscinny, *Le Petit Nicolas* (Paris: Denoël, 1997), 44, 21. In 2004, eighty prevously unpublished Petit Nicolas stories discovered by Anne Goscinny (Goscinny's daughter) were published in the best-selling *Histoires inédites du Petit Nicolas*.
63. Sempé-Goscinny, *Le Petit Nicolas*, 79.
64. Ibid., 87.
65. See Charlotte Ruffault, 'La Bibliothèque rose souffle ses 150 bougies!' interview, available online at http://cultureetloisirs.france2.fr/livres/dossiers/18797459-fr.php?page=5.
66. Marie-Aude Murail, 'Dialogue avec Nadège', in *Littérature de jeunesse, incertaines frontières*, ed. Isabelle Nières-Chevrel (Paris: Gallimard, 2005), 166.
67. See Michel Foucault, *Histoire de la sexualité*, vol. 1, *La Volonté de savoir*, (Paris: Gallimard, 1976).
68. See BBC News item of 2004 online at http://news.bbc.co.uk/2/hi/europe.

CONCLUSION

1. Zep, *L'Amour, c'est pô propre . . .* (Grenoble: Glénat, 1993), 48.
2. Marie-Aude Murail, 'Dialogue avec Nadège', in *Littérature de jeunesse, incertaines frontières*, ed. Isabelle Nières-Chevrel (Paris: Gallimard, 2005), 161.
3. David Gascoigne, *Michel Tournier* (Oxford: Berg, 1996), 168–69.
4. *Guide FNAC. 200 romans jeunesse: La bibliothèque idéale des 7/12 ans* (Paris: FNAC, 2004), 7.

BIBLIOGRAPHY

Aberger, P. 'The Portrayal of Blacks in Jules Verne's *Voyages extraordinaires*'. *French Review* 53 (1979): 199–206.

Alessandrini, Marjorie. *Encyclopédie des bandes dessinées*. Paris: Albin Michel, 1986.

Anderson, R. D. *Education in France 1848–1870*. Oxford: Clarendon, 1975.

Andries, Lise. *La Bibliothèque bleue au dix-huitième siècle: une tradition éditoriale*. Oxford: Voltaire Foundation, 1989.

Ardagh, John. *France Today*. London: Penguin, 1995.

Ariès, Philippe. *Centuries of Childhood*, trans. Robert Baldick. London: Jonathan Cape, 1962.

Ariès, Philippe, and George Duby, eds. *A History of Private Life*, 5 vols. Cambridge, Mass.: Belknap Press of Harvard University Press, 1990.

Atkin, Nicholas. *The French at War 1934–1944*. London: Longman, 2001.

Bancel, Nicolas, Pascal Blanchard, and Laurent Gervereau, eds. *Images et colonies. Iconographie et propagande coloniale sur l'Afrique française de 1880 à 1962*. Paris: BDIC-ACHAC, 1993.

Bastaire, Jean. 'Pour une "lecture-enfant" d'Erckmann-Chatrian'. In *Erckmann-Chatrian. Entre imagination, fantaisie et réalisme: du conte au conte d'histoire*, edited by François Marotin, 19–25. Phalsbourg, France: Editions du Musée de Phalsbourg, 1999.

Beauvoir, Simone de. *Mémoires d'une jeune fille rangée*. Paris: Gallimard, 1958.

Becker, Annette. 'Postface'. In Benjamin Rabier, *Flambeau, chien de guerre*, 65–70. Paris: Tallandier, 2003.

Beer, Gillian. *Darwin's Plots: Evolutionary Narratives in Darwin, George Eliot and Nineteenth-Century Fiction*. London: Routledge and Kegan Paul, 1983.

Bellet, Roger. *L'Aventure dans la littérature populaire au XIXᵉ siècle*. Lyon, France: Presses universitaires de Lyon, 1985.

Bertrand, Marc, *Popular Traditions and Learned Culture in France*, Stanford French and Italian Studies, 35. Saratoga: Anma Libri, 1985.

Bezucha, Robert J., 'An Introduction to the History'. In *The Art of the July Monarchy: France 1830–1848*, 17–48. Columbia: University of Missouri Press, 1990.

_____. 'The Renaissance of Book Illustration'. In *The Art of the July Monarchy: France 1830-1848*, 192–213. Columbia: University of Missouri Press, 1990.

Bléton, Pierre. *La Vie sociale dans la Seconde Empire, un étonnant témoignage de la comtesse de Ségur*. Paris: Editions ouvrières, 1963.

Bouteron, Marcel, ed. *Correspondance avec Zulma Carraud*. Paris: A. Colin, 1934.

Brown, Penny. 'La Chute de l'homme (et de la femme) dans un livre pour les enfants'. *Cahiers séguriens* 2 (2001): 55–58.

_____. 'La Comtesse de Ségur et les contes de fées'. In *La Comtesse de Ségur et ses alentours*, edited by Isabelle Nières-Chevrel, 139–44. *Cahiers Robinson* 9. Artois, France: Université d'Artois, 2001.

_____. *A Critical History of French Children's Literature*. Vol. 1: *The Beginnings, 1600–1830*. New York: Routledge, 2007.

_____. 'Gustave Doré's Magical Realism: The *Nouveaux contes de fées* of the Comtesse de Ségur'. *Modern Language Review*, 95, no. 4 (2001): 964–77.

_____. 'Le Paradoxe de l'Ange gardien, ou les malheurs du Général Dourakine'. *Les Cahiers de la comtesse* 1 (2000): 28–30.

_____. 'Reinventing the Maid: Images of Joan of Arc in French and Children's Literature'. In *The Presence of the Past in Children's Literature*, edited by Ann Lawson Lucas, 41–52. Westport, Conn.: Praeger, 2003.

_____. 'Savoir lire: pouvoir ou perversion? *La Fortune de Gaspard* et le problème de savoir lire dans la littérature enfantine'. *Les Cahiers Séguriens* 3 (2002): 31–37.

Calvin, Jean. *L'Enfant dans la littérature française. De 1870 à nos jours*. 2 vols. Paris: Lanore, 1930.

Caradec, François. *Histoire de la littérature enfantine en France*. Paris: Albin Michel, 1977.

Carpenter, Humphrey, and Mari Prichard. *The Oxford Companion to Children's Literature*. Oxford: Oxford University Press, 1984.

Castex, Pierre-Georges, *Le Conte fantastique en France* (Paris: José Corti, 1951).

Cawelti, John G., *Adventure, Mystery and Romance: Formula Stories as Art and Popular Culture*. Chicago: University of Chicago Press, 1976.

Chanet, Jean-François, 'Erckamnn-Chatrian dans les revues d'enseignement primaire sous la Troisième République'. In *Erckmann-Chatrian. Entre imagination, fantaisie et réalisme: du conte au conte d'histoire*, edited by François Marotin, 329–40. Phalsbourg, France: Editions du Musée de Phalsbourg, 1999.

Chartier, Roger, Dominique Julia, and Marie-Madeleine Compère. *L'Education en France du XVIᵉ au XVIIIᵉ siècle*. Paris, Société d'Edition d'Enseignement Supérieur, 1976.

Chesneaux, Jean. *The Social and Political Ideas of Jules Verne*. Translated by Thomas Wikeley. London: Thames and Hudson, 1972.

Chevalier, Pierre. *La Séparation de l'église et de l'école. Jules Ferry et Léon XIII*, Paris: Fayard, 1981.

Chupeau, Jacques. 'Instruire en amusant: théorie et pratique du récit éducatif à l'époque de la comtesse de Ségur'. In *La Comtesse de Ségur et ses alentours*, edited by Isabelle Nières-Chevrel, 57–65. *Cahiers Robinson* 9. Artois, France: Université d'Artois, 2001.

_____. 'Le Moraliste des enfants: P.-J. Stahl'. In *Un Editeur et son siècle. Pierre-Jules Hetzel. 1814–1886*, edited by Christian Robin, 207–16. Saint-Sébastien, France: Société Crocus, 1988.

Compère, Daniel. *Jules Verne. Ecrivain*. Geneva, Switzerland: Droz, 1991.

_____. *Jules Verne. Parcours d'une oeuvre*. Amiens, France: Ancrage, 1996.

_____. 'Le Robinson suisse relu et récrit par Hetzel'. In *Un Editeur et son siècle. Pierre-Jules Hetzel. 1814–1886*, edited by Christian Robin, 223–32. Saint-Sébastien, France: Société Crocus, 1988.

Cook, Malcolm, ed. *French Culture since 1945*. London: Longman, 1993.

Corsi, Pietro, and Paul J. Wendling. 'Darwinism in Germany, France and Italy'. In *The Darwinian Heritage*, edited by David Kohn, 683–729. Princeton, N.J.: Princeton University Press, 1985.

Couderc, Marie-Anne. *Bécassine inconnue*. Paris: CNRS Editions, 2000.

Crubellier, Maurice. *L'Enfance et la jeunesse dans la société française 1800–1950*. Paris: Armand Colin, 1979.

Darton, F. J. Harvey. *Children's Books in England: Five Centuries of Social Life*. Cambridge: Cambridge University Press, 1982.

Delahaye, Christa. 'Le Joueur et le colporteur: rencontre de deux figures de voyageurs de la seconde moitié du XIXe siècle dans les villes d'eaux'. In *La Comtesse de Ségur et ses alentours*, edited by Isabelle Nières-Chevrel, 49–56. *Cahiers Robinson* 9. Artois, France: Université d'Artois, 2001.

Dennery, Etienne. (ed.) *De Balzac à Jules Verne, un grand éditeur du XIXe siècle*, Exhibition catalogue. Paris: Bibliothèque Nationale, 1966.

Dine, Philip. *Images of the Algerian War: French Fiction and Film, 1954–1992*. Oxford: Clarendon, 1994.

Dufour, Hortense. *La Comtesse de Ségur, née Rostopchine. Biographie*. Paris: Flammarion, 2000.

Dumont, Jean-Louis. *Marcel Aymé et le merveilleux*. Paris: Nouvelles Editions Debresse, 1967.

Eccleshare, Julia. 'Teenage Fiction: Realism, Romances, Contemporary Problem Novels'. In *International Companion Encyclopedia of Children's Literature*, edited by Peter Hunt, 387–96. London: Routledge, 1996.

Escarpit, Denise. *La Littérature d'enfance et de jeunesse*. Paris: Pressses Universitaires de France, 1981.

Evans, Arthur B. 'Jules Verne and the French Literary Canon'. In *Jules Verne: Narratives of Modernity*, edited by E.J. Smyth, 111–39. Liverpool, England: Liverpool University Press, 2000.

_____. *Jules Verne Rediscovered: Didacticism and the Scientific Novel*. New York: Greenwood, 1988.

Evans, I. O. *Jules Verne and His Work*. London: Arco, 1965.

Farr, Michael. *Tintin. Le rêve et la réalité. L'histoire de la création des aventures de Tintin*. Moulinsart, France: Editions Moulinsart, 2001.

Finch, Alison. *Women's Writing in Nineteenth-Century France*. Oxford: Oxford University Press, 2000.

Forsdick, Charles. 'Exoticising the *Domestique*: Bécassine, Brittany and the Beauty of the Dead'. In *The Francophone Bande Dessinée*, edited by Charles Forsdick, Lawrence Grove, and Libby Mcquillan, 23–37. Amsterdam: Rodopi, 2005.

Forsdick, Charles, Lawrence Grove, and Libby Mcquillan eds. *The Francophone Bande Dessinée*. Amsterdam: Rodopi, 2005.

Fourment, Alain. *Histoire de la presse des jeunes et des journaux d'enfants. 1768–1988*. Paris: Edition Ecole, 1987.

Furet, François, and Jacques Ozouf. *Reading and Writing. Literacy in France from Calvin to Jules Ferry*. Cambridge: Cambridge University Press, 1982.

Gascoigne, David. *Michel Tournier*. Oxford: Berg, 1996.

Gasiglia-Laster, Danièle, and Arnaud Laster, eds. *Jacques Prévert. Oeuvres complètes*, vol. 1. Paris: Gallimard, 1992.

Gauthier, Guy. 'Une morale laïque sous le Second Empire: la morale de Stahl dans le *Magasin d'éducation*'. In *Un Editeur et son siècle. Pierre-Jules Hetzel. 1814–1886*, edited by Christian Robin, 189–204. Saint-Sébastien, France: Société Crocus, 1988.

Gemie, Sharif. *French Revolutions, 1815–1914*. Edinburgh: Edinburgh University Press, 1999.

Genette, Gérard. *Palimpsestes. La Littérature au second degré*. Paris: Seuil, 1982.

Gifford, Dennis. 'Popular Literature: Comics, Dime Novels, Pulps and Penny Dreadfuls'. In *International Companion Encyclopedia of Children's Literature*, edited by Peter Hunt, 243–66. London: Routledge, 1996.

Glénisson, Jean. 'Le Livre pour la jeunesse'. In *Histoire de l'édition française*, edited by Henri Martin and Roger Chartier. Vol. 3. *Le Temps des Editeurs, du romantisme à la Belle Epoque*, 417–22. Paris: Promodis, 1986.

Grandhomme, Charles. 'Le Conteur dans les *Romans nationaux*'. In *Erckmann-Chatrian. Entre imagination, fantaisie et réalisme: du conte au conte d'histoire*, edited by François Marotin, 273–89. Phalsbourg, France: Editions du Musée de Phalsbourg, 1999.

Groensteen, Thierry, and Benoît Peeters. *Töpffer: L'Invention de la bande dessinée*. Paris: Hermann, 1994.

Guide FNAC. 200 romans de jeunesse. Paris: FNAC, 2004.

Halls, W. D. *The Youth of Vichy France*. Oxford: Clarendon, 1981.

Hazard, Paul. *Les Livres, les enfants et les hommes* (1932). Reprint, Paris: Hatier, 1967.

Henky, Danièle. *L'Art de la fugue en littérature de jeunesse. Giono, Bosco, Le Clézio, maîtres d'école buissonnière.* Bern, Switzerland: Peter Lang, 2004.

Heywood, Colin. *Childhood in Nineteenth-Century France: Work, Health and Education amongst the 'classes populaires'.* Cambridge: Cambridge University Press, 1988.

Hourihan, Margery. *Deconstructing the Hero: Literary Theory and Children's Literature.* London: Routledge, 1997.

Hughes, Alex. 'Gender Issues'. In *French Culture since 1945*, edited by Malcolm Cook, 241–268. London: Longman, 1993.

Hugon, Anne. 'Conquête et exploration en Afrique noire'. In *Images et colonies. Iconographie et propagande coloniale sur l'Afrique française de 1880 à 1962*, edited by Nicolas Bancel, Pascal Blanchard, and Laurent Gervereau, 18–22. Paris: BDIC-ACHAC, 1993.

Hunt, Peter. *Criticism, Theory and Children's Literature.* Oxford: Blackwell, 1991.

Hunt, Peter, ed. *International Companion Encyclopedia of Children's Literature.* London: Routledge, 1996.

Hürlimann, Bettina. *Three Centuries of Children's Books in Europe.* London: Oxford University Press, 1967.

Iser, Wolfgang. *The Act of Reading.* London: Routledge and Kegan Paul, 1978.

Jan, Isabelle. *On Children's Literature.* Translated by Catherine Storr. London: Allen Lane, 1973.

Judah, Tim. 'Tintin in the Dock'. *Guardian, Weekend* supplement, 30 January, 1999, 8–18.

Kettering, Sharon. *French Society 1589–1715.* London: Longman, 2001.

Kohn, David. *The Darwinian Heritage.* Princeton, N.J.: Princeton University Press, 1985.

Kokkola, Lydia. *Representing the Holocaust in Children's Literature.* New York: Routledge, 2003.

Kreyder, Laura. *L'Enfance des saints et des autres. Essai sur la comtesse de Ségur.* Paris: Schena-Nizet, 1987.

Lacambre, Geneviève, 'Les milieux japonisants à Paris (1860–1880)'. In *Japonisme in Art: An International Symposium*, edited by Society for Study of Japonisme, 43–55. Toyko: Committee of Year 2001, and Society for Study of Japonisme/Kodanska International, 1980.

Lacassin, Francis (ed). *Des enfants sur les routes* Paris: Laffont, 1994.

Lacassin, Francis. *Pour un 9ème art, la bande dessinée.* Paris: U.G.E., 1971.

———, ed. *Des enfants sur les routes.* Paris: Laffont, 1994.

Latzarus, Marie-Thérèse. *La Littérature enfantine dans la seconde moitié du XIXe siècle.* Paris: Presses Universitaires de France, 1924.

Lawson Lucas, Ann, ed. *The Presence of the Past in Children's Literature.* Westport, Conn.: Praeger, 2003.

Le Clézio, Jean-Marie-Gustave. 'J'ai grandi avec ses livres'. In *Jules Verne. L'Odyssée de la terre, Géo*, hors-série, 2003, 6–11.

Le Men, Ségolène. 'Les abécédaires à figures en France au XIXe siècle'. In Glénisson, 'Le Livre pour la jeunesse,' in *Histoire de l'édition française*, edited by Henri Martin and Roger Chartier. Vol. 3. *Le Temps des Editeurs, du romantisme à la Belle Epoque*, 418–419. Paris: Promodis, 1986.

———. *Les abécédaires français illustrés du XIXe siècle*. Paris: Promodis, 1984.

———. 'La Pédagogie par l'image dans un manuel de la Troisième République'. In *Usages de l'image au XIXe siècle*, edited by Stéphane Michaud, Jean-Yves Mollier, and Nicole Savy, 119–27. Paris: Editions Créaphis, 1992.

Leriche, Mathilde. *Cinquante ans de littérature de jeunesse, quatre conférences sur la littérature pour les enfants en France en 1939*. Paris: Magnard et L'Ecole, 1939.

Le Ru, Bénédicte. 'L'Image de la Russie chez la comtesse de Ségur'. In *La Comtesse de Ségur et ses alentours*, edited by Isabelle Nières-Chevrel, 155–64. *Cahiers Robinson* 9. Artois, France: Université d'Artois, 2001.

Lesnik-Oberstein, Karin. *Children's Literature: Criticism and the Fictional Child*. Oxford: Clarendon, 2002.

———. 'Defining Children's Literature and Childhood'. In *International Companion Encyclopedia of Children's Literature*, edited by Peter Hunt, 17–31. London: Routledge, 1996.

Lhoste, Pierre. *Conversations avec J. M. G. Le Clézio*. Paris: Seghers, 1971.

Lloyd, Rosemary. *The Land of Lost Content: Children and Childhood in Nineteenth-Century French Literature*. Oxford: Clarendon, 1992.

Lyons, Martyn. *Le Triomphe du livre: une histoire sociologique de la lecture dans la France du XIXe siècle*. Paris: Promodis, 1987.

Manceron, Gilles. 'Le Missionaire à barbe noire et l'enseignement laïque' in *Images et colonies. Iconographie et propagande coloniale sur l'Afrique française de 1880 à 1962*, edited by Nicolas Bancel, Pascal Blanchard, and Laurent Gervereau, 70–72. Paris: BDIC-ACHAC, 1993.

Marcoin, Danièle. *Le Roman d'aventures à l'école, les héritiers de Robinson*. Paris: Lacoste, 1997.

Marcoin, Francis. 'Autour de la comtesse'. In *La Comtesse de Ségur et ses alentours*, ed. Isabelle Nières-Chevrel, 23–26. *Cahiers Robinson* 9. Artois, France: Université d'Artois, 2001.

———. *La Comtesse de Ségur et le bonheur immobile*. Arras, France: Artois Presses Université, 1999.

Marie, Laurent. 'Le Grêlé 7/13, a (Communist) Children's Guide to the Resistance'. In *The Francophone Bande Dessinée*, edited by Charles Forsdick, Lawrence Grove, and Libby Mcquillan, 74–82. Amsterdam: Rodopi, 2005.

Marotin, François. *Erckmann-Chatrian. Entre imagination, fantaisie et réalisme: du conte au conte d'histoire*. Phalsbourg, France: Editions du Musée de Phalsbourg, 1999.

Martin, Andrew. *The Mask of the Prophet: The Extraordinary Fictions of Jules Verne*. Oxford: Clarendon, 1990.

Martin, Henri, and Roger Chartier, eds. *Histoire de l'édition française*. 4 vols. Paris: Promodis, 1982–86.

Masters, Brian. *A Student's Guide to Saint-Exupéry*. London: Heinemann, 1972.

Mathé, Roger. 'L'Image de l'Indien emplumé et du trappeur dans la littérature populaire du dix-neuvième siècle'. In *Popular Traditions and Learned Culture in France*, ed. Marc Bertrand, 179–209. Stanford French and Italian Studies 35. Saratoga, Calif.: Anma Libri, 1985.

Mauriac, François. *Nouveaux mémoires intérieurs*. Paris: Flammarion, 1965.

Merriman, John. M. ed. *1830 in France*. New York: Franklin Watts, 1975.

Michaud, Stéphane, Jean Yves Mollier, and Nicole Savy. eds. *Usages de l'image au XIXe siècle*. Paris: Editions Créaphis, 1992.

Mistler, Jean. *La Librairie Hachette de 1826 à nos jours*. Paris: Hachette, 1964.

Moré, Marcel. *Le Très curieux Jules Verne*. Paris: Gallimard, 1960.

Murail, Marie-Aude. 'Dialogue avec Nadège'. In *Littérature de jeunesse. Incertaines frontières*, edited by Isabelle Nières-Chevrel, 156–76. Paris: Gallimard, 2005.

Néret, Jean-Alexis. *Histoire illustrée de la librairie et du livre français*. Paris: Lamarre, 1953.

Nières-Chevrel, Isabelle, 'In and Out of History: *Jeanne d'Arc* by Maurice Boutet de Monvel'. In *The Presence of the Past in Children's Literature*, edited by Ann Lawson Lucas, 33–40. Westport, Conn: Praeger, 2003.

Nières-Chevrel, Isabelle, ed. *La Comtesse de Ségur et ses alentours*. *Cahiers Robinson* 9. Artois, France: Université d'Artois, 2001.

Nières-Chevrel, Isabelle, 'Lisières et chemins de traverse. Avant-Propos'. In *Littérature de jeunesse. Incertaines frontières*, edited by Isabelle Nières-Chevrel, 9–27. Paris: Gallimard, 2005.

――――, ed., *Littérature de jeunesse. Incertaines frontières*. Paris: Gallimard, 2005.

Noesser, Laura. 'Le Livre pour enfants'. In *Histoire de l'édition française*, edited by Henri Martin and Roger Chartier. Vol. 4, *Le Livre concurrencé 1900–1950*, 457–541. Paris: Promodis, 1985

Noesser, Laura. (ed.) *Fonds ancien de littérature pour la jeunesse. Catalogue des livres imprimés avant 1914*, Paris: Bibliothèque de l'Heure Joyeuse, 1984.

Nora, Pierre. *Lieux de mémoire*. 3 vols. Paris: Gallimard, 1984.

Odin, Roger. *Jeanne d'Arc à l'école: essai sémiotique*. Paris: Editions Klincksieck, 1980.

Ory, Pascal. *Le Petit Nazi illustré. Une Pédagogie hitlérienne en culture française: 'Le Téméraire' (1943–44)*. Paris: Editions Albatross, 1979.

O'Sullivan, Emer. *Comparative Children's Literature*. Translated by Anthea Bell. Abingdon, England: Routledge, 2005.

Ottevaere–van Praag, Ganna. *Histoire du récit pour la jeunesse au XXe siècle, 1929–2000*. Brussels: Peter Lang, 1999.

————. *La Littérature pour la jeunesse en Europe occidentale (1750–1925)*. Bern, Switzerland: Peter Lang, 1987.

Ozouf, Jacques, and Ozouf, Mona. 'Le Tour de la France par deux enfants. Le petit livre rouge de la République'. In Les *Lieux de mémoire. I. La République*, edited by Pierre Nora, 291–321. Paris: Gallimard, 1984.

Parménie, A., and C. Bonnier de la Chapelle. *Histoire d'un éditeur et de ses auteurs. P.-J. Hetzel (Stahl)*. Paris: Albin Michel, 1953.

Pedley, Alan. 'The Media'. In *French Culture since 1945*, edited by Malcolm Cook, 149–75. London: Longman, 1993.

Perrot, Jean. *Art baroque, art d'enfance*. Nancy, France: Presses Universitaires de Nancy, 1991.

————. *Du jeu, des enfants et des livres*. Paris: Edition du Cercle de la Librairie, 1987.

————. *Jeux et enjeux du livre d'enfance et de jeunesse*. Paris: Edition du Cercle de la Librairie, 1999.

————. 'Patapoufs et Filifers: une aubaine pour la théorie'. In *Littérature de jeunesse. Incertaines frontières*, edited by Isabelle Nières-Chevrel, 214–32. Paris: Gallimard, 2005.

————, ed. *L'Humour dans la littérature de jeunesse*. Paris: Editions In Press, 2000.

Perrot, Michelle, 'The Family Triumphant'. 'The Actors'. In *A History of Private Life*, ed. Philippe Ariès and Georges Duby. Vol. 4, *From the Fires of Revolution to the Great War*, edited by Michelle Perrot, 99–165. Cambridge, Mass.: Belknap Press of Harvard University Press, 1990.

Phillips, Richard. *Mapping Men and Empire: A Geography of Adventure*. London: Routledge, 1997.

Pincet, Yves. 'Erckmann-Chatrian à travers les morceaux choisis dans les manuels scolaires'. In *Erckmann-Chatrian. Entre imagination, fantaisie et réalisme: du conte au conte de l'histoire*, ed. François Marotin, 341–59. Phalsbourg, France: Editions du Musée de Phalsbourg, 1999.

Prost, Antoine. *L'Enseignement en France 1800–1967*. Paris: Armand Colin, 1968.

Proud, Judith. *Children and Propaganda. 'Il était une fois. . . ': Fiction and Fairy Tale in Vichy France*. Oxford: Intellect, 1995.

Ray, Gordon N. *The Art of the French Illustrated Book 1700–1914*. 2 vols. New York: Pierpont Morgan Library/Cornell University Press, 1982.

Renard, Jean-Bruno. *Clefs pour la bande dessinée*. Paris: Seghers, 1978.

Renonciat, Annie. *Livre mon ami. Lectures enfantines 1914–1954*. Exposition des bibliothèques de la ville de Paris. Paris: Mairie de Paris, 1992.

Robert, Marthe. *Roman des origines et origines du roman*. Paris: Gallimard, 1972.

Robin, Christian, ed. *Un Editeur et son siècle. Pierre-Jules Hetzel (1814–1886)*. Saint-Sébastien, France: ACL Edition Société Crocus, 1988.

Sadoul, Georges. *Ce que lisent les enfants*. Paris: Bureau d'Editions, 1938.

Sadoul, Numa. *Entretiens avec Hergé*. Tournai, Belgium: Casterman, 1989.

Sartre, Jean-Paul. *Les Mots*. Paris: Gallimard, 1964.

Schoumacker, L. *Erckmann-Chatrian, étude biographique et critique d'après des documents inédits*. Strasbourg, France: Université de Strasbourg, 1933.

Screech, Matthew. *Masters of the Ninth Art: Bandes dessinées and Franco-Belgian Identity*. Liverpool, England: Liverpool University Press, 2005.

Soriano, Marc. *'Bibliothèque rose ou série noir?'* preface to Comtesse de Ségur, *La Fortune de Gaspard*. Paris: Pauvert, 1972.

_____. *Guide de la littérature pour la jeunesse*. Paris: Flammarion, 1974.

Steel, David. 'Hector Malot, *Sans famille* and the sense of adventure', *New Comparison* 20 (1995): 75–95.

Steins, Martin. *Blaise Cendrars; bilans nègres*. Archives des Lettres Modernes 169. Paris: Minard 1977.

Stephens, John. *Language and Ideology in Children's Fiction*. London: Longman, 1992.

Stephens, John, and Robyn McCallum. *Retelling Stories, Framing Culture. Traditional Story and Metanarratives in Children's Literature*. New York: Garland, 1998.

Strachan, John. 'Romance, Religion and the Republic: Bruno's *Le Tour de la France par deux enfants*', *French History* 18, no. 1 (2004): 96–118.

Strumingher, Laura S. 'Square Pegs in Round Holes: Rural Parents and Primary Schools, France 1830–1880'. In *Popular Traditions and Learned Culture*, edited by Marc Bertrand, 133–147. Stanford French and Italian Studies 35. Saratoga, Calif.: Anma Libri, 1985.

_____. *What are Little Girls and Boys Made of? Primary Education in Rural France 1830–1880*. Albany: State University of New York Press, 1983.

Sussex, R. T. *Henri Bosco, Poet-Novelist*. Christchurch, New Zealand: University of Canterbury Press, 1966.

Thomas-Maleville, Agnès. *Hector Malot. Ecrivain au grand coeur*. Monaco: Rocher, 2000.

Thompson, Harry. *Tintin, Hergé and His Creation*. London: Hodder and Stoughton, 1991.

Todorov, Tzvetan. *Introduction à la littérature fantastique*. Paris: Editions du Seuil, 1970.

Trigon, Jean de. *Histoire de la littérature enfantine de ma Mère l'Oye au roi Babar*. Paris: Hachette, 1950.

Unwin, Timothy. *Jules Verne: Journeys in Writing*. Liverpool, England: Liverpool University Press, 2005.

Vaclavik, Kiera. 'Jules Verne, écrivain . . . de jeunesse: the Case of *Voyage au centre de la terre*', *Australian Journal of French Studies* 42, no 3 (2005): 276–83.

Vierne, Simone. *Jules Verne et le roman initiatique*. Paris: Sirac, 1973.

Vinson, Marie-Christine. *L'Education des petites filles chez la comtesse de Ségur*. Lyon, France: Presses Universitaires de Lyon, 1987.

Warner, Marina. *Joan of Arc: The Image of Female Heroism*. Harmondsworth, England: Penguin, 1983.

Weber, Eugen Joseph. *Peasants into Frenchmen: The Modernization of Rural France 1870–1914.* London: Chatto and Windus.

Zipes, Jack. *The Trials and Tribulations of Little Red Riding Hood. Versions of the Tale in its Socio-Cultural Context.* London: Heinemann, 1983.

_____, ed. *Fairy Tales and Fables from Weimar Days.* Madison: University of Wisconsin Press, 1997.

Zweig, Paul. *The Adventurer: The Fate of Adventure in the Western World.* Princeton, N.J.: Princeton University Press, 1974.

INDEX

A